Venezia 500

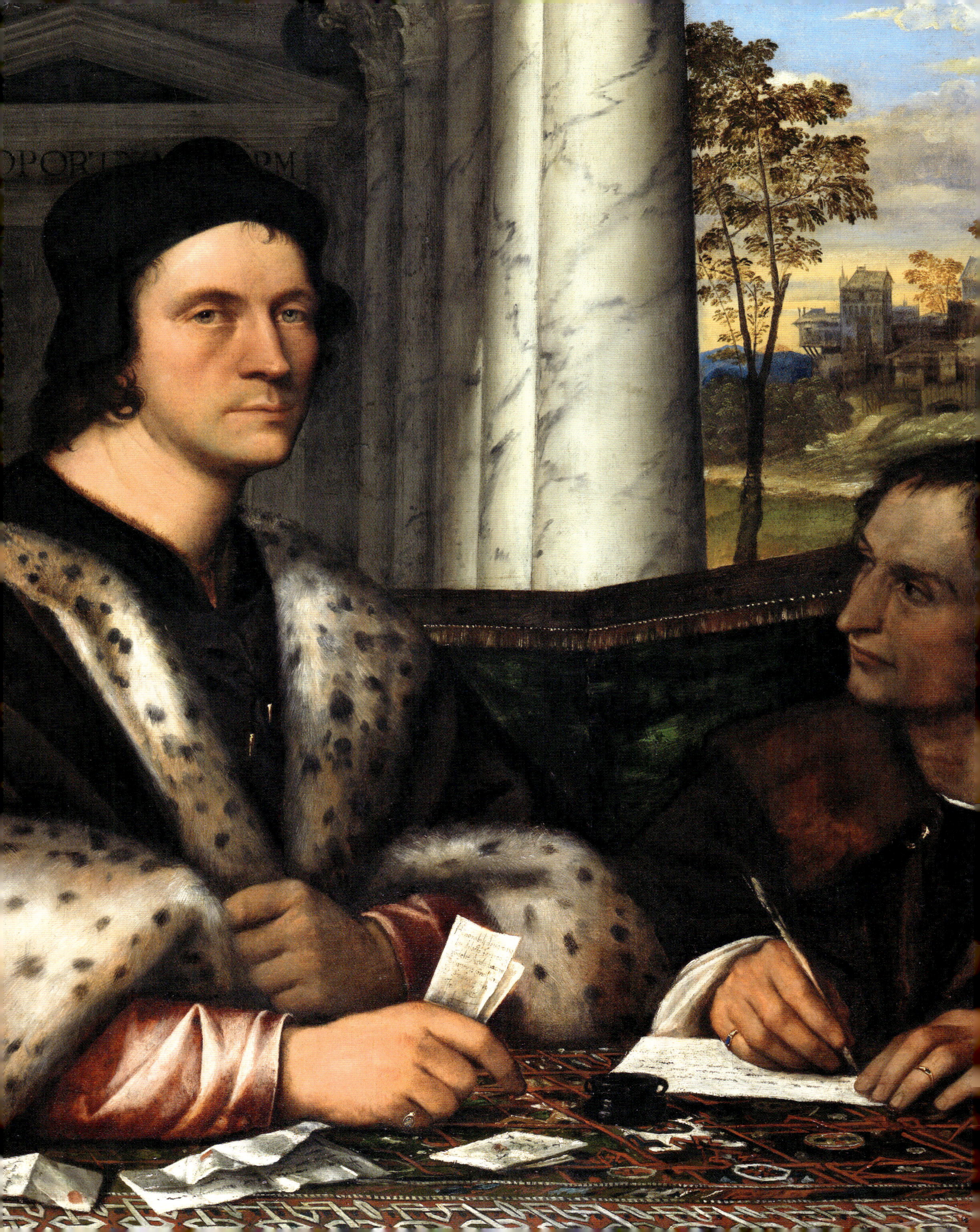

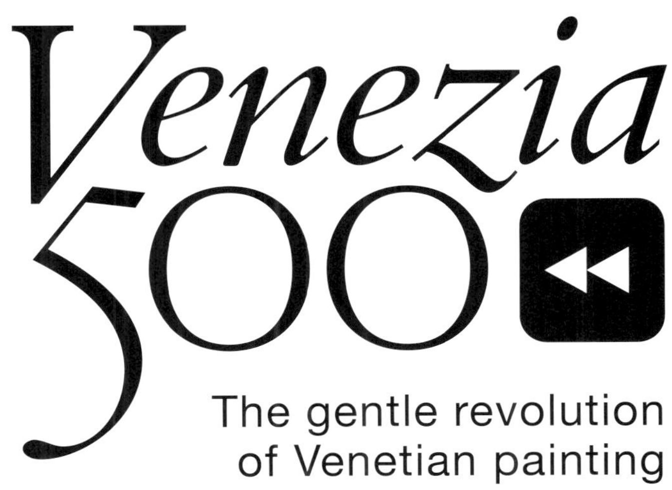

Edited by Andreas Schumacher

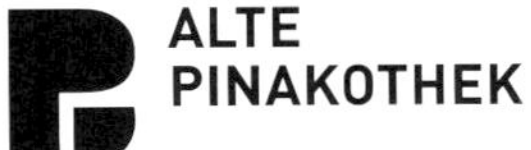

HIRMER

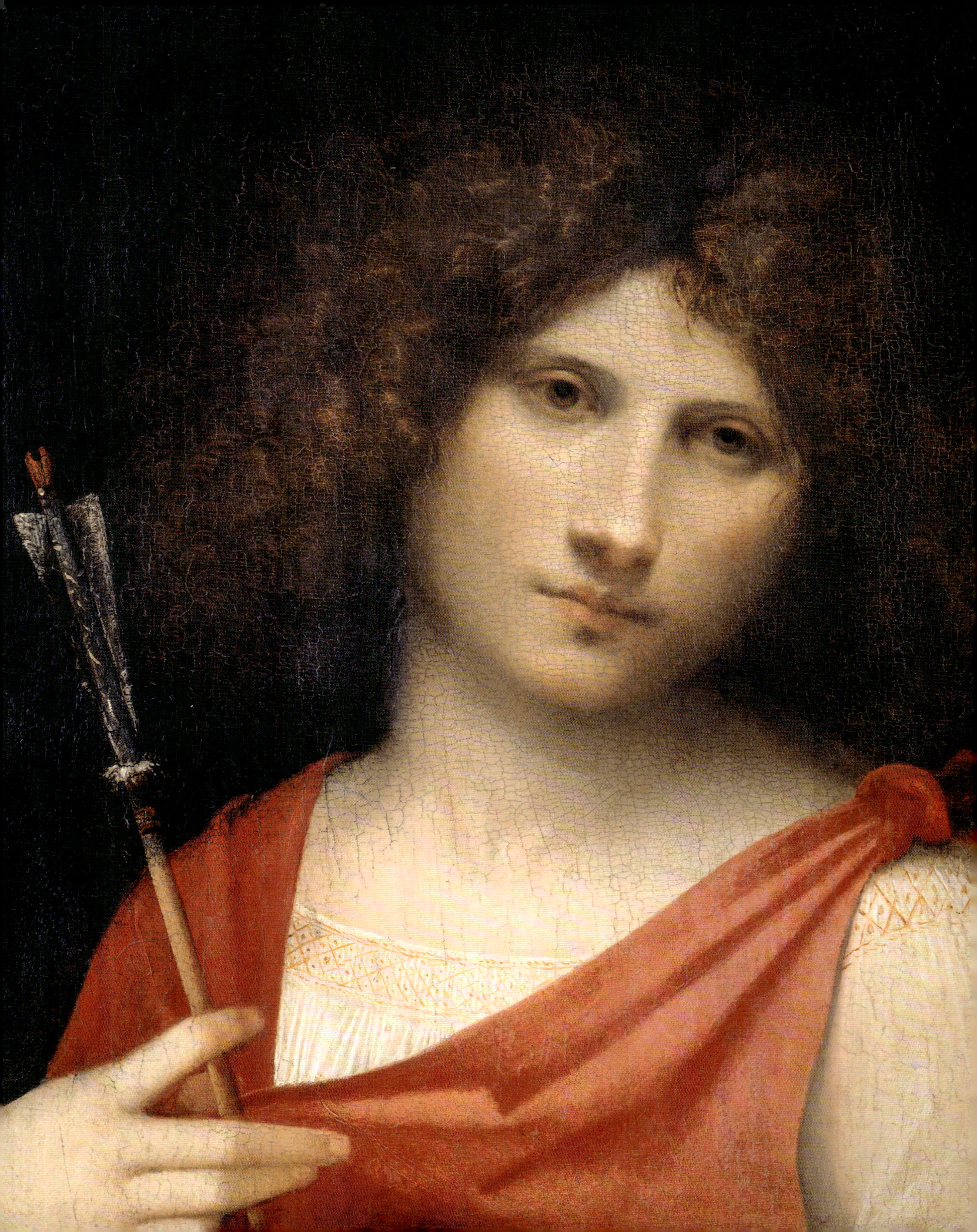

Contents

The catalogue was
sponsored by

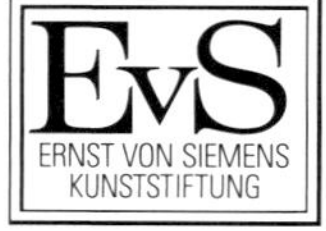

Opening words

Venetian painting has had a profound impact on the development of European art – the works of Giorgione, Titian, Palma il Vecchio and Giovanni Bellini, to name but a few, marked a turning point in the artistic paradigms of the period and facilitated the dissemination of an innovative approach to pictorial composition. This "gentle revolution" had a particular bearing on landscape and portrait painting, whose evolvement the Munich exhibition aims to illustrate.

The Venetian school embodied a distinct conception of landscape, which could serve both as an autonomous protagonist of a work and as a framework for sacral, allegorical and mythological themes. It was no longer merely an ornamental element – rather, it became the focal point of the representation. The works on display not only remind visitors of the beauty of the Italian landscape; they also make us reflect on how essential it is to preserve an environment that is inviting and pleasant for human beings. They bring to mind that landscape is never just nature, but – being the result of centuries of interaction between humans and their environment – is, indeed, also culture. Olive and citrus groves, cypresses, terraces, canals and hills – what we today consider natural landscape is, in fact, the outcome of a harmonious and mutually respectful interplay between human civilisation and the nature that surrounds it. With the topicality inherent in great works and artistic movements, Venetian Renaissance painting also speaks to contemporary sensibilities, pointing to the importance of these aspects: preserving the environment, protecting nature, reducing negative human influences on the landscape and thus combating climate change. These are all highly topical factors in the age of the Anthropocene.

With the innovations of Bellini, Giorgione and their disciples, the portrait was enriched by an essential, psychologically introspective component. The influence such works have had on artists even centuries later is striking – on the German Expressionists of the early 20th century, for instance. These connections prove once again how far-reaching Italo-German artistic associations have always been. The relationships between artists and cultural practitioners, which were established and constantly cultivated through business, trade and politics, expanded over time and continually involved new protagonists.

Among the various sponsors and sources of inspiration of the exchange between Italy and Germany, the Generali Group has assumed an important role. With its contribution to this exhibition, it confirms its special commitment to the development of cultural relations.

In 2024, Italy will be Guest of Honour at the Frankfurt Book Fair – analogously, this high-calibre exhibition in Munich also makes a significant contribution to bringing our countries closer so we can get to know each other even better.

Armando Varricchio
Italian Ambassador
in Germany

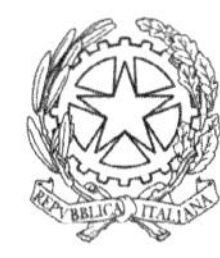

Ambasciata d'Italia
Berlino

Opening words

Giovanni Bellini, Giorgione, Palma il Vecchio, Lorenzo Lotto, Titian and Tintoretto – they all bear witness to a glorious era in Venice's history that has lost none of its artistic radiance to this day. Hardly any other place in the world so movingly unites creative power, inventive spirit and a longing for timelessness.

For centuries, the Serenissima has captivated people with its unique wealth of historical and cultural treasures. Venice was a melting pot of diverse cultures, a central protagonist in the struggle for supremacy in the Mediterranean region and probably the most important trading city in Europe well into the 16th century. The prosperity of its citizens also allowed the arts to flourish, and the painters of the Venetian Renaissance shaped artistic development throughout Europe with their great innovative power.

During the lifetime of these masters, the rebuilding of the Procuratie Vecchie on St Mark's Square as the seat of the procurators created an economically important location whose majestic architecture was to inspire generations of artists.

It was within these historic walls that Generali opened its first branch, just a few weeks after its foundation in Trieste at the end of 1831. The winged Lion of St Mark, the heraldic animal of the Republic of Venice, became its trademark. Then as now, it symbolises our profound attachment to Venice and its art.

After the painstaking renovation of the Procuratie Vecchie in collaboration with the world-renowned architect Sir David Chipperfield, a place of interaction and inspiration was created here. Accessible to all, it is home to *The Human Safety Net* today, Generali's global initiative to help disadvantaged people shape their future.

As a leading insurer in Europe, we have always been committed to human communities and their sustainable well-being. This also includes the protection of our cultural heritage, which is, unfortunately, directly threatened by climate change and all its consequences. We wish to counteract this. In conjunction with our art insurer ARTE Generali and our partners in the EU-funded Erasmus+ programme CHARISMA, we have therefore brought together experts from various scientific disciplines to develop effective solutions to protect valuable works of art and preserve their magic for those who come after us.

For this reason, too, *Venezia 500* is a matter close to our hearts. After 2018, we are pleased to once again sponsor the presentation of an exquisite selection of masterpieces by Italian artists at the Alte Pinakothek in Munich and, at the same time, to set an example of Italo-German friendship. I wish all visitors to this exhibition much enjoyment and an inspiring experience.

Giovanni Liverani
CEO Generali Germany, Austria and Switzerland (DACH)

Lenders

Koninklijk Museum voor Schone Kunsten, Antwerp
Carmen Willems
Dr Nico Van Hout

Fondazione Accademia Carrara, Bergamo
Dott.ssa Maria Cristina Rodeschini
Paolo Plebani

Staatliche Museen zu Berlin
Professor Christina Haak

Gemäldegalerie
Dr Dagmar Hirschfelder
Dr Roberto Contini

Kupferstichkabinett
Professor Dagmar Korbacher

Musée des Beaux-Arts et d'Archéologie, Besançon
Laurence Madeline
Amandine Royer

Museum and Art Gallery, Bristol
Jon Finch
Fran Coles

Szépművészeti Múzeum, Budapest
Dr László Baán

The Faringdon Collection Trust, Buscot Park
Baron Charles Michael Faringdon
Dr Amy Lim

National Gallery of Denmark, Copenhagen
Astrid la Cour

Musée des Beaux-Arts, Dijon
Frédérique Goerig-Hergott

Staatliche Kunstsammlungen Dresden, Gemäldegalerie Alte Meister
Professor Marion Ackermann

Galleria degli Uffizi, Florence
Dr Eike D. Schmidt
Dott.ssa Daniela Parenti

Galleria degli Uffizi, Gabinetto Disegni e Stampe, Florence
Dr Eike D. Schmidt
Dott.ssa Marzia Faietti

Hamburger Kunsthalle
Professor Alexander Klar
Dr Sandra Pisot

Wadsworth Atheneum Museum of Art, Hartford (CT)
Dr Matthew Hargraves
Dr Oliver Tostmann

Museo Civico Amedeo Lia, La Spezia
Dott. Andrea Marmori

The National Gallery, London
Dr Gabriele Finaldi
Christine Riding
Dr Matthias Wivel

The Royal Collection Trust, HM King Charles III, London
Dr Tim Knox
Anna Reynolds
Martin Clayton

Musée des Beaux-Arts, Lyon
Sylvie Ramond

Museo Nacional del Prado, Madrid
Dr Miguel Falomir Faus
David García Cueto

Museo Nacional Thyssen-Bornemisza, Madrid
Professor Guillermo Solana
Dr Maria del Mar Borobia

Pinacoteca di Brera, Milan
Dr James M. Bradburne
Dott.ssa Maria Cristina Passoni

Bayerisches Nationalmuseum, Munich
Dr Frank Matthias Kammel
Dr Jens Ludwig Burk

Sammlung Bernd und Verena Klüser, Munich
Bernd and Verena Klüser

Staatliche Graphische Sammlung München
Dr Michael Hering
Dr Kurt Zeitler

The Metropolitan Museum of Art, New York
Max Hollein
Dr Carmen C. Bambach

National Gallery of Canada, Ottawa
Jean-François Bélisle

Musei Civici, Museo d'Arte Medioevale e Moderna, Padua
Federica Franzoso
Dott.ssa Elisabetta Gastaldi

Bibliothèque nationale de France, Département estampes et photographie, Paris
Laurence Engel

Galerie Canesso, Paris
Maurizio Canesso
Véronique Damian

Musée du Louvre, Paris
Laurence des Cars
Sébastian Allard
Vincent Delieuvin

Musei Civici, Palazzo Mazzolari Mosca, Pesaro
Daniele Vimini
Dott.ssa Francesca Banini

Galleria Borghese, Rome
Prof.ssa Francesca Cappelletti

Musei Capitolini, Pinacoteca, Rome
Dott. Claudio Parisi Presicce
Federica Maria Papi

Musei Civici, Treviso
Dott. Fabrizio Malachin
Dott.ssa Eleonora Drago

Fondazione Musei Civici di Venezia
Mariacristina Gribaudi

Museo Correr
Dott. Andrea Bellieni

Museo di Palazzo Ducale

Gallerie dell'Accademia di Venezia
Dott. Giulio Manieri Elia
Dott.ssa Roberta Battaglia

Albertina, Vienna
Professor Klaus Albrecht Schröder
Dr Achim Gnann

Kunsthistorisches Museum, Vienna
Dr Sabine Haag
Peter Björn Kerber
Dr Francesca Del Torre Scheuch

National Gallery of Art, Washington
Kaywin Feldman
Dr Gretchen Hirschauer

Martin von Wagner-Museum, Würzburg
Professor Damian Dombrowski

Private collection, courtesy of Eckart Lingenauber

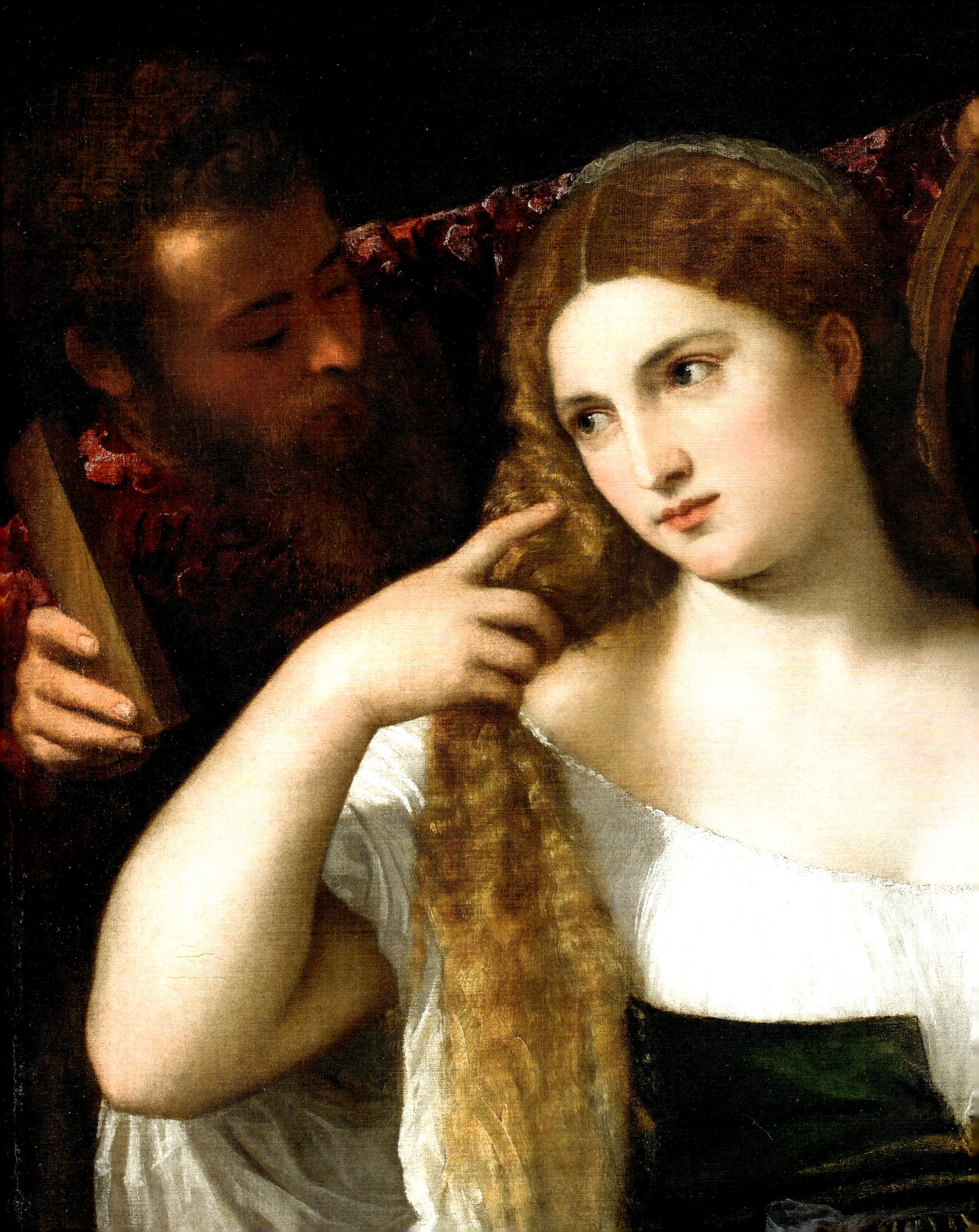

Foreword

"[...] not intellectual but intellect per se": the legacy of Venetian painting

Museum treasures do not explain themselves. They have to be brought up for discussion, interpreted and made comprehensible in order to decipher their meaning, to demonstrate their contemporary relevance and presentness, and to grasp their significance for the future – for each generation anew. In baroque-era galleries, paintings hung on the wall without comment, although a gallery attendant, a curator and a director were part of day-to-day practice even then: they explained the works – and this was certainly not only due to their value. Since the Enlightenment, this discussion and exploration has taken place in a far more in-depth manner; from the 19th century onwards, works of art have also been critically examined in terms of their material content and, moreover, published in substantial catalogues; and for a century now, they have been studied not only with regard to their appearance, but also in terms of their process of creation in a more differentiated manner and using non-destructive scientific methods and imaging techniques.

Today, art historical research is the elementary basis of each and any educational endeavour, while the latter, in turn, forms the societal intention of all contemporary and thus audience-oriented museum work. To this effect, the target audience not only comprises the educated and interested middle class, but also kindergarten children, who we believe ought to be introduced to art at an early age with their ingenuous gaze, and schoolchildren, who can in this way familiarise themselves with ethical, Christian, ancient or contemporary visual themes, as addressees of museum research and its dissemination.

Artists, too, have at all times looked to the works of their professional colleagues from the past and engaged with them critically and constructively; this by no means applies exclusively to those of 19th-century historicism. Wherever creativity was and is effective, it is based on reflection on the achievements of the past. Anyone who might assume that Venetian painting of the 15th and 16th centuries has ceased to impart any creative impetus for many generations, that it no longer has any current significance, or that it should even be regarded as old-masterly and 'finished', will certainly be tempted and led by the following selection of artistic voices to take a differentiated look at Venetian art.

The radical Munich-based painter HP Zimmer belongs to the unforgotten post-war avant-garde. In 1958, he wrote in his diary, referring to some of the artists in our exhibition as well as to works ranging from those at the Alte Pinakothek to those at the Florentine

Uffizi: "The Venetians invented painting, and we will reinvent it. When I was in the Uffizi, I was struck by how delicate and lovely everything was, except for Titian and Tintoretto. [...] I want to combine the expressiveness of Pollock and the elegance of Tintoretto. Tintoretto was the Pollock of the 16th century."[1] Is Venetian painting therefore solely a reference to energetic art? Of course, the Venetians did not invent painting. However, they discovered and celebrated the preciousness of painterly facture, of the make of oil painting, of the structures of the brush and the canvas. Early post-war modernism saw and admired its expressiveness, colourism and innovative power. Artists like Zimmer recognised the enormous creative energy and unbridled imagination inherent in this art. The Venetians stood for the most excellent tradition of figurative painting, while the aforementioned Jackson Pollock stood for the most radical abstraction.

The preceding generation, as Max Beckmann still shows in the last year of his life, had likewise dealt with this centuries-old art. He stated in his diary in New York in 1950: "Der alte Titian großer Eindruck" ("The old Titian great impression"),[2] using the Americanised form of the artist's name, reminiscent of a titan, just as he had enthusiastically noted almost half a century earlier that he was particularly interested in the "Tizians presque tous"[3] – that is, almost all of them. We may assume that this applied not only to the facture of the painting, but also to the ingenious composition and, for example, the complex interactions in compositions involving several or many figures, which can always be read as interpersonal micro dramas.

Paula Modersohn-Becker – at that time still unmarried, hence more precisely: Paula Becker – enjoyed the Louvre in Paris in 1900 and reverently confessed: "Titian reveals himself to me in his nobleness",[4] paying tribute to the Venetian master. A generation older yet again was the legendary Max Liebermann from Berlin, who wittily remarked: "The works of a Titian or Michelangelo [...] are not intellectual but intellect per se".[5] To be intellectual was at that time a sign and expression of a certain compliant superficiality. Intellect per se, on the other hand, is that not something divine?

It was the Venetians who thematised the autonomy and intrinsic value of colour – the brushstroke, the modelling, the nuance. Vincent van Gogh put it amicably: "Colour expresses something in and of itself, this is not to be missed, you must make use of it [...]; when Veronese painted the portraits of his *beau monde* in 'The Wedding Feast at Cana', he had used the whole wealth of his palette of sombre violets, of splendid gold tones on them. Then – there also was a thin sky blue and pearly white [...]. So splendid is this background that it spontaneously emerged of its own accord from a colour calculation."[6] So is it just a matter of cold calculation? Not at all, one would like to retort: it's sheer skill! That was the magic of Venice and its old masters; the colour has a life of its own and was not only used to fill in outlines.

One could go back further and further in the tradition of the best painters, but let us extend no further here than Eugène Delacroix, one of the most brilliant painters of his century. He did not deal with the old Venetians solely on the canvas or in conversation, but also intellectually, reflectively and exploratively in his diary. In 1847, he pondered: "Paolo Veronese does not display the intention, unlike Titian, for example, of creating a masterpiece with every picture. This dexterity in not doing too much everywhere, this apparent lack of concern for detail, which makes for so much simplicity, is due to the habit of decoration",[7] and this in no way expressed a disdain for large decorative commissions. Elsewhere he wrote pensively from his own painting experience: "Titian probably did not know how he would finish a picture."[8] This perception of an open-ended creative process clearly reflected the fact that one (including him, Delacroix, the painter) could and can find traces of procedural changes in the painting process within and on Titian's range of works.

While the older masters such as Bellini or Giorgione usually only meant much to the experts and connoisseurs, it was Titian and his generation with whom those who followed would engage almost tirelessly. And so even a mind like Delacroix could not detach himself from this debate and the ever-new contemplation of the old masters. Accordingly, he muses: "Praise for Titian. [...] Often it is precisely those who least deserve praise who are the subject of eulogies. But praise for Titian! They will tell me that I reminded them of that pious jurist who wrote the *Memorandum in Favour of God*. He can do without my eulogies."[9] Titian, the divine – not Raphael! Titian, the pinnacle of painting? Titian can certainly do without any eulogies. Startled, Delacroix realised: "It seems indeed that these men of the 16th century have left little to do: they were the first to tread the path and seem to have reached the limit in all genres. One is stunned by the strength, the fertility, the universality of these men of the 16th century."[10] Since one does not want to benchmark oneself against that epoch today, this sense of irritation, borne of respect, may be dispensed with.

Bringing Venice and its painting to life requires a wealth of creative forces. Previous exhibitions and catalogues of the Alte Pinakothek were also based on research and aimed at dissemination; they revived the Florentine Renaissance, the Utrecht Caravaggisti and artists such as Anthony van Dyck. It cannot be repeated often enough: museums are non-university research institutions. In this respect, the Pinakothek museums can consider themselves fortunate that they have a broad spectrum of research approaches at their disposal, thanks to the co-operation with the teams of natural science and restoration at the Doerner Institut, allowing questions of intellectual history to be complemented by those of material findings. And yet, in view of the limited staffing, this innovative work would not be feasible on a day-to-day basis if distinguished patrons and sponsors had not helped to expand the circle of contributors at an early stage and to make it possible for these experts to conduct research over several years on the collection, which has never been studied so systematically before. At this point, I would like to express my sincere thanks to the Hubert Burda Stiftung, which provided the initial funding, followed by the Deutsche Forschungsgemeinschaft and the Ernst von Siemens Kunststiftung: the funding awarded by these three parties enables comprehensive research work that could never have been carried out in anything like the same breadth and depth with the permanent staff alone.

Such a project requires a head who, as a passionate and enthusiastic *spiritus rector*, submits applications, oversees funds, supervises personnel, centres research approaches and determinedly overcomes numerous hurdles and resistance: Andreas Schumacher, as head of the collection of Italian painting and as director of collections of the Alte Pinakothek, has managed all this magnificently for this project for several years now and, at the same time, realised this landmark exhibition. This is all the more significant in view of the fact that the years of the pandemic and the still ongoing Russian war of aggression against Ukraine with its repercussions were, and still are, the years during which and due to which we have all had to wrestle with fragmenting and monetarily limiting consequences for any planning for some time now.

The research project on Venetian painting, which will soon result in an extensive collection catalogue, is now taking stock of its first results. It has provided the exhibition, to which this book is dedicated, with important impulses and significant discoveries. The exhibition deliberately does not seek to fan out the broad panorama of art historical and technological research on Venetian painting of the Renaissance. Instead, it directly conveys the outstanding qualities, the special innovative power and the contemporary relevance of the painting of Bellini, Giorgione and Titian, for example, which so fascinated the artists cited above. To this effect, the exhibition concentrates on those genre-specific strengths of Venetian painting that continued to have an impact into the modern age: the art of portraiture and the depiction of landscapes.

In the 15th and 16th centuries, Venice was what Bavaria aspires to be today – namely, a place of innovation and a value-adding commercial exchange. Moreover, the image of mankind of that period is much less remote from our time than it may seem at first. The numerous portraits speak of the enterprising people who helped shape the epoch with their *vita activa*. The conception of man is always an expression of the aspirations of an era: what do we want, how do we show ourselves? Another theme of this exhibition are the questions about the relationship between humans and nature, and landscape as a place of longing and inspiring retreat.

Venice's splendour and fame were largely based on the fact that many people pursued a common goal – namely, to keep the Serenissima flourishing. It is no different with a large exhibition and a catalogue like this one. The endeavour could only be achieved through the intensive teamwork of numerous colleagues from the Bayerische Staatsgemäldesammlungen. My heartfelt thanks go to all of them for their great motivation and tireless energy. In the following, I would like to mention by name those who have been particularly closely involved in the project.

As assistant curator, Annette Kranz played a major role in the conception and preparation of the exhibition. With her great expertise and circumspection, she also accompanied the production of this catalogue. As a curatorial assistant, Theresa Gatarski has driven forward the realisation of the project in all areas with extreme dedication, and has been a valuable support, not least as an image editor and author. Susanne Engelsberger, Angela Cornelius, Ilona von Máriássy and Yvonne Hildwein very carefully and resourcefully carried out important assistance and secretarial tasks. In addition to her work in the research project, Johanna Pawis supported the curatorial team both as an author and adviser.

Jessica Vogelsang and Alexandra Schatz were responsible for the detailed project coordination. Verena Rayer organised the challenging loan procedures. Simone Ebert conceptualised the demanding personal and digital art education. Anke Palden and Alexandra Hiltmair are in charge of the reliable visitor services. Tine Nehler, Jette Elixmann and Verena Sanladerer are to be thanked for their committed press and communications work, and Bianca Henze and Charlotte Neugebauer for the versatile marketing. Barbara Siebert, Katarina Jelic and Constance Huchette planned the extensive programme of events, which they will also accompany.

The restorative measures and art-technological findings at the Doerner Institut are especially thanks to Eva Ortner, Heike Stege, Jan Schmidt, Ulrike Fischer, Johannes Engelhardt, Ronja Emmerich and Anneliese Földes. Important restorations of works in our collection were undertaken by the following freelance restorers: Katharina Geffken, Monika Kneer, Daniela Sieber, Barbara Staudacher and Caroline Vogt.

The museum and exhibition technology team carefully set up the exhibition. In the photography department, Sibylle Forster and Nicole Wilhelms produced numerous new photographs. Thanks also go to the local administration under the direction of Benjamin Roger, the team of the security and operations department as well as all the staff in central services for their dedicated cooperation.

In this volume, an international circle of renowned authors present current research on Venetian Renaissance painting in the first decades of the 16th century. It is a special pleasure to see how vividly their texts present the interplay between artists and their patrons as well as the shared ideals and achievements so specific to the lagoon city. For their profound and inspiring contributions, my heartfelt thanks – also on behalf of Andreas Schumacher as editor – go to Theresa Gatarski, Johannes Grave, Chriscinda Henry, Henry Kaap, Annette Kranz, Antonio Mazzotta, Johanna Pawis and Catherine Whistler.

Hirmer Verlag has produced this beautiful catalogue; it was realised with much care and precision by Jutta Allekotte as project manager and Lucia Ott as graphic designer. Uta Barbara Ullrich is to thank for the excellent German editing; the apt translations from English and Italian are by Birgit Lamerz-Beckschäfer and Rita Seuß. For the English edition of the volume, Julian Jain translated from German and Laura Bennett from Italian; the careful English editing was done by Ariane Kossack.

The exceptionally inspiring and instructive design of the exhibition architecture is thanks to Juliette Israël. The elegant lettering was designed by Silke Weigl and Sebastian Struch, and produced and mounted by Annette Martin. With their design of the communication media, Agentur Parat.cc gave the exhibition its face. Ursula Vorwerk and Martin Beyer wrote the audio guide texts at Linon Medien. Paolo del Panta, the editor of *All About Italy,* developed the cooperation with partners and sponsors with great commitment. We would thus like to thank the following collaboration partners for their support and cooperation: Orchesterakademie der Münchner Philharmoniker, Yehudi Menuhin Live Music Now München e.V., Staatstheater am Gärtnerplatz Garibaldi, Eataly, Air Dolomiti and The Charles Hotel.

For important advice, stimulating discussions and support, the project team would like to thank Jaynie Anderson, Jens Burk, Caroline

Campbell, Marco Cavarzere, Roberto Contini, Francesca Del Torre Scheuch, Gabriel Dette, Bernd Ebert, Hans Ellermann, Gretchen Hirschauer, Annette Hojer, Oliver Kase, Peter Kerber, Eckart Lingenauber, Giulio Manieri Elia, Antonio Mazzotta, Rebecca Müller, Elke Oberthaler, Paolo del Panta, Marco Pesarese, Priscilla Pfannmüller, Alexander Röstel, Neville Rowley, Petra Schäfer-Andreoli, Alexandra Schumacher and Oliver Tostmann.

Even six months before the opening, securing essential funds to finance the exhibition was a challenge. This makes the constant support from the Herbert Schuchardt-Stiftung all the more valuable, without whose wonderful help all the major projects of the Alte Pinakothek would no longer be feasible. I would like to thank Generali Deutschland AG and its chairman Stefan Lehmann for its committed support as main sponsor. For their outstanding support, I would like to express my heartfelt thanks to the Ernst von Siemens Kunststiftung and its secretary general Martin Hoernes as well as to the Hubert Burda Stiftung, its board of directors and Dr Hubert Burda. I am also grateful to the Karl Thiemig-Stiftung and its board, the Stiftung Mittelsten Scheid, Verena Klüser and Dr Wilhelm Winterstein for their generous support. Consorzio Prosecco DOC got involved as a project partner, and Marina Rinaldi as a sponsor.

A number of private individuals and companies from the circle of the Pinakotheks-Verein have come forward to support the restoration of paintings from the Venetian collection of the Alte Pinakothek. The following should also be mentioned here: Eyb&Wallwitz Vermögensmanagement, Charlotte and Nikolaus von Bomhard as well as Isabel and Andreas Gocke. I would like to express my sincere thanks to Elisabeth zu Sayn-Wittgenstein, chairwoman of the Pinakotheks-Verein, and all members of the board for this initiative and for further facilitating discussions. I would also like to thank the Free State of Bavaria and the taxpayers who provide the initial foundations for the fulfilment of museum tasks by ensuring that the ongoing operation of our museums is secured at all times.

It is a great pleasure that, despite a one-year postponement of the exhibition and necessary adjustments to the concept, we have succeeded in bringing together so many precious works of the Venetian Renaissance on loan in Munich. Together with the curator, I would especially like to thank the numerous colleagues who welcomed our project idea with great interest and goodwill and who now place their trust in the exhibition as lenders.

Museums have long ceased to be temples for visitors kneeling in worship in front of great art; instead, they are social spaces or so-called third places where one enters into conversation about art and the human condition, about history and the present, about questions of humanity, experiences of humanity and images of humanity. May the *Venezia 500* project provide the opportunity for all this and have a long-lasting impact. For some years now, it has no longer been a matter of course to be able to launch such major undertakings, and it has become all the more important to give them the space they deserve.

I wish you, dear readers, all the happiness of seeing and understanding. To all the aforementioned, to all our partners and supporters, I offer my heartfelt thanks. The final thanks, however, are due to Andreas Schumacher as well as all the contributors and supporters for their belief that this project is as necessary as it is forward-looking and that it will ultimately be everlasting.

Professor Bernhard Maaz
General Director of the
Bayerische Staatsgemäldesammlungen

Venice's longing for land

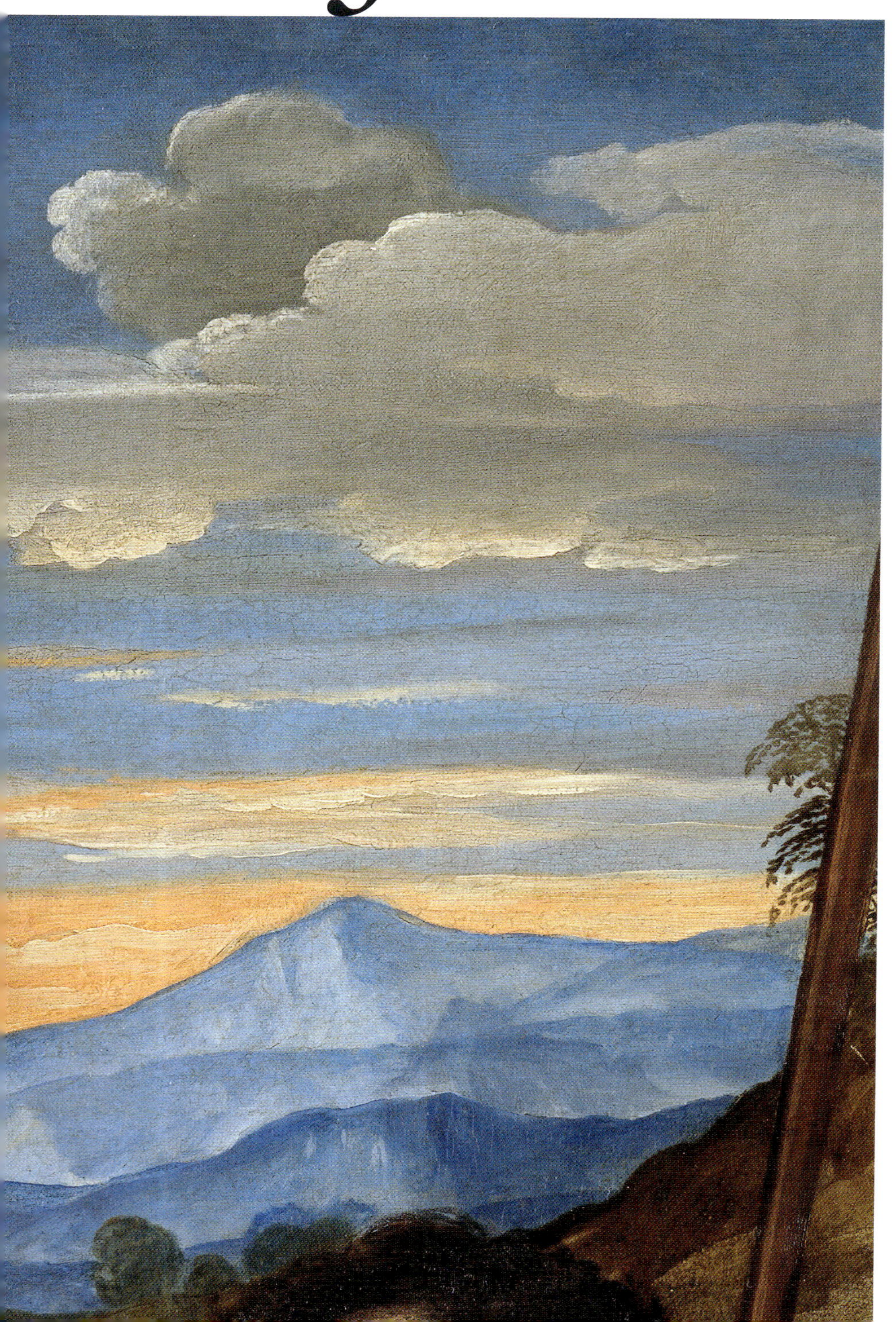

How the dream of Arcadia revolutionised landscape and portrait painting: an introduction

ANDREAS SCHUMACHER

All the paintings we present in this volume are of Venetian origin. Their specific innovative features, which have made them the protagonists of the current exhibition at the Alte Pinakothek, are due to the specific social and cultural conditions of the lagoon city. And yet none of these works depicts the city of Venice, so artfully built in the water, or the lagoon itself – neither the sacral and profane histories do so, whose real 'protagonist' is the landscape, nor the portraits with their window-view backdrops. Instead, the painters invite the viewer to let their gaze wander across the expanse of lush, hilly landscapes, leading it ever deeper and up to the peaks of the southern Alps. In many instances, sun-coloured skies stretch across the horizon and set a strong example for the fact – so intensively dwelt upon by art historians – that Venetian painting is uniquely distinguished by the atmospheric reproduction of the phenomena of colour and light.

The yellow-red, pink, white and deep-blue hues of the sky, so convincingly composed by the painters on the basis of their studies of nature, was an important inspiration for the scenography of our exhibition in Munich. Even more essential to the decision-making process in this regard, however, were the unmistakable appearance and the uniquely homogeneous colour tone of the city of Venice. Both provided a colour gradient that now forms the background of the exhibits in many places in the presentation and transfers the atmosphere around the works' place of origin to the Alte Pinakothek. It was probably not so much the green hue of the mainland, the *Terraferma*, in all its nuances, but primarily the richly varied play of colours in the materials of their home city that honed the Venetian painters' extraordinary sensitivity for colour and surface qualities: this applies above all to the glowing marble and the warm tones of the bricks as well as the consonance of the architecture with the light blues and muted greys of the sky and water, doubled by the reflections of the water. Moreover, local craft products – mosaics, glass, silk fabrics and other textiles, for example – as well as the colourful variety of international goods, such as spices, pigments, porcelains, precious stones and carpets, provided a strong impetus for a differentiated perception of colour tones and all the optical effects associated with them.

Contrary to what the works brought together in this volume and in the exhibition suggest, the artists' attention was also focused on the architectural form and social life of the Serenissima. They celebrated Venice's glory in great campaigns of decoration for the Doge's Palace or the *Scuole* (lay confraternities) with monumental views of the central locations as well as the gatherings and festivities celebrated there. In doing so, they anticipated the triumph of the 18th-century *vedute*, which, as souvenirs in many residences and country estates throughout Europe, proclaimed Venice as a particularly ambitious creation by the hand of man. Even the foundation soil has been laboriously wrested from nature here, while all building materials invariably had to be brought in from outside. Nothing is in its natural place in the literal sense. Hardly any city can thus be a more suitable symbol of civilisation than Venice and simultaneously so impressively demonstrate the great achievements as well as the high fragility of this very civilisation. This can be directly experienced by travellers today as it was five hundred years ago. Despite the threat of decay, the resulting protective measures and the steadily decreasing number of inhabitants, the fascination for its unique urban fabric still belies the fact that this city, even far from its heyday as a maritime power, is for better or worse intrinsically linked to the water, representing a singular existence that in earlier times found its meaningful expression in the annual solemn marriage of the Doge to the sea as part of the Festa della Sensa on Ascension Day.

For all its beauty, even those spending only a few days in Venice experience how demanding life can be here, and not just during floods. One quickly feels cramped or trapped. The narrow and dark alleys, which hardly offer any sense of orientation, can have an oppressive effect. The view is always obstructed if one doesn't happen to be in a large square, on a bridge or by the banks of a canal. In rainy or stormy weather, it is almost impossible to escape the damp and cold. And although the city has gardens and parks to offer, including not only the famous Giardini, a lack of greenery for the eye becomes apparent. There is quite simply a lack of natural land areas to satisfy the need for repose and free movement.

Five hundred years ago, these challenges were, of course, accompanied by far more restrictions and numerous existentially threatening events. The city's vulnerability was emphatically brought to mind time and again – for example, during epidemics such as the plague that broke out in 1503/04 and 1510, but mainly in the case of warlike conflicts that challenged both its dominance as a maritime and trading power as well as its so vital mainland possessions. Venice's prosperity, based on overseas trade, was severely affected by defeats in the wars against the Ottoman Empire (1499–1503) and by the shift in trade routes resulting from the discovery of America (1492) and the opening up of the sea route to India (1498). In addition to epidemics, famines and destructive fires destroying the Fondaco dei Tedeschi in 1505 and the Rialto market in 1514 shook the proud city society as well. Especially drastic for the period relevant here was the Battle of Agnadello lost on 14 May 1509. With this defeat against the European powers united in the League of Cambrai (the Holy Roman Empire, the Papal States, France, England, Spain and various Italian states), Venice forfeited its large territories in northern Italy. Only a few decades earlier, with the Peace of Lodi in 1454 and the Treaty of Bagnolo in 1484, it had fought for the greatest expansion of its mainland possessions, which were of the utmost importance not least for the food supply of the lagoon city. This now stood in contrast to the loss of almost the entire *Terraferma*; the League's troops advanced as far as Mestre. This experience was a collective trauma and undoubtedly had a decisive influence on the patrons and artists who, despite the political events, set off together into the golden age of Venetian painting.

The paintings, drawings and prints presented in this catalogue bear witness to how much the Venetians yearned for green land and open nature; for gardens, a large number of which - as Jacopo de' Barbari's (1440/50 or c. 1470–before 1516) famous plan shows (see pp. 31–32) - were also found in the urban area; for the refuge of their villas and country estates; for the areas of agriculture and animal husbandry; as well as for wild nature with its watercourses, forests, rocks and mountains. This longing was emphatically cultivated within the elite circles that dominated innovative artistic activity, as will be explained below. The discourse on literary and philosophical questions, the contemplation of pictorial works and the making of music together formed the source of inspiration and, at the same time, the basis of reception for the novel, enigmatic paintings referred to as "poesie" with which Giorgione (1473/74–1510) above all others was to revolutionise the painterly representation of landscape.

The works of Giovanni Bellini (c. 1435–1516) were an essential prerequisite for the establishment of landscape panoramas as a pictorial theme in their own right – as seen in the large-format drawings by Giulio Campagnola (c. 1482–c. 1516) and his adopted son Domenico Campagnola (c. 1500-1564), presented in this volume by Catherine Whistler (cat. 32, 34–36; also see p. 87, fig. 2; p. 89, fig. 3). Bellini's devotional pictures (cf. cat. 1, 22, 23) as well as some of his rare secular works, including the four enigmatic allegories completed around 1485/95 (cat. 5a–d), depict man and nature in harmonious union. They leave no doubt that the vast landscapes, which present meticulously studied details of flora and fauna, are not merely decorative backgrounds for the figurative protagonists, but also convey meanings and moods, while having a very deliberate effect on the process of viewing. In this volume, Johannes Grave shows that the rich, symbolic details in Bellini's landscapes offered a wide range of material for the Christian allegorical interpretation practised by his contemporaries, but did not necessarily serve a clearly defined goal in the sense of a precisely outlined message. Thus, Bellini's depictions of a nature created by God and shaped by man encouraged viewers to let their gaze wander through the picture, as if on an extended excursion, thanks to the elusive openness of the contexts of meaning. Instead of finding a system of signs that could be clearly deciphered according to the patterns of the early modern language of images, the recipients were encouraged to explore the depictions in an imaginative and associative manner. By intensified viewing and pondering, they thus reached a state of meditative contemplation favourable to devotion.

It is precisely this state that St Jerome achieves through his retreat into the great outdoors. At least this is what the depictions of the Christian hermit emphasise, which, under the influence of humanist teachings and the ecclesiastical reform movement, enjoyed great popularity in northern Italy for a long time from the middle of the 15th century onwards, especially among Venetian collectors. The two small-format devotional paintings by Giovanni Bellini and Cima da Conegliano (1459/60–1517/18) – representing two highlights of the selected works in this exhibition (cat. 1, 2) – situate the reading or penitent saint between rugged rock faces in the foreground of the pictures, while their middle and backgrounds comprise pure landscape paintings: here, the hilly countryside of Veneto stretches out with its waters and a characteristic town of the region, surrounded by extensive fortified walls, while mountain ranges bound the horizon. In Bellini's scene with Jerome, one even thinks of a real city of the *Terraferma*, Marostica, in the province of Vicenza. If this saint were not so closely associated with the longing of the owners of such paintings to find strength and creativity through relaxing escapes into nature, one would suspect that the artists were only attracted to this subject because it offered them an opportunity to demonstrate their talent for atmospheric landscape portraits.

The curiosity and ability of the masters working in Venice around 1500 to make detailed observation of nature an elementary component of their art resulted essentially from their good knowledge of Early Netherlandish painting. Their achievements informed collectors' demands and were accordingly reflected in the observations that Marcantonio Michiel (1484–1552) made in the art collections of his hometown. In his *Notizia d'opere del disegno*, in which he compiled his impressions, he for the first time identified the landscape ("paese") as an essential, even primary pictorial subject. He did not only praise Giorgione's pioneering atmospheric-poetic art of depiction in this field, but also emphasised Bellini's achievements, for instance, as exemplified in his much-admired *St Francis in the Desert* (see p. 76, fig. 2), a work of the highest perfection, including a rich selection of natural elements, which only at first glance appears all too fond of detail. The Venetian painters at the beginning of the 16th century must also have been keenly aware of the artistic potential of meticulous analytical study of nature demonstrated by Leonardo da Vinci (1452–1519) and Albrecht Dürer (1471–1528); for Leonardo sought refuge in the lagoon city in 1500 and Dürer's art not only met with a resounding response during his two stays there (1494/95 and 1505–1507), but also attracted a great deal of long-term attention due to the *Feast of the Rosary*, painted for San Bartolomeo in 1506 and, in particular, his prints. The fundamental importance of the direct study of nature stimulated in this way, not least for the persuasive power of Titian's landscapes (c. 1488/90-1576), is revealed by their drawing-led preparation, as exemplified by the New York drawing with a group of trees presented in the prelude to the exhibition (cat. 30).

Giorgione's *The Tempest* (see p. 72, fig. 1) marks the beginning of a new chapter in European landscape painting: the painter has freed himself from the traditional task of rendering landscape solely as a space for religious or mythological content and devoted himself to the challenge of developing an artistic expression for creative nature itself in the first place. Giorgione chooses the transitory moment of a thunderstorm to capture on canvas, for the first time, the all-encompassing and unifying effect of the specific atmosphere of a fictitious natural scene. The enigmatic pictorial characters suggest a definite message, which the painter, however, consciously resists just as much as the traditional effort to capture divine creation in detail in a coherent picture. On the contrary, he demonstratively claims for his art the freedom of poetry, whose reception – as can only be briefly outlined here – provided the decisive impetus for the powerful evolution of Venetian landscape painting already initiated by Giovanni Bellini.

At the meetings of the humanist circles that were so central to this development and are presented in this volume primarily by Chriscinda Henry, a common literary interest dominated alongside the contemplation of art and music making. In the homes of collectors and patrons, artists, musicians, singers, authors, publishers and scholars met and participated intensively in the rediscovery of ancient pastoral poetry. Their knowledge of ancient poetry, such as Theocritus's *Idylls* and Virgil's *Bucolics*, undoubtedly made them particularly receptive to the contemporary bestseller of bucolic literature: the romance titled *Arcadia* by the Neapolitan Jacopo Sannazaro, which first appeared – initially as a pirated edition – in Venice in 1502 and 1504. The text, formulated in prose and verse, evokes the Arcadian paradise sung about in Virgil's pastoral poems, where the autobiographical hero Sincero finds refuge after fleeing the city due to political unrest and disappointed love. With their affinity for art, the Venetian patricians recognised themselves in Sincero, driven by a longing to experience originality and tranquillity, beauty and sensuality. They strove to regain lost freedom, creative power and true love, to finally answer for themselves the question of the deeper meaning of life. The escape from the reality of their city, which was shaped by economic and social constraints, could of course take on a very tangible form with stays in country estates and the villas of the *Terraferma;* however, the dominant feature and causal factor for the artistic work under discussion here was the fashion cultivated in the circles described above to immerse themselves in fictitious alternate worlds. This spiritual escapism ranged from contemplative study to communal art experiences and pastoral games.

For the wealthy and educated patrician Gabriele Vendramin (1484–1552), for example, in whose possession Michiel saw Giorgione's

The Tempest in 1530, it was clear that he had found himself in his *camerino* or *studiolo* while reading and contemplating art. His collection gave him peace and tranquillity in his working life, Vendramin noted in his will. Based on such testimonies, Stephen J. Campbell has convincingly reconstructed that the cultural elite of Venice at the start of the 16th century, under the impression of their reading of Lucretius and Virgil, considered reading and collecting to be particularly conducive to individual moral education, because both freed the mind from worldly worries and disturbances. Just as important to Vendramin as the quiet, contemplative engagement with the books and works of art surrounding him was the lively discourse in a circle of like-minded people, who, for example, collectively puzzled over the *Tempest* scene, enticing an imaginary excursion into the landscape of the painting. The young man in the left foreground of the picture, identified by his clothing and staff as a wandering urban patrician, immediately offered himself as a figure for identification; his demonstrative pondering expression, which seems to be triggered by the encounter with the female figure sitting naked on the ground nursing a child, directly connected to the longings of the viewers nurtured by bucolic and Petrarchan poetry. Regardless of whether the enigmatic female figure was interpreted as a nymph-like creature of nature or as the divine embodiment of beauty, love and maternal power – namely, as Venus Genetrix – the Arcadian landscape image unmistakably set the tone for the recipients' sensual projections evoking the lost paradise.

Fig. 1 Titian, *Boy with Pipe*, c. 1510/15, Windsor, The Royal Collection, HM King Charles III

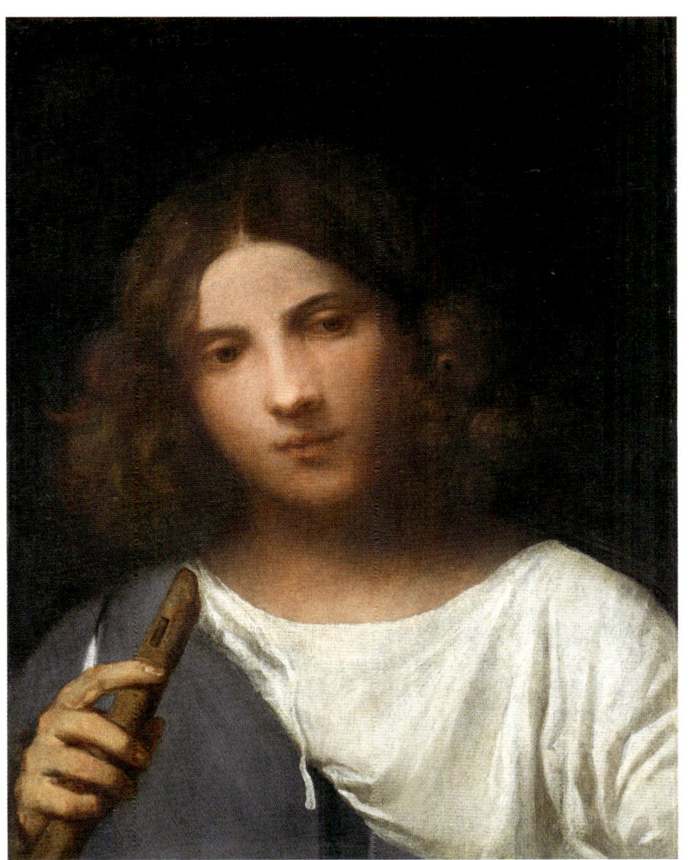

The painting *Concert Champêtre*, which Titian created (see p. 167, fig. 3) when the trauma caused by the Battle of Agnadello was still fresh, is, like Giorgione's *The Tempest*, an icon of allegorical pastoral landscape painting in early cinquecento Venice. And as Chriscinda Henry has recently pointed out, it proves to be a perfect mirror image of the dreamed up and acted out Arcadian pastoral fantasies influenced by literature. Like Giorgione's protagonist in *The Tempest*, Titian's main figure, the lute-strumming young man, wears striped stockings. These reveal him to be one of the young patricians of humanist spirit, who flaunted their association in alliances of friendship through extravagant fashionable costume. The *Concert Champêtre* undoubtedly depicts a member of the so-called Compagnie della Calza, perhaps even the commissioner of the painting himself. Titian shows his luxuriously dressed protagonist with a red beret in a *Terraferma* idyll. He takes little notice of the accompanying nymphs, who are first and foremost symbols of his yearning, but leans intimately towards a shepherd of the same age, characterised by wild, frizzy hair; as his alter ego, he is the focus of all his interest. In this encounter, the city meets the countryside, art meets nature.

Through the illustrations of ancient and contemporary bucolic texts, Arcadian themes became established in Venetian pictorial art, including the motif of the shepherd in particular, which sometimes had strong homoerotic connotations (cf. cat. 10–12). The music-making shepherd was a popular role model when it came to praising an artist – and this did not only apply to poets and musicians. First and foremost, Giorgione and Sebastiano del Piombo (c. 1485–1547), as reported by Giorgio Vasari (1511–1574), attracted attention with their musical talent. Their skill on the lute facilitated their access to the circles of patrons and ensured them a relevant function in the pastoral game. Seductive portraits of ideally handsome youths, such as Giorgione's *Boy with Arrow* (cat. 62) or Titian's *Boy with a Pipe (The Shepherd)* (fig. 1), are rooted in this context and are, as Theresa Gatarski explains in the present volume, closely related to the much-discussed ideal female portraits variously expressed in Venetian painting (cf. cat. 52, 53, 57–59; see also p. 160, fig. 2). For as in the case of the *belle donne*, inspired by the love poetry of Petrarch (1304–1374) and contemporary treatises on female beauty, the creators and recipients of these male portraits (cf. cat. 61) made the claim, influenced by Neoplatonic teachings, to follow a longing for divine beauty and knowledge that goes far beyond the earthly, painfully unfulfilled desire for love.

In this sense, the female nudes in the *Concert Champêtre*, which oscillate between a real and an imagined image, embody the contents and aims of pastoral longings. They convey what for contemporary recipients was a very worldly – but at the same time also poetic and philosophical – attraction of such approachable divine beauty as the one Giorgione rendered sleeping in a landscape in his famous *Sleeping Venus* painting (c. 1508/10) in Dresden. The portrait *Young Woman at*

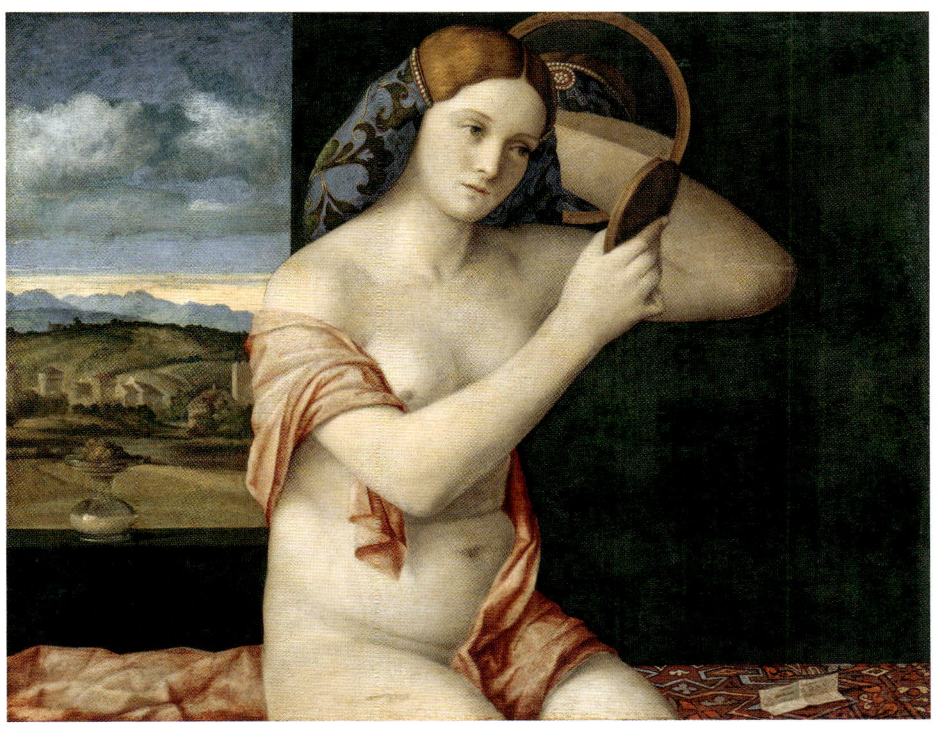

Fig. 2 Giovanni Bellini, *Young Woman at Her Toilette*, 1515, Vienna, Kunsthistorisches Museum

Her Toilette (fig. 2), signed by Giovanni Bellini in 1515, displays almost all facets of the depiction of Venetian beauties. While it at first seems to be connected to the numerous portrait-like *belle donne* and, among these, especially to Titian's variations on the theme (cat. 55, 57–59), it additionally evokes ancient and contemporary depictions of Venus and pastoral scenes on account of the nudity, the grasp of the hair, the mirror and the landscape. Admittedly, the viewers, whose roles and gazes Bellini consciously included in the calculated impact of the picture, are at first offered a very tangible erotic conception instead of a sublimation of the scene: they see themselves in the role of voyeurs peering into the room of a real Venetian lady who does not notice them, being absorbed in her own reflection in the mirror while wrapping her hair in a sumptuously decorated hairnet that marks her as a married woman. In view of the idealised features of the young woman and the artificiality of the entire arrangement, however, there is ultimately no doubt that the painter has not portrayed an individual personality here, but rather sought to artistically express an idea of divine beauty in such a way that the portrait, just like the motifs around it, including first and foremost the carpet and the glass vase but also the landscape, turns the creative potential of his art itself into its subject. As in the case of the window views of the *Terraferma*, which form the backdrops in numerous Venetian portraits of the first decades of the cinquecento (cf. cat. 14, 21, 66, 79–83; also see p. 201, fig. 8), the landscape, conceived here as a picture within a picture, can be read as a metaphor for the extraordinary power of painting, which is able to reproduce or even surpass nature not only in all its manifestations, but also in terms of its very conception.

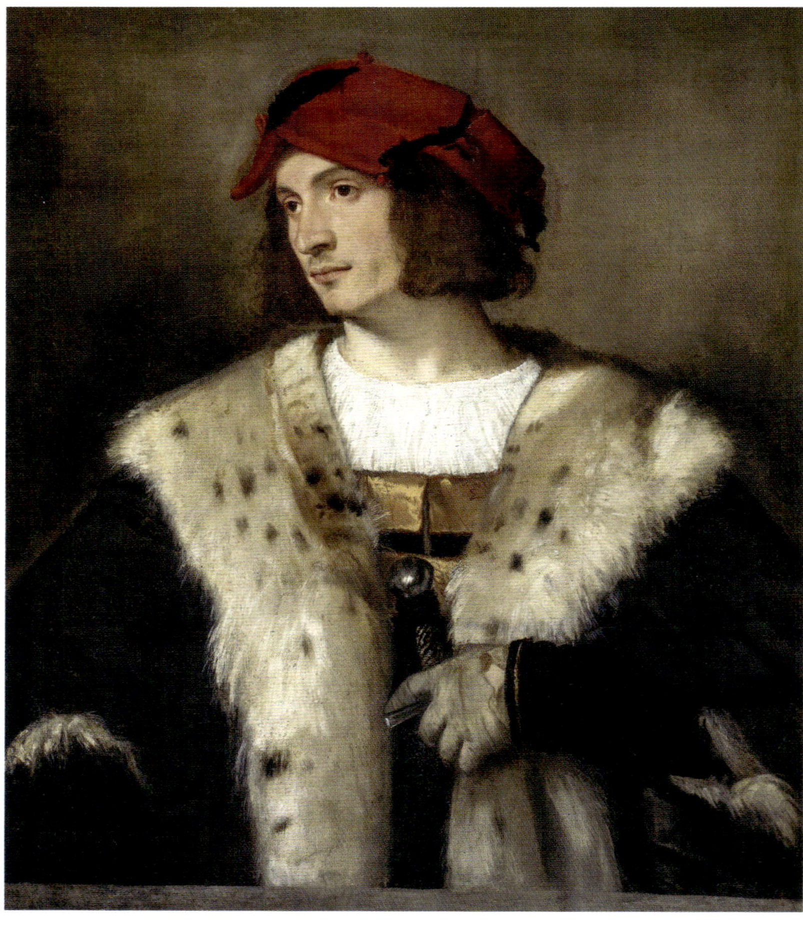

Fig. 3 Titian, *Portrait of a Man in a Red Hat*, c. 1510/20, New York, The Frick Collection

The collectors and recipients of the novel pictorial creations presented here attracted attention and harsh criticism in equal measure through their self-confident elitist demeanour and especially their melancholy pursuit of contemplativeness. Conservative spokespersons of the city accused them of disregarding the virtues supporting the common good of the republic, of not devoting themselves adequately to the political offices they held, and of no longer pushing decisively enough the factors so elementary to the preservation of power, seafaring and trade. The *Portrait of a Man in a Red Cap* by Titian in the Frick Collection in New York (fig. 3) is a pointed example of how the escapism cultivated by the rising generation of patrons and artists led to a new self-portrayal that ostentatiously broke with traditional role models. People now refrained from presenting themselves in their public, social position, preferring instead a private appearance that reflected personal interests and desires or even youthful beauty and nonchalance as a sovereign yet sensitive individual. Accordingly, the young patricians no longer had themselves portrayed in the traditional and rather simple garb of the elites, but in courtly, elegant and preferably black clothing with luxurious accessories – the stranger in Titian's New York portrait, for example, wears a noble red cap that connects him with the lute player in the *Concert Champêtre*. The patrons' desire for an approachable reproduction of their personality, which was shaped by their own longings and often manifested itself as melancholic and contemplative introspection, corresponded to the painters' constant endeavour to also depict the character of their counterparts through their art, going beyond their outer appearance. With the lyrical form of male portraits, the Venetians gave European portraiture a pioneering innovation, prominently represented in the exhibition, not least with Titian's now restored *Portrait of a Man* (cat. 15) in Munich. The genesis, specific expression and reception of Venetian portrait art in all its facets are comprehensively discussed in the present volume by Henry Kaap, Antonio Mazzotta and Annette Kranz. The fact that Giorgione's work soon unfolded its effect in the field of portrait art with just as much revolutionary force as in landscape painting can be shown in the presentation at the Alte Pinakothek by means of a small but concise group of portraits, which, as the contribution by Johanna Pawis breaks down, also includes a (re)discovery that is important for the oeuvre of this enigmatic painterly genius (cat. 43).

Viewing the faces of the personalities sensitively characterised by Giorgione and his artist colleagues – who in turn look back firmly at us viewers – enables an almost immediate encounter with the cultural elites of Renaissance Venice, despite a temporal distance of 500 years. The portrait art of the old masters opens the way for a fascinating journey through time: the portrayed personages become so close to life, body and soul that we feel transported back half a millennium. The intensity of this encounter grows in the presented context with the awareness that we find pivotal desires of these persons reflected in the lyrical and idealised portraits as well as in the Arcadian landscapes. Moreover, the topicality of these same desires is unbroken, since they revolve, as briefly shown here and explained in more detail in the following contributions, around the profoundly human striving for contemplation and beauty, for love and knowledge, and thus around the great longing to live in harmony with creation.

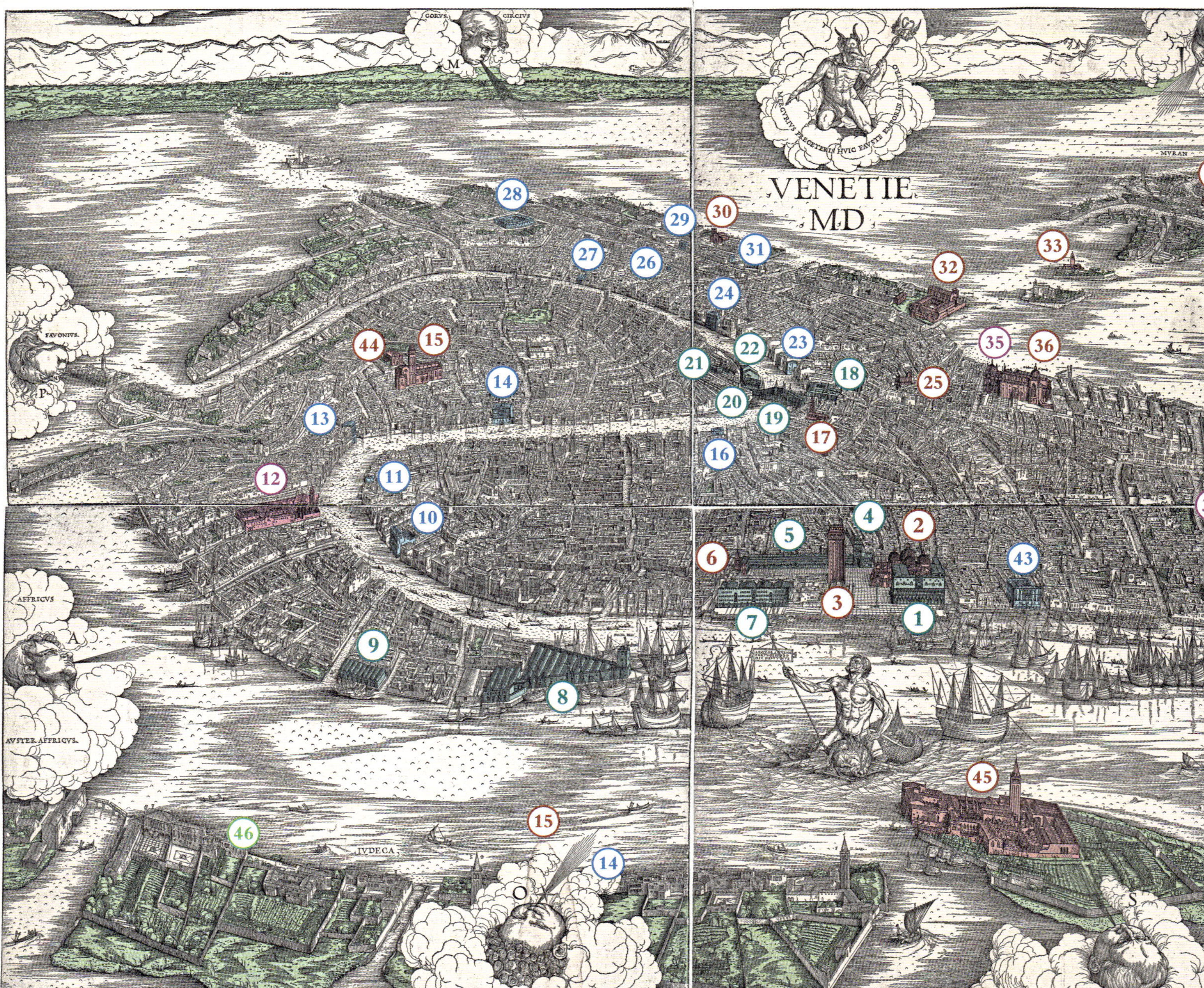

1. **Palazzo Ducale** Doge's Palace and seat of government
2. **San Marco**
3. **Campanile di San Marco**
4. **Torre dell'Orologio** Clock tower
5. **Procuratie Vecchie** Administrative seat of the procurators
6. **San Geminiano**
7. **Fondaco del Frumento o Granai di Terranova** Public granary and health department
8. **Dogana del Mar** Customs facilities
9. **Saloni del Sale** Municipal salt depots
10. **Palazzo Malombra** From 1531: Palazzo Corner della Ca' Granda
11. **Ca' del Duca** Workshop for Titian's state commissions until 1531
12. **Santa Maria della Carità** Church, convent and the first Scuola Grande
13. **Palazzo Foscari**
14. **Palazzo Pisani-Moretta**
15. **Santa Maria Gloriosa dei Frari** Franciscan church and convent
16. **Palazzo of Leonardo Dandolo** From 1551: Pietro Aretino's residence
17. **San Bartolomeo** Church of the German merchants
18. **Fondaco dei Tedeschi** German trading post
19. **Rialto Bridge**
20. **Loggia dei Mercanti** Merchants' lodge
21. **Banco Giro di Rialto** State and private banks
22. **Official seat of the Camerlenghi** (Treasurers) **and the Rason Vecchie** (Fiscal authority)
23. **Palazzo Bolani** From 1529: Pietro Aretino's residence
24. **Ca' d'Oro**

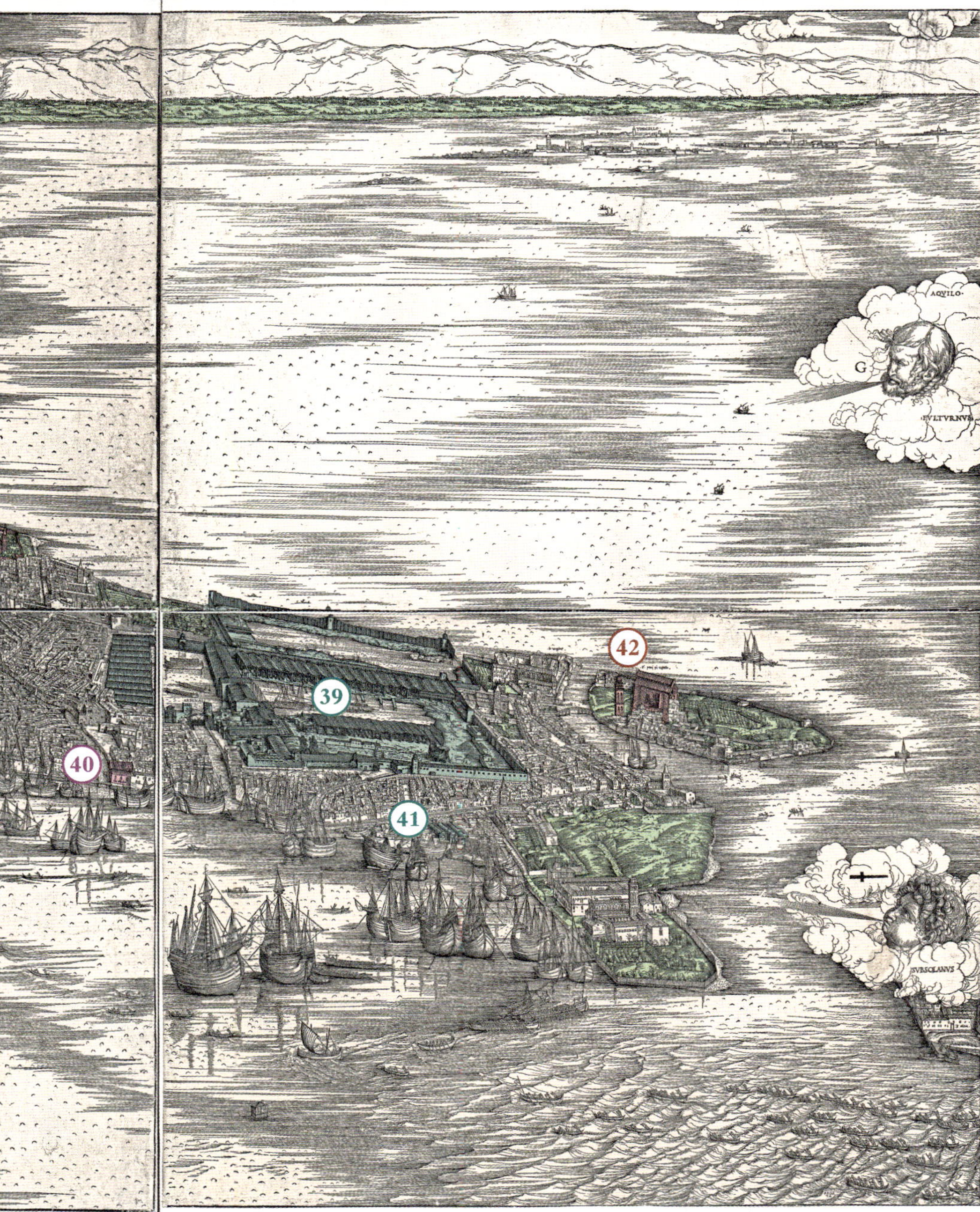

- Public buildings and monuments
- Churches and convents
- Private *palazzi* and residences
- *Scuole* and *ospedali* (confraternity buildings and charitable institutions)
- Gardens

(25) **Santa Maria dei Miracoli**

(26) **Palazzo Vendramin a Santa Fosca** Residence of the collector Gabriele Vendramin

(27) **Palazzo Loredan** Today Palazzo Vendramin-Calergi

(28) **Campo del Ghetto Nuovo** Jewish quarter

(29) **Later Casa-Bottega of Jacopo Tintoretto** Residence and workshop

(30) **Church of Madonna dell'Orto** (Madonna of the Orchard)

(31) **Later residence of the agent and patron Carlo Maggi**

(32) **Church and convent of the Order of the Crociferi with Ospedale** (Residential home for single women)

(33) **San Michele in Isola** Camaldolese church and convent

(34) **Basilica dei Santi Maria e Donato di Murano**

(35) **Scuola Grande di San Marco**

(36) **Santi Giovanni e Paolo** Dominican church and convent

(37) **San Francesco della Vigna** Franciscan church and convent

(38) **Scuola Dalmata dei Santi Giorgio e Trifone** Lay confraternity of immigrants from Istria and Dalmatia

(39) **Arsenale** Shipyard and fleet base

(40) **Ca' di Dio** Charitable widows' home

(41) **Corte Colonne** Municipal housing for retired seafarers

(42) **San Pietro in Castello** Church and seat of the Patriarch of Venice

(43) **Palazzo Dandolo** From 1536: Palazzo Gritti

(44) **San Rocco**

(45) **San Giorgio Maggiore** Benedictine church and convent

(46) **Gardens and villas of Giudecca**

ART

1475/76: **Antonello da Messina** in Venice

1479: **Gentile Bellini** at the court of Sultan Mehmed II in Constantinople; **Giovanni Bellini** receives commission for renewing the frescoes of the Sala del Maggior Consiglio in the Doge's Palace

c. 1480: **Giovanni Bellini** completes the painting *St Francis in the Desert*, which was already admired by his contemporaries for its detailed depiction of nature

1488: **Alvise Vivarini** successfully applies for the post of "Painter of the Republic in the Doge's Palace"

1490/98: **Vittore Carpaccio** creates an imaginative and colourful panorama of Venetian city life for the Scuola di S. Orsola depicting monumental scenes from the legend of St Ursula

1494/95: **Albrecht Dürer** in Venice

CONTEMPORARY EVENTS

1479: After 16 years of war, the Republic of Venice signs a peace treaty with the Ottoman Empire under Sultan **Mehmed II**

1484: Treaty of Bagnolo; the Venetian Republic reaches its greatest territorial expansion in northern Italy

1486: **Agostino Barbarigo** is elected Doge

1489: **Caterina Cornaro** abdicates in favour of Venice as Queen of Cyprus

1492: **Christopher Columbus** lands in the Bahamas ("Discovery of the Americas")

1494: The Italian campaign of King **Charles VIII** of France marks the beginning of a phase of armed conflict on the Italian peninsula that lasts almost four decades

from 1494: **Aldus Manutius** prints books with Greek letters in Venice; texts from classical antiquity gain new, widespread appeal

1498: **Vasco da Gama** discovers the sea route to India

1499: Sultan **Bayezid II** attacks the Venetian possessions in the Aegean Sea

1501: **Leonardo Loredan** is elected Doge

1503: For a peace settlement with the Ottoman Empire, Venice accepts large territorial losses in the eastern Mediterranean Sea; as a result, the Republic expands its territorial policy to open up new resources on the *Terraferma*

1504: Publication of **Jacopo Sannazaro's** pastoral poem *Arcadia*

1506: A new law regulates membership of the political and social elite of Venice (entry in the *Libro d'Oro*)

1508: Emperor **Maximilian I** and King **Louis XII** of France ally against Venice at Cambrai; the Pope and the English and Aragonese kings later join the alliance (League of Cambrai)

1509: France declares war on Venice; Pope **Julius II** excommunicates the Maritime Republic; Venice is defeated by the League of Cambrai at Agnadello and loses all mainland possessions

1500: Publication of **Jacopo de' Barbari's** woodcut with a bird's-eye view of Venice; **Leonardo da Vinci** in Venice

from 1500: Venice's pigment sellers jointly form their own trade

1505–1507: **Albrecht Dürer** in Venice

c. 1505/10: **Giorgione** paints *The Tempest*, a pivotal work of landscape painting that remains enigmatic to this day

from 1508: **Giorgione** and **Titian** work on the exterior frescoes of the Fondaco dei Tedeschi, the trading post of the Germans at the Rialto Bridge

1509: **Giovanni Cariani** is documented as a painter in Venice

1510: **Giorgione** dies of the plague raging in Venice; **Palma il Vecchio** is documented as a painter in the city

1511: **Sebastiano del Piombo** leaves Venice for Rome; **Cima da Conegliano** fails in his attempt to privilege the profession of figure painters within the painters' guild

1517: **Titian** receives a broker's patent which, in addition to tax benefits, also includes the privilege of painting all official portraits of the Doge

1518: Unveiling of **Titian's** *Assunta* (*Assumption of the Virgin*) in the Frari Church; **Paris Bordone** is documented as a painter in Venice

from 1520: Giovanni Girolamo Savoldo is documented as a painter in Venice

1525: **Lorenzo Lotto** returns to Venice after stays in the Marches, Rome and Bergamo

1527: After the Sack of Rome by the troops of **Charles V**, intellectuals and artists seek refuge in Venice, including **Jacopo Sansovino**, **Michele Sanmicheli**, **Sebastiano Serlio** and **Pietro Aretino**

1516: Venice assigns Jewish families fleeing from armed conflicts on the *Terraferma* an enclosed quarter in Cannaregio – the Ghetto

1517: By the end of the wars against the League of Cambrai, Venice has regained almost all its former possessions

1520: Soon after **Martin Luther's** posting of his theses in Wittenberg, the first Protestant groups form in the liberal confessional climate of Venice

1521: **Antonio Grimani** is elected Doge

1523: **Andrea Gritti** is elected Doge; his strategy of "renovatio urbis" transforms the cityscape through Renaissance architecture modelled on central Italian designs

1524: Collapse of the wooden Rialto Bridge, decision to build a new bridge in stone

1545: **Francesco Donà** is elected Doge; convening of the Council of Trent with the aim of containing Protestantism

1540: Venice has a population of 129,971, including 4,457 *nobili*

1539: **Pietro Lando** is elected Doge

1537–1540: Sultan **Suleiman I** conquers the last remaining Venetian possessions in the Peloponnese

1530: **Charles V** is crowned Holy Roman Emperor in Bologna

1529: Peace of Bologna; Venice's improved relations with the *Terraferma* are reflected in the culture of the *villeggiatura*

1548: **Titian** with Emperor **Charles V** at the Imperial Diet in Augsburg; **Jacopo Tintoretto's** *The Miracle of the Slave* for the Scuola di San Marco causes a sensation in Venice, Pietro Aretino publicly criticises the artist for the "swiftness of his brushstroke"

1545: **Titian** with Pope **Paul III** in Rome

1539–1542: **Francesco Salviati** and **Giorgio Vasari** introduce a mannerist style of Tuscan–Roman origin to Venice

1536/37: Start of construction of the Zecca (mint), the Biblioteca Marciana and the Loggetta on St Mark's Square according to **Jacopo Sansovino's** plans

1534–1539: **Titian's** monumental painting for the lay confraternity of San Maria della Carità transposes the *Presentation of the Virgin at the Temple* into the landscape of the *Terraferma*

1533: **Titian** is ennobled by Emperor **Charles V** and appointed court painter

1529: **Michelangelo** in Venice

The new golden age

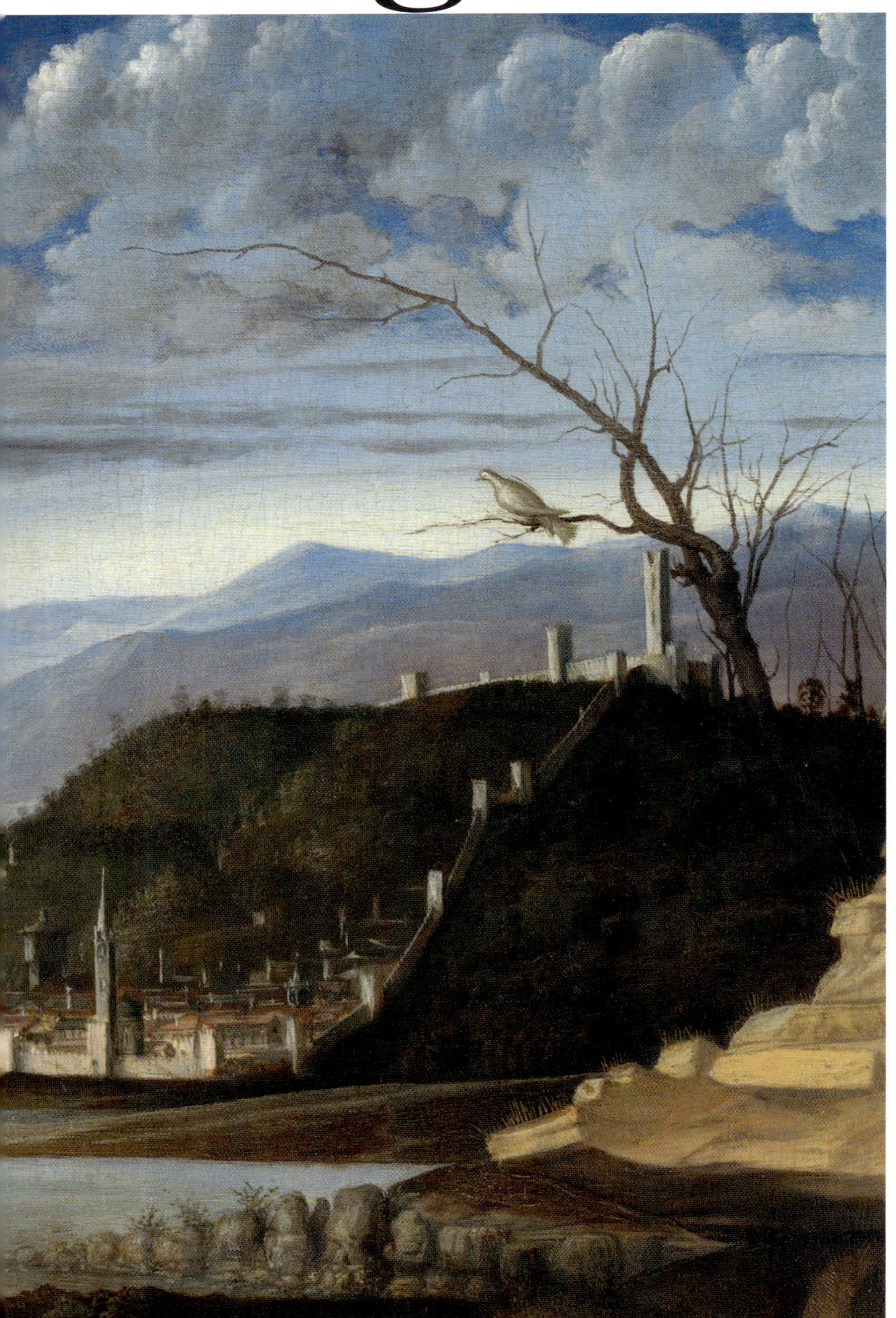

Domestic art collection and Arcadian desires

CHRISCINDA HENRY

"Let your house be […] above all […] a workshop of liberality, a refuge for those in need, a dwelling place for friends, a hospice for foreigners, [and] an academy of philosophers, all of whose halls and gateways, galleries and arcades, resound day and night with wisdom, echo with poetic and oratorical utterance, ring with philosophical truths, where Apollo with his nine sisters [the Muses] may for perpetuity establish a home."[1]

These inspiring words by the Venetian humanist Francesco Negri (1452–1523) appear in his encomium to the Venetian aristocracy, *De moderanda venetorum aristocratia*, which was composed in 1493/94 and originally dedicated to Doge Agostino Barbarigo.[2] Excerpted from a section of the text on "the home as a sacred institution", the epigraph calls on Venetian patricians and elite *cittadini* (citizens) to fashion their private dwellings as welcoming spaces of intellectual and cultural refuge. The humanist topos deployed by Negri justifies conspicuous consumption in the private sphere by relating it to hospitality and the noble social virtues of *magnificentia* (magnificence) and *liberalitas* (liberality) as originally laid out by classical authors, most notably Aristotle in the *Nicomachean Ethics*.[3]

At the time Negri penned these words in at least partial emulation of a set of mentalities and practices already well ensconced at the Italian courts of Naples, Milan, Urbino, Ferrara and Mantua, a small but significant group of precocious Venetian collectors and connoisseurs had already begun to reimagine the private home as a physical and material expression of individual taste and knowledge to be shared with others. Fortuitously for posterity, one of these individuals, the patrician Marcantonio Michiel (1484–1552), compiled a set of unpublished notes, the *Notizia d'opere del disegno*, that document some – although nowhere close to all – of the impressive private art and antiquities collections being amassed in Venice, Padua, Milan and elsewhere in northern Italy between around 1490 and 1540.[4]

The select group of 22 men whose homes Michiel visited in Venice and Padua, along with other Venetian individuals whose collections are documented through wills, probate inventories and other documentary sources, began in the late 15th century to look beyond the kinds of pictures – devotional images of holy figures and family portraits – that traditionally hung on the walls of Venetian homes towards more novel and varied forms of artistic expression.[5] By the first decades of the 16th century, these adventurous Venetian patrons and collectors had engendered a rapidly diversifying art market somewhat analogous to – and closely connected with – that of the cities in the southern Netherlands.[6] As in Antwerp, the new cultural terrain and focus on acquisition, display and the expression of an individual's cultural and intellectual interests created ideal circumstances in Venice for artists to experiment with novel artistic subjects drawn from pagan mythology, ancient history beyond the Christian Bible, literature and contemporary life.

Michiel assembled the *Notizia* from a series of home visits he conducted between 1521 and 1543.[7] The notes present a small cadre of distinctly "modern" Venetian and Paduan collectors – mostly patrician and some citizen-class merchant gentlemen, government officers and bureaucrats, highly placed ecclesiasts, humanist scholars and resident foreigners – as a savvy, sophisticated and closely connected community of connoisseurs with a pronounced taste for both antiquities and contemporary art by northern European and central Italian in addition to local Venetian and Paduan artists. Within his small sample, Michiel traces an intimate, interlaced network of art ownership between Venice and Padua, making special mention of gifts, trades and loans between collectors, noting when drawings, paintings, medals, coins, cameos, engraved gems and ancient statues passed from one owner to another as well as when copies and casts after and preparatory drawings for a given artwork changed hands. He also remarks on the competitive spirit between collectors, most famously Isabella d'Este's (1474–1539) frustrated pursuit of "a picture of a night scene, very beautiful and unique" painted by Giorgione (1473/74–1510), who had recently died. The Venetian collectors who owned these rare works, now rendered even more precious, refused to sell no matter the offering price.[8]

Later 16th-century accounts regarding two of the Venetian collectors Michiel visited – the patrician Gabriele Vendramin (1484–1552) and the *cittadino* Andrea Odoni (1488–1545) – point to the role played by art and other collectable objects of material culture in domestic sociability and what should properly be considered the early salon culture of Venice. In his celebratory guidebook, *Venetia, città nobilissima et singolare* (1581), Francesco Sansovino singles out Vendramin's palace in the parish of Santa Fosca in Cannaregio as "the former meeting place of the virtuosi of the city [...] because there lived Gabriele, the greatest lover of Painting, Sculpture and Architecture [...] who collected various things by the most famous artists of his time [...] by Giorgione da Castelfranco, Giovanni Bellini, Titian and Michelangelo".[9] Giorgio Vasari (1511–1574), in the context of describing the fresco decoration on the facade of Odoni's palace, now lost, anthropomorphises the *casa* itself as "a friend and gathering place of virtuosi" and construes the prominent armoured figures of Minerva and Apollo painted by Girolamo da Treviso to either side of the *piano nobile* balcony as the symbolic guardians of Odoni's hospitality towards knowledge and the arts.[10] Such examples clearly resonate with Negri's call for Venetian elites to establish their homes as dwelling places for Apollo and the Muses.[11]

Unlike their more tradition-bound ancestors, when this new class of artistic patrons and collectors had their portraits painted by the young generation of Venetian artists that included Giorgione, Vincenzo Catena, Titian, Giovanni Cariani and Palma il Vecchio, they did so with an ethos of artful self-fashioning modelled to some degree on the mainland nobility and captured in literary form by Baldassare Castiglione in his *Libro del cortegiano* (largely written between 1508 and 1517, published in Venice in 1528). Their portraits evoke a fresh sense of intimacy and interiority and reflect the personal sensibilities, taste and interests of the sitters, rather than document the public offices they held or the key life events they had achieved, such as marriage or military honour. In the *Notizia*, Michiel attributes Vendramin's portrait – painted around 1517 when he was in his early 30s – to Giovanni Cariani (c. 1485/90–1547), a contemporary of Titian (c. 1488/90–1576) and Sebastiano Luciani, later del Piombo (c. 1485–1547). Jaynie Anderson has identified this portrait with the likeness of an elegant young man dressed in black and holding a glove from the holdings of the Palais Fesch – Musée des Beaux Arts in Ajaccio, although most scholars assign it to Titian (fig. 1).[12]

Whether to be identified as Vendramin's portrait by Cariani or not, the painting in Ajaccio typifies a pronounced trend in early 16th-century Venetian portraiture, when elite men chose to be portrayed not in the traditional *toga* or *vesta*, the austere floor-length

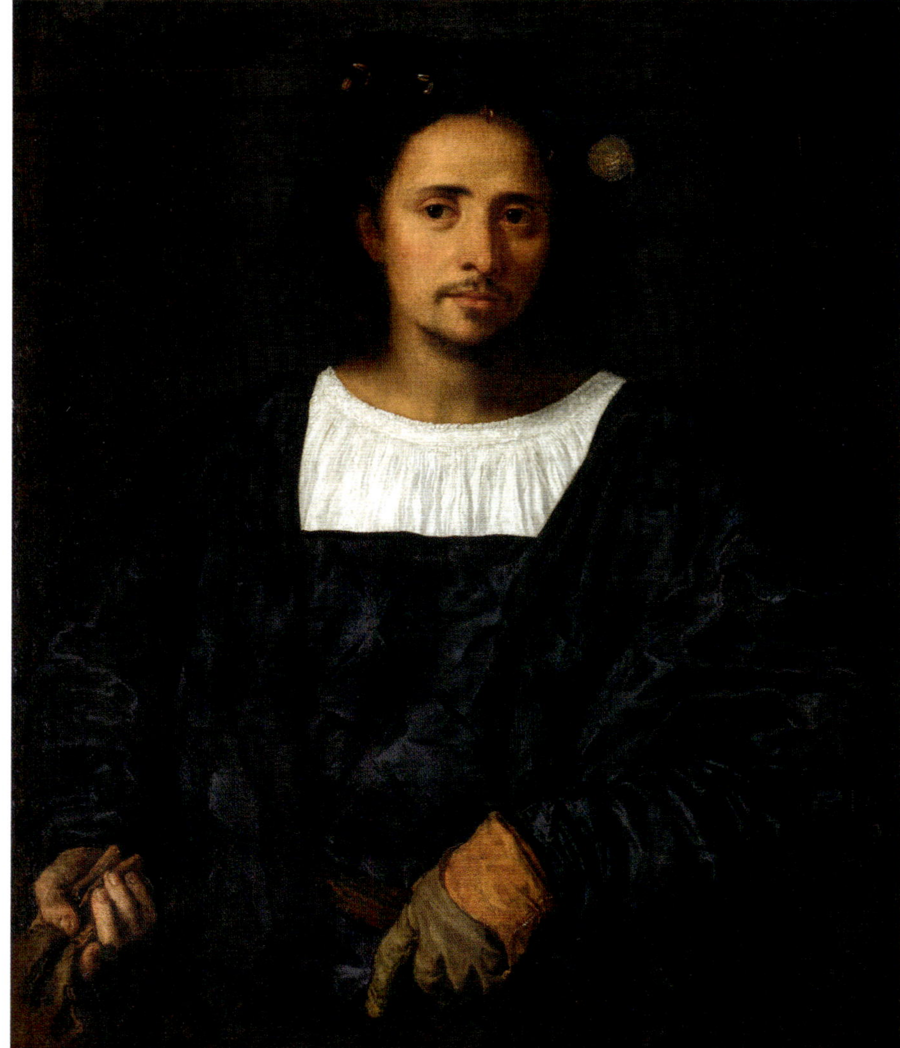

Fig. 1 Titian (or Giovanni Cariani?), *Portrait of a Man with a Glove*, c. 1517, Ajaccio, Palais Fesch – Musée des Beaux Arts (on loan in Paris, Musée du Louvre)

robes worn in public by adult members of the patrician political class, but in fashionable, courtly ensembles of all black, "the most graceful colour for clothing" according to Castiglione.[13] As Marianne Koos and others have amply demonstrated, such portraits are often characterised by a uniform dark or neutral background suggestive of an interior space, an informal or even intimate character, a contemplative or psychologically animated expression and a sense of physical movement, rather than the rigid profile or formal frontal view of earlier portraits.[14] The lightly bearded man in the Ajaccio portrait gazes inquisitively out at the beholder. He wears a fashionably large *berretto tondo,* a round beret with wide laced-up flaps, which is accented with a gilt hat badge in the style of the northern Italian nobility. The meticulously stitched double-faced leather gloves serve as a further marker of his gentility, and his active pose – holding one glove as if he just removed it – epitomises the graceful nonchalance signified by Castiglione's term *sprezzatura*.

Linked to the characterisations by Negri, Sansovino and Vasari of patrons' hospitality towards the arts and intellectual culture is the information we have about artists and their sociable presence in the homes of Venetian collectors like Vendramin and Odoni, some of whom were certainly also their direct patrons. In his biographies of the Venetian painters Giorgione and Sebastiano del Piombo, Vasari mentions the "musical performances and gatherings" to which the two artists were regularly invited as virtuosi, or individuals of exceptional talent, learning and skill.[15] Vasari emphasises that Giorgione and Sebastiano were sought after primarily for their singing and lute playing, which they frequently practised in the homes of noblemen, as well as for their conversation skills, a claim reiterated by Paolo Pino (rec. 1534–1565) and later Carlo Ridolfi (1594–1658).[16]

Albrecht Dürer (1471–1528) describes first-hand the contemporary Venetian social and cultural milieu he enjoyed while residing in Venice between 1505 and 1507 in remarkably similar terms. In a letter home dated February 1506 to his closest friend, the humanist scholar Willibald Pirckheimer, Dürer enthuses: "How I wish you were here at Venice! There are so many nice men among the Italians who seek my company more and more every day – which is very pleasing to one – men of sense and knowledge, good lute-players and pipers, judges of painting, men of much noble sentiment and honest virtue, and they show me much honour and friendship."[17] In another letter to Pirckheimer of the following October, Dürer claims, not without a hint of exaggeration, that within this Venetian network of scholars, musicians, gentlemen connoisseurs and artists, he is treated as a gentleman, a social equal to his patrons, whereas at home in Germany he is considered a parasite: "Here I am a gentleman, at home only a parasite."[18] It does not prove difficult to identify the kind of noble, knowledgeable and virtuous Venetian connoisseurs to whom Dürer here refers: Gabriele Vendramin owned numerous prints by Dürer, including *The Engraved Passion* (1507–1513) and *The Life of the Virgin* (c. 1504–1511) series, as well as a portrait Dürer painted in Venice in 1506, mistakenly later thought to be a self-portrait.[19]

What would Vendramin's *ridotto*, as celebrated by Sansovino, and the concerts and gatherings of noblemen and virtuosi mentioned by Vasari have been like? The term *ridotto* came into use in Venice by the mid-16th century to designate a habitual, salon-like gathering in the home of an informal and flexible character, whereas earlier 16th-century Venetian sources, such as the *Diarii* by Marin Sanudo (1466–1536), commonly use the verb form, as in "se reduceva" (they gathered privately) to describe musical and other domestic gatherings.[20] Rodolfo Baroncini provides a succinct characterisation of the phenomenon: "ridotti were simply gatherings of cultivated men (or those with the ambition to appear as such) where one could enjoy, listen to and discuss musical performances, poetry recited in the vernacular and in Latin, and learned philosophical, medical and scientific analyses."[21] I would only qualify this assessment to say that cultivated women, such as poets, singers and musicians, some of them courtesans, were also participants in such groups, if to a lesser extent than men.[22]

Beyond artists and musicians, the virtuosi who attended the home gatherings hosted by Vendramin, Odoni and other similar individuals would likely have included a fluid roster of learned and talented individuals such as poets, writers, publishers and humanist scholars. On the guest list would have been the host's friends, acquaintances and professional colleagues, both locals and foreign visitors, among them other like-minded collectors and connoisseurs. From contemporary accounts and texts such as Castiglione's *Libro del cortegiano* and Paolo Cortesi's *De Cardinalatu* (1510), we know that topics of conversation included the theory and interpretation of art, architecture, music and poetry as well as the *paragone*, or comparison, of the relative merits of these arts.[23] Carefully displayed objects – ancient and modern sculptures, paintings, maps, globes, books, vases, musical and scientific instruments, *naturalia* – provided the material touchstones for discussions between owners and their erudite interlocutors, as confirmed in texts such as Antonfrancesco Doni's *I Marmi* (1552).[24]

Michiel's descriptions of artworks and accounts of their manufacture, subject matter, size and authorship also imply detailed conversations between himself, the various owners and others, including artists and agents. Michiel was a respected collector of painting and sculpture himself as well as a friend of the publisher Aldus Manutius, prominent Paduan and Venetian intellectuals and artists, including the painters Giovanni Bellini, Titian, Sebastiano, Vincenzo Catena, the sculptor Andrea Riccio, the painter-illuminator Guido Celere and the painter-illuminator-engraver Giulio Campagnola.[25]

The artworks, antiquities and other collectable objects stored and displayed within Venetian Renaissance homes – Islamic metalware, Chinese porcelain, specimens of exotic flora and fauna, maps, globes, portraits of popes and Ottoman sultans – indexed people and places far beyond the urban confines of Venice.[26] In a similar way, artworks in a range of media with classical pastoral and related mythological subjects could evoke for Venetian collectors the lost golden age of Theocritus's *Idylls* and Virgil's *Bucolics*, and perhaps even the promise for a new era of peace, harmony and plenty after the devastating and destabilising years of the War of the League of Cambrai (1508–1516).[27] Pastoral became the Renaissance cultural mode par excellence for social elites, musicians, artists and other virtuosi who sought to foster ideal and escapist communities through theatre, literature and art that were invested in ancient culture and the ideal of civilised *otium* (leisure).[28] Venetian presses began publishing the major classical pastoral works in the late 15th century, with exquisitely illustrated editions of Virgil's *Bucolics* first appearing in Latin as part of his *Opera* in the 1470s, followed by Aldus Manutius's influential editions of Theocritus's *Idylls* in Greek in 1496 and Virgil's *Bucolics* in the complete pocket-sized edition of his *Opera* in 1501.[29]

Modern literary works inspired by these classics soon followed. After circulating in manuscript form, Jacopo Sannazaro's *Arcadia* appeared (unillustrated) in several pirated print editions in Venice in 1502 and 1504, and in authorised form in Naples in 1504.[30] Local production of pastoral prose and poetry in the vernacular also flourished. The Ferrarese poet Antonio Tebaldeo (1462/63–1537) lived in Venice from 1502 to 1511 and his *Opera*, largely comprising sonnets and pastoral eclogues that were frequently set to music, was published there in four editions from 1500.[31] Wealthy Venetian collectors prized luxury copies of pastoral texts, particularly Virgil's *Bucolics* but also Theocritus's *Idylls* and Sannazaro's *Arcadia*.[32] It was through the miniature paintings that illustrated them – whether in manuscripts, incunabula or printed editions by Manutius and others – that the pastoral iconography of Arcadia recognisable in the paintings, drawings, engravings and sculptures of Cima da Conegliano, Andrea Previtali, Giorgione, Giulio and Domenico Campagnola, Titian, Sebastiano, Palma, Riccio and others first entered Venetian visual culture.[33]

Another crucial and authentic point of reference for these artists were the ancient sculptures, vases, medals, coins and cameos amassed in Venetian and Paduan collections during the late 15th and early 16th centuries, some of which featured pastoral and related mythological subject matter.[34]

This essay explores the ways in which Michiel's *Notizia* can help to flesh out the rich associations and potential meanings of Venetian pastoral imagery through just one iconographic example, *Daphnis* of around 1513/15 now housed in the Alte Pinakothek, Munich (cat. 13), which, although scholars have proposed other artists, is persuasively attributed to Palma il Vecchio (c. 1480–1528).[35] Following this single figure across multiple Renaissance art collections and different artistic media and historical epochs reveals a complex circuit of cultural transmission that, I argue, must have deeply enriched the imaginative aesthetic experience and sociable intellectual discourse of collectors and their friends and associates, including artists. The subject of the small painted panel in Munich derives from classical pastoral poetry and its rustic, remote world populated by satyrs, nymphs, sylvan deities and shepherds, who live together in a *locus amoenus* or delightful place – whether Theocritus's Sicily or Virgil's Arcadia – which remains untouched by civilisation and its harms. In the Munich painting, as in Venetian pastoral imagery more generally, the landscape is transformed to resemble the rolling green hills, woods, streams and Alpine vistas of the Venetian *Terraferma*.

Despite the traditional title of the painting, the youth seated in the foreground playing the syrinx is almost certainly human, as he lacks the short horns and pointed ears that differentiate contemporary representations of fauns, Greco-Roman mythological beings that were part human and part goat. Strikingly, and unusually for depictions of shepherds during this period, he is nude but for the cerulean-blue cape tied at his neck that falls in animated folds from his shoulders.[36] David Alan Brown has identified him as Daphnis, the beautiful Sicilian herdsman traditionally considered the inventor of bucolic poetry, whose sweet music and tragic death are the subject of Theocritus's first *Idyll*.[37] Beyond Theocritus, an erudite Venetian audience would have known Daphnis through Virgil's fifth eclogue, in which the shepherds Menalcas and Mopsus mourn his death in song and eulogise his musical talent to the point of deification. As Paul Joannides has demonstrated, contemporaries could also have been familiar with the ancient romance

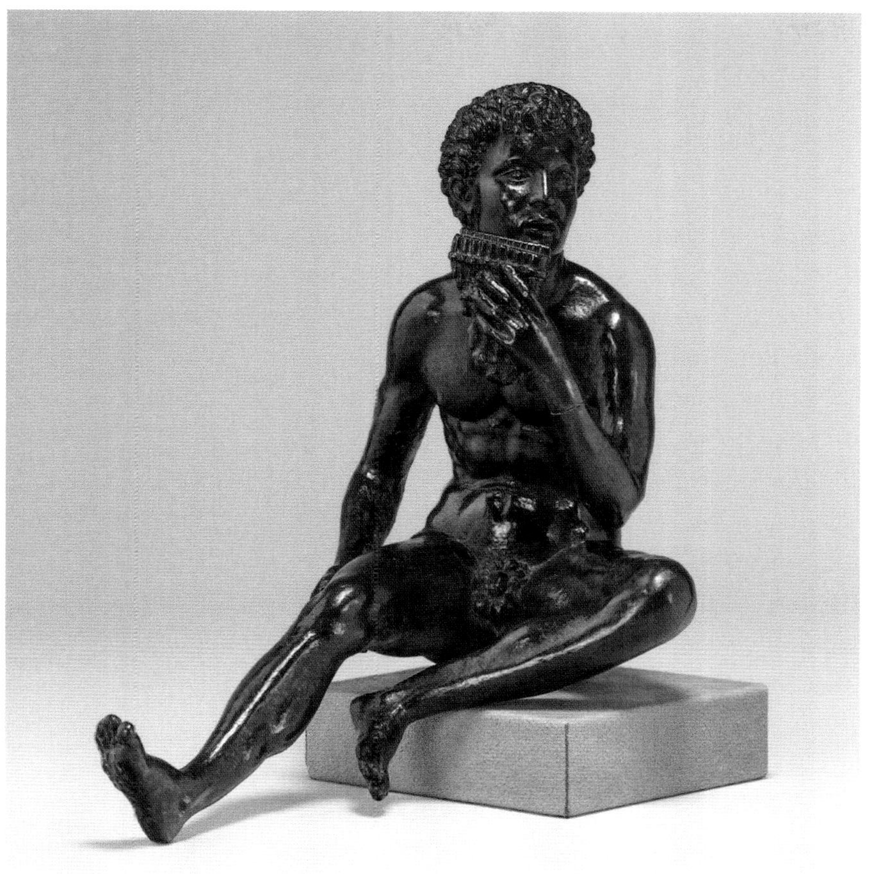

Fig. 2 Andrea Riccio, *Shepherd Playing the Syrinx*, c. 1520, Baltimore, Walters Art Museum

novella *Daphnis and Chloe* attributed to the Greek writer Longus, eschewing tragedy for a joyous tale of the pair's childhood, love affair and marriage.[38] While the grazing deer in the landscape of the Munich painting could be seen as a reference to the pacific effect of Daphnis's music as described by Virgil, even perhaps loosely evoking lines such as: "Wolves lay no ambush for the flocks, no nets wait to betray the deer: Daphnis loves peace", there is no feature of the painting's iconography that confirms a specific identification with Daphnis over any other Arcadian shepherd seated in a grove and playing the sweet melody of his pipe.[39]

As has been noted on occasion by scholars, the beautiful, curly-haired youth in the Munich painting bears a strong resemblance in both pose and physical appearance to a small bronze statuette by the Paduan sculptor Andrea Riccio (1470–1532), the *Shepherd Playing the Syrinx*, owned by the Walters Art Museum, which dates to around 1520 (fig. 2).[40] Interestingly, Edgar Peters Bowron arrived at his identification of the statuette's subject as Daphnis long before Brown's independent proposal regarding the figure in the Munich painting, although in the case of the sculpture there is even less specific iconographic evidence to confirm it.[41] Riccio returned to the same subject on at least one other occasion during his career, the evocative *Shepherd with Syrinx*, a version of slightly modified pose and smoother finish now in the Louvre, which may date to the early 1520s.[42] He also produced a closely related statuette of a faun, distinguished by short horns, delicately pointed ears and a small tufted tail, now known through two later copies by other artists.[43] These unique (non-serialised) sculptural repetitions and variations on a theme point to the general popularity of the subject matter among Riccio's humanist-minded collectors in Padua and Venice. Michiel confirms the presence of "many bronze figurines [that are] modern works", whether by Riccio or "the hand of diverse masters", in a number of the collections he visited, and on one occasion specifies that they "come from the antique".[44]

In terms of coming from the antique, Philip Rylands and Jeremy Warren have separately suggested that the Munich panel and the Riccio statuettes may be derived from a common antique source, which would help explain the unexpected nudity of the human figure in the painting. Over the course of several decades, Michiel documents the presence of two marble sculptures in several Venetian collections that fit the bill.[45] He first saw a figure of "the god Pan, or a faun in marble who sits on a tree trunk, and plays the pan pipes, two feet high, and an ancient work", in the home of the *cittadino* collector Francesco Zio in 1521.[46] Later, in 1531, Michiel mentions "a faun in marble who sits on a rock outcropping and plays the pan pipes, a foot and a half in size with the right arm broken off", in the collection of the patrician Antonio Foscarini, noting that it had formerly been owned by Zio, although the dimensions are smaller by half a foot, the tree trunk has been replaced by a rock and the fragmented arm is new.[47] Finally, in 1543, when Michiel visited the home of patrician Michele Contarini, he singles out "a Faun, or rather a nude shepherd of marble [...] sitting on a rock reclining [...] playing a double-reeded pipe, an ancient work, whole and praiseworthy".[48] The connoisseur also traces an auspicious lineage of ownership for the sculpture, emphasising that Michele had inherited the "elegant houses" of the revered patrician humanist and poet Pietro Contarini, known as "the philosopher", and "his son Francesco Zen."[49] Pietro bequeathed the faun to Michele in his 1527 testament – and, later, in a codicil to his own testament of 1550, Michele bequeathed the sculpture to Gabriele Vendramin, his "most dear patron and friend", in repayment of a sizable debt, revealing just how precious knowledgeable collectors considered it.[50]

It is not unusual for Renaissance sources to refer to fauns and shepherds somewhat loosely and interchangeably as does Michiel. While Palma's painting would seem to relate more closely to the sculpture owned by the Contarini rather than the "god Pan, or a faun" owned by Zio, the shepherd in the Munich painting seems to sit on a tree stump like the figure in Zio's sculpture, while the original small supports for the Walters and Louvre statuettes do not survive.[51] Such discrepancies highlights the important point that sculptures like Riccio's and paintings like Palma's were intended not as exact copies of ancient works but as creative emulations or, as in music, variations on a theme. Warren has proposed that a Roman imperial statue of a seated nude faun playing the flute – now housed in the Fitzwilliam Museum, Cambridge – may in fact be one of the marbles seen by Michiel (fig. 3).[52] And indeed, its dimensions, iconography and condition – it has a broken right arm – do correspond well, although not exactly, with Michiel's description of the Zio or Foscarini marble, and its rough-hewn base could easily be construed as a rock outcropping.

In tracing this nexus of intermedial translation and adaptation from ancient marble(s) to Renaissance bronzes and panel painting, it is important to note that this example is not unique. Scholars have hypothesised a similar phenomenon regarding Michiel's descriptions of ancient sculptures in other Venetian collections. For example, Vendramin owned a marble figure of a "clothed Nymph who sleeps in a reclining position", which Millard Meiss first proposed could have provided the model for Giorgione's and Titian's *Sleeping Venus* of around 1507 now in the Gemäldegalerie Alte Meister, Dresden.[53] Vendramin also owned a "half-bust of a girl, the head of a girl, the head of a boy [...] ancient works [...] another little head of a girl in marble".[54] All these sculptures could easily have inspired some of the bust-length paintings of generic, idealised and vaguely *all'antica* shepherds, youths and young women made by Giorgione, Titian, Palma, Tullio Lombardo, Riccio and other artists across the first decades of the 16th century.[55] Such potential use of ancient sculpture as a touchstone that inspired inventions in art of the early cinquecento across media and scale fits well within what Stephen J.

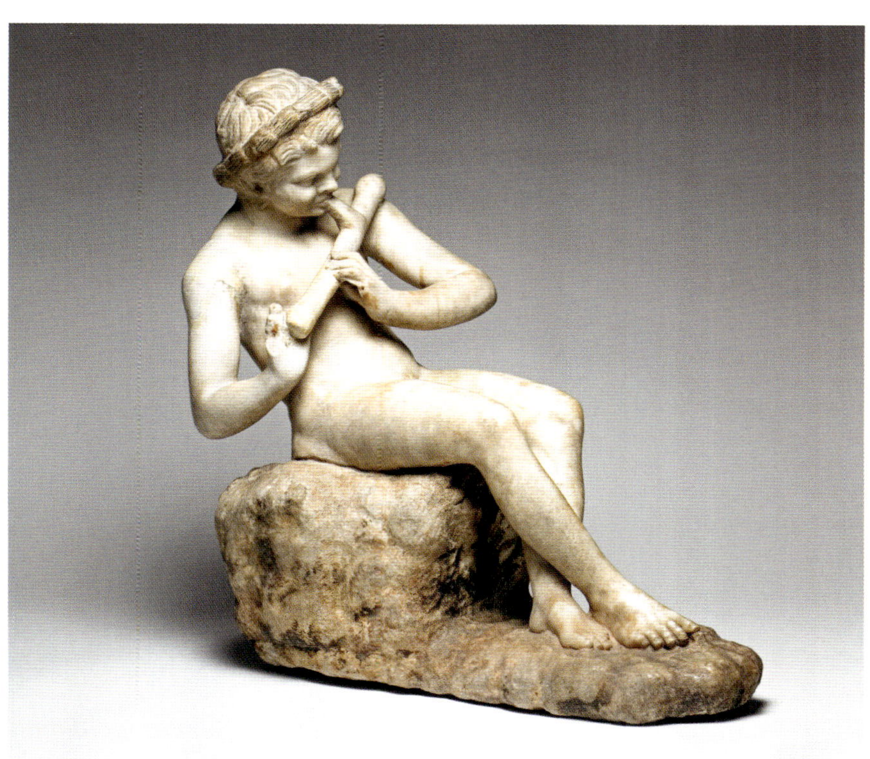

Fig. 3 *Young Faun Playing the Flute*, Roman, first century AD, Cambridge, Fitzwilliam Museum

Campbell has termed a humanist "aesthetics of grafting", which informed northern Italian and especially Veneto art around the turn of the 16th century, and was characterised by self-referentiality, a fascination with materiality and a tendency to illusionistically combine different artistic media into a complex montage.[56] "Grafting" is also a useful idiom through which to consider Palma's prominent inclusion of a musical anachronism within his composition, the finely carved and ornately decorated cittern standing in the right foreground, which is wholly out of time and place in such a rustic and presumably ancient Arcadian setting. As Brown rightly remarks, the cittern, or *cetera* in Italian, was a stringed instrument much appreciated in Renaissance courtly and humanist circles for its associations with the classical Greek cithara.[57]

Palma's painted cittern can be further identified as a unique work of art of the type signed by master instrument makers and collected by connoisseurs in the Renaissance because it features the classicising motif of an elaborately carved grotesque finial in the form of an animal skull.[58] The pointed juxtaposition in the Munich painting of the shepherd playing the syrinx and the modern cittern standing unattended on the ground establishes a visual paragone familiar from Sannazaro's preface to *Arcadia* – namely, the contrast between the rustic wind instruments fashioned from natural materials played by shepherds and nymphs in Arcadia and the luxury stringed instruments played by amateur and professional Renaissance musicians at courts and in urban palaces and proudly displayed in these settings when not in use.

Sannazaro makes the outcome of the comparison, framed as a sort of abstract musical competition, clear when he declares that "the wax-bound reeds of shepherds proffer amid the flower-laden valleys perhaps more pleasurable sound than do through proud chambers the polished and costly boxwood instruments of the musicians".[59] In staking this claim, Sannazaro inverts the traditional Platonic hierarchy, in which chorded instruments are superior, because their sonic harmony is mathematically proportional and thus related to the music of the spheres, while wind instruments are inferior because they lack such proper harmony, but also because they cannot be accompanied by voice and were thus argued to lack poetry.[60] The Munich painting, which leaves the cittern idle on the ground, would seem to be the perfect illustration of Sannazaro's argument for the "more pleasurable sound"[61] of waxed reed pipes played in outdoor settings over that of costly chamber instruments. This alleged superiority derives from the sensuous quality and therapeutic value attributed to pastoral music, which could even be described as a potent form of natural magic for the powerful effects it had on listeners. In his *Idylls*, Theocritus describes the shepherds' music in the sensual terms of lips placed on the soft and fragrant waxed mouthpieces of rustic instruments – for example, in the first *Idyll* when Daphnis celebrates his "pretty pipe, this pipe of honey breath, of wax well-knit round lips to fit" (*Idyll* 1, 128).[62] With frequent references to the intimate physicality of breath and whispering, the effect of pastoral music on its audience in Theocritus and Virgil is soporific, often bears erotic connotations and simulates the soothing "green" effects of nature.

Through this juxtaposition of low- and high-order instruments, one played and the other not, the Munich painting could have prompted recondite reflection on ancient and modern music, theory and instruments as well as on the perceived hierarchies of musical instruments and musical and poetic genres. This is just the sort of specialised conversation topic one might expect to come up in, for example, Vendramin's *ridotto* or in the home of a collector who prized both works of art and rare and luxury musical instruments, such as the Venetian *cittadino* Michele Vianello.[63] Such a setting would also furnish one possible explanation for the small dimensions and thin panel support of the Munich painting, both of which prove exceptional within Palma's oeuvre.[64] These unusual features suggest that the painting was originally part of a piece of furniture and, as such, it could have been accompanied by other panels, which is typical of furniture ornamentation. Intriguingly, scholars have proposed that other Venetian furniture paintings with similar dimensions and related subject matter may have decorated musical instruments, their protective cases or the wooden storage chests in which they were stored when not in use.

Among these examples, perhaps the most closely related to Palma's single panel in Munich in terms of theme and format are the *Scenes from Tebaldeo's Eclogues* of around 1510 attributed to Andrea Previtali (c. 1470/80 [1476?]–1528 [?]) and now housed in the National Gallery, London (fig. 4).[65] The four individual scenes from Tebaldeo's second eclogue are paired and stacked vertically on two separate panels, which likely functioned as the *sportelli* (doors) to a small cupboard or adorned a musical instrument with cabinet-like doors or possibly the wooden case of an instrument.[66] They represent key moments from Tebaldeo's second eclogue, in which the lovelorn shepherd Damon broods over his unrequited love for Amaryllis, is questioned by his friend Thyrsis about the cause of his melancholy, takes his own life and is discovered by Thyrsis.

Brown has similarly, but in a more hopeful vein, interpreted the Munich painting as depicting a passage from Longus's *Daphnis and Chloe*, in which the young herdsman, singing of his awakening love,

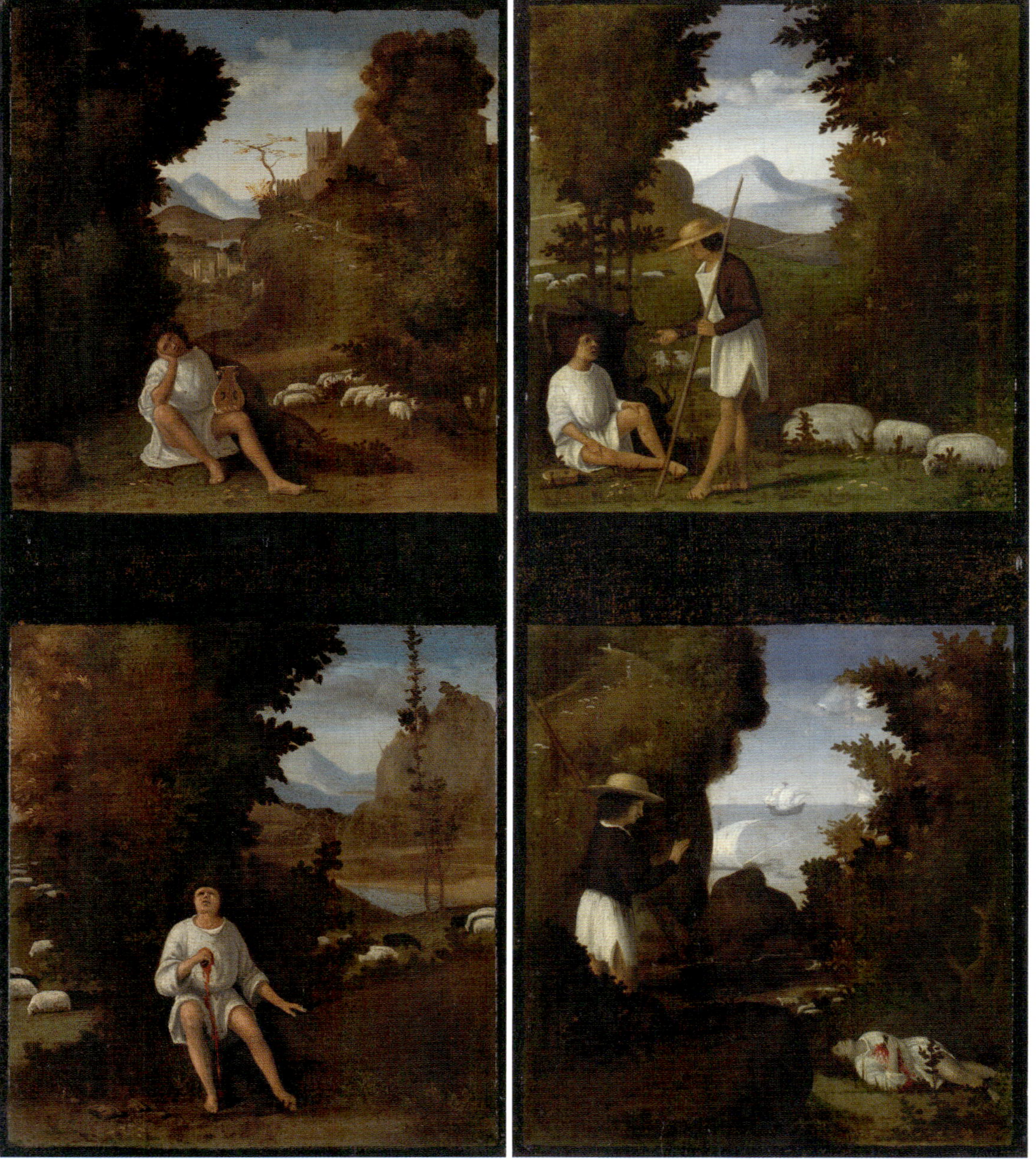

Fig. 4 Andrea Previtali, *Scenes from Tebaldeo's Eclogues*, c. 1510, London, The National Gallery

"appears nude and playing the pipes, as in the Munich picture".[67] In the introduction to his *Dialogo della musica* (1544), the writer Antonfrancesco Doni evokes just the sort of informal domestic gathering in which Tebaldeo's eclogues could have been sung to the accompaniment of a lute or cittern surrounded by precious paintings, sculptures and ornamented furniture with pastoral subjects, along with erudite conversation on their themes and potential meanings.[68] Doni concludes his vivid description of secular music as a leisured pastime with an idealised description of its somatic and spiritual benefits that resonates with Palma's sun-dappled landscape and beautiful boy shepherd playing his pipes: "And feeding the body that way with a sweet repose, we will nourish the soul again with a delicate sweetness, indeed with a divine sustenance."[69]

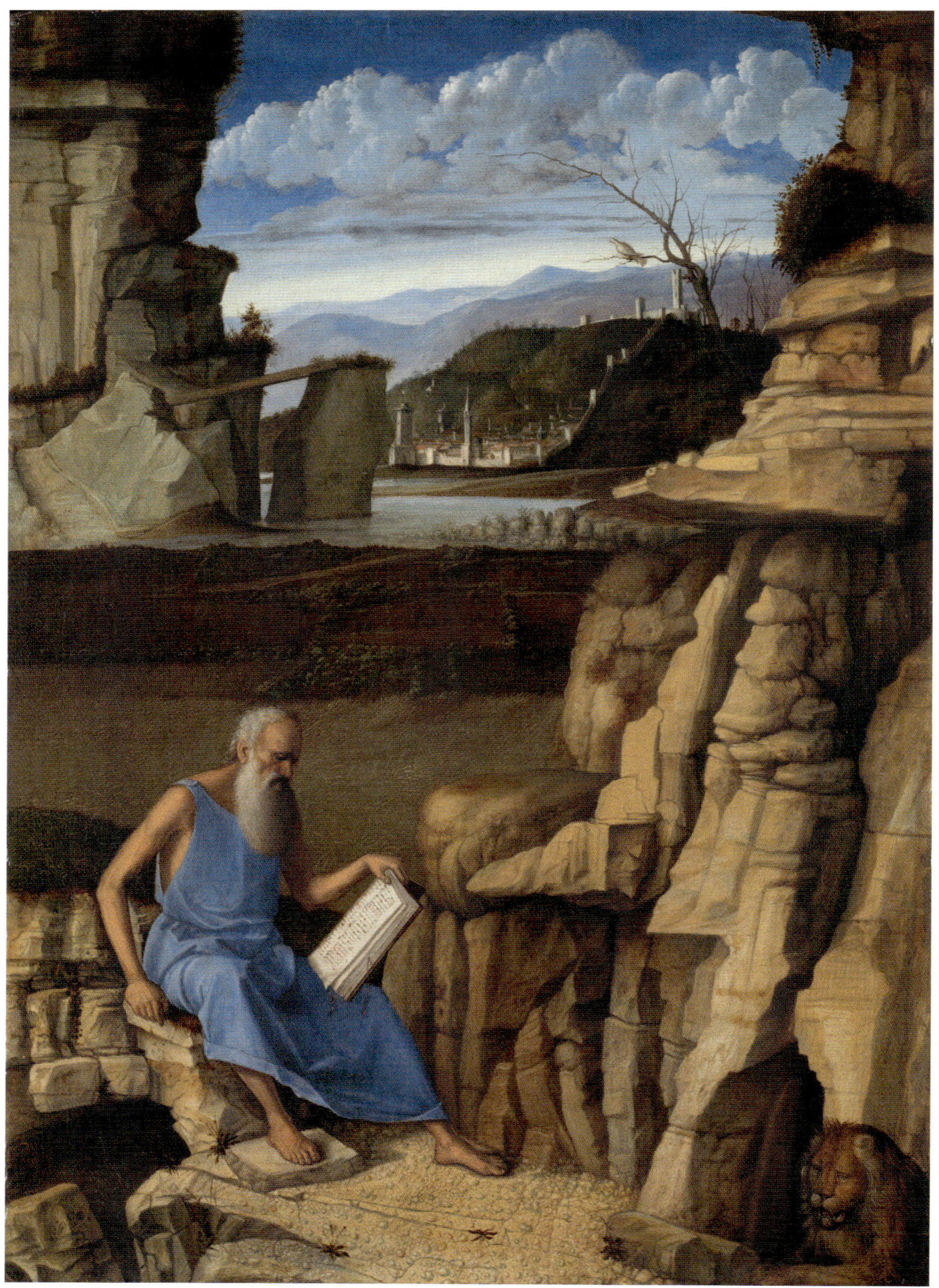

1 Giovanni Bellini, *St Jerome Reading in a Landscape*, c. 1480/85, London, The National Gallery

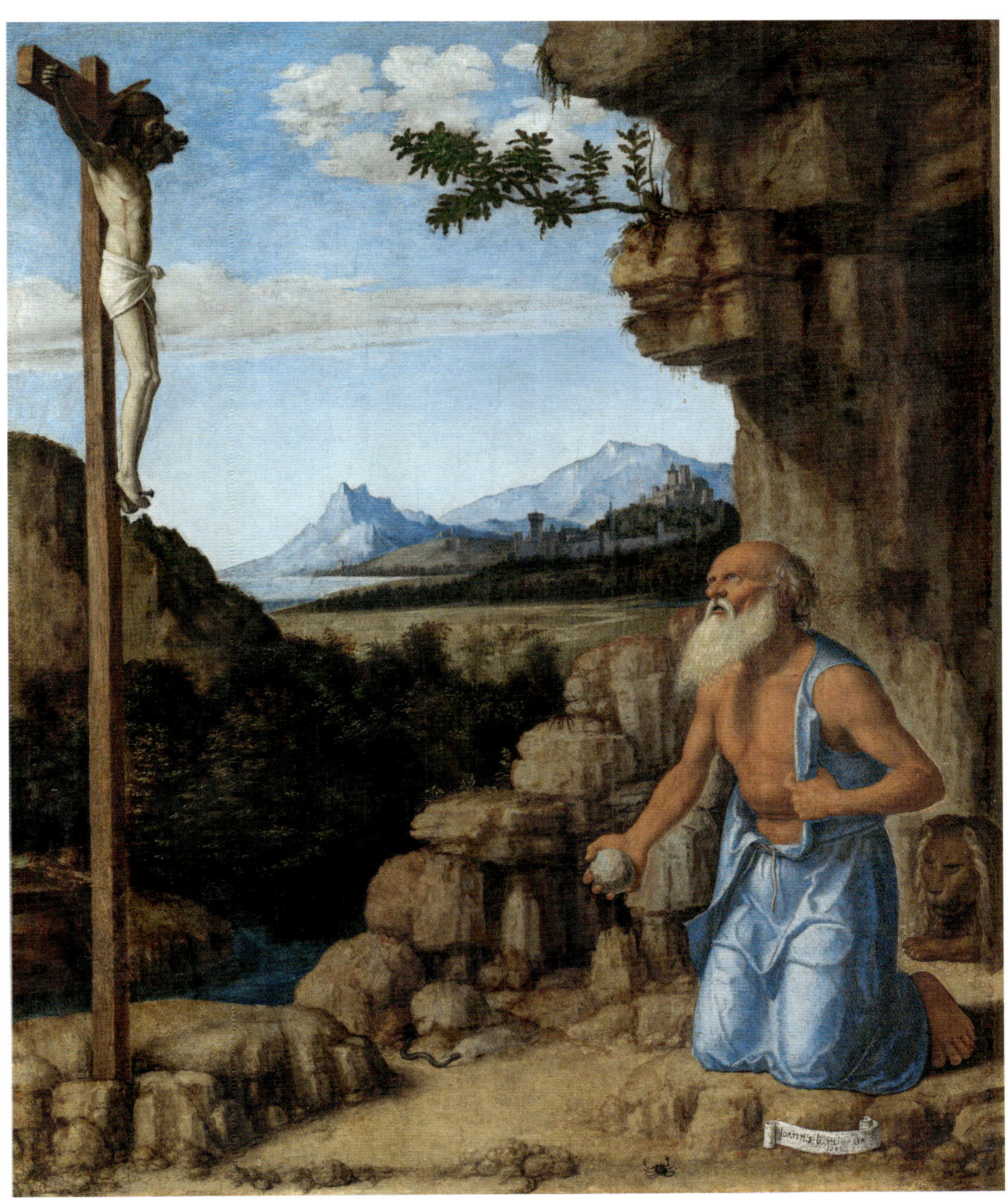

2 Giovanni Battista Cima da Conegliano, *St Jerome in the Wilderness*, c. 1500/05, Washington, D.C., National Gallery of Art

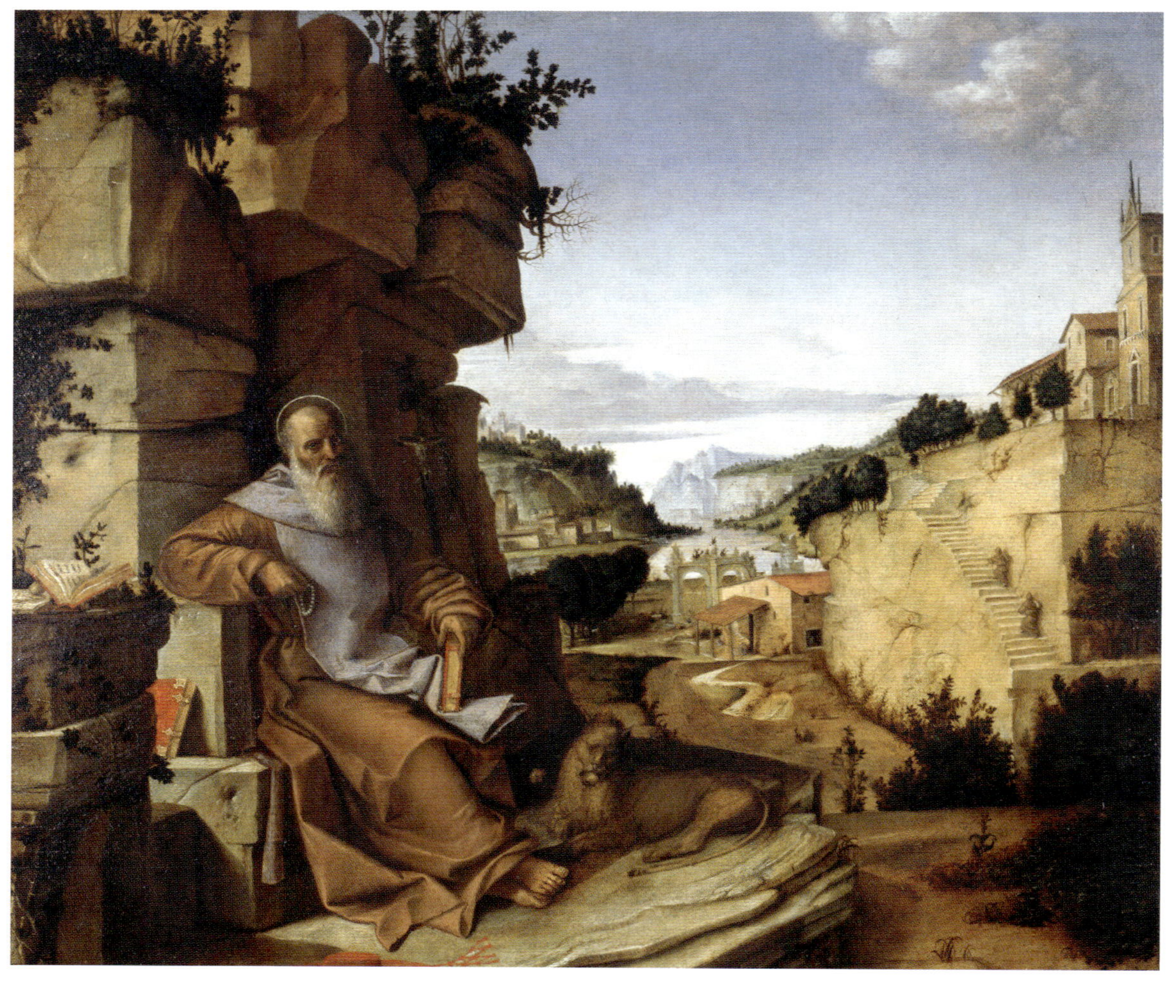

3 Bartolomeo Montagna, *St Jerome in the Desert*, c. 1500/02, Milan, Pinacoteca di Brera

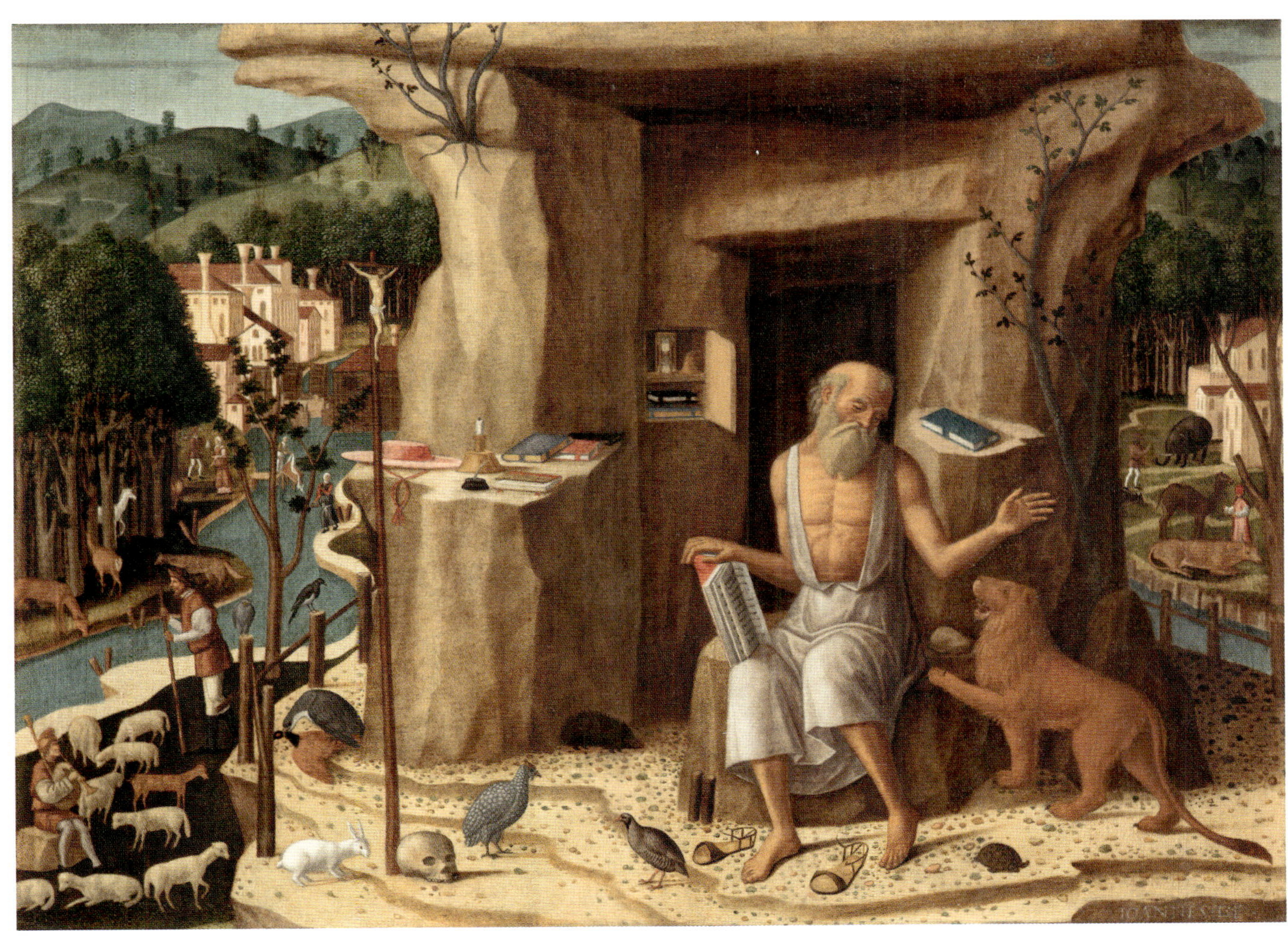

4 Giovanni di Niccolò Mansueti, *St Jerome in a Landscape*, 1505–1520, Bristol, Museum and Art Gallery

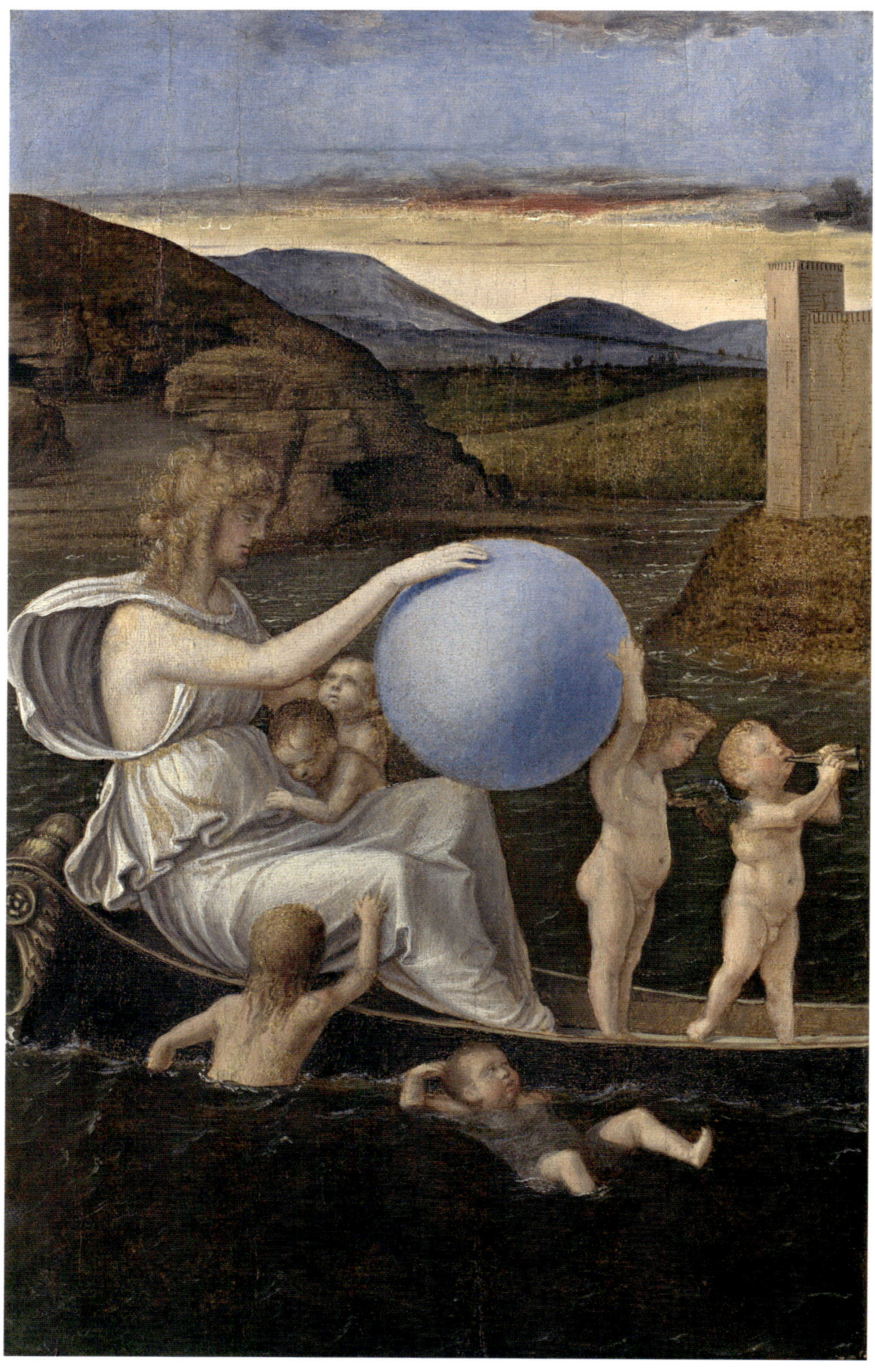

5a Giovanni Bellini, *Malinconia*, c. 1485/95, Venice, Gallerie dell'Accademia

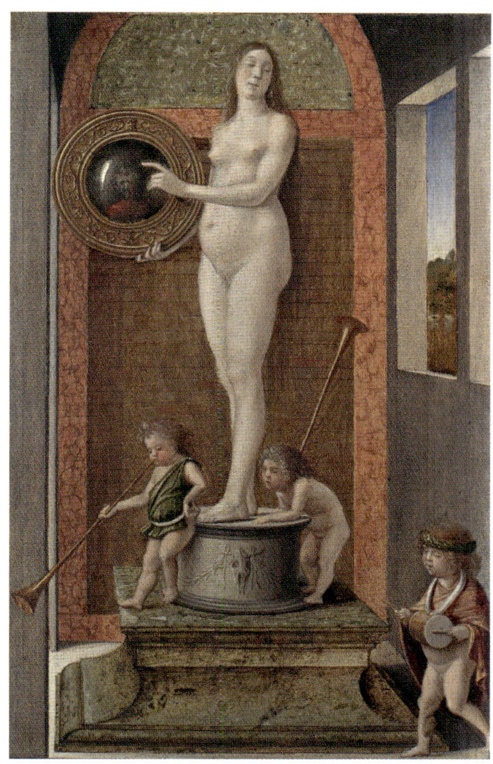

5b Giovanni Bellini, *Vanitas*, c. 1485/95, Venice, Gallerie dell'Accademia

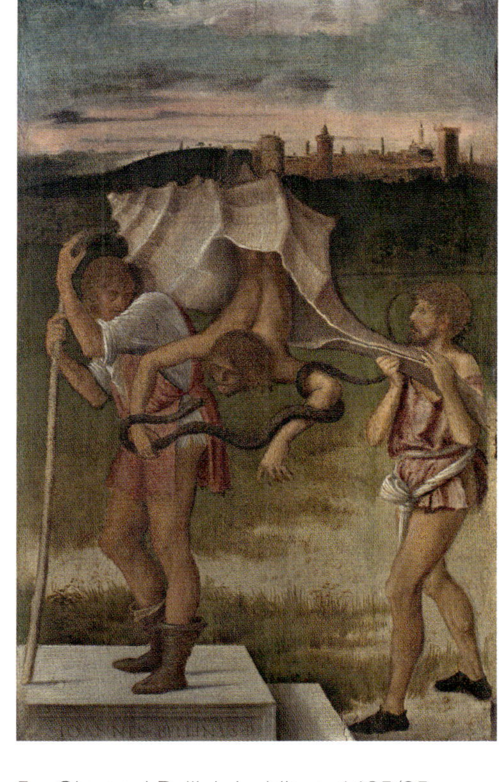

5c Giovanni Bellini, *Invidia*, c. 1485/95, Venice, Gallerie dell'Accademia

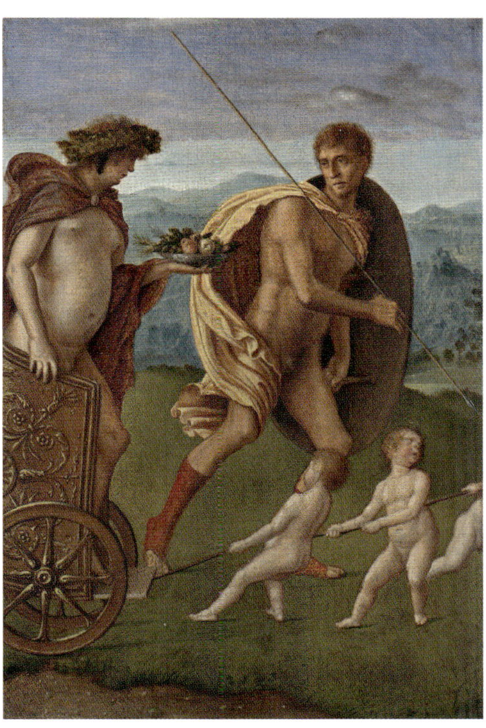

5d Giovanni Bellini, *Bacchus*, c. 1485/95, Venice, Gallerie dell'Accademia

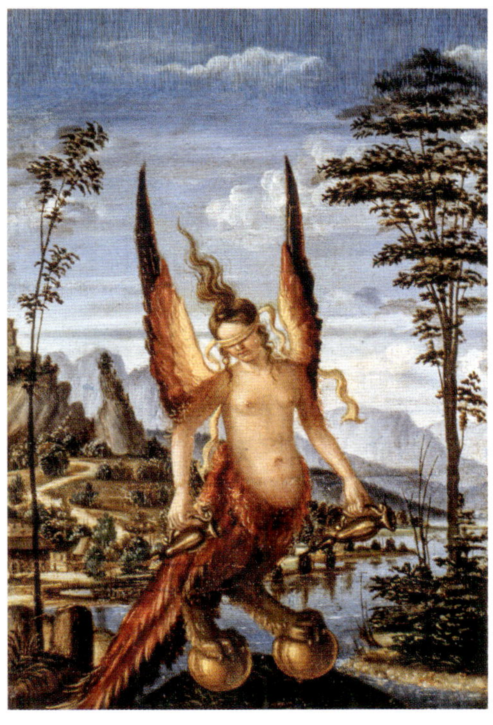

6 Andrea Previtali, *Allegory of Fortune*, c. 1490, Venice, Gallerie dell'Accademia

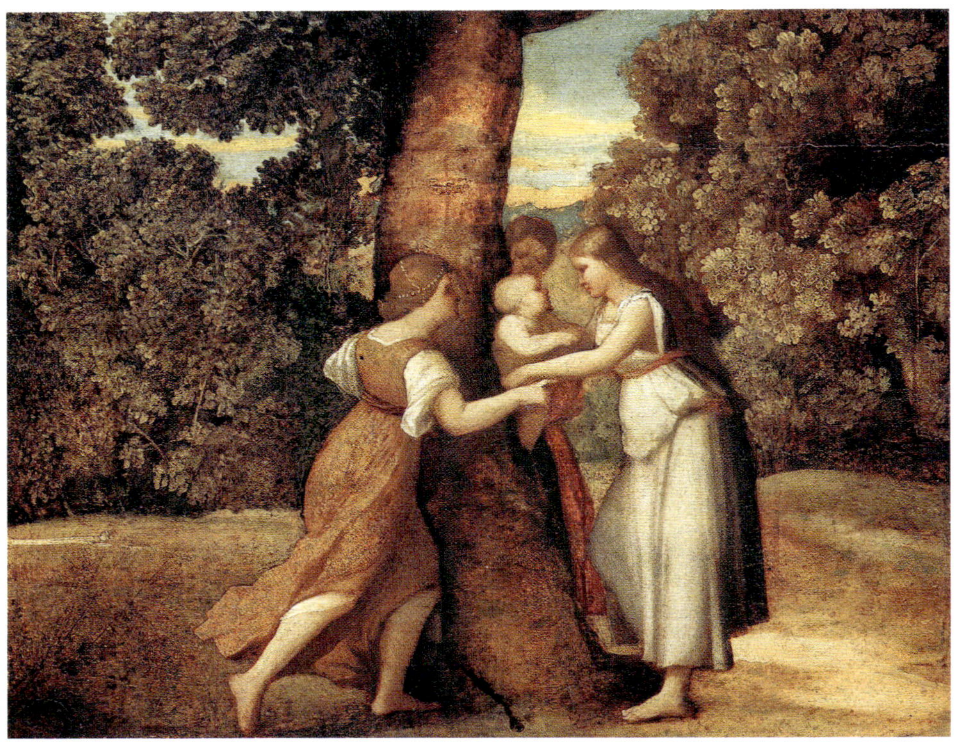

7a Sebastiano del Piombo, *Birth of Adonis*, c. 1505, La Spezia, Museo Civico Amedeo Lia

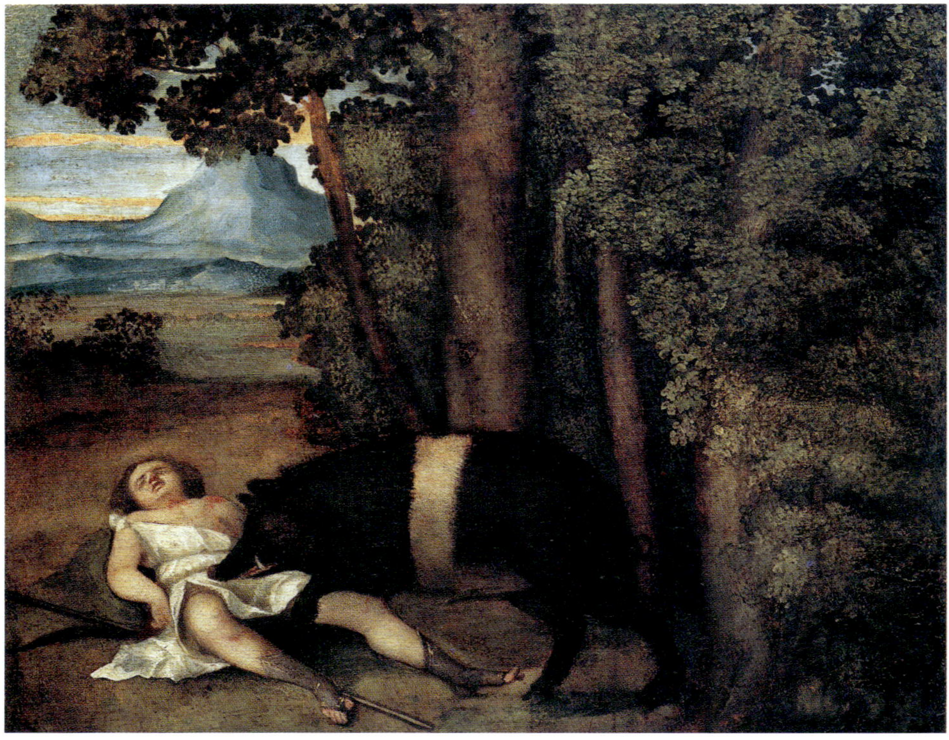

7b Sebastiano del Piombo, *Death of Adonis*, c. 1505, La Spezia, Museo Civico Amedeo Lia

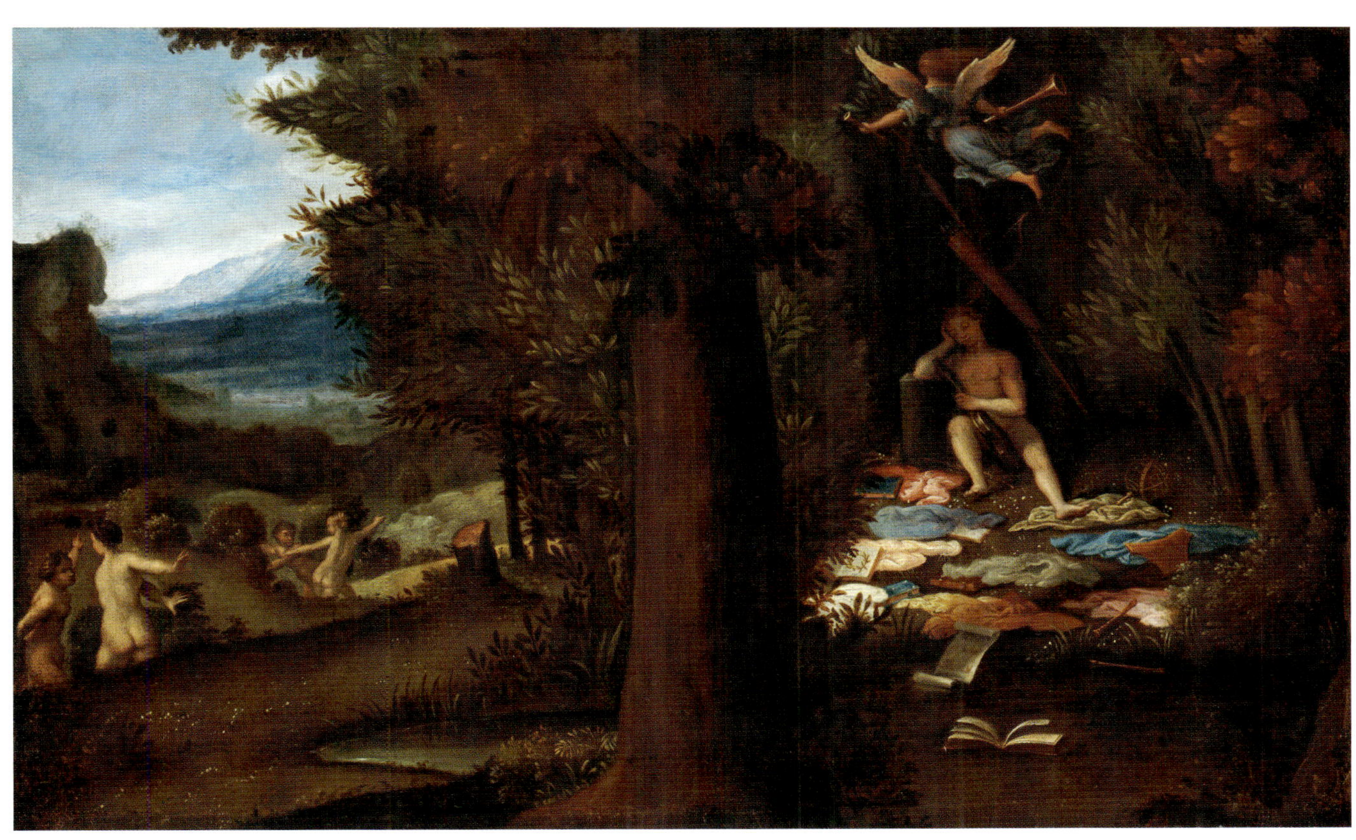

8 Lorenzo Lotto, *Sleeping Apollo with Fame and the Muses*, c. 1549, Budapest, Szépművészeti Múzeum

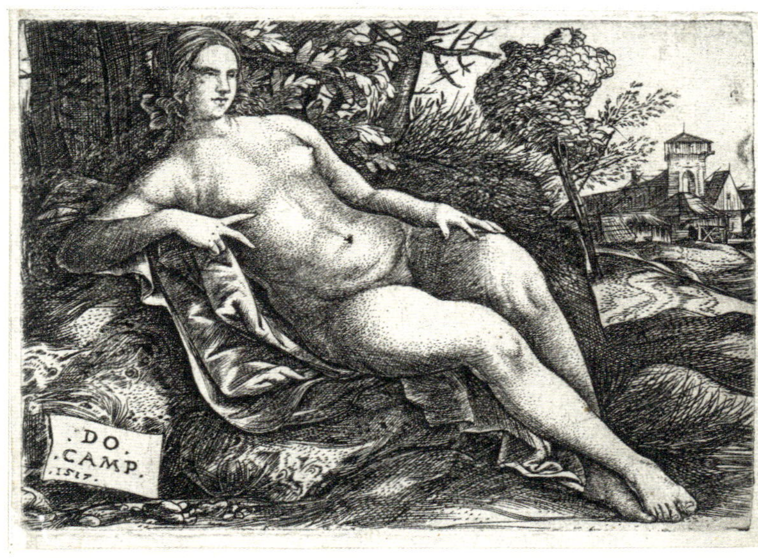

9 Domenico Campagnola, *Resting Venus in a Landscape*, 1517, Berlin, Staatliche Museen, Kupferstichkabinett

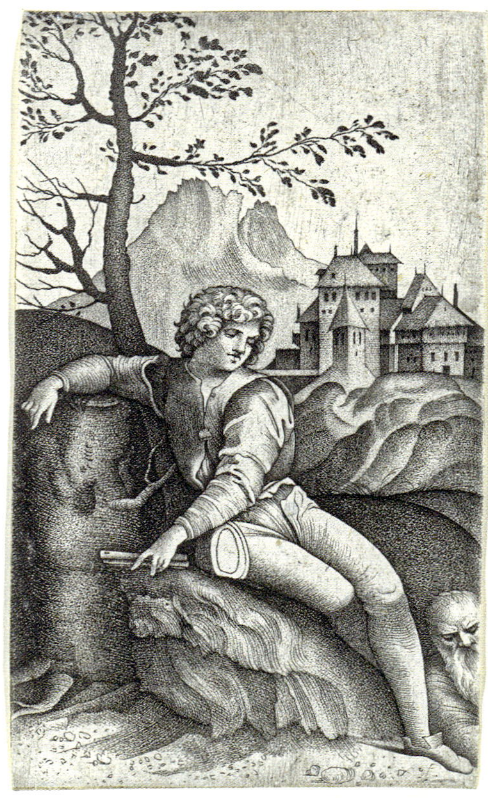

10 Giulio Campagnola, *Young Shepherd*, c. 1509/12, Munich, Staatliche Graphische Sammlung

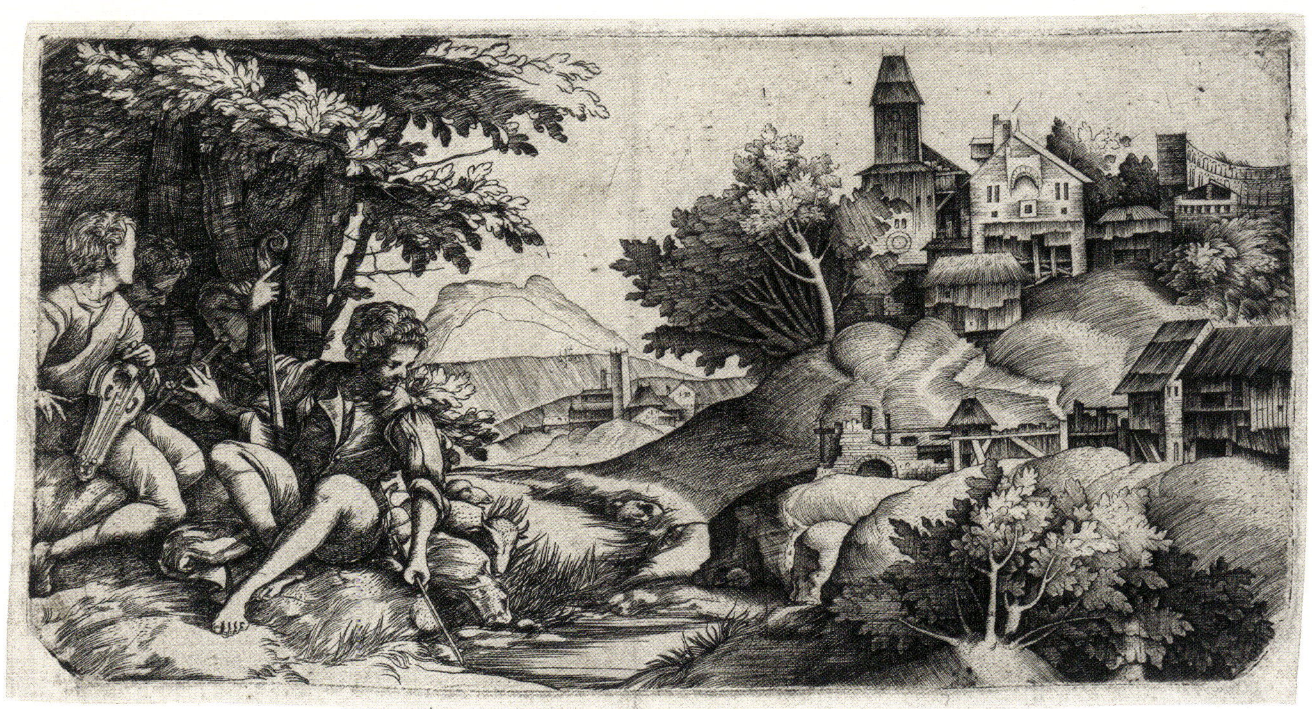

11 Domenico Campagnola, *Concert by a Brook*, c. 1516/17, Berlin, Staatliche Museen, Kupferstichkabinett

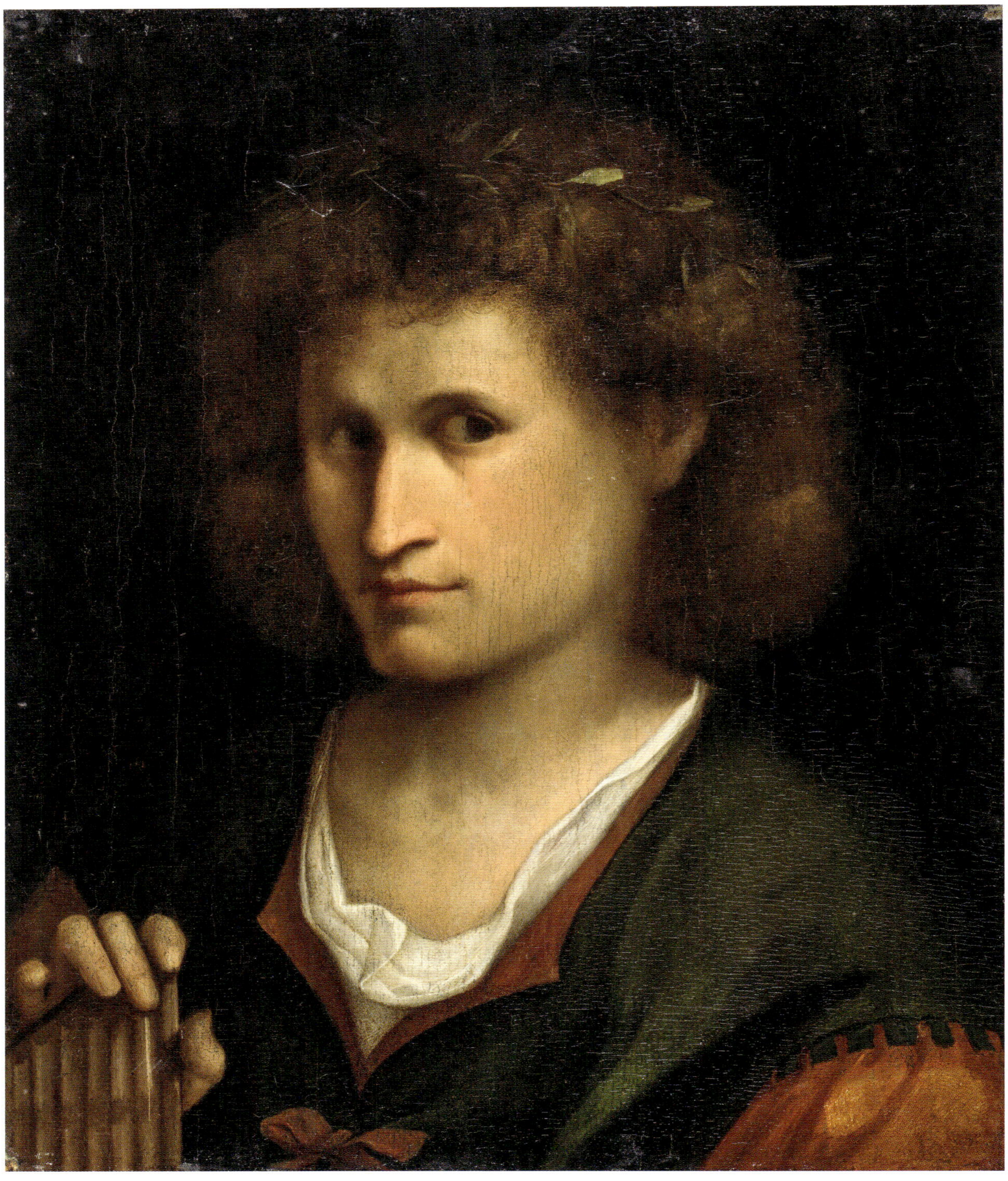

12 Palma il Vecchio, *Shepherd with Panpipe*, c. 1525, Private collection

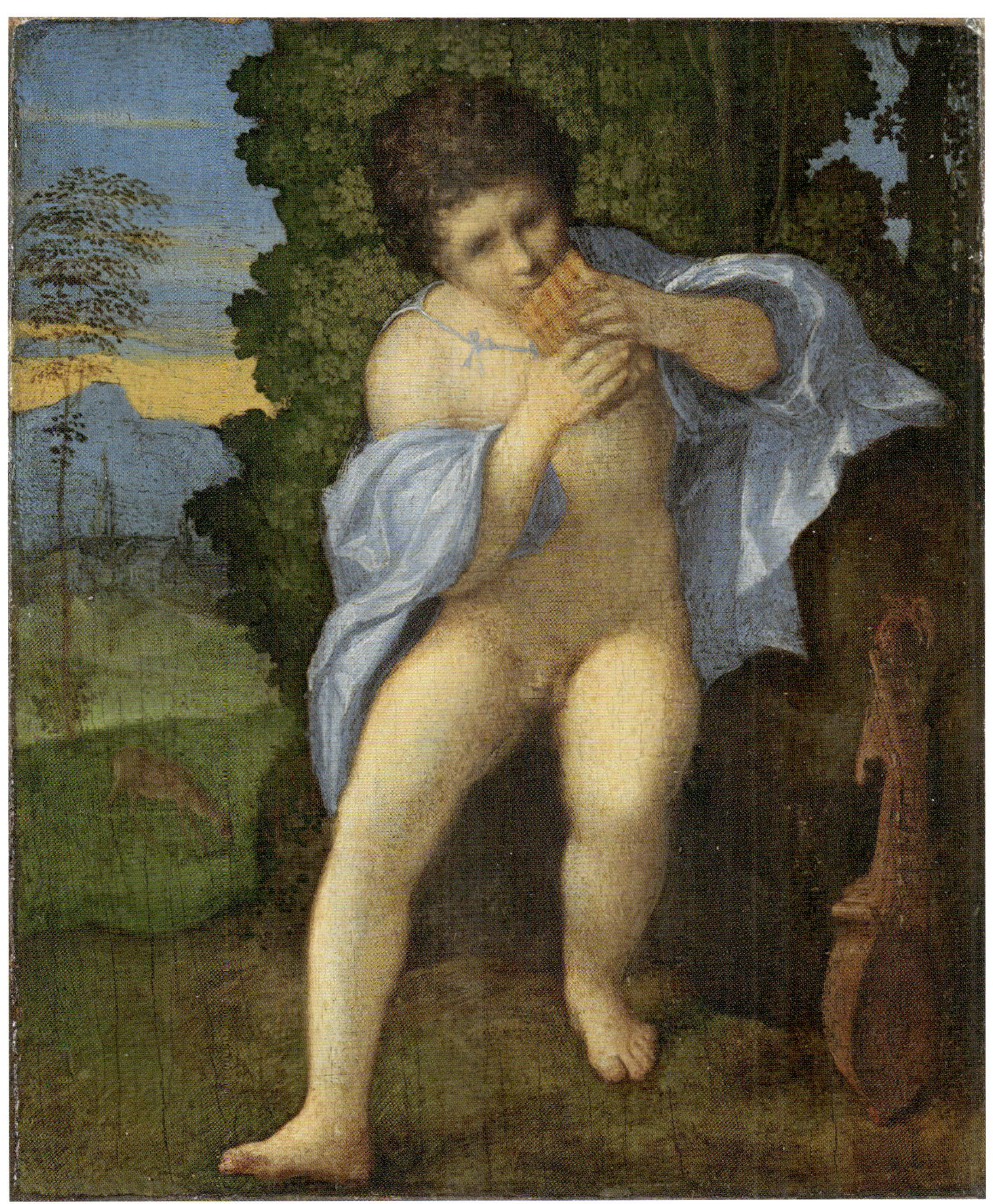

13 Palma il Vecchio, attribution, *Daphnis*, c. 1513/15, Munich, Bayerische Staatsgemäldesammlungen, Alte Pinakothek

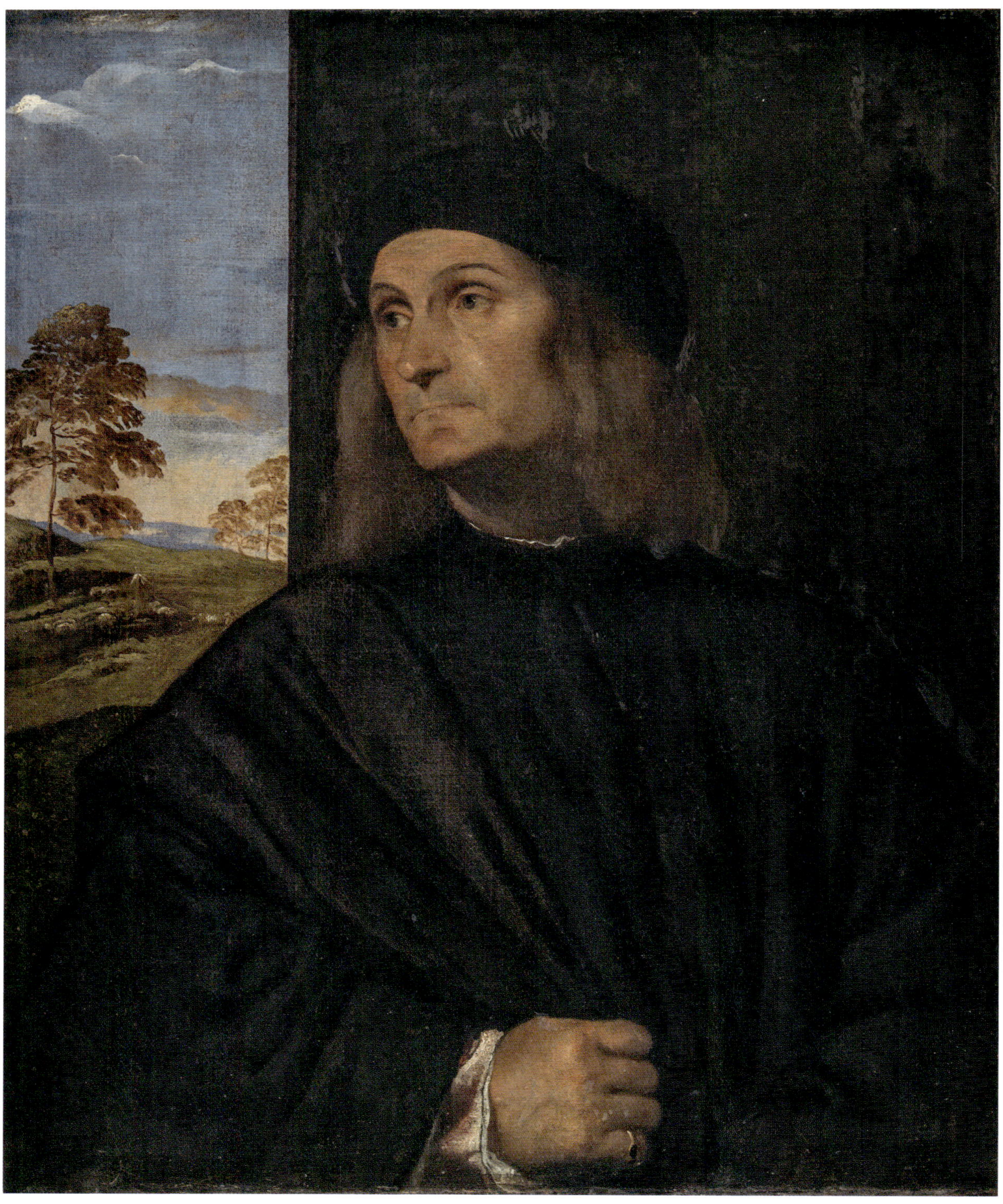

14 Titian, *Portrait of Giovanni Bellini*, c. 1511/12, Copenhagen, National Gallery of Denmark

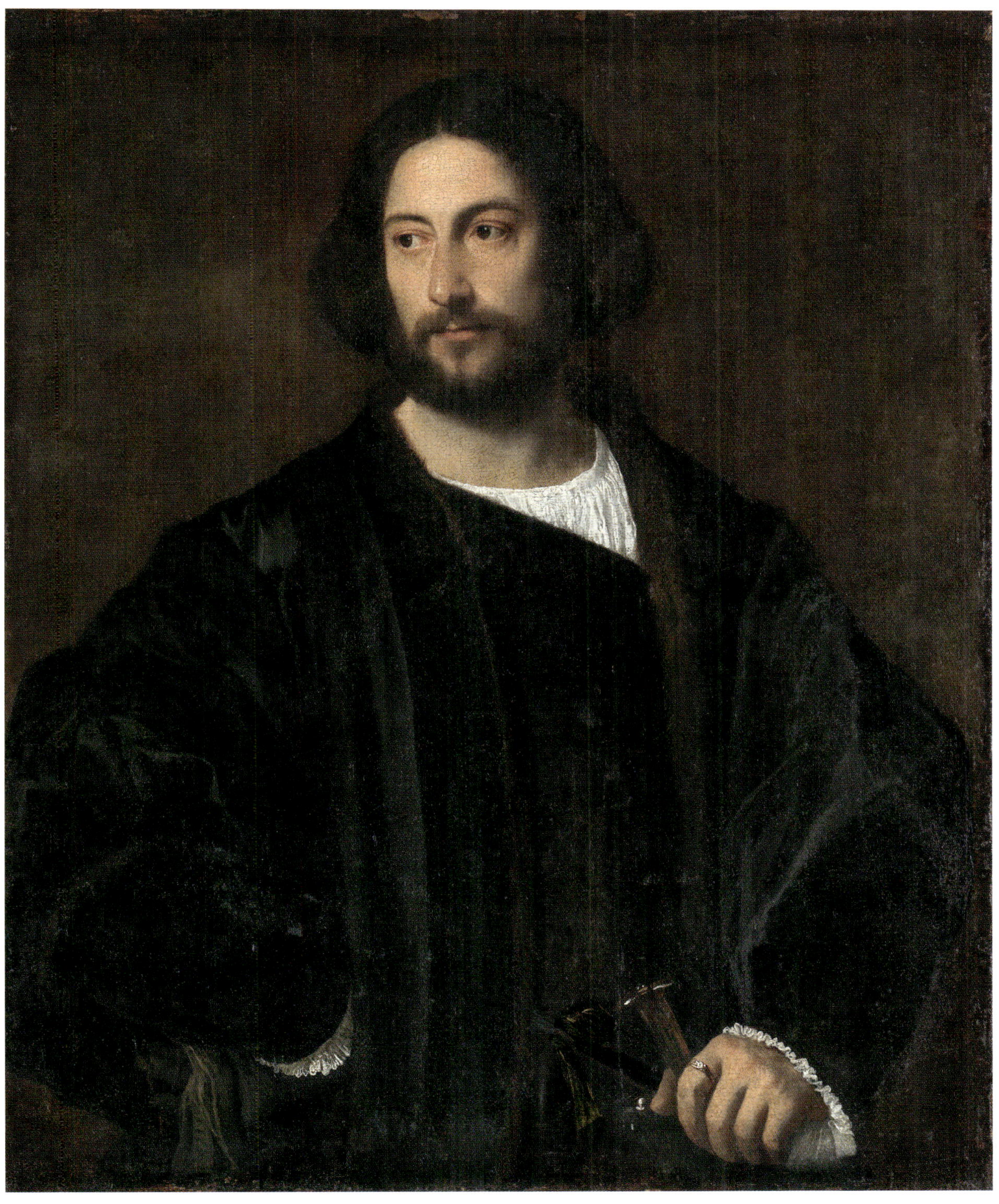

15 Titian, *Portrait of a Man*, c. 1520/22, Munich, Bayerische Staatsgemäldesammlungen, Alte Pinakothek

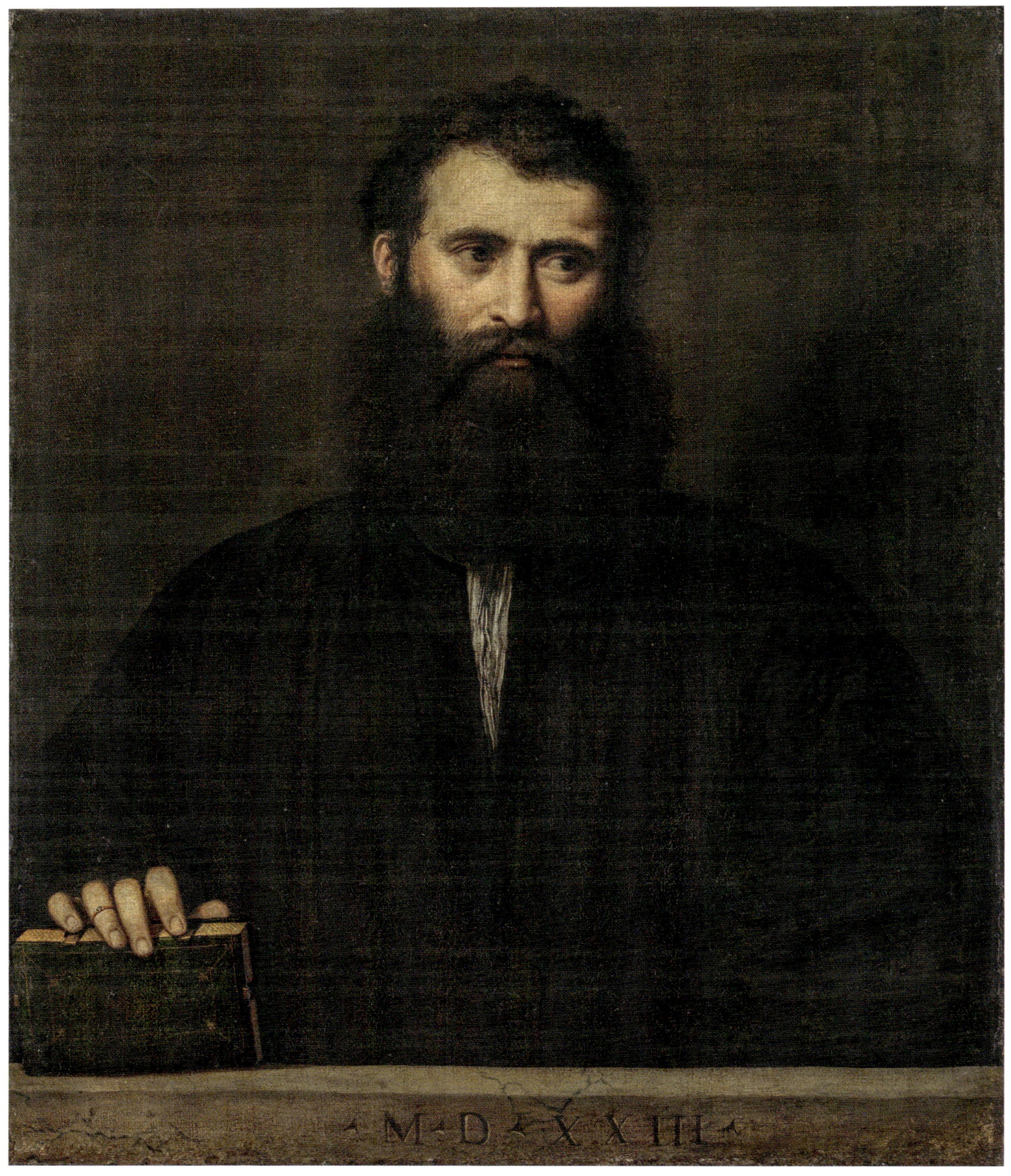

16 Paris Bordone, *Portrait of Giulio Manfron*, 1523, Munich, Bayerische Staatsgemäldesammlungen, Alte Pinakothek

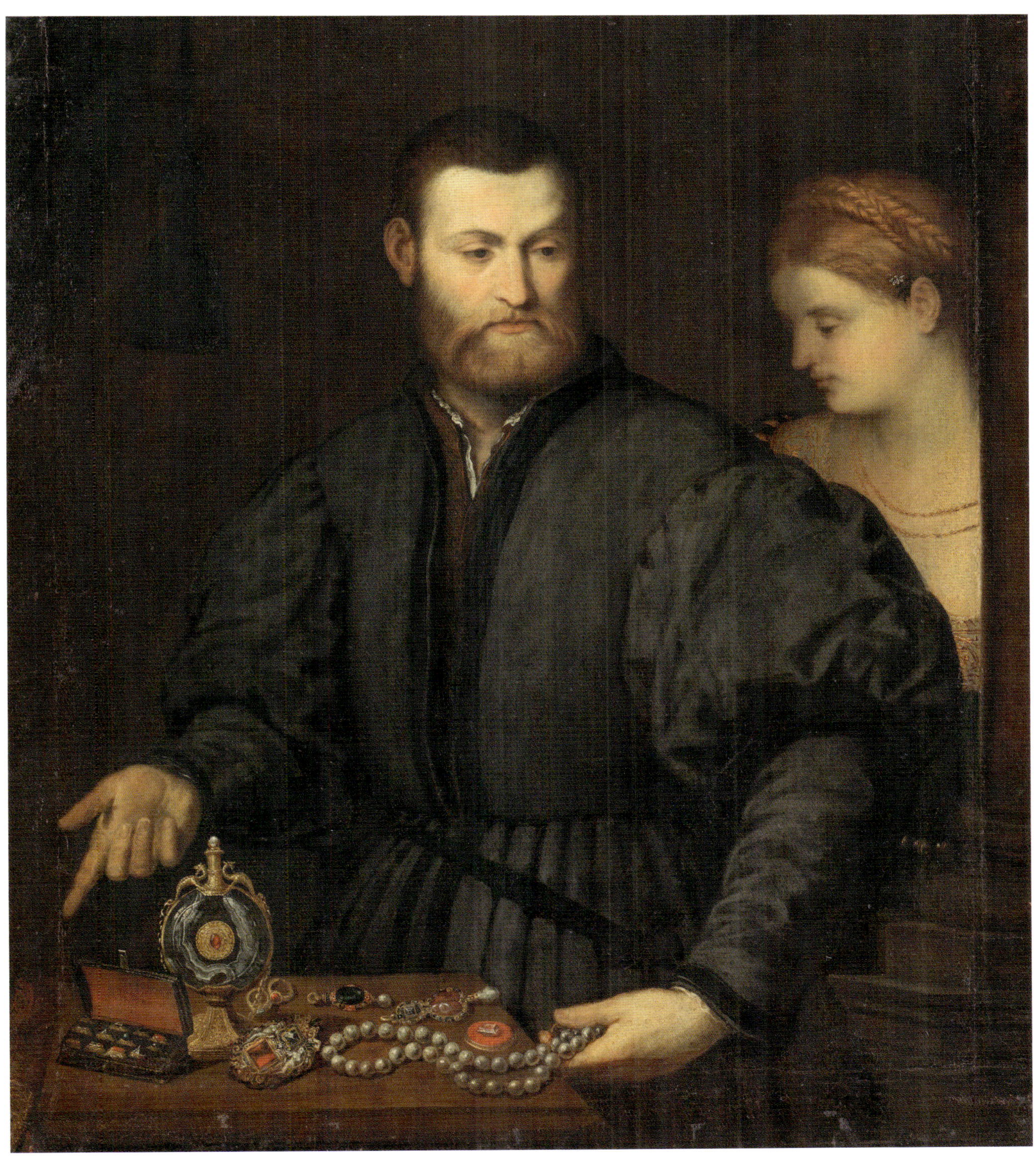

17 Paris Bordone, *Jeweller with a Lady*, c. 1530/35, Munich, Bayerische Staatsgemäldesammlungen, Alte Pinakothek

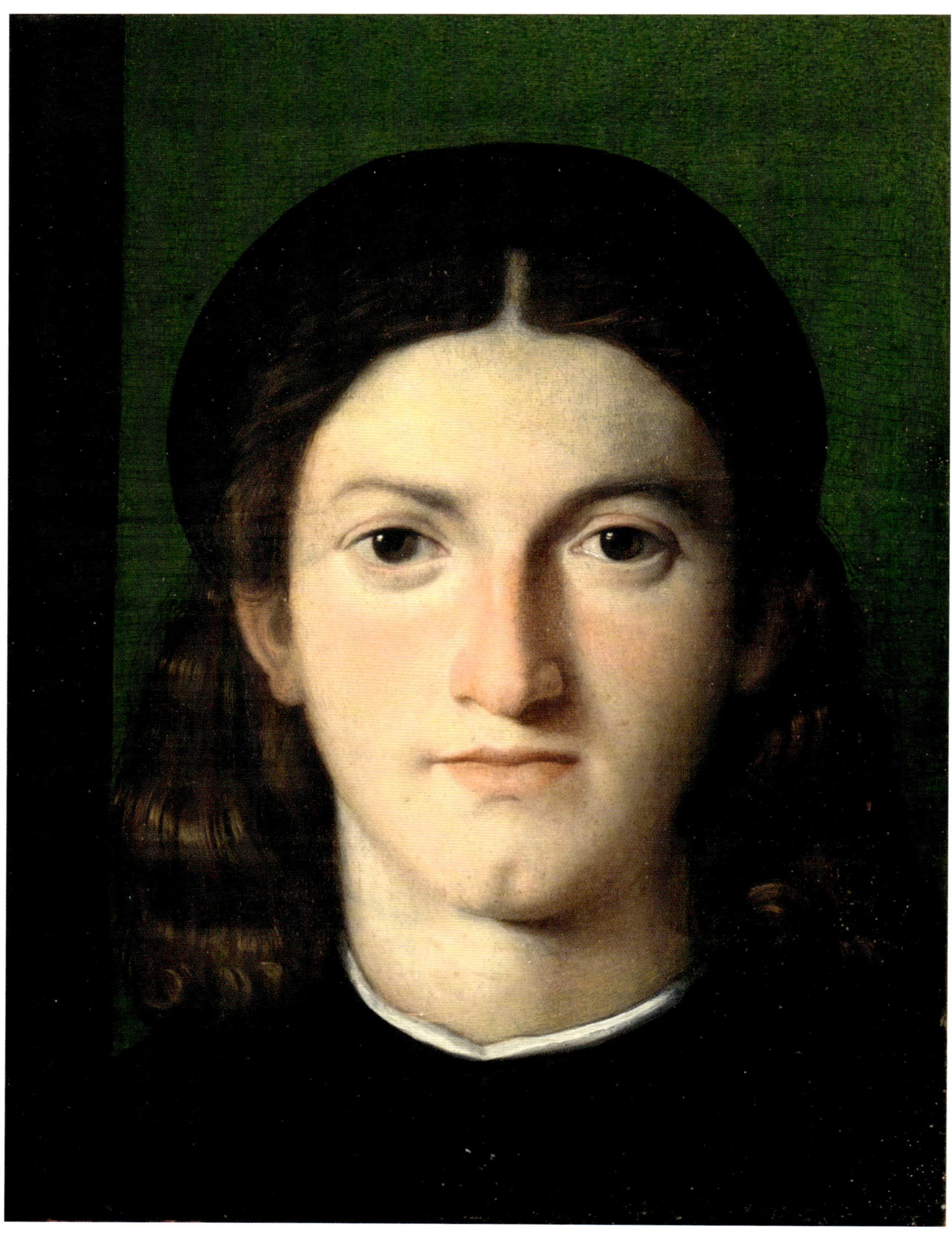

18 Lorenzo Lotto, *Portrait of a Young Man*, c. 1509/10, Florence, Galleria degli Uffizi

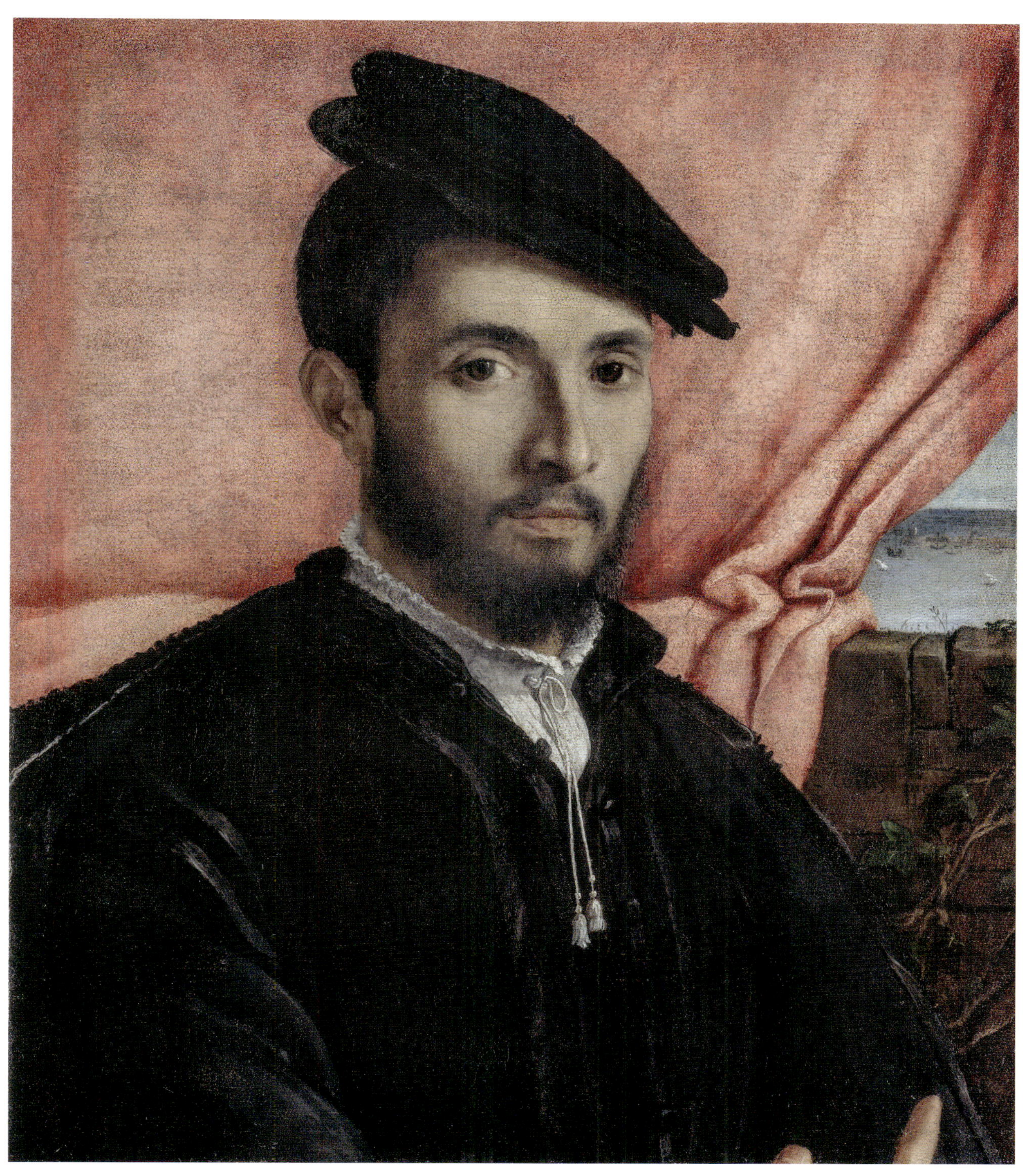

19 Lorenzo Lotto, *Portrait of a Young Man*, c. 1534/35, Berlin, Staatliche Museen, Gemäldegalerie

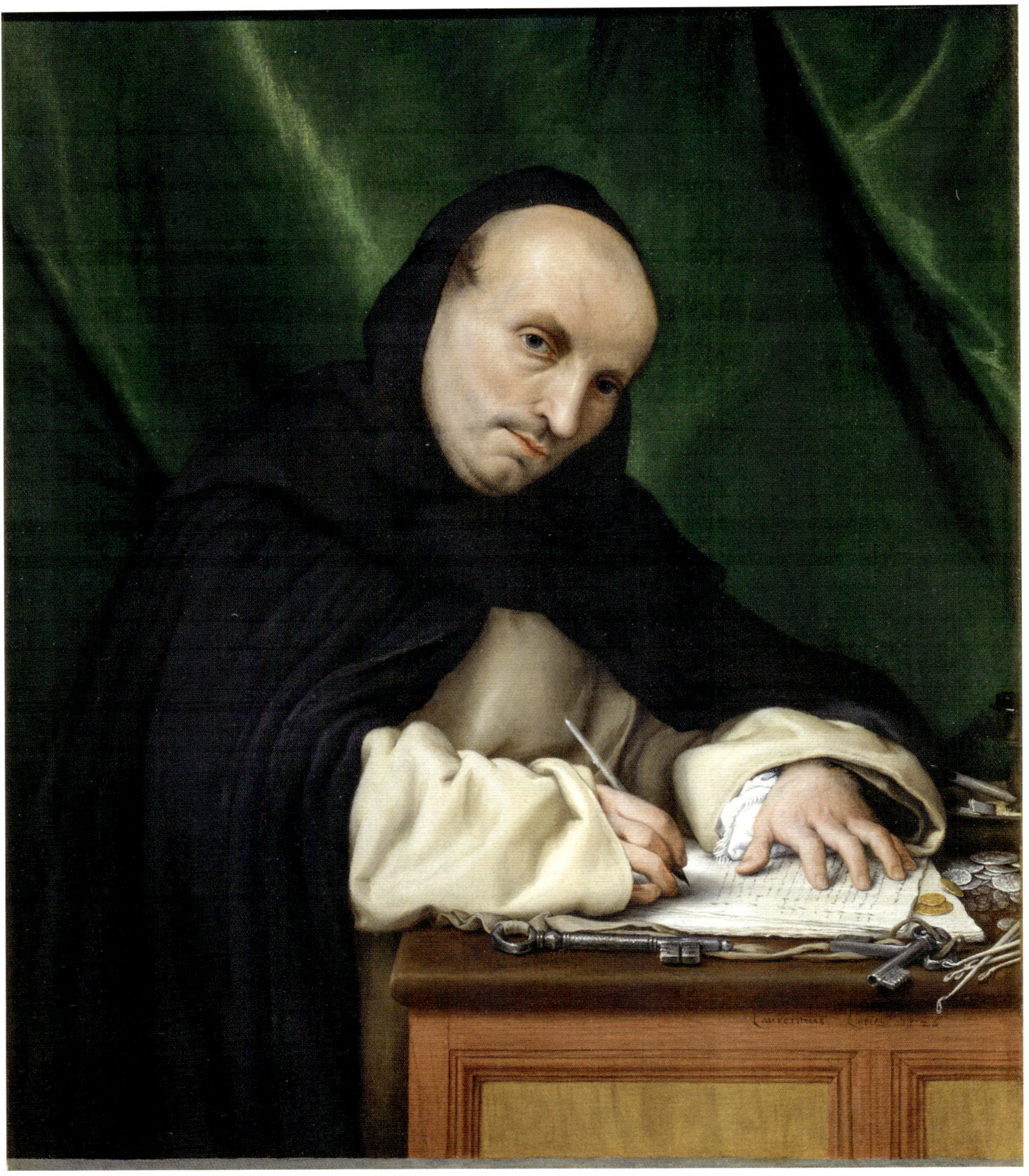

20 Lorenzo Lotto, *Portrait of a Dominican Friar (Marcantonio Luciani?)*, 1526, Treviso, Musei Civici

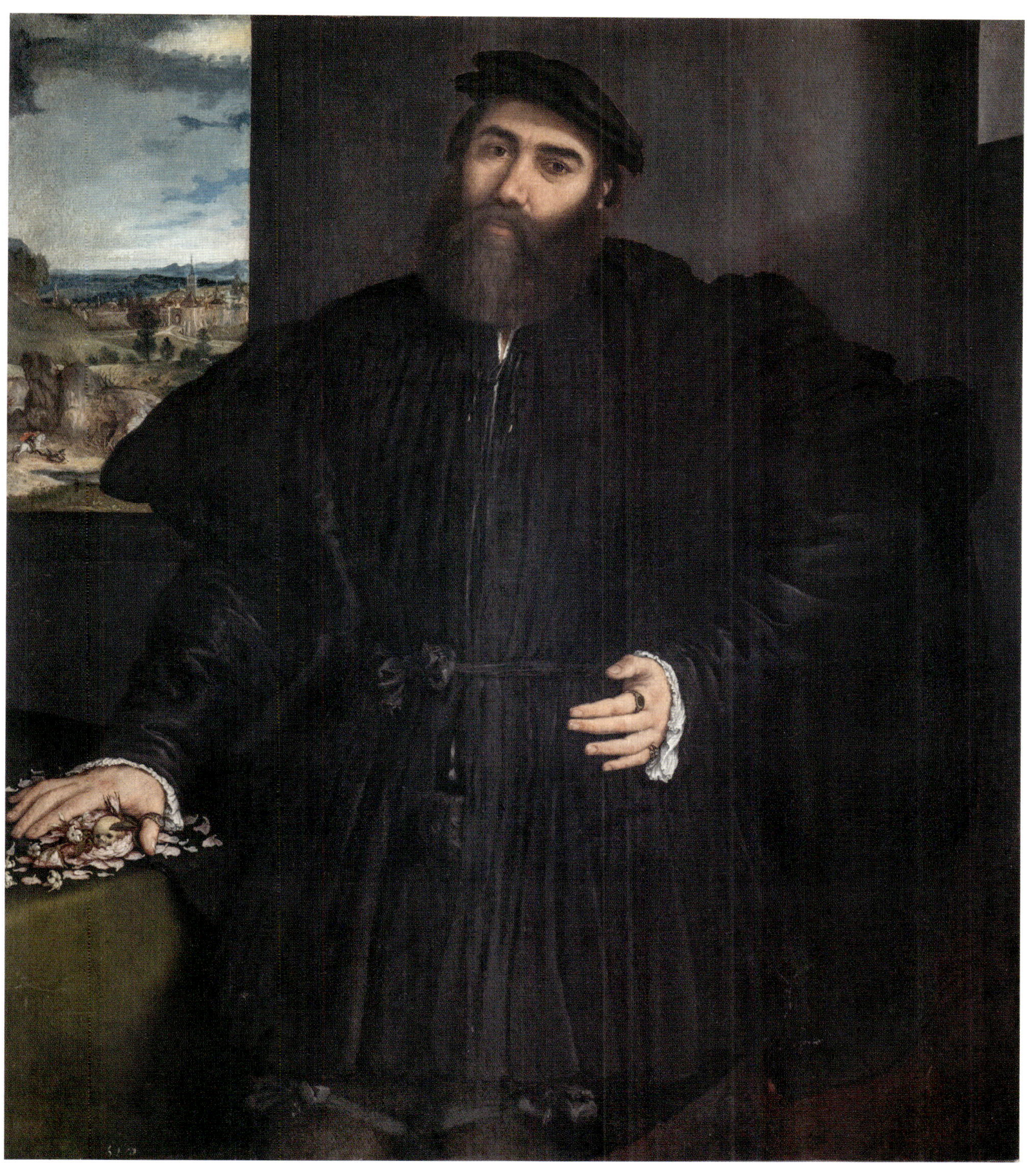

21 Lorenzo Lotto, *Portrait of a Gentleman (Mercurio Bua?)*, c. 1535, Rome, Galleria Borghese

The wandering gaze

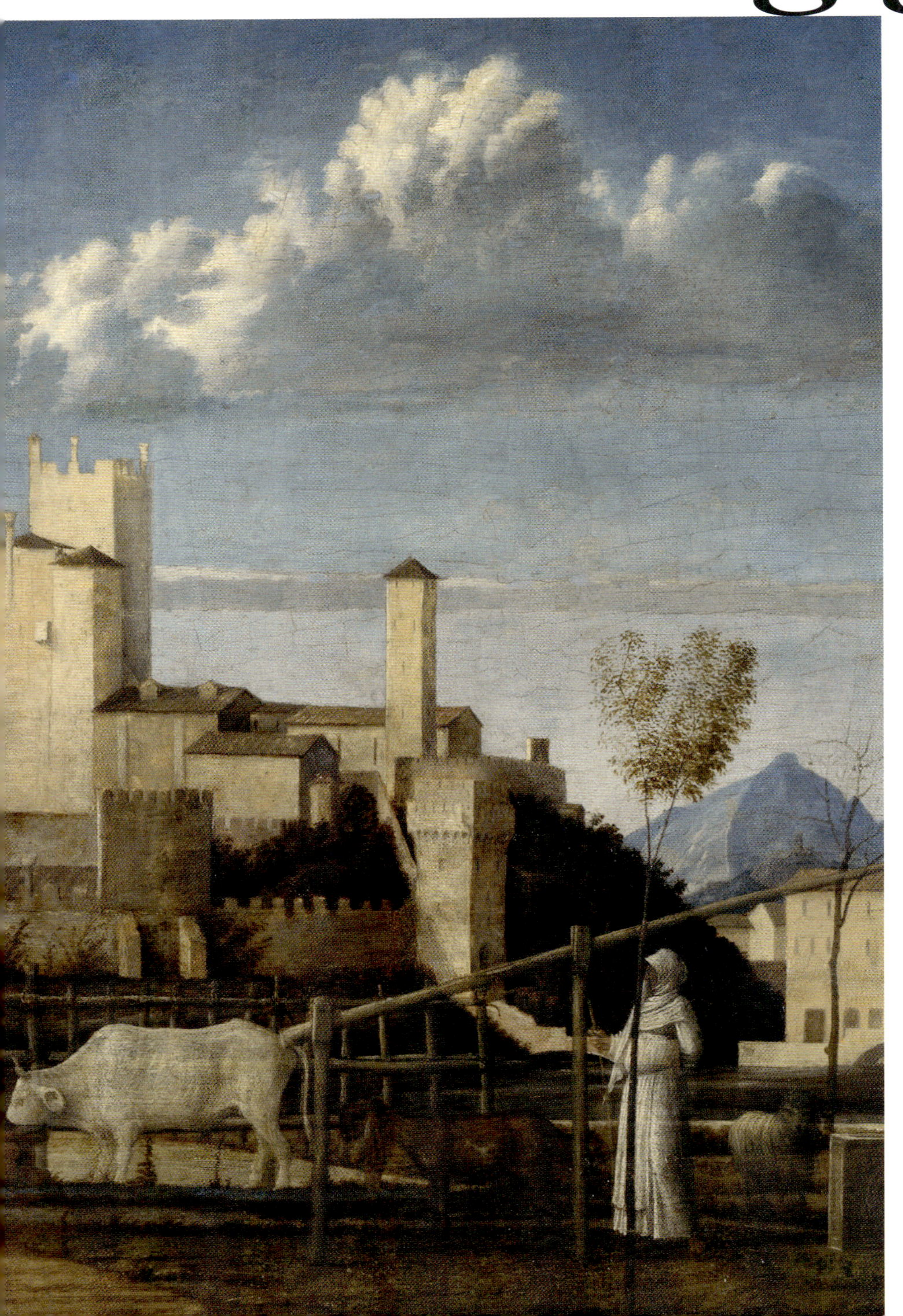

A new Venetian pictorial concept and its roots in late medieval piety

JOHANNES GRAVE

Salvatore Settis recently wrote of a "revolutionary novelty of […] pictorial language"[1] when he characterised Venetian painting of the period around 1500 and summarised a long-standing corpus of research to which he himself contributed substantially. In his opinion, paintings by the later Giovanni Bellini (c. 1435–1516), the early deceased Giorgione (1473/74–1510) and the young Titian (c. 1488/90–1576) cannot be derived solely from early Renaissance painting, which had developed in the 15th century and whose theoretical foundations seem to have been handed down in Leon Battista Alberti's (1404–1472) treatise *De pictura* (1435/36).[2] The understanding of images articulated in Venetian painting around 1500 differs, as Settis suggests, from what was known until then. It is at odds, for example, with the established demarcation between an intellectually sophisticated pictorial narrative (*historia*) and the religious devotional picture. In the paintings of Bellini, Giorgione and Titian, Settis discovers decidedly poetic qualities. The works they created around the turn of the century suggest deeper thoughts that cannot, however, be deciphered with certainty; they are rich in allusions, work with metaphorical fields of meaning and invite the viewer to a long, attentive and pleasurable gaze.

The fact that Venetian painting of the late 15th and early 16th centuries developed in a very independent, dynamic and innovative way has been consistently observed and appreciated in art historical research. Nevertheless, for a long time, it was difficult to grasp the characteristics of this art. To describe it merely as a stance that deviated from the standards of the Florentine Renaissance was bound to remain unsatisfactory. What, however, is this painting aiming at, if it obviously follows other expectations and guiding principles?

Thoughtful beholding instead of encoded messaging

Settis's reflections fit into a strand of recent art historical research that – despite continuing controversies and unanswered questions – is gradually outlining a genuinely Venetian understanding of the image. This is not intended to construct a fundamental, intrinsic difference, as it were, between Venice and Florence. Instead, it delineates a polyphonic Renaissance painting practice, which cannot be measured solely by the supposed standard of Florentine art and Alberti's treatise. The characteristically Venetian understanding of the image can be concisely and pointedly described as follows: Venetian painters and their audience did not simply lack consistency and rigour in their orientation towards the pictorial concepts typical of Florentine painting, but developed a different, independent conception of the possibilities of visual representation. At the centre of this understanding lies not so much a precise and reliable communication of certain thoughts or an intellectual-scholarly ambition, but rather a pictorial reception in which viewing and contemplation are combined in a special way. In addition to what a depiction allows us to see and reflect upon – namely, the characters, plots and the meanings conveyed with them – what counts at least as much in Venetian pictorial culture is that a picture stimulates its audience to a specific action and an unusual experience: thoughtful beholding.

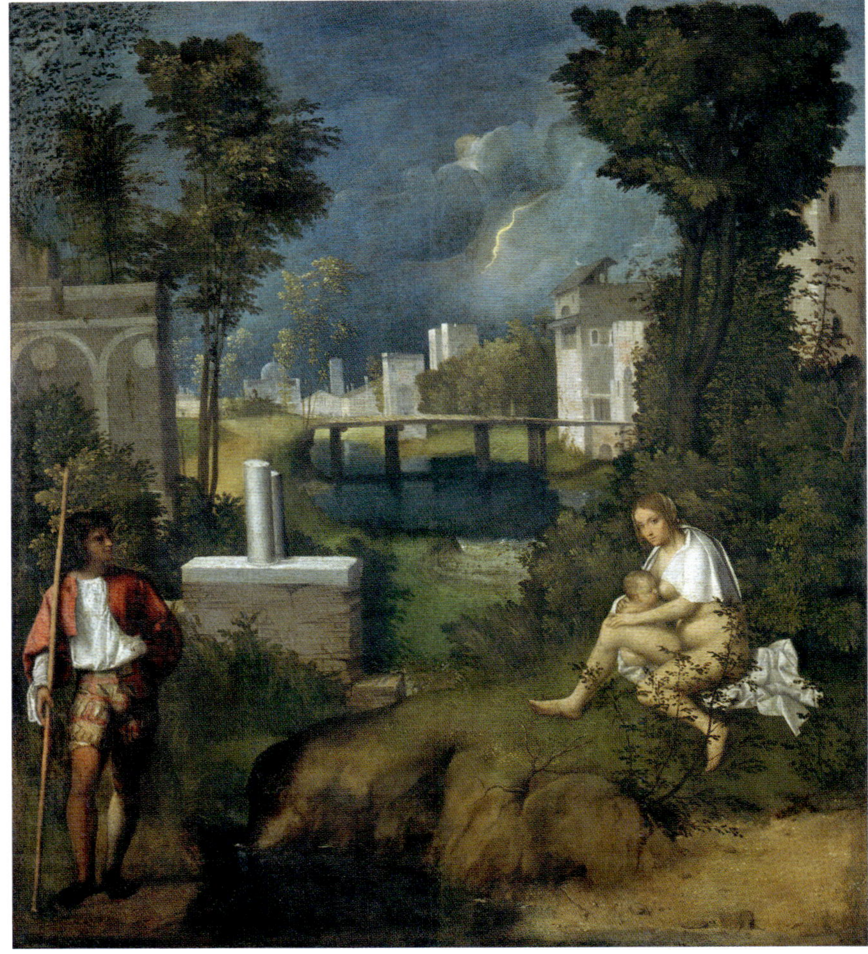

Fig. 1 Giorgione, *The Tempest*, c. 1505/10, Venice, Gallerie dell'Accademia

Like hardly any other painting, Giorgione's *The Tempest* (fig. 1) stands for "the revolutionary novelty of [...] pictorial language" of which Settis writes. The work continues to provoke attempts at interpretation to this day. More than 50 interpretations, some of them very different, can now be traced,[3] and the series of ever new suggestions as to which sources could shed light on the painting and its content is never-ending.[4] This unusual diversity is not merely due to chance. For

Giorgione's painting is particularly emphatic in inviting far-reaching attempts at interpretation. Individual pictorial motifs as well as their composition quickly catch the eye and raise the question of their meaning: why is the woman naked? What is signified by the man's conspicuous clothing and his staff as well as the fact that he is standing at some distance from the woman and child? Why are the figures, whose identities are not immediately obvious, shown in a natural setting adorned with ruins and not in the city, which can be seen in the middle and background? What is the significance of the thunderstorm, which immediately draws the eye with its lightning? And how can we explain the visual relationships that connect the man with the woman and them, in turn, with us? Are the viewers also assigned a certain role? When the painting is viewed for a longer period of time, more and more new details emerge – for instance, the seemingly unmotivated piece of wall with the two strangely clean-cut column stumps, which are so demonstratively placed in the picture and characterised in a strikingly specific manner that they can hardly be mistaken for mere incidental details. Further questions result from the seemingly incoherent distribution of the pictorial elements. The way they are placed in relation to each other does not help deciphering, but, on the contrary, makes understanding more difficult. The fact that the mother is breastfeeding her child when a thunderstorm is approaching makes little sense – and how the man on the left relates to her remains open. The many figures and details in Giorgione's *The Tempest* therefore seem like individual words whose meaning is unclear and which lack a comprehensible syntactic link.

Numerous attempts at interpretation on the part of art history respond to this almost provocatively disconcerting plethora by taking recourse to presumed literary references and other contextual knowledge to establish clarity and coherence that fails to emerge from the actual viewing of the painting. Such interpretations "search" for an external key that makes it possible to uncover a connection which is not evident in the painting itself and to derive a precise, binding meaning from the painting. However, the number of contributions that were sceptical about efforts to completely decipher the painting or that related the work to literary writings in another way remained rather limited.[5] Yet it is precisely here that a promising alternative could be sought. For insofar as Giorgione was guided by texts when working on his painting, he may not necessarily have perceived them as a guideline from which his depictions could be completely and definitively explained. Rather, he could have understood his painting as an equivalent to a form of meaning generation cultivated in literary writings – namely, in the poetry of so-called Petrarchism. Dan Lettieri, for example, has suggested that Giorgione drew primarily on the multilayered and metaphorical qualities of poetry such as Jacopo Sannazaro's *Arcadia* (1480s, printed in 1504) and that, in other words, he wanted to stimulate the viewer's own imagination and associations.[6]

Art historical research has far from approached a consensus in the interpretation of *The Tempest*. However, it seems not only tempting but also plausible that this ongoing search for meaning, which keeps producing new variants of interpretation, could come close to the original function of the work. Gabriele Vendramin (1484–1552), in whose collection the painting is first documented in 1530 and who may have commissioned it in the first decade of the 16th century, was, like Giorgione, part of an educated and culturally sophisticated milieu in which intellectually stimulating conversation on works of art was probably also cultivated.[7] In the scholarly and art-interested circles of Venice, the appeal of pictures that appear decidedly enigmatic and encourage playful disputes about various presupposition-rich interpretations was probably recognised.[8] For such a practice of viewing pictures, the question of whether the painter himself has based his painting on a clearly contoured story or message would be secondary. It would, indeed, be much more important to ensure a good balance between the challenging, enigmatic specificity of the details and a multifaceted interpretability of the picture as a whole. It is precisely for this kind of playfully serious search for meaning, in which the participants can demonstrate the sharpness of their gaze and at the same time their erudition, that Giorgione's *The Tempest* is uniquely suited. The figure characterisation and pictorial structure correspond perfectly to such a presumed function of the painting.

Landscape and allegorical thinking

The very first mention of Giorgione's *The Tempest* betrays a certain perplexity in view of the subject and its message. When the Venetian scholar and art collector Marcantonio Michiel (1484–1552) recorded some notes on Vendramin's collection in 1530, he described the painting as a "small landscape on canvas with the storm, the gypsy [a label externally imposed on Romani people] woman and the soldier" ("paesetto in tela cun la tempesta, cun la cingana et soldato").[9] Michiel thus attempted to identify the most important figures, but did not speculate on what narrative they might illustrate. It is noteworthy that he referred to the work as a "paesetto" and thus associated it with a term that anticipates our understanding of landscape. Whereas previously the word "lontani"/"luntani" (literally: "that which is far away") had been used to designate natural settings in pictures,[10] Michiel's notes provide early examples of how the conceptual field of "paese"/"paesaggio" is formed, in which a modified conception of landscape in pictures is obviously expressed. While "lontani" mainly referred to spatial distances, the term "paese" seems to assign a stronger intrinsic value to the landscape element and to make nature worthy of the image in a new way.

In fact, the landscape depiction in Giorgione's *The Tempest* is of fundamental importance if one assumes that the painting's function is to challenge different attempts at interpretation. For it is, above all, the embedding of the figures in a natural scenery that enabled the painter to distribute the individual, highly evocative motifs across the picture's space and surface in such a way that clearly legible relationships and plots do not immediately emerge between them. The depiction of nature also reinforces the mysteriousness of the entire work by not conspicuously marking which detail needs to be explained at all and which motif could prove to be a more or less random and incidental prop of the landscape. To this effect, it is difficult to draw a line between the pictorial elements, which ought to be deciphered within the framework of an overall interpretation, and the motifs, whose task is to form the setting of the depicted scene without themselves harbouring deeper layers of meaning.

Giorgione's *The Tempest* was not the only painting that Michiel described using the semantic field "paese"/"paesetto". A few years earlier, on the occasion of a visit to the collection of the Venetian patrician Taddeo Contarini (c. 1466–1540), he had already used the word "paese" several times. One of Giorgione's paintings, still known today as *The Three Philosophers* (c. 1508/09, Vienna, Kunsthistorisches Museum), is described by Michiel as an "oil painting on canvas with the three philosophers in a landscape" ("tela a oglio delli 3 phylosophi nel paese").[11] In addition, he cites – again on a work by Giorgione – a "landscape on canvas with the birth of Paris and the two shepherds" ("tela del paese cun el nascimento de Paris, cun li dui pastori").[12] However, the use of this early concept of landscape is not limited to Giorgione's creations. Rather, it is also encountered in the note to a

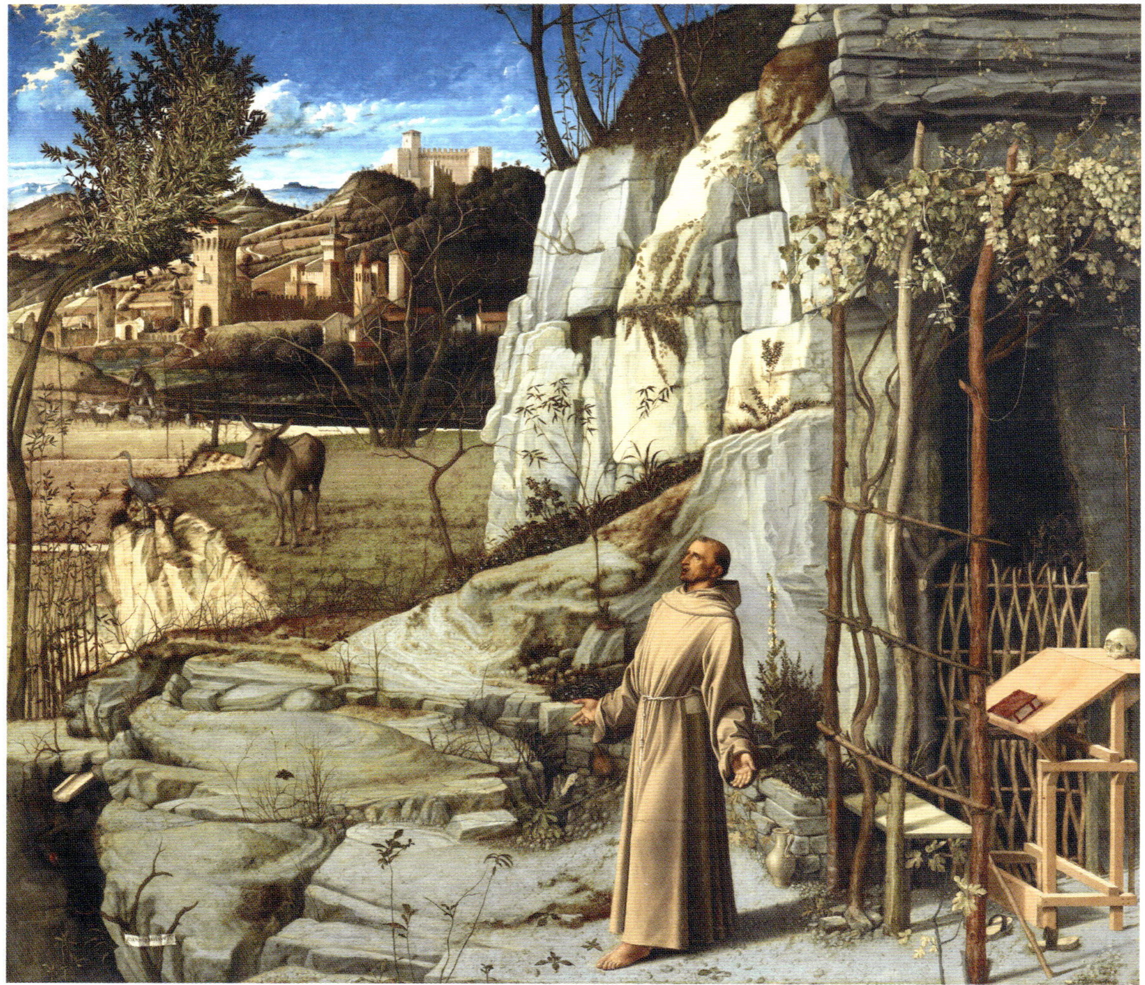

Fig. 2 Giovanni Bellini, *St Francis in the Desert*, c. 1475/80, New York, The Frick Collection

painting that has been identified with good reason with Giovanni Bellini's famous painting in the Frick Collection in New York (fig. 2): "The panel in oil of St Francis in the wilderness was the work of Zuan Bellino, begun by him for Mr Zuan Michiel; it has a marvellously composed and detailed landscape" ("[...] un paese propinquo finito e ricercato mirabilmente").[13]

The fact that Michiel speaks of "paese" in both Giorgione's enigmatic paintings and Bellini's depiction of the saint may draw attention to similarities between these paintings. Indeed, the landscape is of great importance in both cases. Both Bellini and Giorgione create – measured against the conventions of the quattrocento – convincingly coherent landscape spaces that extend far into the depths of the pictorial space and boast a wealth of detail. The question therefore arises as to whether the landscapes of the two painters can also be ascribed a comparable aesthetic function. However, we first need to take a closer look at Bellini's use of the depiction of nature.

There is no doubt that Bellini wanted to draw the viewer's attention to the numerous animals and plants, but also to rock formations, springs and watercourses as well as clouds and light. There is hardly a spot on the picture surface that does not present some detail of the rendering of nature that can attract interest. The fact that St Francis is depicted as comparatively small and off-centre in the composition additionally contributes to triggering a process of contemplation that does not let the gaze linger on the protagonist alone, but lets it wander over the whole scene. The saint's behaviour no less supports the viewer's impulse to turn to the landscape in all its diversity, as he too directs his attention to nature, here presumably to the unusual light phenomenon in the upper left corner.

Despite all the controversies, recent art historical research has not disputed the fact that Bellini's depictions of nature – both in his *St Francis* and in many other paintings – are closely connected with the religious content of the pictures. In their analysis of the work in New York, several art historians have hoped that the numerous detailed motifs in the natural scenery would shed light on the question of which moment from St Francis's life or which aspect of his personality is at the centre of the representation. Since the saint's posture and the situation in which he is shown do not reliably tie in with familiar iconographic traditions and cannot be elucidated beyond doubt by recourse to written sources, the idea that a key to understanding the picture might lie in the many, strikingly sharply drawn details at first seems only logical.

It would be going too far here to present even in outline the often very complex and presupposition-rich analyses that aim to locate presumed written sources of the painting's concept and to unlock its deeper meaning.[14] Quite a few of these interpretative efforts attempt to underpin the approach of Millard Meiss, who in 1964 assessed Bellini's painting as an unusual depiction of the stigmatisation of the saint,[15] by evaluating the rendition of nature. At times, these efforts, in their utmost seriousness, display an unintentional humour – for example, when the plants are not only determined with botanical precision, but their growth and inflorescence are also used as an occasion to determine the exact time of day and season of the event depicted by Bellini.[16]

Such a detective-deciphering approach must, however, fail in its attempt to provide unambiguous clarification, as it ignores the pictorial structure and its consequences for the reception process.[17] For Bellini already plays with the extraordinary potential inherent in a detailed depiction of nature. His painting offers a stupendous natural continuum whose unity in terms of content and aesthetics is secured not least by the colouring and the skilful use of light.[18] All details are integrated into a comprehensive context that gives their presence in the pictorial space an unconstrained, natural justification. At the same time, however, the animals, plants, rocks, watercourses and fences, even in the distant background, are rendered in such sharp detail that they subtly attract attention. In doing so, the viewer's gaze can move effortlessly and casually from one motif to the next, as the dense, almost seamless distribution of the many details constantly offers new inputs for beholding and thinking. Allowing oneself to be drawn into this process, one's gaze does not follow clearly marked paths in the painted landscape. Rather, it is obviously up to the viewer to decide when to go to which detail and where to linger longer.

The sharpness of detail and the positioning of the many precisely captured and therefore easily identifiable animals, plants and other natural phenomena almost inevitably raise the question of whether these motifs can be linked to further meanings. Pious and educated contemporaries of Bellini will have quickly made associations. This applies, for example, to details such as the solitary donkey in the middle ground or the tree stump near the saint's right hand, which almost demonstratively shows that it has been felled, while remaining recognisable as a fig tree thanks to the large leaf. In order to gain a deeper, figurative meaning from such motifs, various possible contexts of reference could be considered: viewers could recall legendary traditions about the life of St Francis, think of well-known biblical texts or fall back on the rich heritage of Christian allegorical interpretation, which, although it had been fed by biblical guidelines, had long since expanded far beyond them. By the end of the Middle Ages at the latest, the practice of allegorical interpretation had reached such a degree of differentiation that all plants and animals could be interrogated for a transferred meaning, for example, in order to reflect on the Christian story of salvation or on personal virtues and vices. When Bellini included in his painting an abundance of easily distinguishable plants such as laurel, fig, vine, mullein, aster, bindweed and iris as well as numerous animals such as donkeys, rabbits, sheep, cranes and kingfishers, he offered viewers a rich, hardly exhaustible repertoire of potentially allegorical motifs.[19]

The painter could also count on a great willingness to interpret such details in Christian terms, because this hermeneutic approach to nature was firmly anchored in late medieval piety. Alongside the Holy Scriptures, God's creation was considered his second revelation; it was therefore necessary to read the book of nature and ask for the meaning behind earthly phenomena. This comprehensive culture of allegorical interpretation was widely practised and rehearsed – in sermons, treatises and edifying writings as well as in prayers, poetry, songs and pictures, and not least in encounters with the great outdoors. Comprehensive compendia (e.g. Bartholomaeus Anglicus's *De proprietatibus rerum* [c. 1242/47], the *Speculum maius* of Vincent of Beauvais [c. 1247/60] and *Summa de exemplis ac similitudinibus rerum* of Giovanni da San Gimignano [c. 1300/10]) recorded a spectrum of possible meanings in the late Middle Ages almost impossible to survey. It is particularly noteworthy that the objects to be interpreted were usually assigned several, sometimes sharply contradictory meanings, so that a lion could stand for both Christ and the devil.[20] On closer inspection, however, this practice is only logical, for every allegory started with concrete properties of animals, plants or other phenomena. As soon as an object had several properties, the possibilities for reading it had to multiply. This openness to multiple interpretations could also be accompanied by a greater focus on the precise observation of nature; God's book of nature was only accessible to those who were prepared to perceive the abundance of phenomena with all their different qualities. The late medieval allegorical interpretation of nature is thus characterised by two tendencies that are of interest with regard to Bellini's painting: on the one hand, an increasingly detailed and precise perception of nature and, on the other, a practice of interpretation that reckoned with several options for meaning from the outset. In allegorical reading, believing Christians could therefore not merely repeat rehearsed attributions of meaning, they also had to become active in beholding and thinking themselves in order to experience a hermeneutical freedom.

Visual landscape and viewing time

Bellini's depiction of St Francis must have seemed a plausible and attractive proposition to viewers familiar with such a practice of allegorical interpretation. In my opinion, the painting does not direct the focus to the decoding of a complex programme, but rather to a thoroughly free and associative movement of seeing and thinking. It triggers a process of

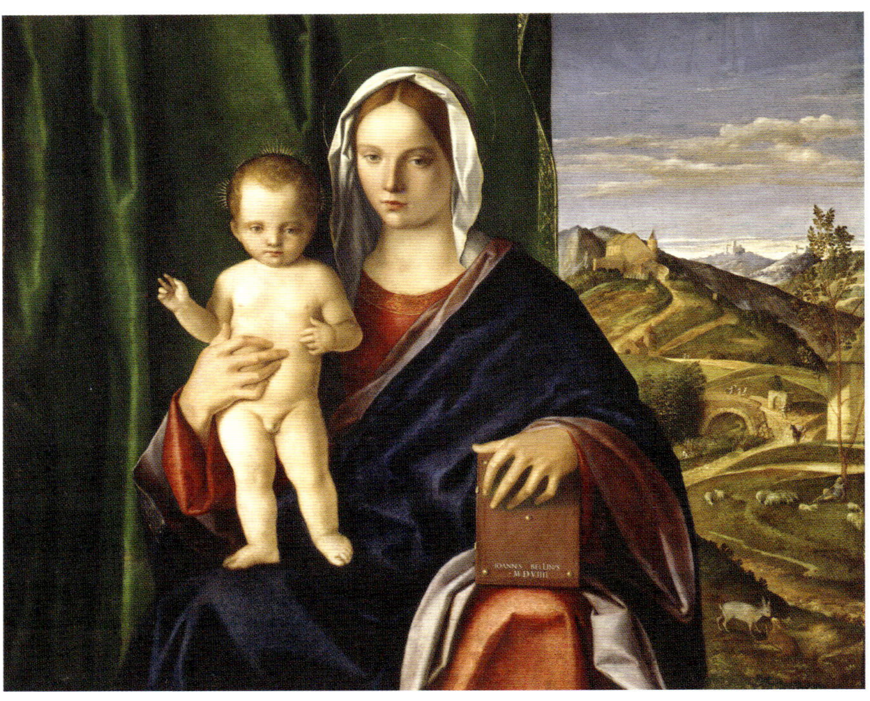

Fig. 3 Giovanni Bellini, *Virgin and Child*, 1509, Detroit, Institute of Arts

beholding that is not solely oriented towards a clearly predetermined goal and a final insight. There is no doubt that any meaningful engagement with the image will always keep St Francis in mind. The way in which the saint is integrated into the richly detailed landscape, however, suggests that he is not the centre of a network of highly specific, hidden clues – instead, with his own attitude of prayerful attention to nature, he exemplifies the practice that is also recommended to the viewer.

The fact that Bellini did not want to encode a complex, precisely defined message with his depictions of nature but, on the contrary, offered illustrative material for a thoroughly open-ended allegorical interpretation also emerges from his practice of using plants and animals as modular components in a large number of paintings. Not infrequently, he inserted a natural motif almost unchanged into different contexts, so that it would be implausible to assign very specific and simultaneously binding content to each detail. Thus, the same pair of hares seen in the lower right corner of the *Virgin and Child* from Detroit (fig. 3) is also encountered in the *Resurrection of Christ* (c. 1500/10, Fort Worth, Kimbell Art Museum) and in a *St Jerome* found in Washington (fig. 4).[21] Since other depictions of the church father by Bellini's hand – for instance, a painting in the Uffizi in Florence (c. 1480/85) and a work in the National Gallery in London (cat. 1) – are without this detail, the impression is reinforced that the artist applied a rather loose connection between the details of nature and the central subject. This broadened the scope that Bellini's contemporaries could explore when dealing with the many natural motifs. Without immediately encountering frustrating contradictions, they were able to try out various aspects of allegorical interpretation in analogy to the doctrine of the four senses of Scripture and relate individual motifs accordingly to the life of Christ or a saint, to the

Christian history of salvation, to moral considerations or also to eschatological aspects.

As a rule, Bellini's plants, animals and other natural motifs invite an allegorical reading without displaying a decidedly enigmatic character. However, the painter also created works that approach Giorgione's *The Tempest* in this respect. This applies to the *Madonna of the Meadow* in London (fig. 5) with the fight between the bird and the snake in the middle ground on the left and the strange cloaked figure at the draw well on the right as well as to the much-interpreted *Sacred Allegory* (fig. 6).[22] The latter, in particular – with its very individually characterised but not consistently reliably identifiable figures, with their disconcerting arrangement in the pictorial space and with a veritable wealth of meaningful details in the vast landscape – anticipates essential means of design in Giorgione's works.

This suggests that a path could lead from Bellini's landscapes of meditation to Giorgione's enigmatic creations. What the former had brought to fruition in an innovative pictorial development of medieval practices of allegoric reading could be taken up by the latter and brought closer to a learned humanist milieu equipped to incorporate other literary and mythological allusions beyond Christian allegoric interpretation.

Fig. 4 Giovanni Bellini, *St Jerome in the Desert*, 1505, Washington, D.C., National Gallery of Art

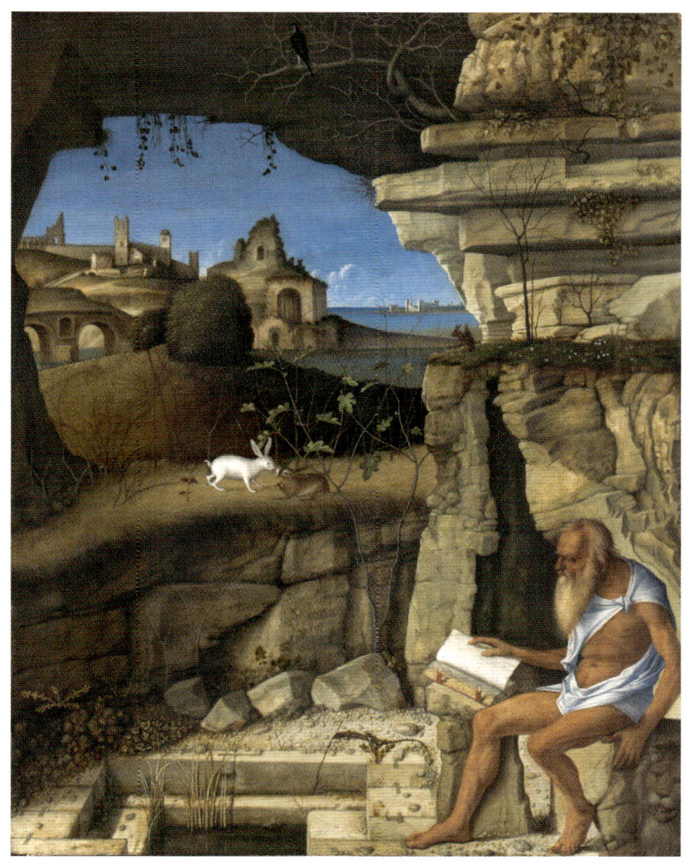

If we may assume that Bellini and Giorgione were not primarily concerned with a specific message, but with the process-orientedness and performativity of beholding, interpreting and thinking, then they developed a remarkable pictorial concept that is indeed strikingly different from the conception of the image that had been put forward by Alberti and had become widespread, above all, in Florence. For the paintings of both artists imply an understanding of images that does not conceive them solely as a means of communication or a system of signs, but as highly developed and refined instruments of a sophisticated practice of contemplation. In doing so, the process of seeing and thinking has greater relevance than its result, the concrete thoughts and conclusions.

In a conversation reported by the humanist Pietro Bembo (1470–1547), Bellini seems to have claimed a similar idea for the creation of his paintings. Bembo had endeavoured to convince the artist to paint a picture commissioned by the Margravine of Mantua, Isabella d'Este, on condition that he adhere to an iconographic programme to be agreed upon beforehand. In a letter of 11 January 1506, however, Bembo reported to Mantua that Bellini was not to be won over for too precise specifications; the painter was "accustomed, as he says, always to wander around at will in the pictures" ("uso, come dice, di sempre vagare a sua voglia nelle pitture").[23]

In the quotation handed down by Bembo, the aimless wandering, designated by the term "vagare", refers to the production of the picture, which, however – as Bellini specifically added – is committed to the purpose of satisfying the viewer. It therefore seems tempting not to confine the relative openness of this wandering to the painter, but to consider it also for the reception of the picture. Such a thought would imply that

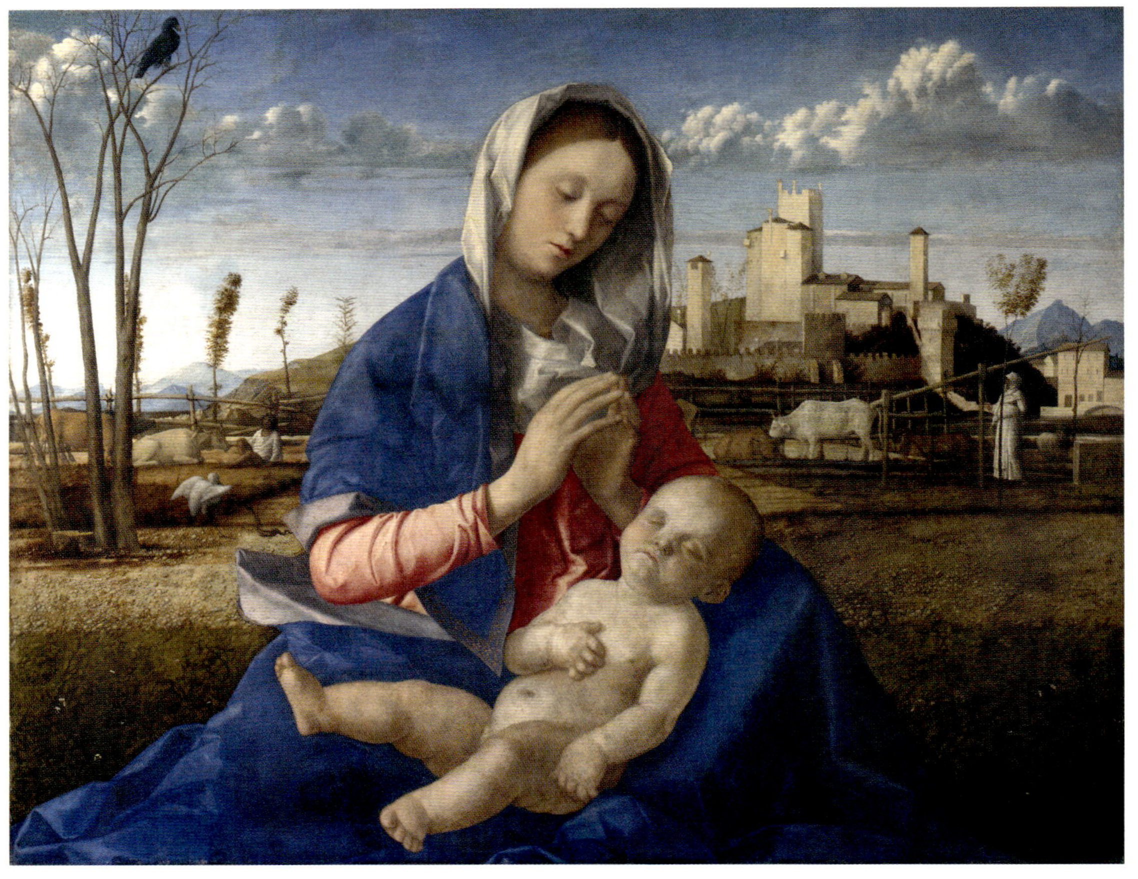

Fig. 5 Giovanni Bellini, *Madonna of the Meadow*, c. 1500/05, London, The National Gallery

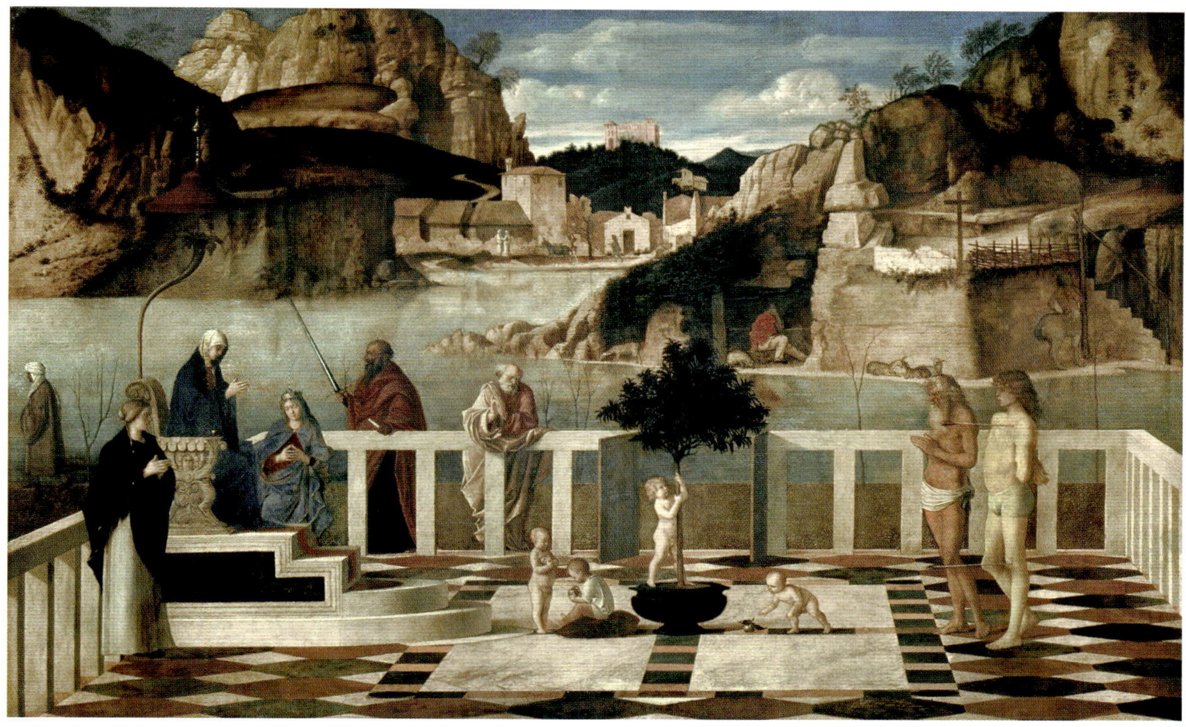

Fig. 6 Giovanni Bellini, *Sacred Allegory*, 1480s, Florence, Galleria degli Uffizi

paintings, despite all their immobility and immutability, shape time in an eminent sense. Understood in this way, they not only serve communication, but rather invite a manner of seeing and thinking and thus stimulate experiences that extend in time and whose processual quality has a value of its own. How this process takes place is not solely at the discretion of the viewer; it is essentially determined by the picture itself, what is depicted in it, but also by the formal design and structure of the work. Pictures have a specific reception-aesthetic temporality; in other words, they can give rise to special, meaningful experiences of time.[24]

In the decades around 1500, a unique laboratory-like situation developed in Venice in which this insight could take shape. It is precisely the comparatively traditional cultural practice of Christian allegorical interpretation from which essential impulses were taken to arrive at a new conception of the possibilities of the image, which was to be of great importance for the art of the early modern period. Pictures – as Venetian painting shows – cannot be reduced to being manifestations of a clearly predetermined meaning. First and foremost, they are objects of open, temporally extending contemplation and reflection, which grant their viewers a different, freer participation than solving a puzzle.

Innovation and experimentation

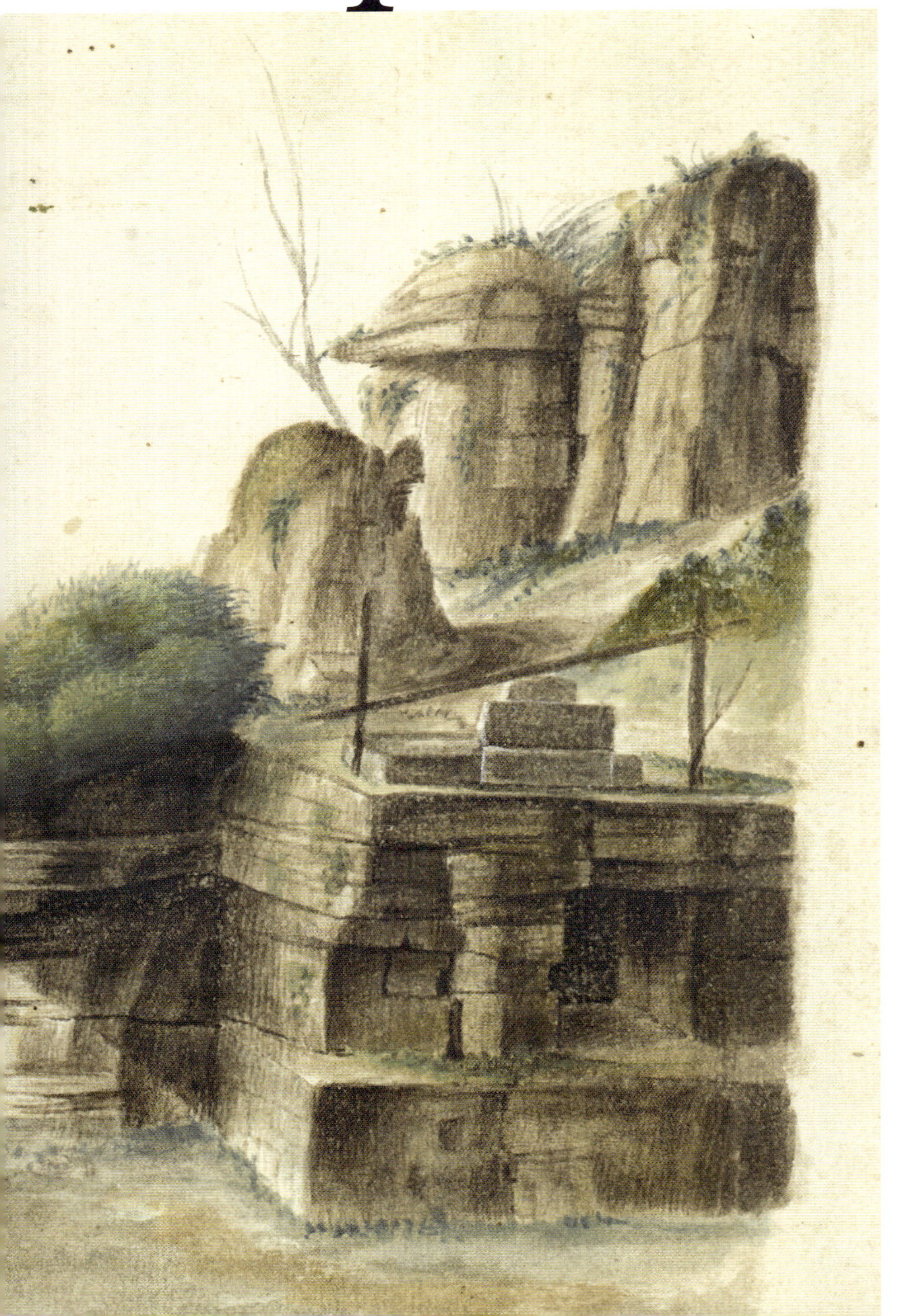

Landscape in early 16th-century Venetian prints and drawings

CATHERINE WHISTLER

When Marcantonio Michiel (1484–1552) noted the painting by Giovanni Bellini (c. 1435–1516) that he had seen in the house of Taddeo Contarini in Venice in 1525 – the *St Francis in the Desert* (see p. 76, fig. 2), now in the Frick Collection, New York – his recollection was of a beautiful landscape representing the wilderness that filled the entire picture right into the foreground. In recording another painting on the same visit, Giorgione's (1473/74–1510) *Three Philosophers* (1508/09; Vienna, Kunsthistorisches Museum), Michiel was impressed by the treatment of the imposing craggy outcrop and the rays of the sun.[1]

By the 1520s, Venetian art lovers were attuned to the delights of such representations, not least because of the innovative exploration of landscape in prints and drawings in the early 1500s that helped to shape a new genre in artistic production. The aspects that caught Michiel's attention – such as the filling of the visual field with natural elements, providing an inviting experience, and the contrasts of wild or rocky stretches with luminous skies – were already characteristic of engravings and independent drawings, notably by Giulio Campagnola (c. 1482–c. 1516) and by his adoptive son, Domenico Campagnola (c. 1500–1564), who were each in their separate ways major protagonists in the development of the Venetian landscape in small-scale monochrome works of art.

A sophisticated graphic artist, Giulio was also a manuscript painter and a talented musician. He was the son of a Paduan humanist, Girolamo Campagnola, whose erudite friends praised the young man's gifts and abilities. Giovanni Aurelio Augurello wrote vividly of the appeal of Giulio's landscapes with their mountains, valleys, hills and streams in his poem, *Chrysopoeia*, published in 1515. Having settled in Venice by 1507, Giulio was part of a circle of writers and humanists who also appreciated the achievements and innovations of Giorgione. Indeed, in his finely considered technique and his sensitivity to atmosphere and mood, Giulio comes close to Giorgione in terms of poetic refinement, as is evident in his *Nymph in a Landscape* (fig. 1). In that

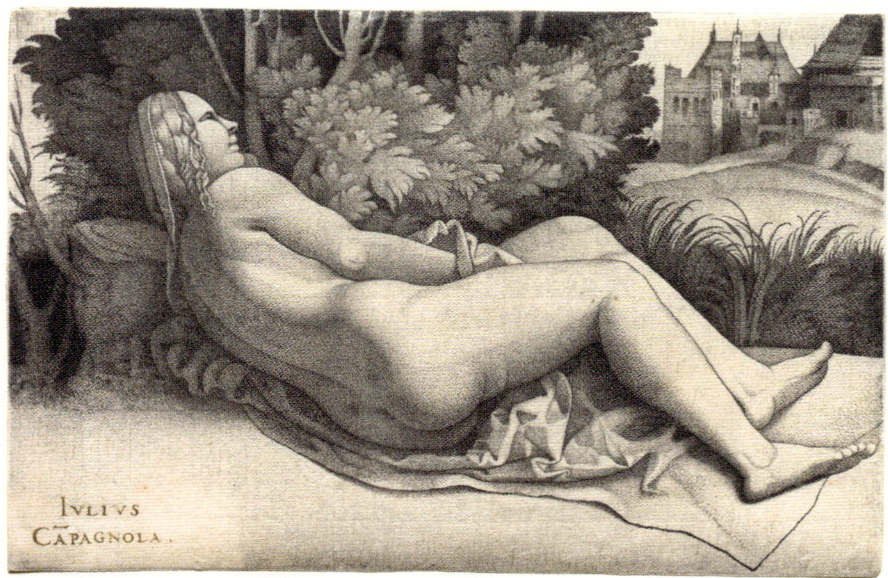

Fig. 1 Giulio Campagnola, *Nymph in a Landscape*, c. 1508/09, Cleveland, The Cleveland Museum of Art, Department of Prints and Drawings

enigmatic image of around 1508/09, the linear qualities of engraving are softened by an experimental technique of dots and flickering marks, where contours are blurred and forms are shaped through soft tonal modelling. Such stippled flecks appear in manuscript painting, creating indeterminate spaces around antique-style motifs, and Giulio brought this *pointilliste* mode to some of his prints, accentuating their antique resonances. Immersed in her own verdant, sensuous world that fills much of the visual field, contrasting with the distant architecture, the figure of the nymph is impervious to the gaze of the viewer or to that of an imaginary wanderer in the landscape. As an engraving, albeit in a small edition, Giulio's image reached a wider audience than that of a Giorgionesque painting of such a subject. Moreover, the innovative technique was itself admirable at a time when fine prints by masters such as Andrea Mantegna (1430/31–1506) or Albrecht Dürer (1471–1528) were avidly collected in Venice. Rather than being surrogates for paintings, prints were desirable as embodying the qualities of good *disegno*, meaning inventiveness and virtuosity in representation and craftsmanship. Venice's thriving print culture offered opportunities for experimentation with new subject matter and techniques in a medium unbounded by traditional conventions, while explorations in painting of landscape with allegorical and mythological themes were matched by innovations in types of *disegno*. As striking monochrome representations, their inked marks demanding close scrutiny, both prints and drawings created convincing and immersive 'green worlds' on paper.

Both Giulio and Domenico were attentive to nature's variety in constructing their fictive Veneto landscapes, alternative worlds of verdant delights where natural and human forms would interact. In a refined drawing with two men in conversation in a woodland setting near a rustic Veneto town (fig. 2), Giulio used meticulous strokes of the pen with dense cross-hatching in parts to model the varying motifs of trees, foliage, grassy slopes and wooden or stone buildings. The sheet is filled with appealing naturalistic detail that allows the viewer's gaze to rove and explore, enjoying the contrasts of dark woodland and luminous distant mountains or of rustic occupations and the presence of the antique. Without disturbing the beauty of the drawing, the contours are finely pricked for the transfer of the design to another surface; it was intended as a model for an engraving, yet could still be admired by a future owner. An engraving was produced by Domenico Campagnola with typical variations, notably in the figures, which have now become an entire group of musicians (cat. 11). The Venetian-born Domenico, who was of German origin, took his master's name. While his date of birth is uncertain, he may already have been collaborating on print projects by about 1515, and his first dated works are from 1517. Importantly, Domenico's talents in *disegno* saw him forge a professional path in designing and making prints and drawings,

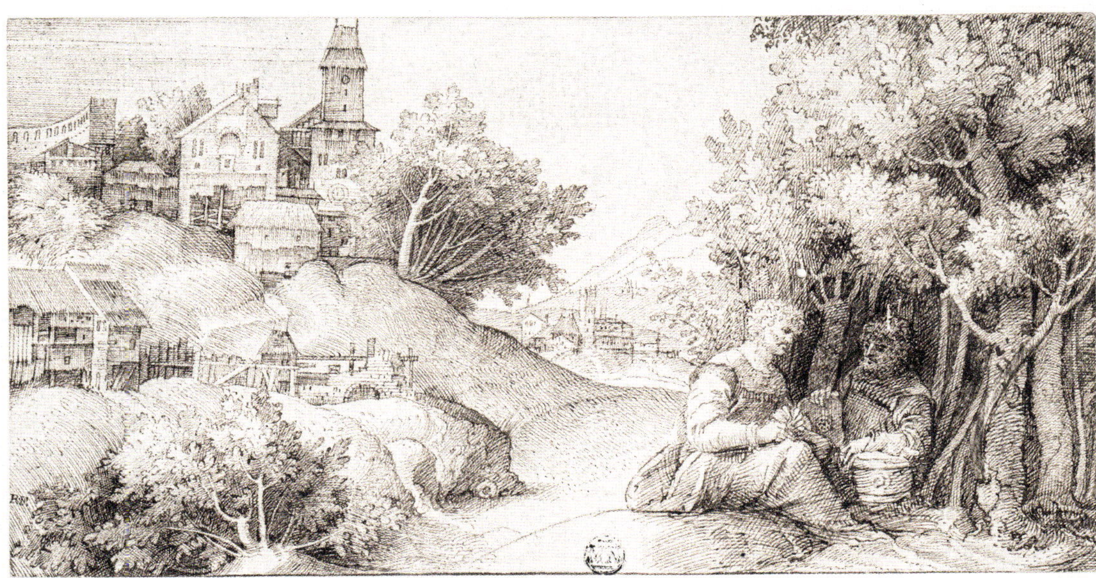

Fig. 2 Giulio Campagno a, *Landscape with Two Men Sitting near a Copoice*, c. 1510/15, Paris, Musée du Louvre, Département des Arts Graph ques

building on Giulio's achievements by producing independent landscape compositions that appealed to cultivated collectors.

Wild and rugged elements appear in some of Giulio's engravings, with atmospheric skies stretching behind: for example, in *The Astrologer* (c. 1509), the contemplative protagonist is seated in front of a blasted tree stump with a steep rocky mound from which trees grow in a twisting clump; the dragon-like monster, redolent of northern European art, and other details refer to political misfortunes. Domenico would make this strenuous, craggy aspect a more dramatic feature of his prints and autonomous drawings throughout his career. His later depiction of St Jerome in penitence in the wilderness includes the striking motif of a rock formation that creates a natural bridge, which seems to pulsate with verdant life (cat. 32). One feels the graphic energy in the varied strokes of Domenico's pen, used with different pressures to create a sense of animation as well as conveying the fall of light on foliage, tree bark and rocks. This attention to the arboreal as well as the emphasis on the wildness and ruggedness of the landscape is a strand running through Domenico's independent drawings. Prominent rocky outcrops are seen in compositions such as an early signed drawing in the British Museum, London (inv. 1848.1110.10), or a later expansive landscape in the Albertina, Vienna (cat. 35), where in each case travellers contend with the hardships of journeys through difficult terrain. In these drawings, strongly delineated modelling suggests impending storms, as the skies seem partly darkened by changing weather. In other independent sheets, Domenico's skies are radiantly luminous, with the blank paper standing for bright light, as in his undulating, panoramic landscape where the distant water reflects the calm stillness of the sky (fig. 3). Unlike the nuanced approach and refined air of Giulio's prints and drawings, those of Domenico make a vivid impact, with forceful, confident marks that seem to carve out a light-filled, dynamic space. In his mature career, Domenico's vision of landscape is above all distinctive in that he uses sinuous, swerving lines and strokes to convey the rhythmic forms of trees, the rolling stretches of ground, and breezy, atmospheric skies – with a finely judged tension between spirited surface patterning and representational depth.

Both Giulio and Domenico were attracted by northern European prints, which circulated widely in Venice, and particularly the approach to landscape in the engravings and woodcuts of Albrecht Dürer. The filling of the visual field with vibrant lines and appealing detail seen in prints by Dürer such as the *Virgin and Child with the Monkey* (c. 1498) or the *Sea Monster* (c. 1498) was exemplary for Giulio as much as for the younger Domenico in their immersive landscapes; Giulio incorporated many specific landscape motifs or details from Dürer in his engravings that would be recognised and enjoyed by his friends and patrons, in a spirit of astute emulation and appropriation akin to literary practices. By contrast, for Domenico, the robust and vital line of the German artist was of great importance in the formation of his style in landscape drawings, together with the innovative zest that Titian brought to Venetian graphic art. Meanwhile, the cross-currents between the prints of Dürer and Venetian achievements of the early 1500s are vividly epitomised in the expressive engraving of *The Virgin Nursing the Christ Child at the Foot of a Tree* (cat. 31) by Jacopo de' Barbari (1440/50 or c. 1470–before 1516). If the German artist was the primary lexicographer of arboreal material for the early 16th century, then his vocabulary is brilliantly adapted in the extraordinary treatment of the venerable tree, the thick, spreading roots of which shelter and protect Mary as she feeds her baby. This motif is given life by the variegated curving marks of Jacopo's burin, which trace the bulging forms and the dark recesses of the tree trunk and its root system, exploring the rough texture of the bark, and the thrusting stump of a

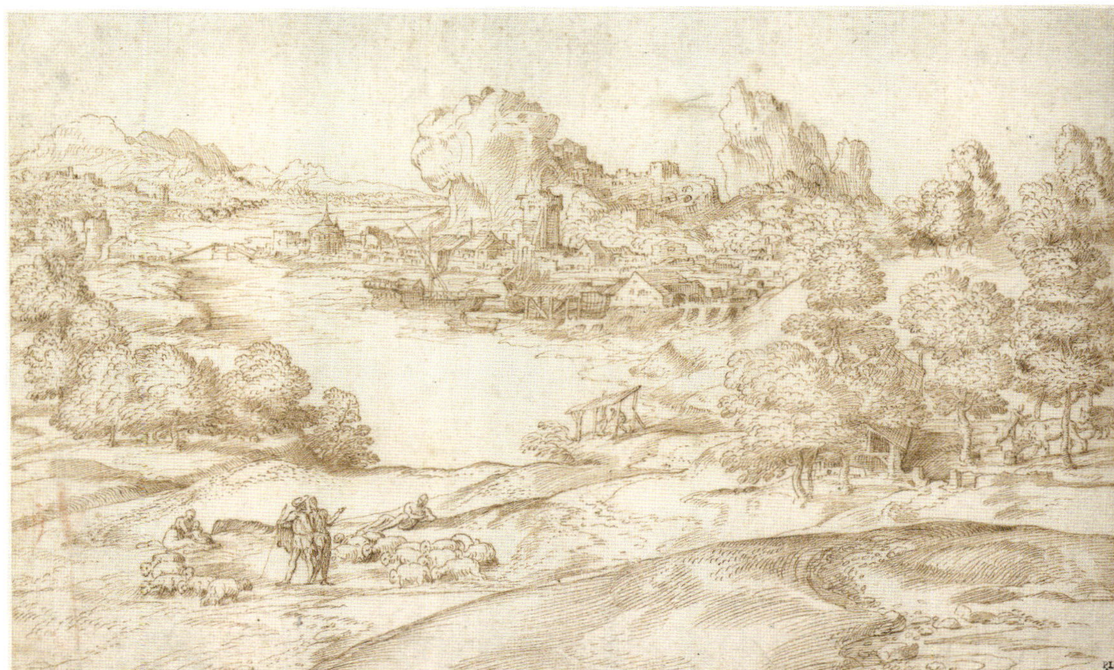

Fig. 3 Domenico Campagnola, *Landscape with Herdsmen*, c. 1550, Paris, Fondation Custodia, Collection Frits Lugt

lopped branch. Yet in a different graphic mode reminiscent of Mantegna, Jacopo used fine, rhythmic lines to define the complex, elegant folds of classicising drapery that enclose Mary's body, differentiating her from the powerful natural form of the tree. Living and dead trees endow devotional subjects with symbolic and Biblical weight; Jacopo here presents a distillation of familiar medieval subjects, the Madonna of Humility, with Mary shown seated on the ground, together with the Madonna lactans, where Mary is offering her breast to the Child, but with an innovative arboreal setting that fuses powerful naturalism and symbolism in a highly economical composition. For Jacopo, whose intellectual and aesthetic interests were closely aligned, the print medium opened a path in creative experimentation. Here, the language of nature's proud forms – the majestic tree that rises towards the heavens – is vividly explored in ways that Titian would also embrace.

Landscape backgrounds in religious paintings had long been distinctive in Venetian art for their beauty and naturalism. Looking back to Giovanni Bellini's paintings (see p. 76, fig. 2), his appealing and convincing *lontani* or landscape settings with realistic detail were stimulated by the drawings of his father Jacopo (c. 1400–1470/71) as well as by his interest in Flemish art and his own observation of nature, as seen in his exacting pen drawing of a cow, a study of form, action and environment (Florence, Galleria degli Uffizi, Gabinetto Disegni e Stampe, inv. 779Orn). The few autograph drawings by Giovanni provide little indication of his study of landscape, although the *Nativity* of about 1480 attributed to him includes a decisively handled representation of a rocky hillside (London, Courtauld Institute of Art, Gallery, inv. D78.P.G.79). The extensive fertile landscapes in his paintings were newly interpreted by Girolamo Mocetto (c. 1470–after 1531) in engravings such as *The Baptism of Christ*, based on the altarpiece (1500–1502) by Bellini in S. Corona, Vicenza, but possibly also on lost drawings of landscape motifs by the master. Apart from their intrinsic visual interest as graphic works, such prints effectively disseminated Bellini's inventiveness in landscape. A different kind of response to Bellini and to northern art is seen in the striking and unusual watercolour study, generally attributed to Marco Basaiti (c. 1470–rec. 1530; cat. 29). The attention to striated rocks, their geological structures eroded by time, finds resonance in the art of Mantegna and Carpaccio (c. 1465–1525/26), but the gentle effects of light and shade, with hazy areas where the cliff and rock formations meet with water and are reflected there, are far closer to the luminous and contemplative landscapes of Bellini – from the *Resurrection of Christ* of about 1475–1479 (Berlin, Staatliche Museen, Gemäldegalerie) to the *Sacred Allegory* of the Uffizi of perhaps 1498 to 1500 (see p. 83, fig. 6). While the question of authorship and precise dating remains unresolved, this enchanting study is a rare survivor; it differs from the freshly handled observational studies in watercolour made by Dürer in the mid-1490s, since its eloquence lies in the creation of a fictive landscape evoking the tranquillity of a wild, overgrown terrain where crags and jagged rocks meet calm water and some vestiges of habitation may be present. We are immersed in Bellini's vocabulary of naturalistic motifs that could be deployed, for example, in a painting of St Jerome in the wilderness, while the choice of coloured washes of subdued values gives a meditative effect appropriate for devotional paintings. Recent research on colour in drawing practices in the Veneto suggests that there is more to learn regarding the use of such washes in the 1500s.[2]

In writing to Isabella d'Este, Marchioness of Mantua, about plans for a *Nativity* by Bellini in 1502, her Venetian agent Michele Vianello cited "qualche luntani et altra fantaxia", associating landscape with imaginative exploration.[3] This similarly applies to Giorgione, whose captivating poetic landscapes have justly been celebrated. His innovative spirit is evident in a remarkable drawing, which scholars have long believed is by his hand, following the early attribution recorded by Padre Sebastiano Resta (1635–1714; fig. 4). Although red chalk was used in Venice at least from the 1490s in preparatory studies – including a fascinating study of rocks and vegetation housed in the Uffizi (Gabinetto Disegni e Stampe, inv. 464P) – this drawing is rare as a seemingly autonomous landscape subject. The distinctively Veneto setting includes a fortified town of the type seen in the backgrounds of many paintings – and identifications of it have been proposed, most recently, as the Castel San Zeno in Montagnana. But, as with the complex architecture in Giulio's *Astrologer*, the passage or journey between habitation and wildness is the salient element. A single seated figure appears in the foreground, perhaps a traveller or pilgrim with his staff, who leans forward slightly, protected by an ample hooded cloak. While he may be a shepherd, there is no indication of flocks, although the winding river and bridge, and the thick clumps of trees provide the kind of rustic setting for a shepherd and his song found in pastoral

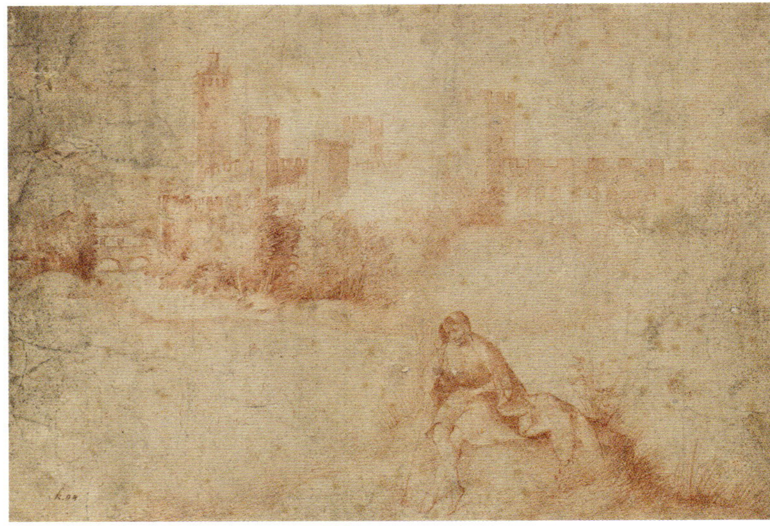

Fig. 4 Giorgione, *View of Castel San Zeno (?), Montagnana, with a Seated Figure in the Foreground*, c. 1507/10, Rotterdam, Museum Boijmans Van Beuningen, Prentenkabinet

poetry. The motif of his crossed legs may allude to the antique, since Bacchus, Pan and satyrs were often depicted in their revels, seated or standing with legs casually crossed; such references to the denizens of the woodlands, and to nature as the realm of Pan, are intrinsic to the genre of the poetic landscape. The bird flying above is probably an eagle, a noble predator with many symbolic connotations that also evokes the more violent forces of nature. It is unlikely that Giorgione had a literary text in mind; this is an individual artistic creation of, or response to, an imaginative world where landscape actively inspires reflection. The delicate rendering of volume and texture with fine touches of the red chalk, combined with the deeper tonalities produced by stronger pressure and dense shading, make this a virtuoso drawing, despite its worn condition. Titian may have known of this work when he drew vigorously in pen and ink to create a rustic scene with Veneto farm buildings by a river in a fragmentary sheet of c. 1510 (Florence, Galleria degli Uffizi, Gabinetto Disegni e Stampe, inv. 937P). This was made in two moments: Titian overlaid his initial thoughts for the scene, adding with strong curvilinear strokes the motif of a proud eagle, seen in profile directly above as a presence dominating the landscape. He used broadly hatched modelling to accentuate and extend the rugged hills, which rise sharply to merge with the eagle's form and upward movement.

The imaginative and nuanced approach to landscape seen in the exquisite works by Giulio Campagnola, Giorgione and Jacopo de' Barbari discussed above is closely bound up with the poetic and antiquarian interests of the tightly knit circles of humanists and art lovers who were their patrons; these artists also had musical, intellectual or mathematical interests. A culture of intimate appreciation is signalled by Giulio's placing of a hand-written inscription on some of his prints (fig. 1), suggesting that they were gifts to friends and emphasising the close relationship between prints and drawings. Titian's early interest in landscape drawings is rooted in this type of exploration, but his graphic art takes flight in new directions, as is evident in the autonomous

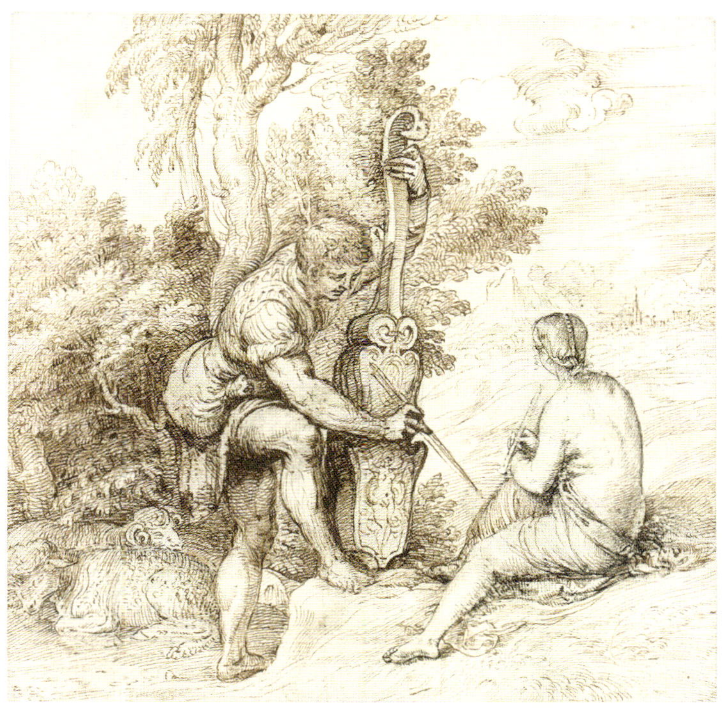

Fig. 5 Titian, *Two Musicians in a Landscape*, c. 1508, London, British Museum, Department of Prints and Drawings

drawing of *Two Musicians in a Landscape* (fig. 5). A fertile wooded landscape with a flock of sheep at rest is the locus for music making and for states of desire and distance; this is the territory of classical poetry, recalling Theocritus and Virgil, where the shepherd musician can act as the poet's persona, while the landscape is a green dream world where love can be pursued. These topics of joy, longing and melancholy amidst verdant nature were expanded by Petrarch (1304–1374), whose poetry was championed by Pietro Bembo (1470–1547). In tune with these broad themes, Titian may have begun with the idea of the nymph lost in reverie, her intricate hair style recalling classical types, before building a more elaborate composition with a slightly larger-scale male figure. At this second moment (which may have been quite close to the first) he also used a different batch of ink, a little darker in tone; these elements have suggested to some art historians that the drawing is by two separate artists, but it is entirely coherent with Titian's pen style around 1508–1510, which can be sensitive yet agile, with broad handling at times. In rounding out the athletic figure of the shepherd, Titian made a playful visual comparison between his muscular, weight-bearing leg and the sinuous strength of the tree trunk behind. He used rapid, springing strokes for the shepherd and his highly ornamented viola da gamba which includes a female nude in its decoration, wittily articulating the man's thoughts as he pauses in his playing, his hands caressing the expensive instrument. Separating himself from the enigmatic and often erudite landscape compositions of Giorgione and Giulio Campagnola, Titian infuses this drawing with ingenuity and wit. His shepherd is a performer who may be conjuring the nymph into being, and he gestures suggestively with the bow, although the figures do not touch. Titian may have been exploring ideas that took full shape in the painting known as the *Concert Champêtre* (see p. 167, fig. 3), although the drawing is an autonomous work. His attention here to the character of trees recurs in drawings, notably in a design of c. 1514 in which the twisting forms of venerable and younger trees, including one stalwart lopped trunk, create an impenetrable clump growing from a steep hillside, whose uneven curving forms suggest the pulsing shapes of tree roots (cat. 30).

Titian's adventurous spirit in terms of drawing style and iconography is seen in the sinewy, agile forms of the satyrs in an autonomous pen drawing of c. 1510 (fig. 6). In including a celestial disc, he may have referred to Giulio's *Astrologer* engraving, with its subtleties of technique and interpretation. However, his approach with the pen is now impetuous, and the grassy landscape becomes a sensuous space, as the satyrs' bodies are intertwined and their hairy legs are inseparable from the blades of grass. This approach no doubt provided inspiration for Domenico Campagnola in his early drawings, where the subject matter and treatment veers away from the classical and poetic themes that Giulio so sensitively embraced. In fact, in the early *Concert by a Brook* engraving mentioned above (cat. 11), Domenico's graphic exuberance changes the atmosphere and subject of the original design. The sense of repose created around the two men in Giulio's drawing (fig. 2), one of whom turns the leaves of a small book while the other holds musical instruments, is in tune with the meditative, embedded relation of the Venetian humanist to the countryside. Instead, Domenico's youthful figures of shepherd musicians – who are on a larger scale than their counterparts in the drawing – seem to dominate their environment, occupying the space with a more forceful graphic presence. A deliberate disjunction of scale also occurs in the scene with a boy fishing (fig. 7), a carefully executed sheet perhaps of c. 1516 where the landscape with weary travellers unfolds with curving lines evoking gentle hilly terrain in winding rhythms. There, the disjunction focuses the viewer's attention on the intensely concentrated youth who has cast his fishing line. Domenico's sense of the fictional 'green world' as a space for licence and transgression is embodied in a group of independent drawings with pairs of sprawling youths as protagonists (cat. 34), where his themes of tangled male intimacy could be explored in conversation by viewers of the drawings. He inscribed his name prominently on some of these early landscapes, including one of two youths

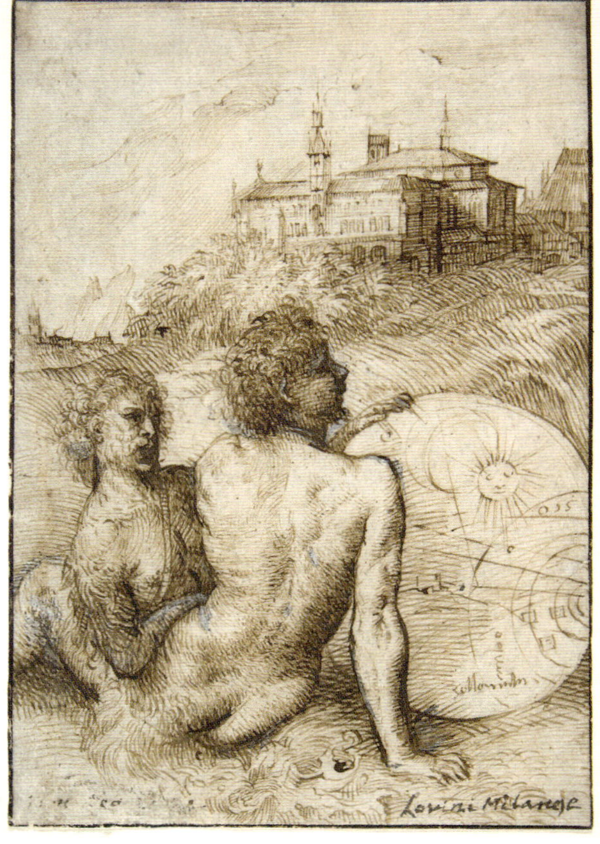

Fig. 6 Titian, *Two Satyrs in a Landscape*, c. 1510 (?), New York, The Metropolitan Museum of Art, Department of Drawings and Prints

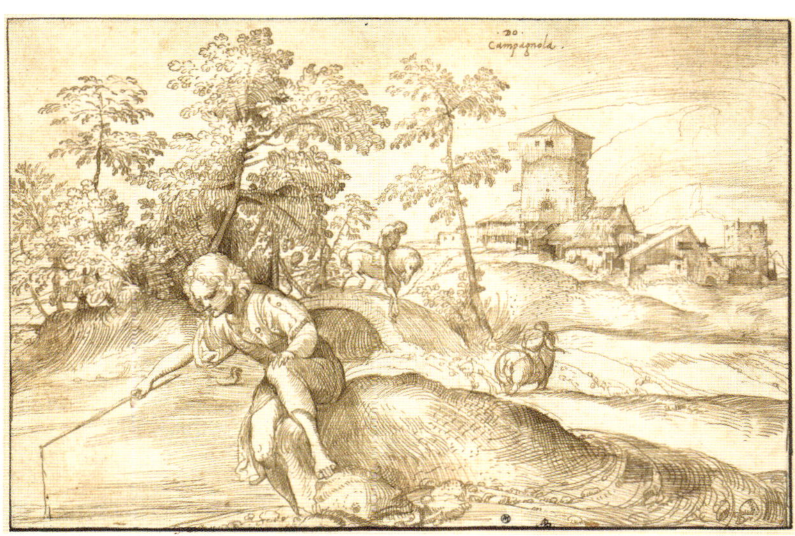

Fig. 7 Domenico Campagnola, *Landscape with a Boy Fishing*, c. 1516, Washington, D.C., National Gallery of Art, Department of European Prints and Drawings

in a close exchange (London, British Museum, Department of Prints and Drawings, inv. 1895,0915.836), suggesting their destination of an art lover's collection. This signified Domenico's pride in inventiveness and authorship, perhaps emulating Giulio who had placed epigraphic-style signatures on some prints, while further emphasising the autonomous nature of the handmade drawing. Possibly, once his reputation had become more established, and after Giulio's death, Domenico did not need to continue this practice. In his maturity, his landscape drawings have the crispness and luminosity of engravings or woodcuts. Drawings and prints were often kept together by collectors, as the evidence of inventories shows, so that direct comparisons could be made between landscape compositions in drawing and in prints.

From 1516/17, Domenico was closely engaged with print production, which was marked by novelty and experimentation not least in the grand-scale woodcut. In Titian's design for *The Submersion of Pharoah's Army in the Red Sea* of around 1517, the powerful graphic line of the woodcut was taken to its full potential in ways that impressed Domenico and other contemporaries (fig. 8). Here Titian envisaged an extraordinary scene where the explosive forces of nature would be represented in turbulent skies and ferocious waves. This terrifying vision, articulated through assertive, even audacious graphic marks was distant from the Venetian contemplative landscape in style as in subject. While tumult and ferocity were not generally represented in independent landscape prints and drawings, the vigorous and decisive ink mark that activates the blank space of the paper remained a strong element in both Titian's and Domenico's production in the following decades.

Throughout his career, Titian was stimulated by the imaginative potential and the representational challenges of the drawn and printed landscape – exploiting, for instance, the dynamic language of the thick, swelling woodcut lines that fill the visual field in his extraordinary design for the mid-century *St Jerome in the Wilderness* (perhaps executed by Niccolò Boldrini or Giovanni Britto). He could adopt a finer mode in drawing, such as the beautiful sheet of c. 1515–1525 where a huntsman, probably St Eustace, is privileged with a vision of the crucifix between the antlers of a deer in a covert of trees (fig. 9). While charging the pen strongly with ink for some parts of the design – notably, in accentuating the kneeling figure's attitude of yearning devotion or in rendering the thickly leaved haunt of the deer – Titian drew sensitively in other parts to create contrasts of finish, with freely sketched elements and finely articulated details. He also exploited the value of the blank paper in the economy of his composition. Some very light squaring suggests a preparatory purpose, yet the drawing retained its value as an autonomous work that would appeal to art lovers interested in airy landscapes made with gestural sensitivity. Titian was highly aware of the interests of collectors in graphic art, continuing to produce independent landscape drawings late in his career. He also collaborated closely with the engraver Cornelis Cort to ensure that superb compositions such as *St Jerome in the Wilderness* of 1565 would circulate as engravings, bringing home to a wide European audience his powers of *disegno* in representing light-filled, verdant landscapes.

As innovative graphic artists, Giulio Campagnola, Domenico Campagnola and Titian created landscape scenes of enduring beauty and enchantment, with Giulio pursuing delicacy and originality in his graphic techniques. In their drawings, Domenico and Titian in different ways reacted to the sinuous graphic forms of the woodcut and the deeply curving grooves of engravings, making distinctive works of

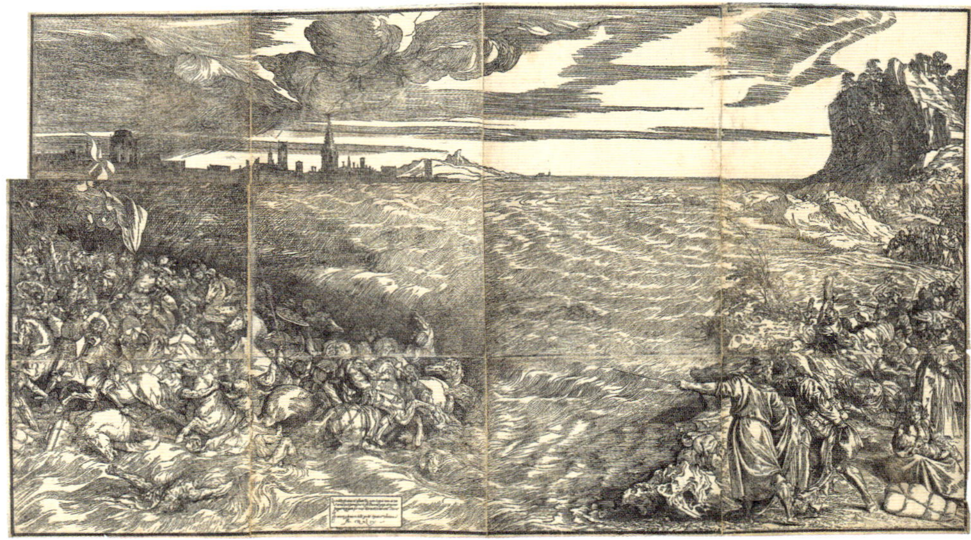

Fig. 8 Titian, *The Submersion of Pharaoh's Army in the Red Sea*, c. 1517, Washington, D.C., National Gallery of Art, Department of European Prints and Drawings

art that were treasured by collectors of the 17th and 18th centuries. The captivating prints that they designed (and in Domenico's case, actively produced) would be highly influential in the evolution of the genre of the independent landscape in Europe.

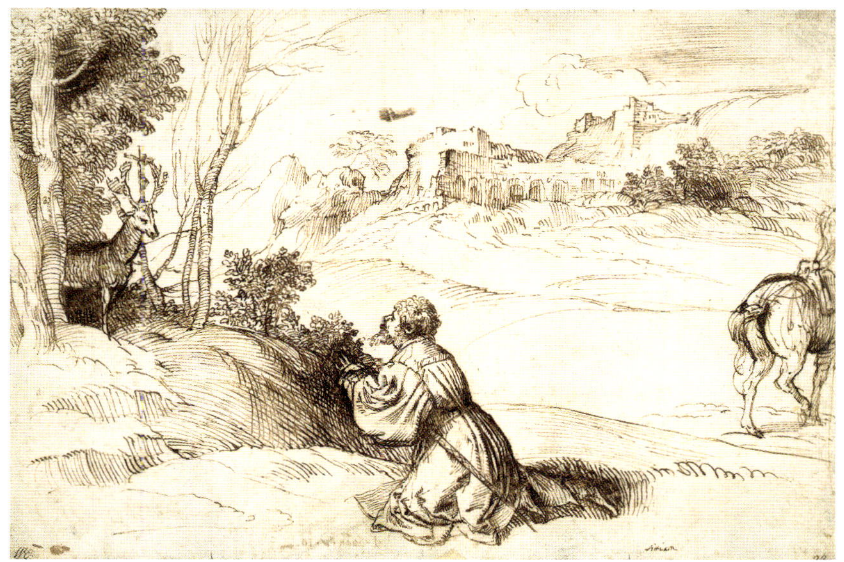

Fig. 9 Titian, *St Eustace (or St Hubert?) in a Landscape*, c. 1515/25, London, British Museum, Department of Prints and Drawings

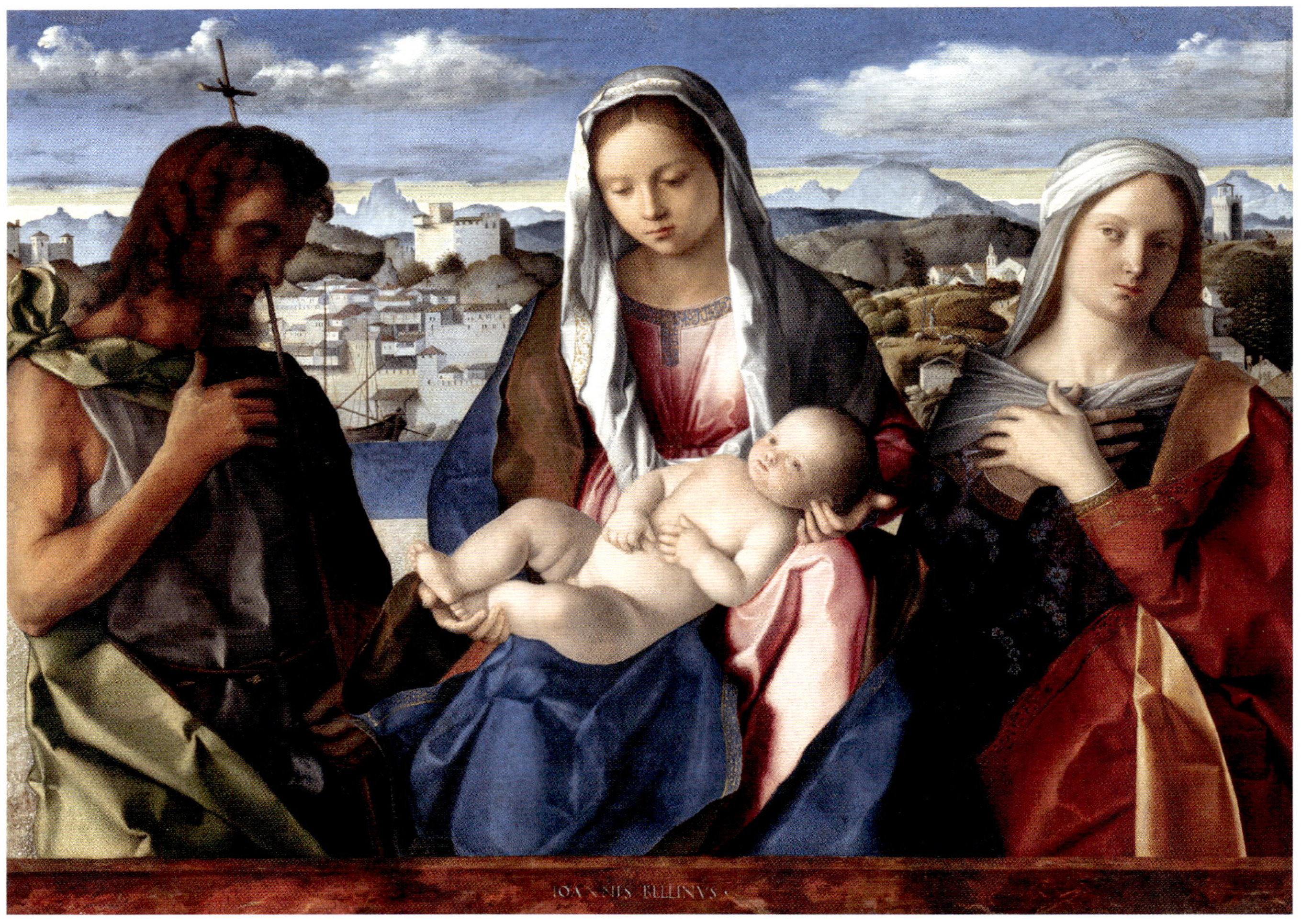

22 Giovanni Bellini, *Virgin and Child with St John the Baptist and an Unknown Saint*, 1500–1505, Venice, Gallerie dell'Accademia

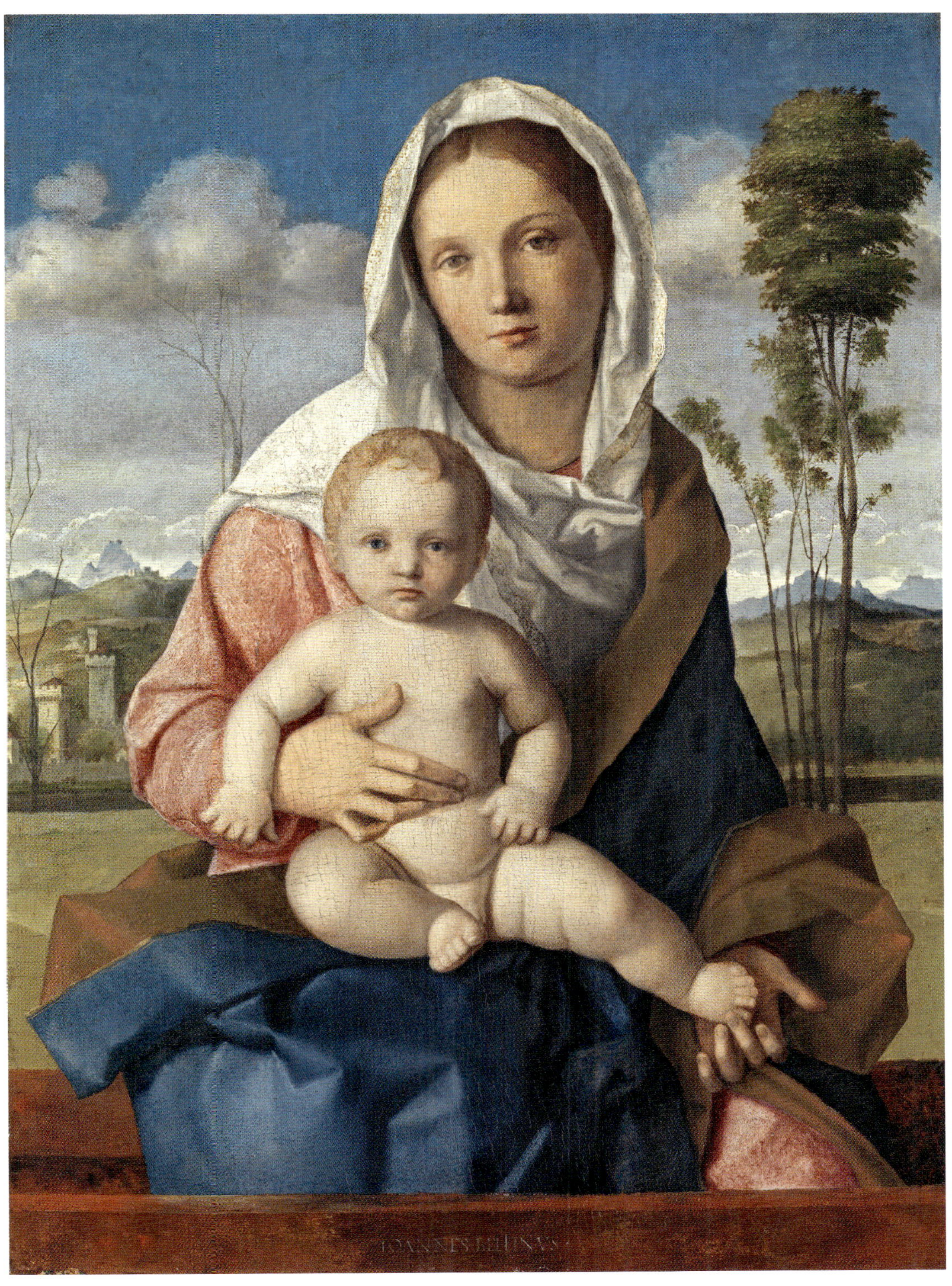

23 Giovanni Bellini, *Virgin and Child in a Landscape*, c. 1508, Munich, Bayerische Staatsgemäldesammlungen, Alte Pinakothek

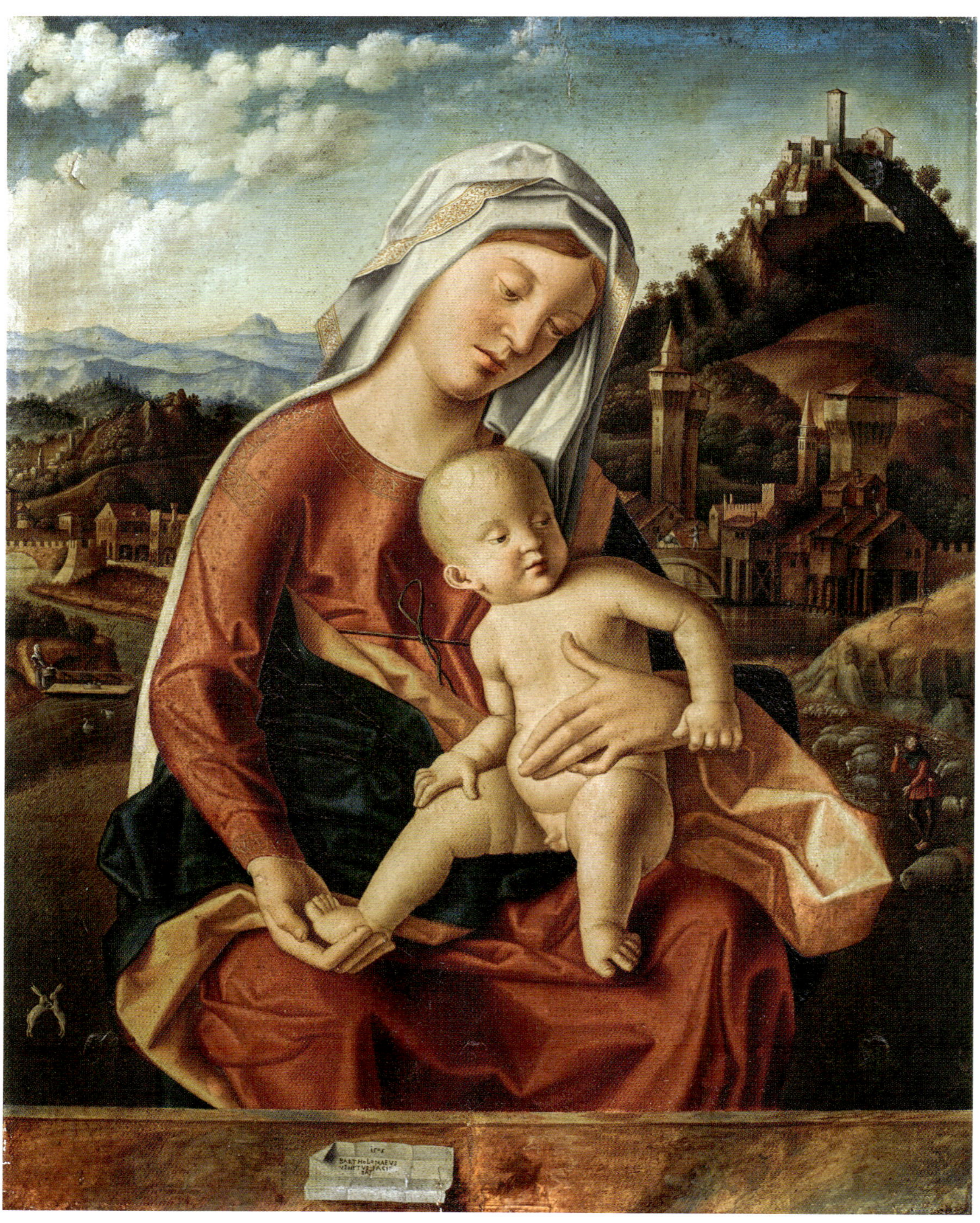

24 Bartolomeo Veneto, *Virgin and Child*, c. 1505, Bergamo, Accademia Carrara

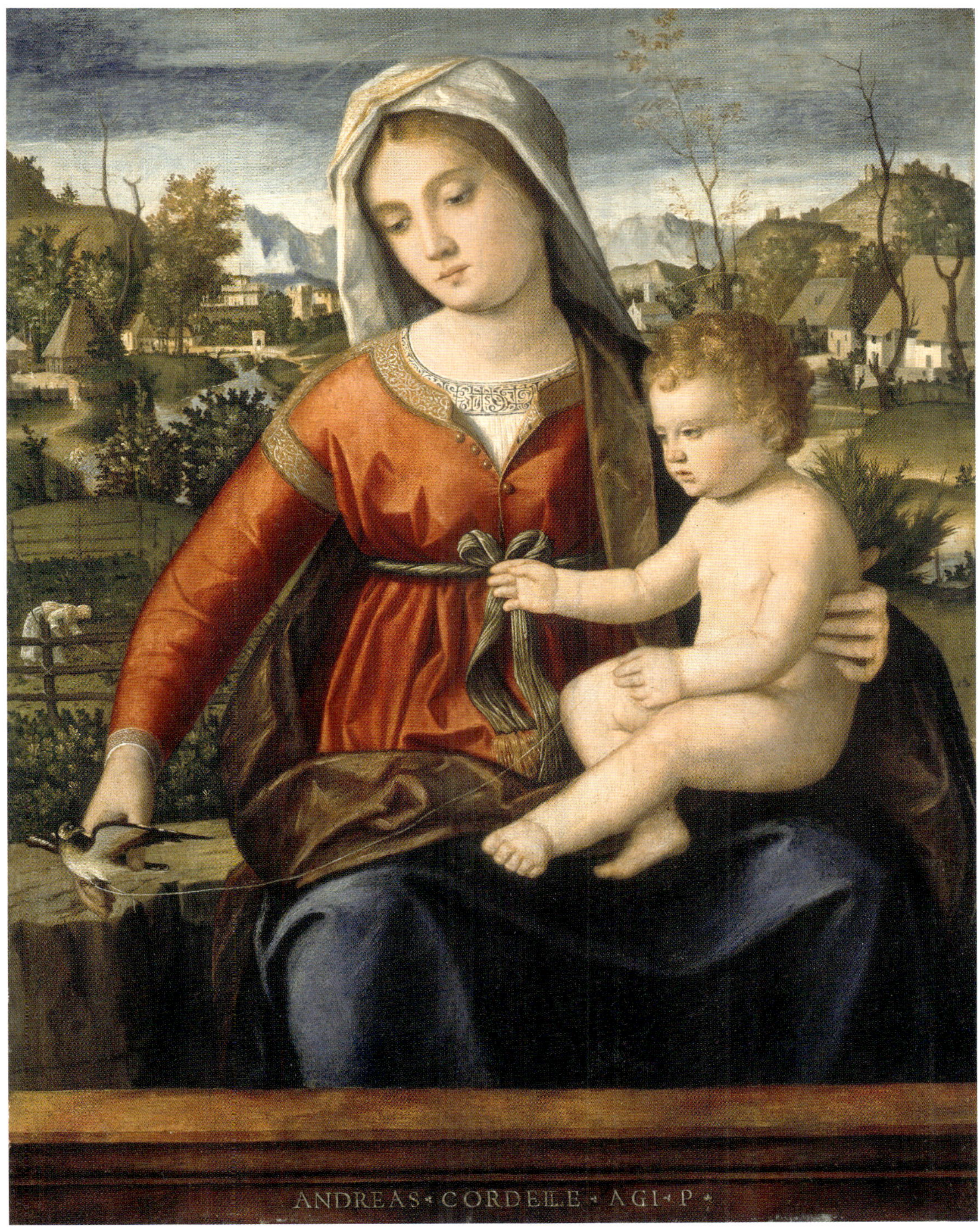

25 Andrea Previtali, *Virgin and Child*, c. 1502, Munich, Bayerische Staatsgemäldesammlungen, Alte Pinakothek

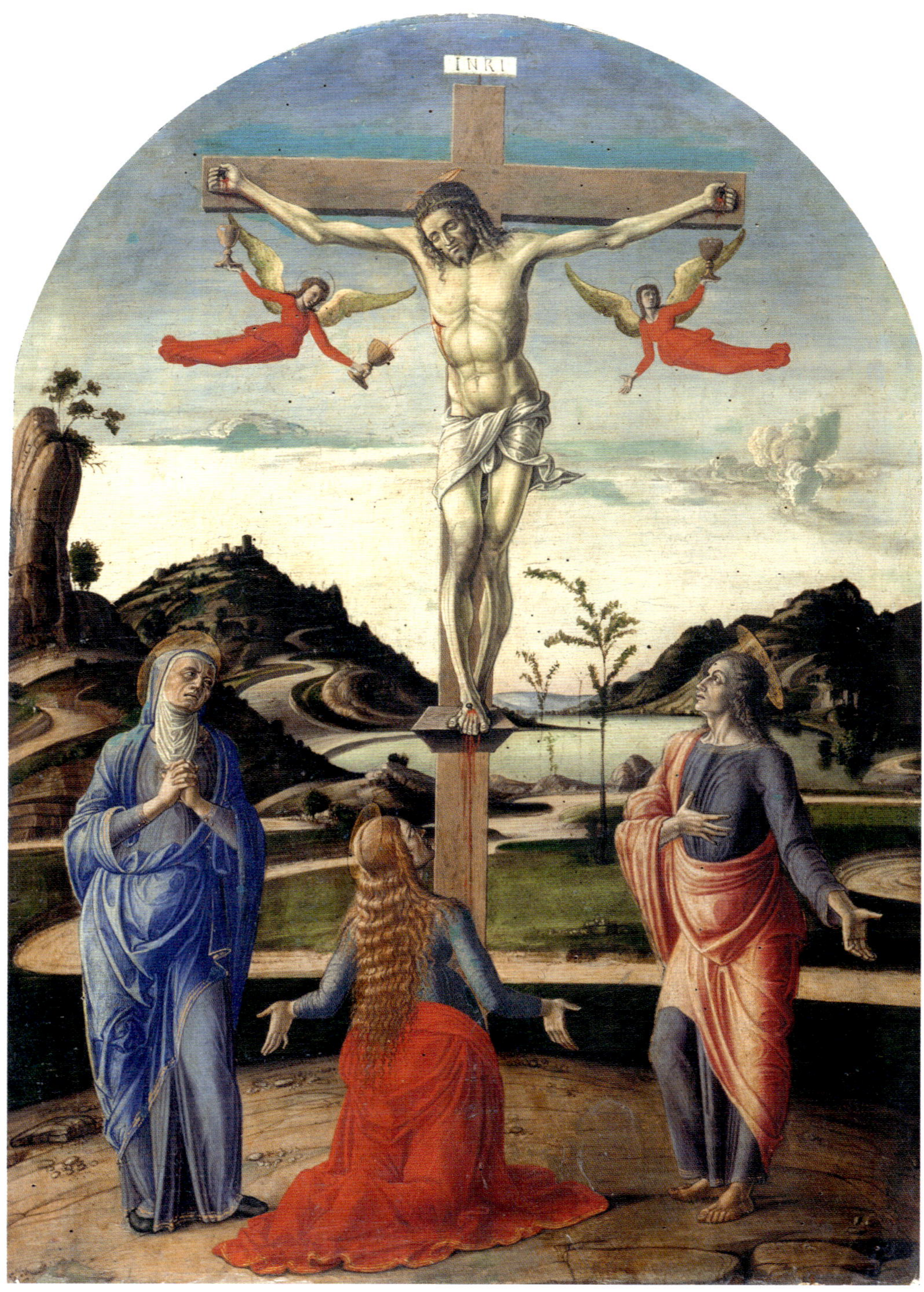

26 Alvise Vivarini, *Crucifixion with the Virgin Mary, Mary Magdalene and St John,* c. 1470, Pesaro, Musei Civici, Palazzo Mazzolari Mosca

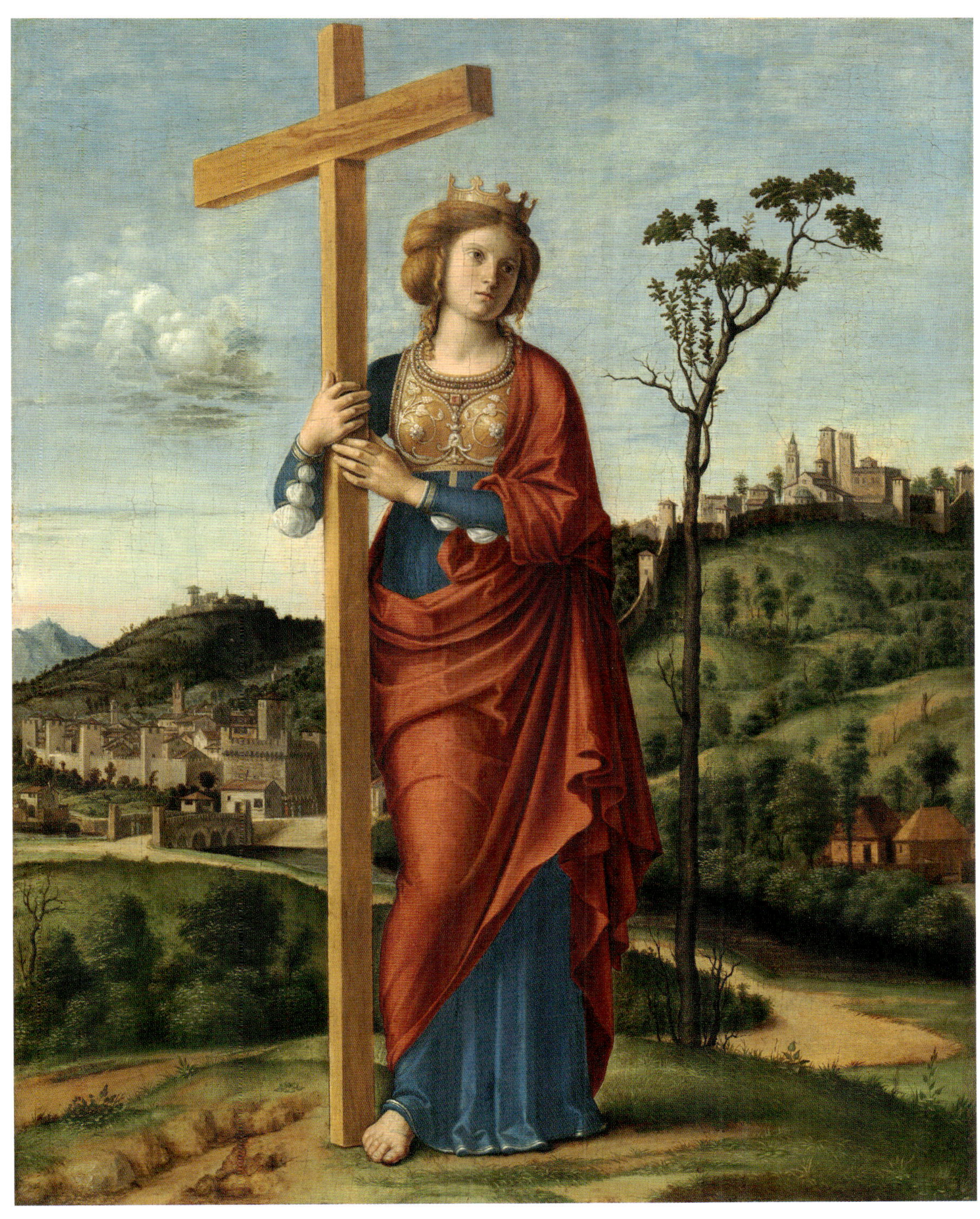

27 Giovanni Battista Cima da Conegliano, *St Helena*, c. 1495, Washington, D.C, National Gallery of Art

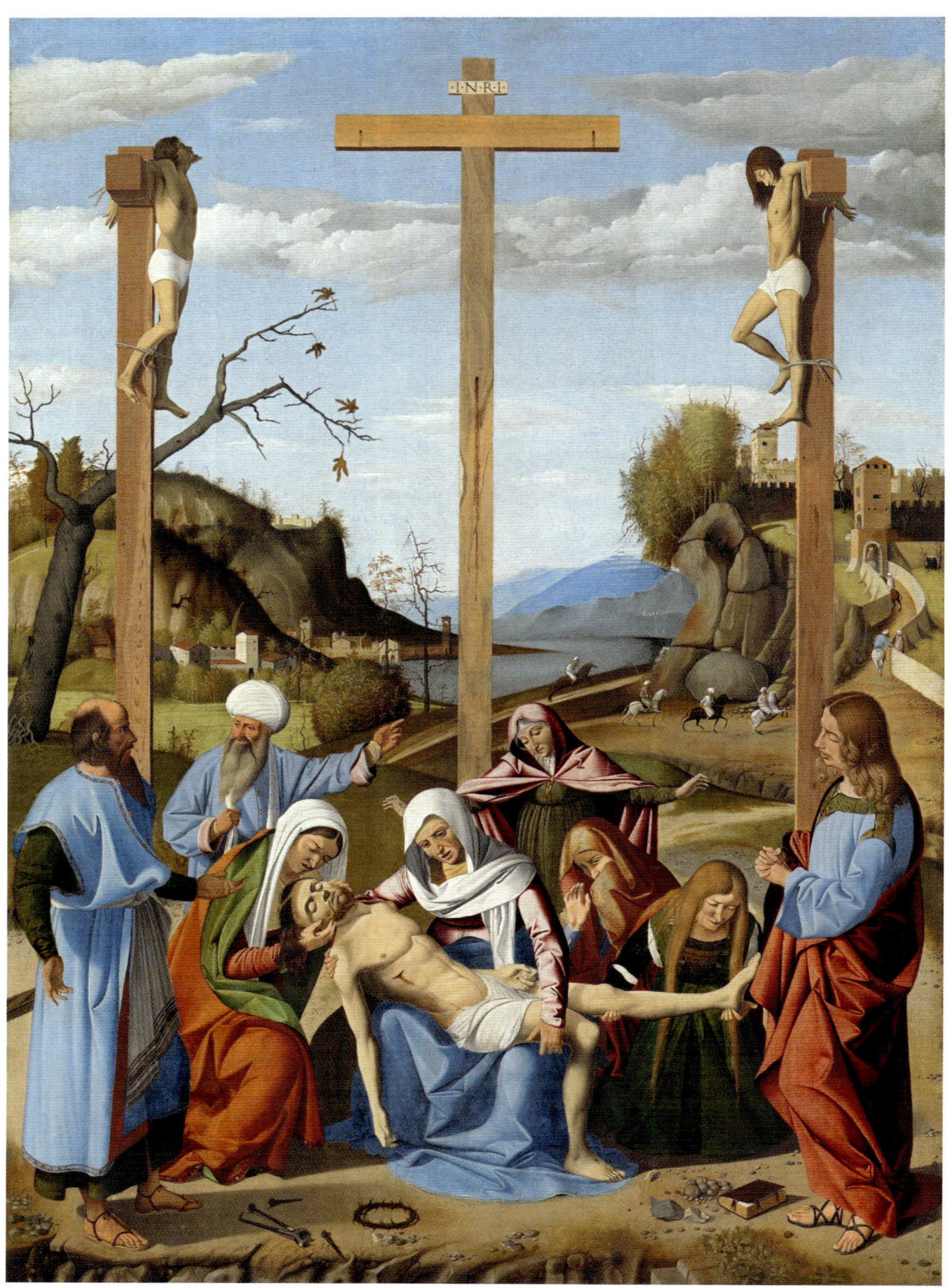

28 Marco Basaiti, *Lamentation of Christ*, c. 1506, Munich, Bayerische Staatsgemäldesammlungen, Alte Pinakothek

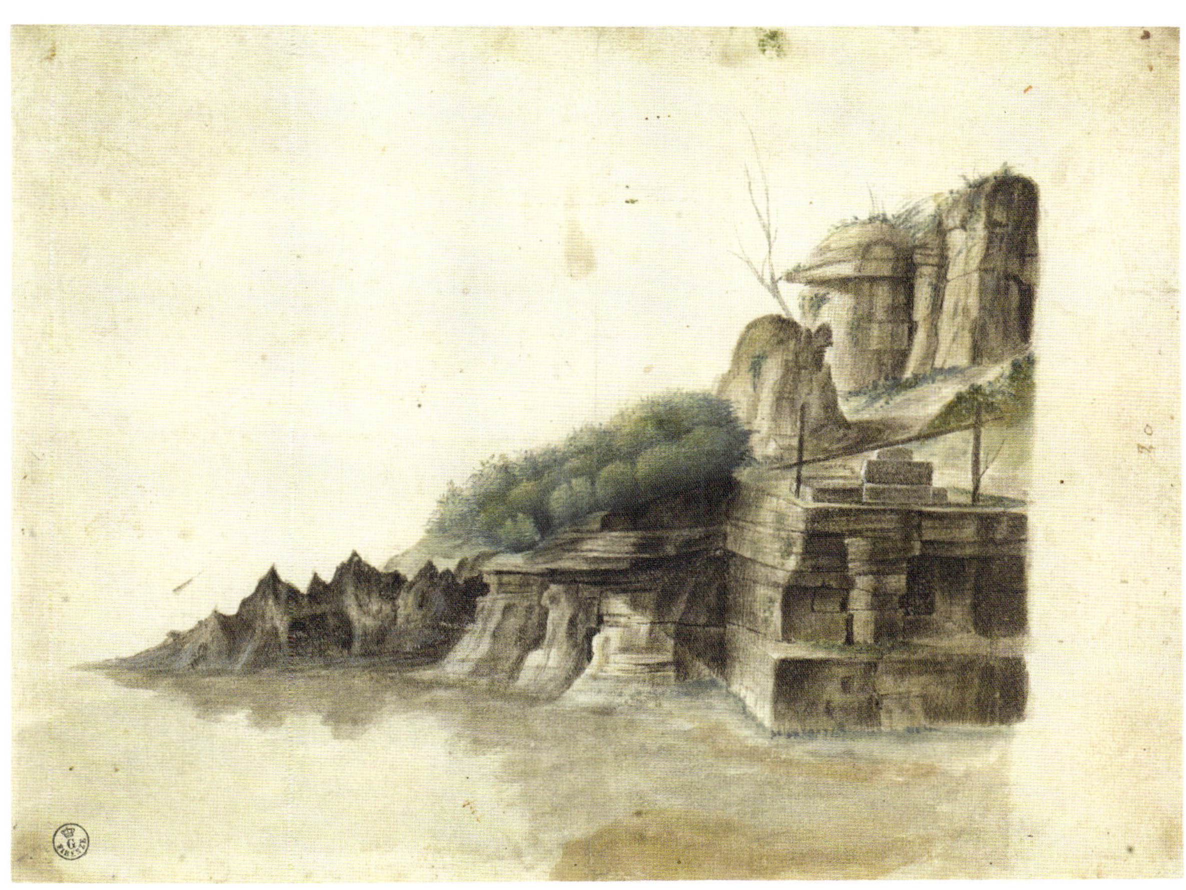

29 Marco Basaiti, attribution, *Rocky Shoreline*, c. 1500/10, Florence, Galleria degli Uffizi, Gabinetto Disegni e Stampe

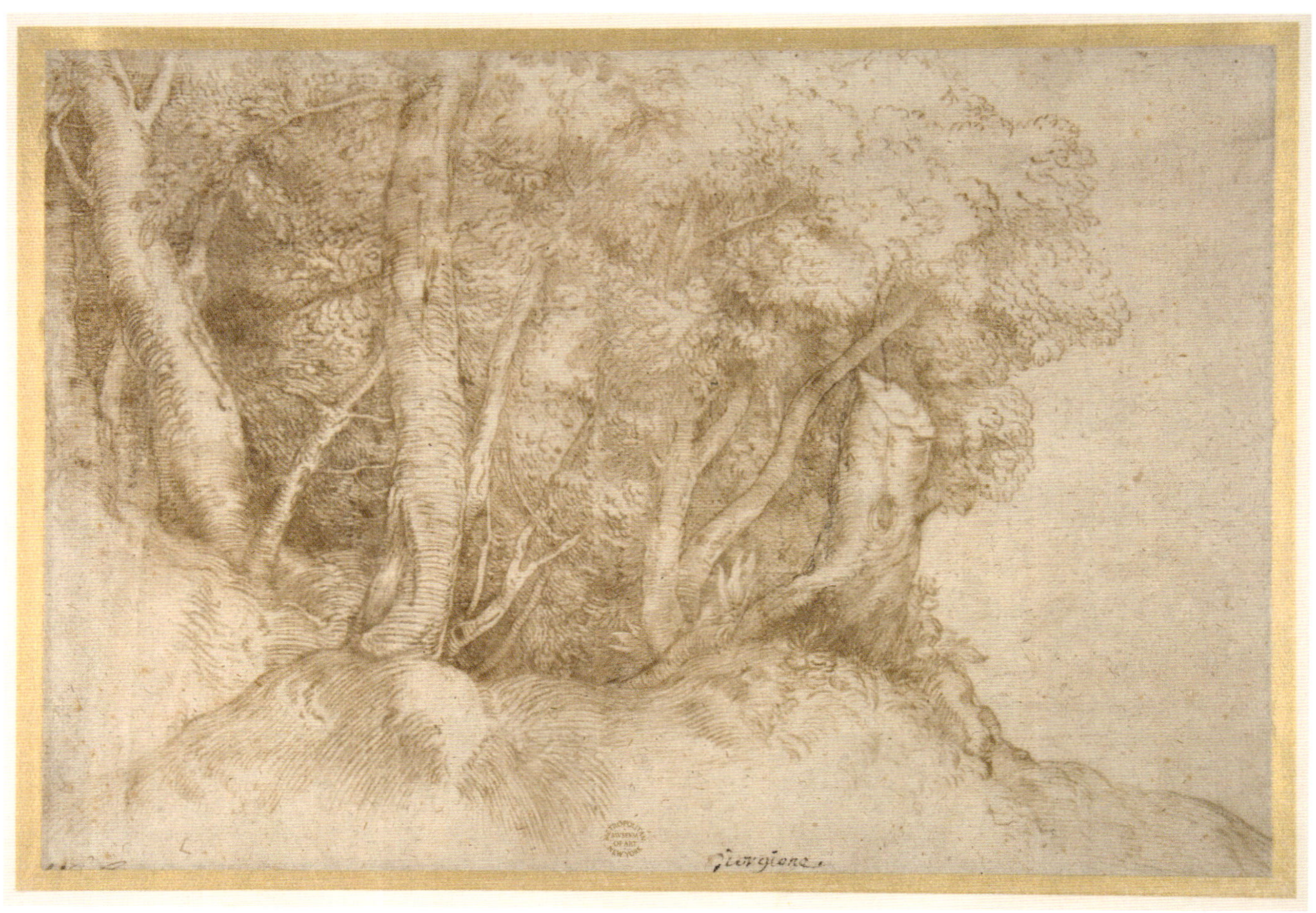

30 Titian, *Group of Trees*, c. 1514, New York, The Metropolitan Museum of Art, Department of Drawings and Prints

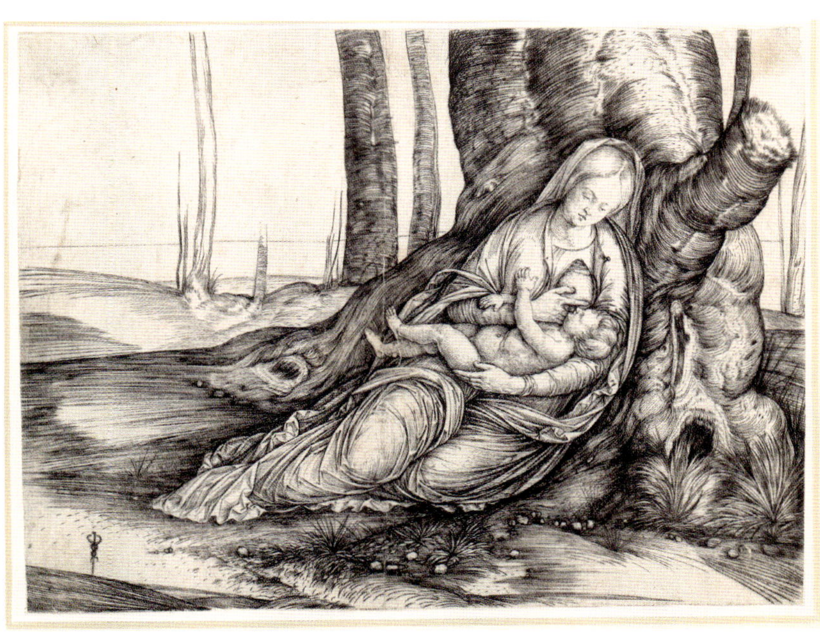

31 Jacopo de' Barbari, *The Virgin Nursing the Christ Child at the Foot of a Tree*, end of 15th/beginning of 16th century, Vienna, Albertina

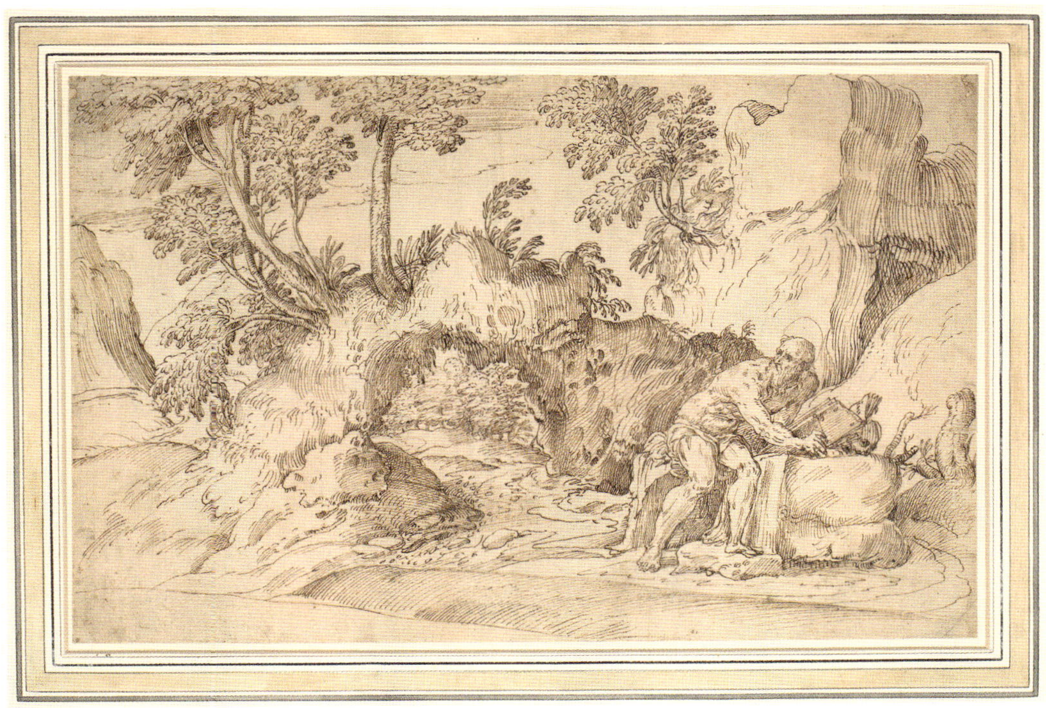

32 Domenico Campagnola, attribution, *St Jerome in the Wilderness*, 1540–1560, Windsor, The Royal Collection, HM King Charles III

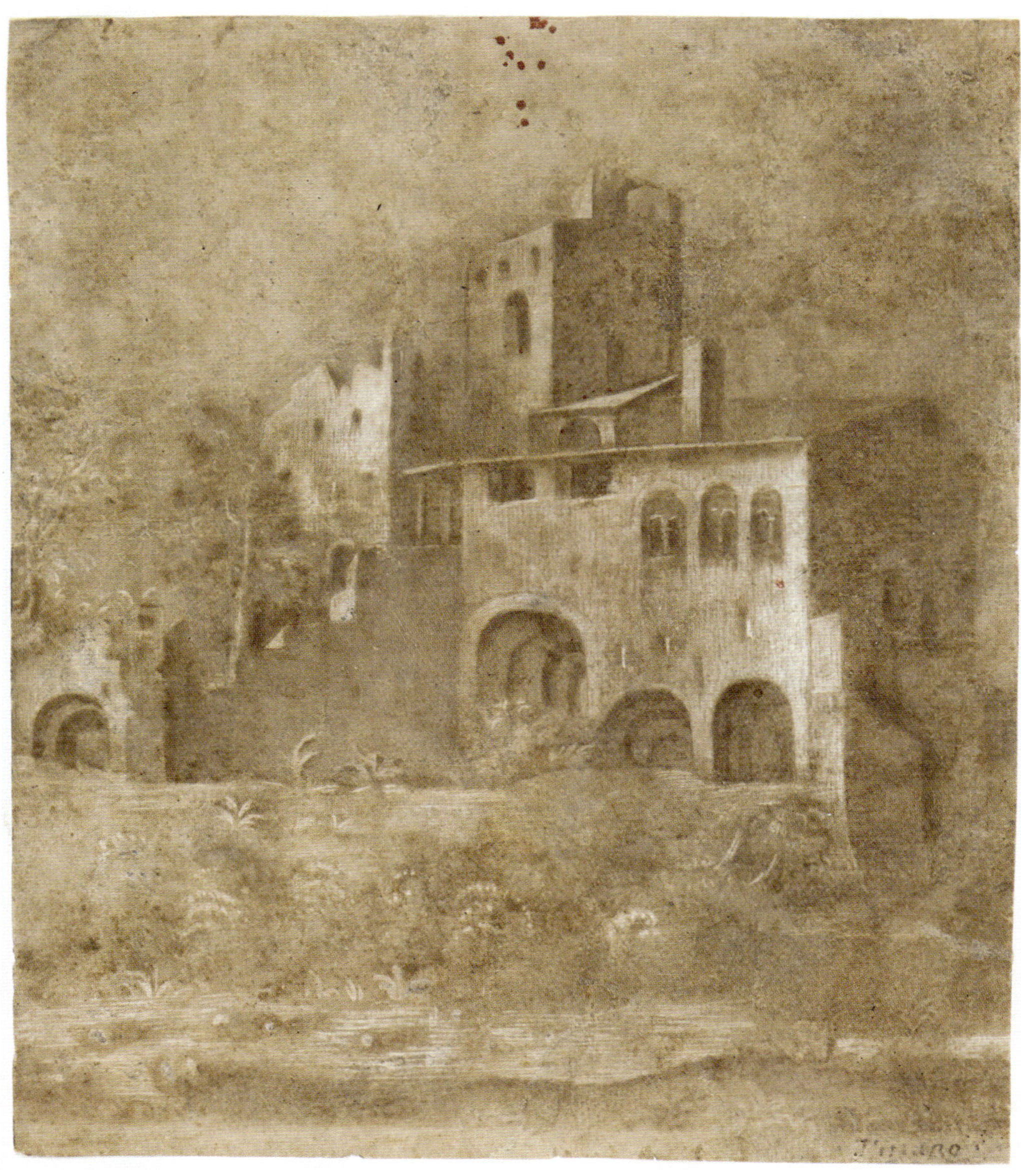

33 Giorgione, *Architectural Ensemble by a River*, c. 1500, Munich, Sammlung Bernd und Verena Klüser

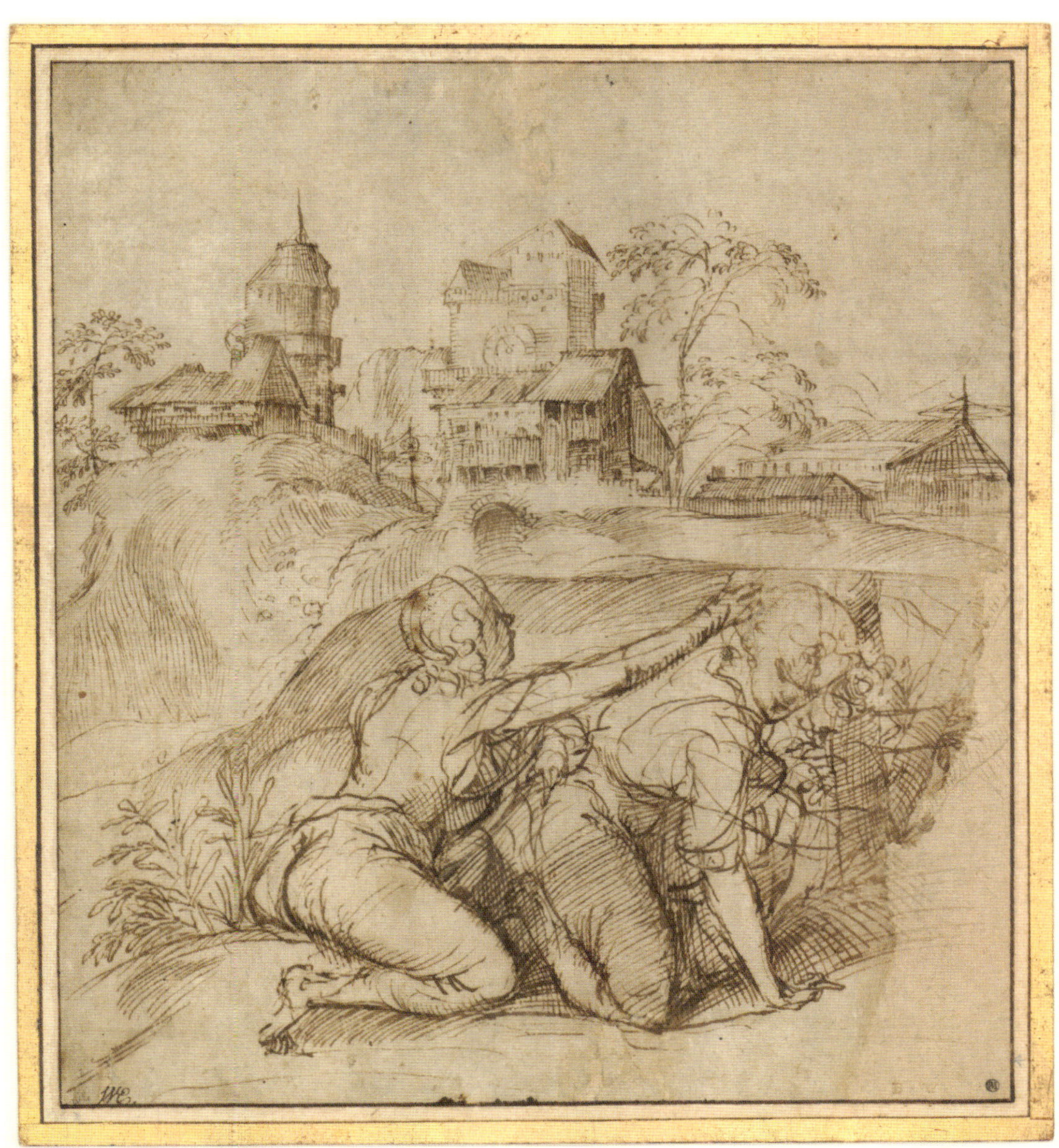

34 Domenico Campagnola, *Two Kneeling Youths in a Landscape*, 2nd quarter 16th century, Vienna, Albertina

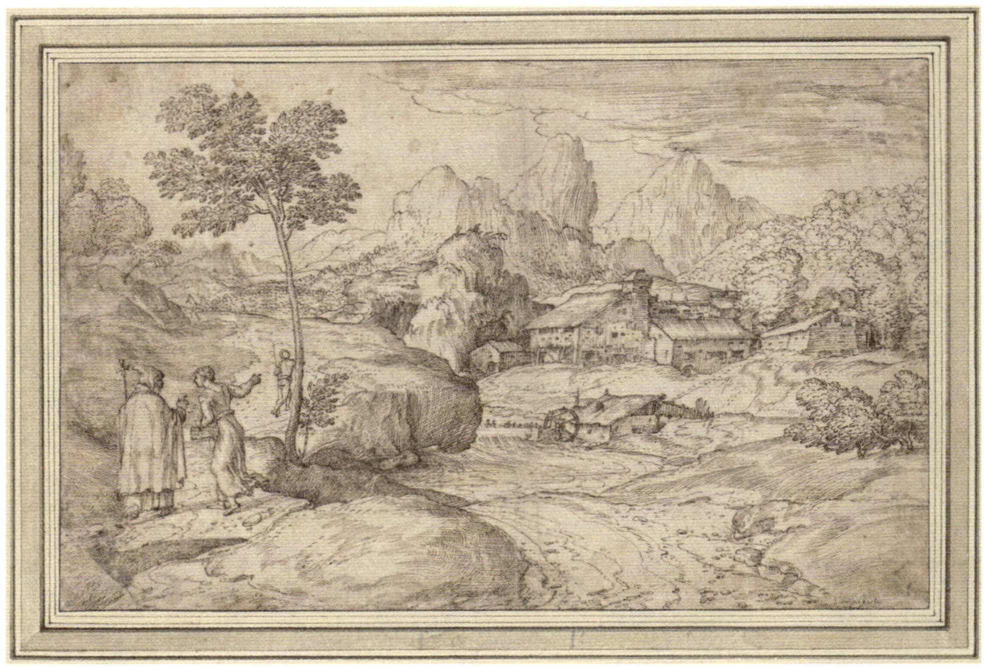

35 Domenico Campagnola, *Mountainous River Landscape with a Farmstead*, 2nd quarter 16th century, Vienna, Albertina

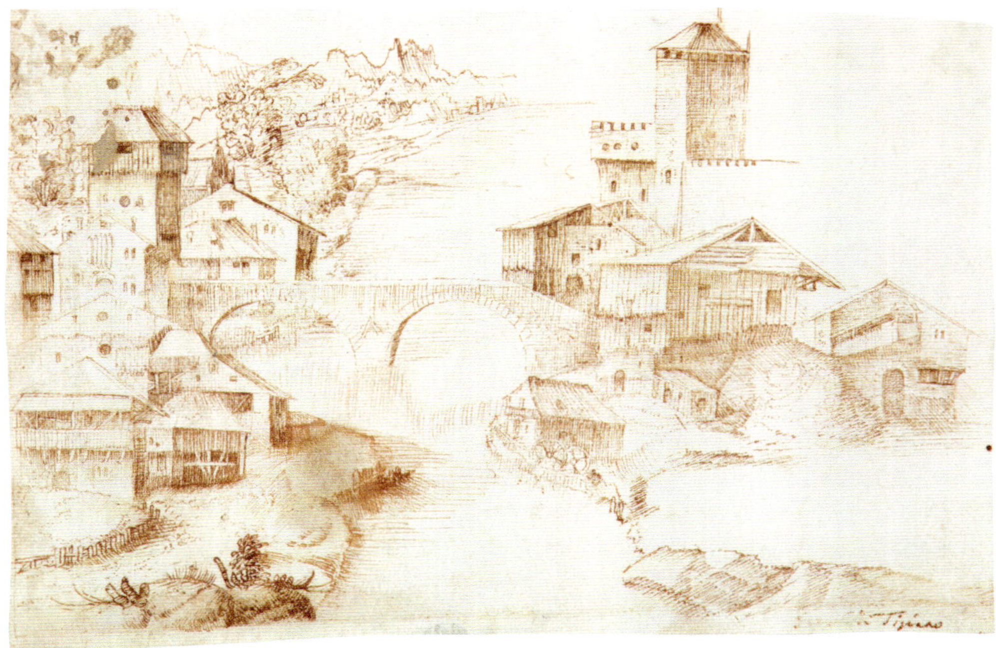

36 Giulio Campagnola, *River Landscape with Buildings and a Bridge*, 1st quarter 16th century, Munich, Sammlung Bernd und Verena Klüser

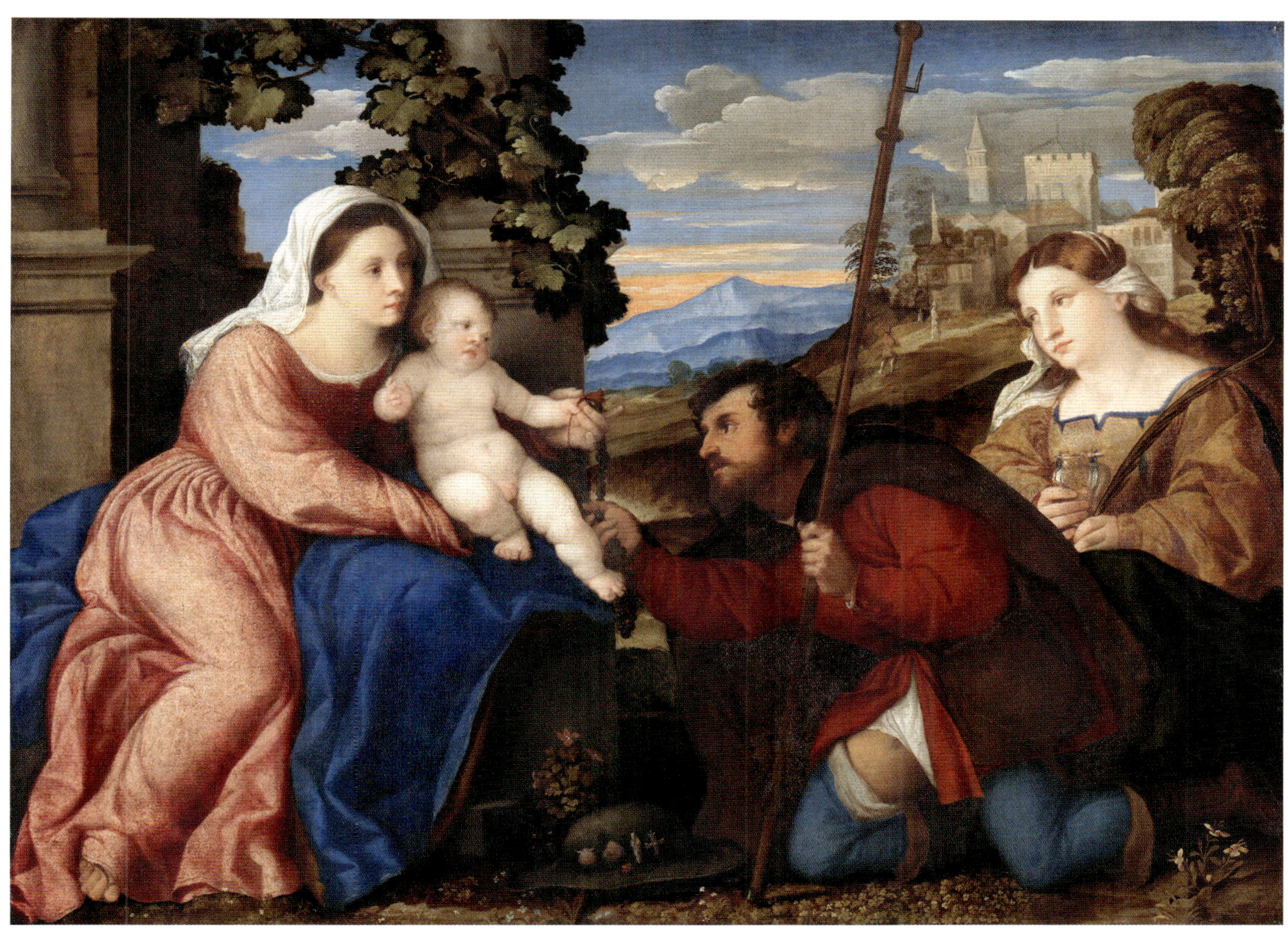

37 Palma il Vecchio, *Virgin and Child with St Roch and Lucia*, 1513/15, Munich, Bayerische Staatsgemäldesammlungen, Alte Pinakothek

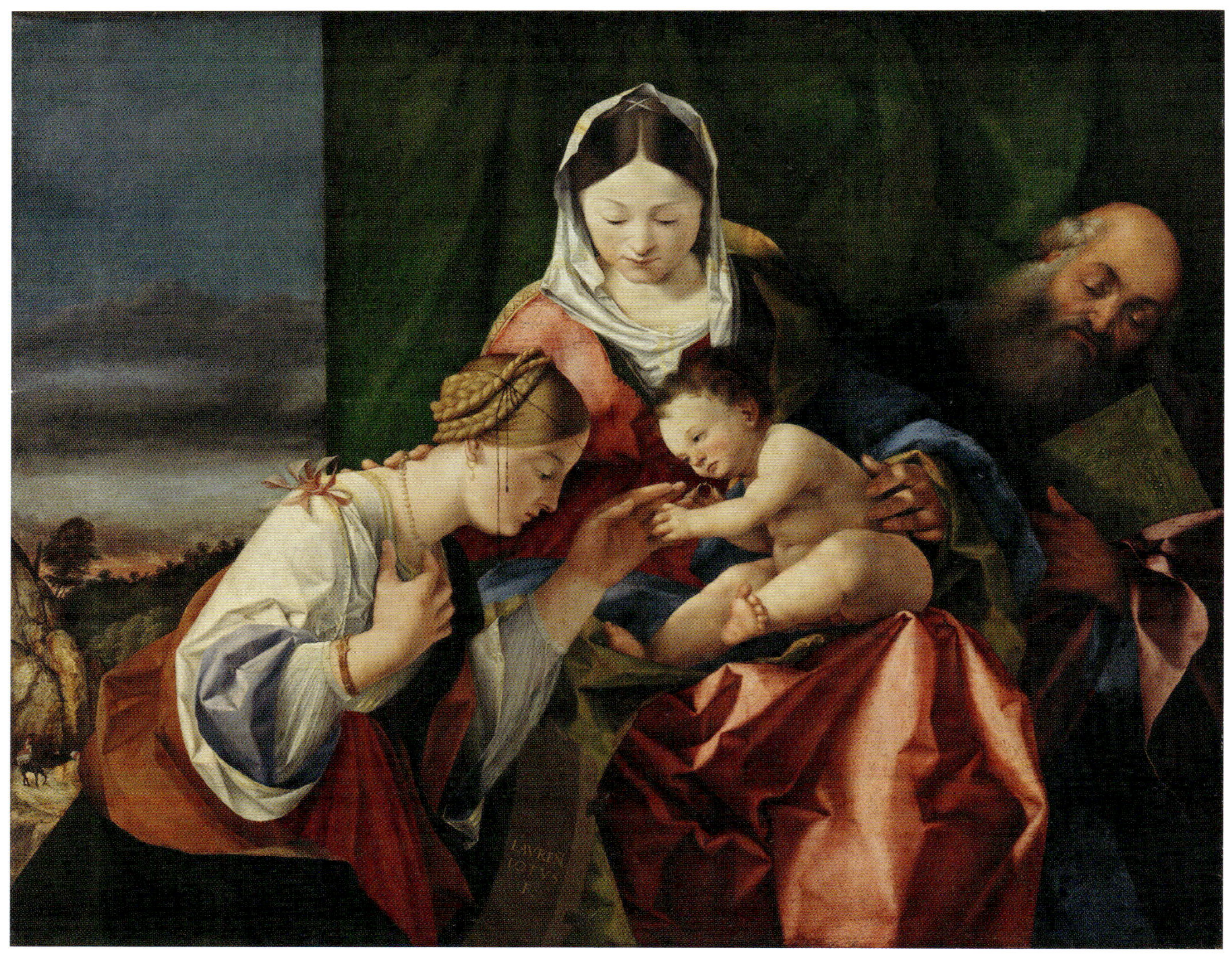

38 Lorenzo Lotto, *Mystical Marriage of St Catherine*, c. 1506, Munich, Bayerische Staatsgemäldesammlungen, Alte Pinakothek

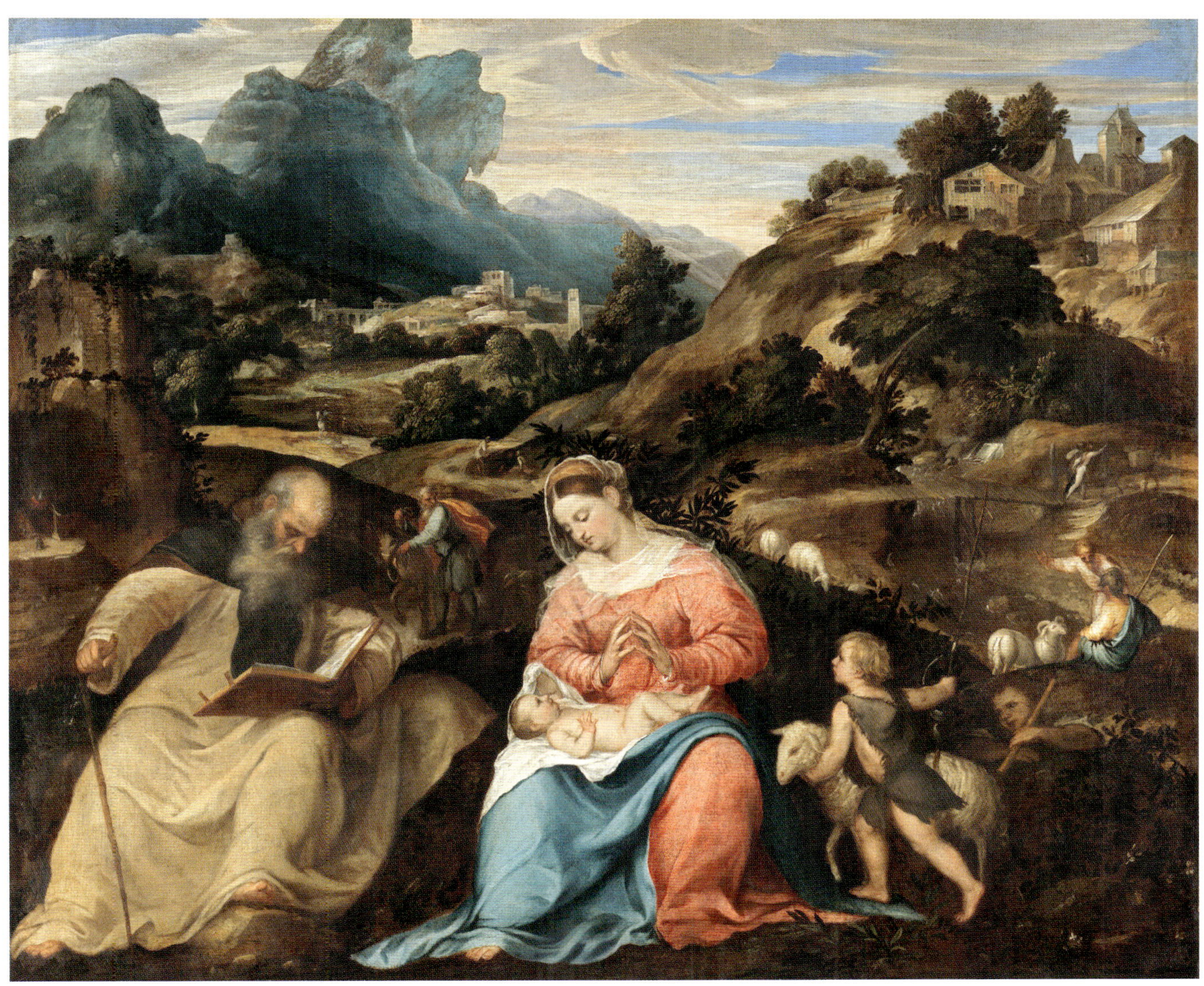

39 Giovanni Cariani, attribution, *Virgin and Child with St Anthony the Abbot and John the Baptist as a Boy*, c. 1540, Munich, Bayerische Staatsgemäldesammlungen, Alte Pinakothek

Giorgione's Portrait of a Young Man

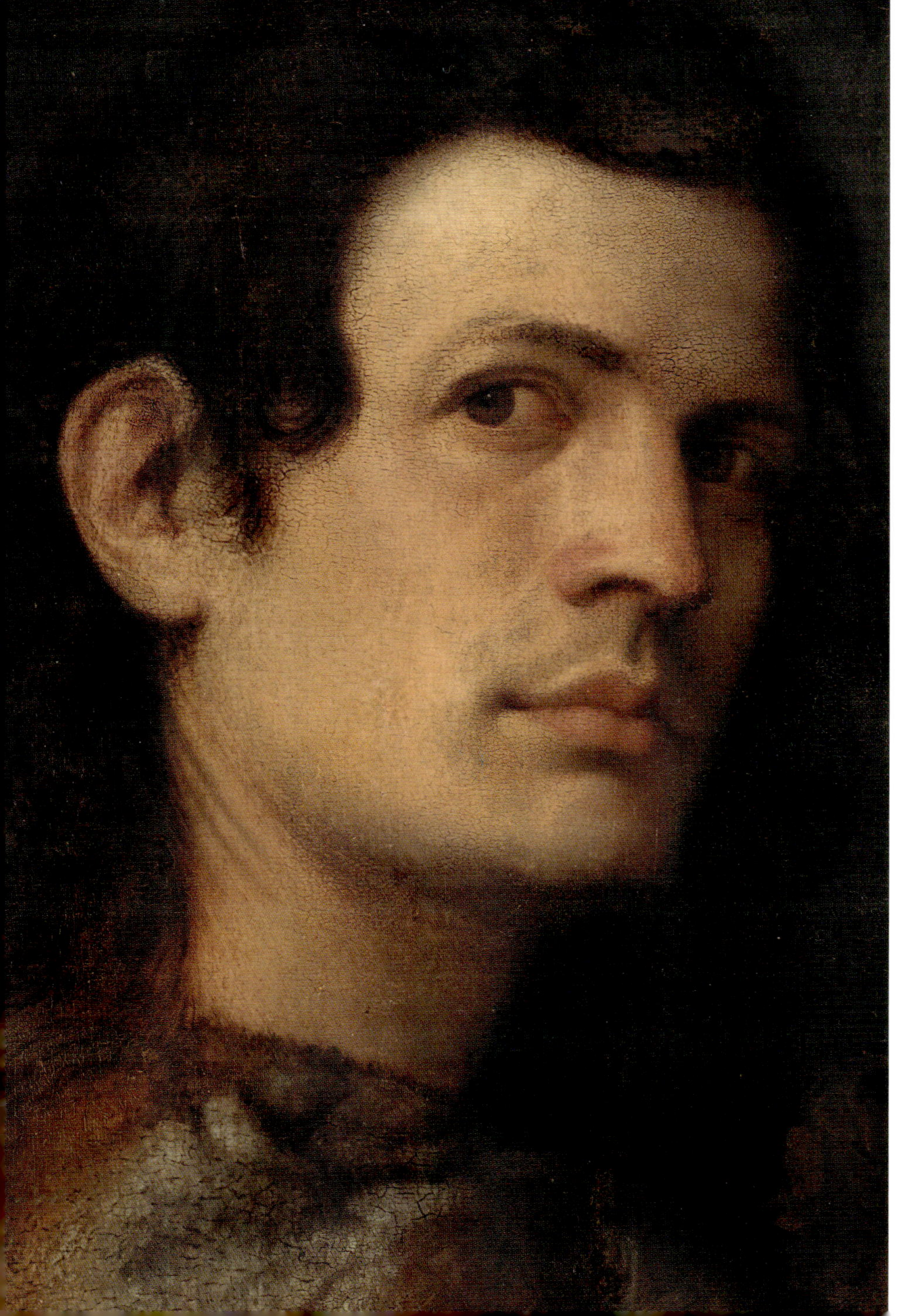

The "looking-over-the-shoulder" portrait and its prehistory

ANTONIO MAZZOTTA

In an enclosed and dimly lit, semi-abandoned architectural setting, overrun with climbing plants, a young man is captured as if in a snapshot. He turns towards us, looking back over his shoulder, the twist in his body underlined by the folds of skin on his neck (cat. 40). The gloves in his hand, perhaps recently removed, his broad back covered by a fox fur, and the red quilted sleeve are astonishing details that characterise the lower half of the painting. The upper half is focused around the gaze, from "coffee-coloured" eyes, interrogative and inquisitive at the same time, and the large ear, which appears to be listening to us, but in haste (the head slightly tilted forward gives the impression that the man is walking to the right), as if, despite the tightly closed mouth, he were trying to say "tell me now, or stay silent".[1]

The ability of a painter to infuse the element of listening into portraiture had already been emphasised as an imponderable quality in the late 15th century – in Milan at the time of Ludovico Sforza, Il Moro – in a famous sonnet by Bernardino Bellincioni, published posthumously in 1493, celebrating Leonardo da Vinci's (1452–1519) *Portrait of Cecilia Gallerani* (c. 1486, Kraków, National Museum).[2] For the poet, it seems as if the artist had "depicted her in his painting / as if she were listening and not speaking". Leonardo's *Portrait of Cecilia Gallerani* has always been considered a revolutionary portrait in its compositional cut and the – entirely Florentine – spiral and dynamic twist of the figure. So much so that on 26 April 1498, it stimulated the need in Isabella d'Este, Marchioness of Mantua, to see it alongside "certain beautiful portraits by the hand of Zoanne Bellino" (c. 1430–1516), which must have seemed much more static to her in their ethereal, fixed nature and indifference to the "noises" of the real world.[3]

The idea of movement captured (like a snapshot, as we might put it today) in late 15th-century portraits – at a time when, it is important to remember, full-length life-size portraits did not yet exist (and would have lent themselves less to the search for poses so focused on psychological aspects) – was the preserve, it could be said, of Leonardo. In the jargon of Italian art history, *Portrait of Cecilia Gallerani* has been defined as one of the prototypes of the *ritratto di spalla* – literally, "shoulder portrait" – a broad and fairly generic category, while the *Portrait of a Young Man* belongs instead to a very specific subgenre of this portrait category, much better defined by the "looking-over-the-shoulder" formula. This phrase refers to a compositional method typical of the "modern manner" and which is intrinsically linked to the theme of listening, given the immediate and spontaneous gesture of the head twisting to address us.[4] Leonardo was also an absolute innovator in this subgenre. In particular, the magical drawing at the Royal Library in Turin (fig. 1) should be referred to, which, for Bernard Berenson, was "one of the finest achievements of all draughtsmanship" (and who are we to argue?).[5] Much has been written about the dating of this drawing and its relationship with the angel in Leonardo's two versions of the *Virgin of the Rocks* altarpiece (c. 1483, Paris, Musée du Louvre; c. 1490, London, The National Gallery), yet it is correct to consider it a portrait in all respects (and therefore not purely preparatory for the angel), produced in around 1490 and constituting one of the most accomplished and (final) outcomes in the parable of Leonardo as a metal-point draughtsman.[6] The pose of Leonardo's figure, reversed compared to the *Portrait of a Young Man*, is the same, with the back visible, although in shadow, and the deliberate, powerful act of turning around (almost to the point of cricking his neck), the twisting neck underlined by two biting graphic lines in the absolute synthesis of that area. However, this immortalised, frozen action is pervaded by an intangible *charis* or grace, a quality that Pliny the Elder pointed out in Apelles's painting[7] in the first century AD and which Leonardo (and thus later Giorgione [c. 1473/74–1510]) undoubtedly succeeded in making his own.[8] One painted consequence of this drawing – albeit a "shoulder portrait", yet not exactly "looking over the shoulder" – is the famous *Belle Ferronière* (c. 1490–1492, Paris, Musée du Louvre), which bears huge

Fig. 1 Leonardo da Vinci, *Head of a Young Woman*, c. 1490, Turin, Biblioteca Reale

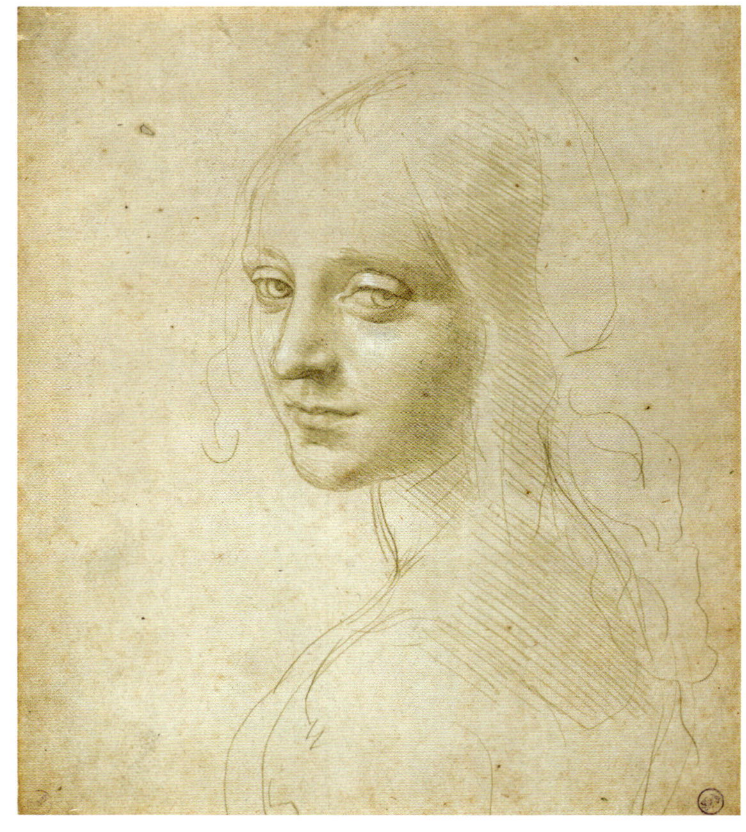

specific importance in the history of portraiture in general in terms of its influences and consequences (and also on Giorgione: see, for comparison, the almost identical pose of the *Old Woman* (c. 1503, Venice, Gallerie dell'Accademia).

The close correlation between Leonardo and Giorgione, written about from Giorgio Vasari (1511–1574) onwards, evidently takes place following the Tuscan's brief stay in Venice in the first few months of 1500.[9] One of the paintings most indebted to Leonardo by Giorgione, which today is almost universally attributed to him, is *The Three Ages of Man* (c. 1500/01, Florence, Palazzo Pitti, Galleria Palatina), with the still entirely Leonardesque typological figure of the old man posed in a "looking-over-the-shoulder" twist.

At this point in the history of Venetian art there emerges a painting that has always appeared as an absolute masterpiece, despite being relatively undervalued by many (albeit not all) critics. Although it is not a portrait, its pose (and even its architectural backdrop) and composition link it closely to the *Portrait of a Young Man* in Munich – we are referring to *Christ Carrying the Cross* of the Kunsthistorisches Museum in Vienna (cat. 41).[10] It is impossible not to trace this magnificent painting back to a juncture between Venice and Leonardo (we need only think of Leonardo's famous drawing of *Christ Carrying the Cross*, c. 1490, Venice, Gallerie dell'Accademia, inv. no. 231), sometime immediately after 1500.[11] In the cascading hair (fig. 2), depicted with Flemish meticulousness, we seem to glimpse Leonardo's studies of water in motion. The relationship between the Vienna and Munich paintings is indissoluble, even though the two extreme twists express something subtly different. The Viennese *Christ* seems surprised by our presence and his half-opened mouth appears to be admonishing us with a whisper, whilst the steadfastness and even silent aggression of the young man in the Munich portrait has already been mentioned. It is as if we were imagining the same artist at work, a few

Fig. 2 Cat. 41 (detail)

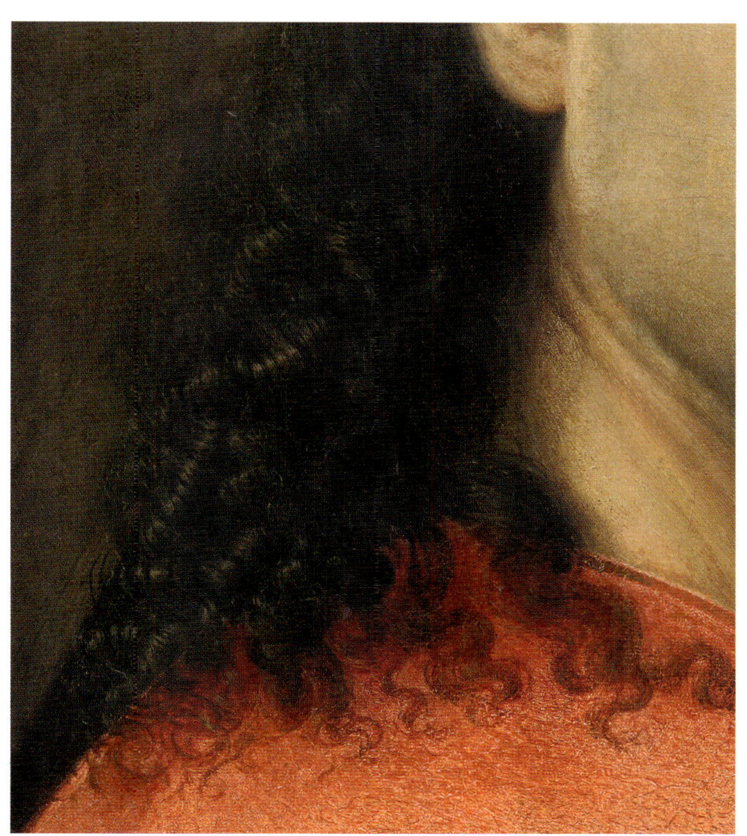

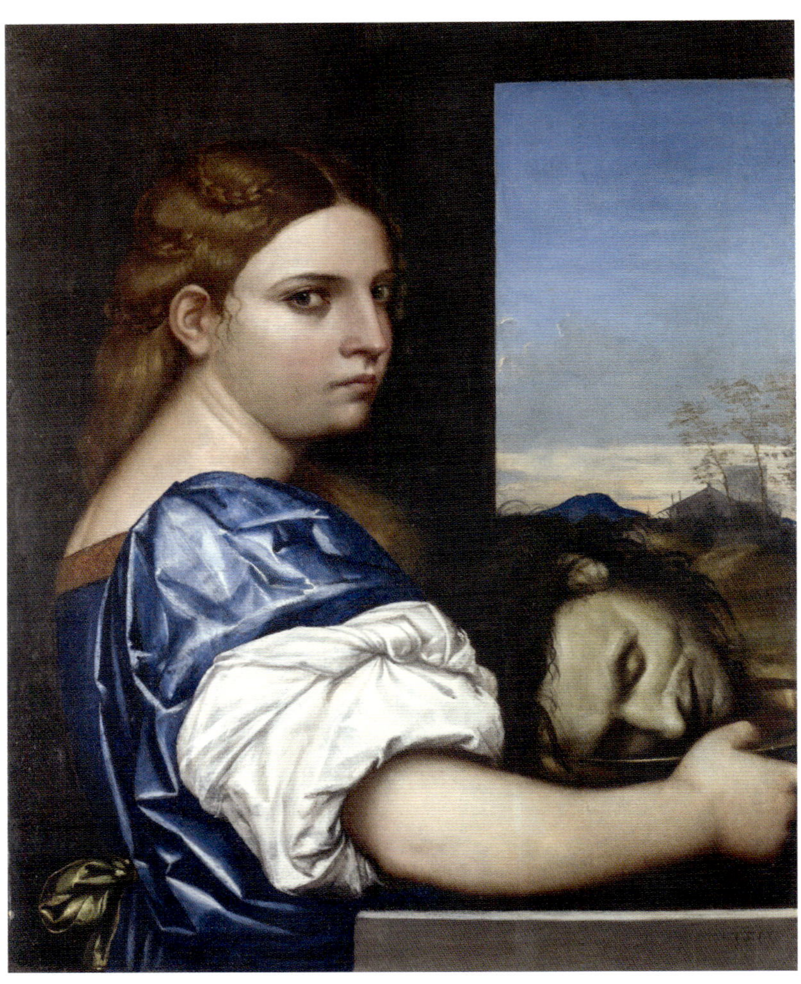

Fig. 3 Sebastiano del Piombo, *Salome*, 1510, London, The National Gallery

years later, on the same "looking-over-the-shoulder" formula, but shifting from a religious subject (albeit permeated by a notable stamp of portraiture in the features of the face) to a portrait, in which the "close-up" effect appears less extreme and the composition more monumental. For me, it appears evident that *Christ Carrying the Cross* is a much older work – still bearing traces of the 15th century (the red sleeve with the broken, angular, almost Flemish folds) – than the *Portrait of a Young Man*, in which the light appears to have become sulphurous and fiery compared to a more crystalline vision of the *Christ*. Never has Pordenone (c. 1483/84–1539), still recently indicated as the artist of the Vienna painting, ever painted with these lenticular, Leonardesque qualities that retain much of the 15th century.[12]

The practice of the "looking-over-the-shoulder" pose, or rather "portrait from behind", was used by Giorgione on various occasions in the early 16th century: for example, the terminology used in Marcantonio Michiel's 1528 description of Giorgione's portrait of Gerolamo Marcello is very effective. The sitter is described as "armed, showing his back, up to his belt, and turning his head"[13], a passage sometimes associated with the painting now housed at the Kunsthistorisches Museum in Vienna (inv. no. GG 1526), which critics consider one of the clearest points of contact between Giorgione and Leonardo.[14]

Coming back to the *Portrait of a Young Man*, however, it might seem as if we were taking it for granted that it was painted by Giorgione, something that is not undisputed, even in recent art literature. It has, in fact, long been identified as a self-portrait by Palma il Vecchio (c. 1480–1528) described by Vasari, who points out a particular "girar d'occhi" (a turning of the eyes towards the viewer) in that painting.[15] But this hypothesis comes up against two insurmountable obstacles:

the quality of something that has all the credentials to be considered "one of the masterpieces of the century", which was never achieved, not even remotely, by the admittedly excellent Palma; and the apparent age of the sitter, in his early 20s, which seems incompatible with the period of Palma's career in which it is said to have been painted, in the middle of the second decade of the 16th century, when the artist would have been around 35 years old.[16] The other attribution that still comes up today is that of Sebastiano del Piombo (c. 1485–1547); however, a comparison with another of his Venetian works posed in a similar way, and dated 1510, such as *Salome* in the National Gallery in London (fig. 3), is enough to make us understand that Sebastiano's art lacks that pulsating realism, that Dürerian component so powerful in the Munich portrait.[17] Having said that, the twist and volume of the body in the *Salome* are typical of Sebastiano's poetry and become part of a pure exercise in plasticism – note the arc "drawn" by the female figure's back – which is already proto-Michelangelesque, leading to a formalistic departure from reality that is even psychological.

The huge importance to the Venetian art world of the Munich portrait, the *Portrait of a Young Man,* is confirmed by works that clearly draw inspiration from it. An almost literal quotation (in which the fox fur becomes that of a lynx) appears in *Christ Among the Doctors* (fig. 4), datable not long after 1510, by Rocco Marconi (died before 13 May 1529), in which the painter typically offers a sampling of Giorgionesque pastiches, declaring the full extent of his lack of inventiveness.[18] Another work generated by *Portrait of a Young Man* – even in the quilted satin (which has become green) – is the *Lira da Braccio Player* in the Kunsthistorisches Museum in Vienna (fig. 5), which confused a connoisseur as great as Johannes Wilde to the point that he believed the two works to be *modello* and derivation created

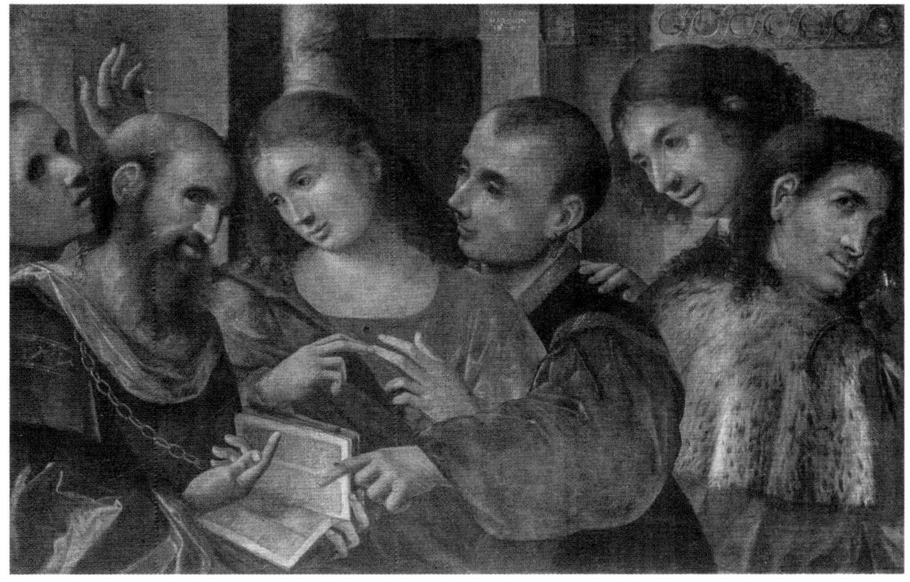

Fig. 4 Rocco Marconi, *Christ Among the Doctors*, c. 1510–1515, formerly Verona, Collection Bragantini

by the same anonymous "Meister der Selbstbildnisse" (master of self-portraits) active in the first half of the 16th century.[19] The Vienna painting, for which the recent reference to Domenico Capriolo (c. 1494–1528) appears convincing, as a partial derivation does not capture the profound formal (and anatomical) characteristics of the *modello.* It slavishly repeats aspects such as the folds of the neck, despite the fact that the difference in the orientation of the chest tells us that a twist should not really be there: this is no longer realism, but is already manner.[20] In addition, it is almost grotesque to see how the element of listening, rendered so subtly and poetically in the Munich painting, has been translated into vulgar prose in the image of a man who looks out at us slightly dazed as he tunes his viola da braccio (and listens to the instrument rather than to us).

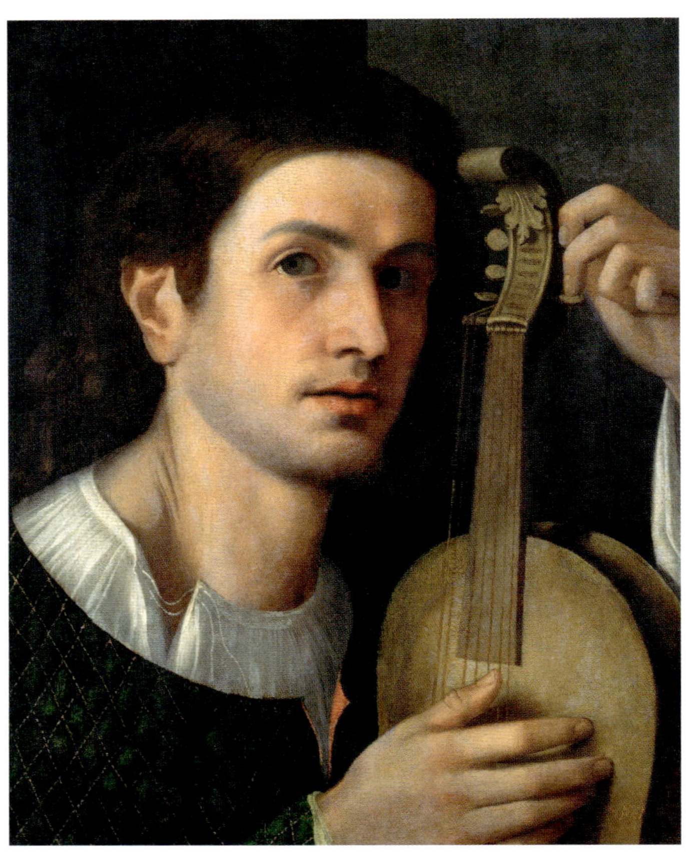

Fig. 5 Domenico Capriolo, *Lira da Braccio Player*, c. 1515, Vienna, Kunsthistorisches Museum

There are also grandiose interpretations of the Munich portrait, however, and they are offered by Giorgione's greatest follower – Titian (c. 1488/90–1576) – to whom, for that matter, it had even been attributed, although not particularly convincingly.[21] One of the most famous "looking-over-the-shoulder" portraits by Titian is *Man with a Quilted Sleeve* (c. 1510) in the National Gallery in London, most likely identifiable as the portrait of a member of the Barbarigo family mentioned by Vasari.[22] Titian's sitter conquers the space with all the confidence, self-esteem and surety of someone who dominates and has no need to listen – in this sense, the Munich painting can be seen to contain a synthesis of all the profound artistic differences between the personalities of Giorgione and Titian. The unceasing influence of the London painting over the centuries is evidenced by the large number of copies and derivations as well as its impact on the portraiture of Van Dyck (and consequently on English portraiture) and Rembrandt – the painting was in Amsterdam around 1639/40, where it inspired at least two self-portraits (one engraved, the other painted) by the great Dutch artist.[23] During the 17th century, thanks in part to the *modelli* of Titian (and Giorgione), still admired a century later, the "looking-over-the-shoulder" pose became canonical in portraiture,

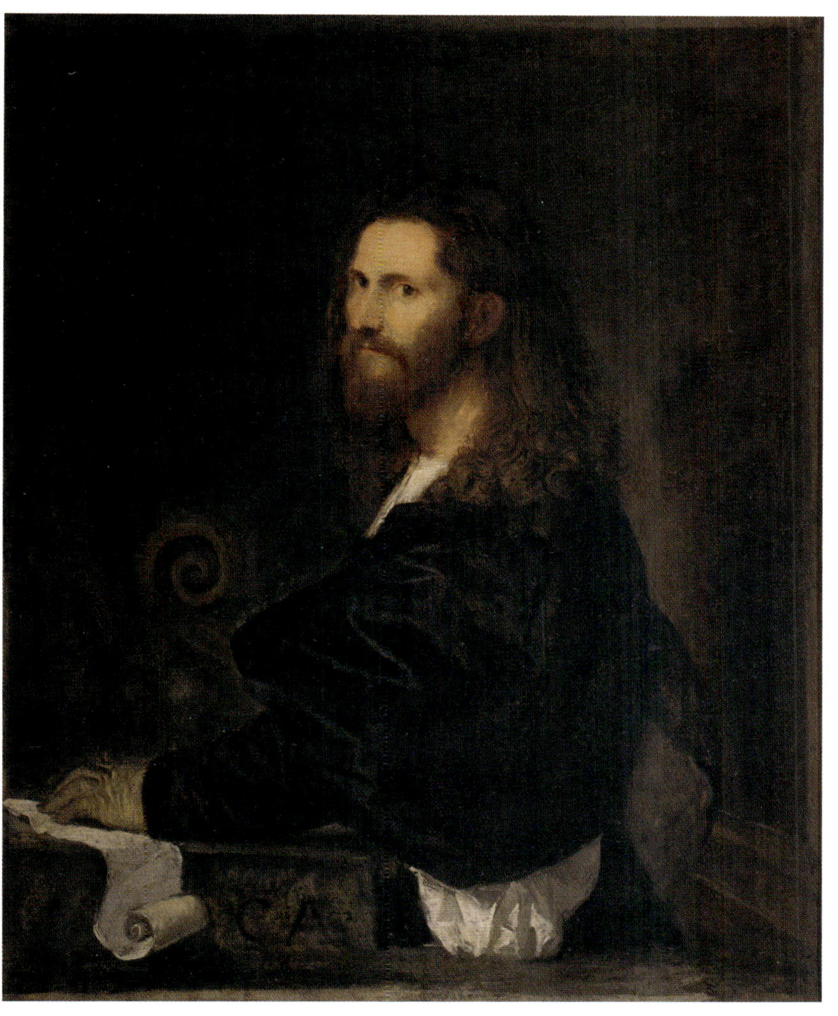

Fig. 6 Titian, *Portrait of a Musician*, c. 1513, Rome, Galleria Spada

although not without continuing to create problems for those portrayed: Samuel Pepys, for instance, painted by John Hayls in 1666 (London, National Portrait Gallery), wrote in his diary: "I sit to have it [the painting] full of shadows and do almost break my neck looking over my shoulders to make the posture for him [Hayls] to work by".[24]

Another painting by Titian, less known and less discussed, seems to have been inspired even more intensely by Giorgione's *modello*, due in part to the presence of dimly lit architecture in the background, "framing" the composition: the beautiful (and possibly unfinished) *Portrait of a Musician* at the Galleria Spada in Rome (fig. 6). Here, Titian – albeit with an even more monumental cut of the figure around the waist – seems to want to salvage all the uncertainties of Giorgione, in a posthumous tribute to the late master.[25] The entirely Venetian fate of the painting now in Munich (cat. 40) tells us that, for a few years at least, the work remained in Venice, where it was admired.[26]

Apparently, the figure cannot be identified with any certainty; reference to the painting as a portrait by Giorgione of "a German from the Fuchera family with a fox fur on his back, from the side, in the act of turning around" only dates back as far as the time of Carlo Ridolfi (1648), who referred to the portrait once it had ended up in Antwerp in the Van Veerle brothers' collection.[27] It is possible that Ridolfi, who was well informed about the Van Veerle collection, may have proposed a forced reading – to provide a pedigree for a work that was, after all, on the market at that time – of a passage from Vasari, who, in the *Vita* of Giorgione, mentions "a head coloured in oils, a portrait of a German of the Fugger family", which was part of his book of drawings (and therefore, with all probability, was a small work on paper, certainly not a panel).[28] At about the same time, around 1650, we know that Wenzel Hollar had engraved the painting – in counterpart – in a first state with the (from today's perspective) absurd and still inexplicable identification of the 14th-century Tuscan painter Buonamico Buffalmacco; in the second state, he switched to a Fugger identification, in all likelihood adjusting his approach based on Ridolfi's comments (and helping make his passage almost appear true, still today).[29] Given that the assumptions are so weak, it seems superfluous to try to track down a specific Fugger at all costs; it could be Ulrich (born in 1490) or Anton (born in 1493).[30]

Also in the Van Veerle collections, Ridolfi remembers another, now lost, painting by Giorgione that Vasari saw (and described in detail) in the studio of the patriarch Giovanni Grimani sometime earlier, in 1566: "a much larger head, portrayed from nature; [...] holding the red cap of a commander, and there is a cape of fur, below which is one of the old-fashioned doublets. This is believed to represent a military leader".[31] The work was fortunately immortalised by Federico Zuccari (1539/40–1609), an artist in the pay of the Grimani around the time of Vasari's visit, in a beautiful drawing (fig. 7).[32] The subject, cut at the waist, is not captured "from behind" or "looking over the shoulder", but almost frontally, "in majesty", according to a tried-and-tested scheme in Venice – especially by Titian – primarily from the mid-1510s onwards. His aura of screamed desperation (despite his head thrown back slightly, he turns his pathetic gaze towards us) has led this lost original to be traced back to Giorgione's last years. As rightly pointed out by Alessandro Ballarin, this composition contributes greatly to consolidating the attribution of the Munich portrait to Giorgione. A close comparison between the faces (figs 8, 9) seems to demonstrate that the two men had a very similar physiognomy, an aspect that suggests it may even be the same person (a Grimani?), immortalised in two paintings that differ in terms of pose and composition, but are similar, a year or two apart.[33]

Fig. 7 Federico Zuccari (after Giorgione), *Portrait of a Man*, c. 1563–1565, Berlin, Staatliche Museen, Kupferstichkabinett

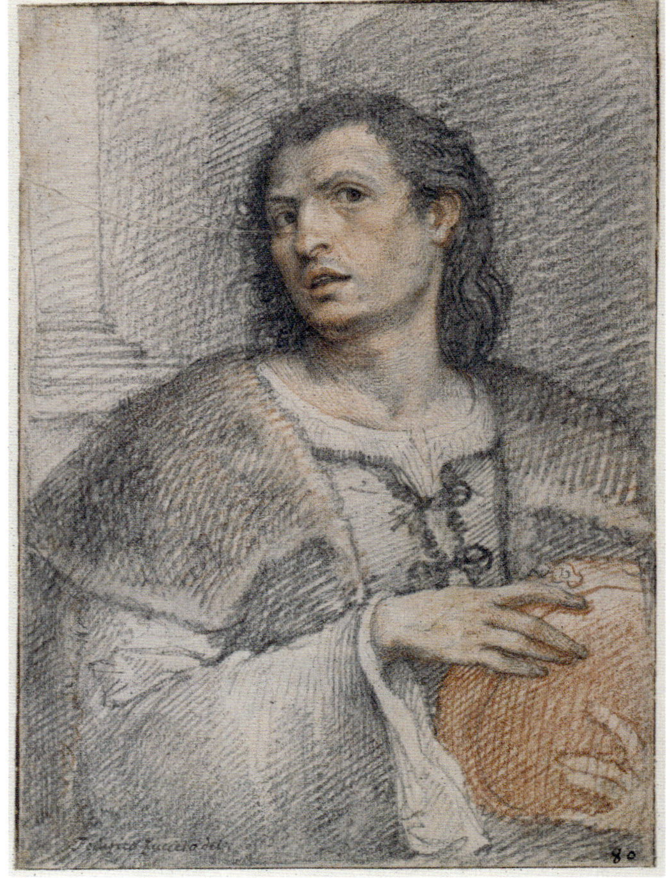

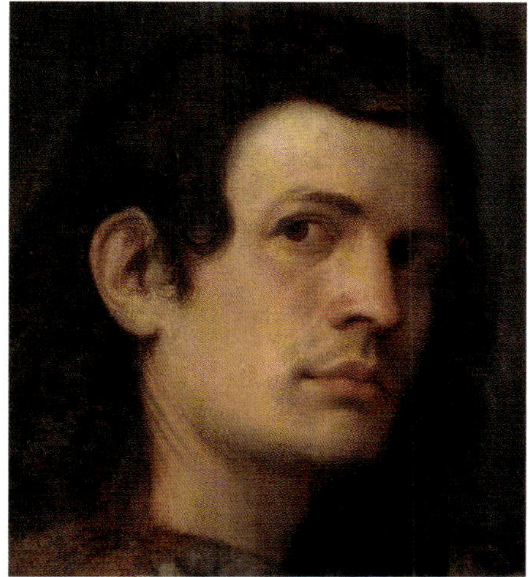

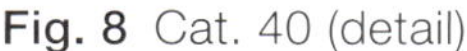

Fig. 8 Cat. 40 (detail)

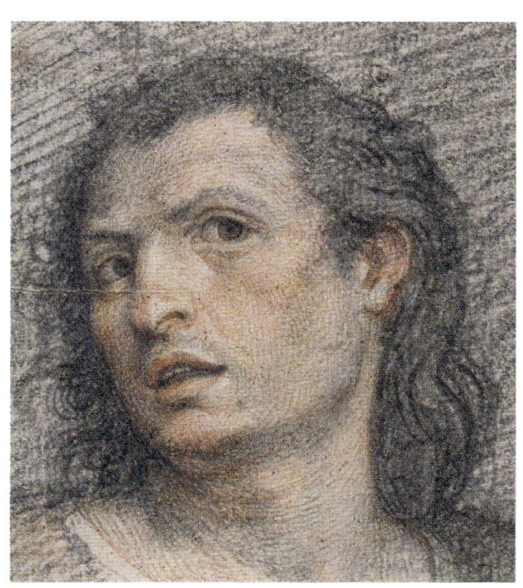

Fig. 9 Federico Zuccari (after Giorgione), *Portrait of a Man* (detail), c. 1563–1565, Berlin, Staatliche Museen, Kupferstichkabinett

At this point, we should turn to a painting that, thanks to an old black-and-white photograph by Federico Zeri (who had catalogued it as "Giorgione?"), has been lying in my Munich *Portrait of a Young Man* folder for years.[34] The work in question is a *Philosopher/Astronomer with a Pupil* at the Bayerische Staatsgemäldesammlungen in Munich, which has for some years been on display in the Grüne Galerie at the Munich Residenz (cat. 43). My association was based principally on the similar "looking-over-the-shoulder" pose of the teacher, whose dress is characterised by a fur (in this case, a lynx) and my thoughts had leant vaguely towards Pordenone, not being familiar with its painted matter. Upon later receiving a colour photograph, I was extremely excited to see the image of such a splendid, chromatically complex painting, damaged in places, but still dazzling, especially in terms of the unforgettable hands, and the boy's head and scarf (unfortunately, the latter has been affected by a reduction of a few centimetres of canvas on the left).[35] The proto-Caravaggesque aura of the astronomer, and above all of the pupil, initially made me question that this was an early 16th-century Venetian painting; I changed my mind only once I had had the opportunity to see the picture in real life, with the light effects on the gilded bronze astrolabe in the foreground, which can only be imagined in Giorgione's Venice at this level and with this skill (fig. 10). The boy's clothing, although darkened, is a magnificent green (copper

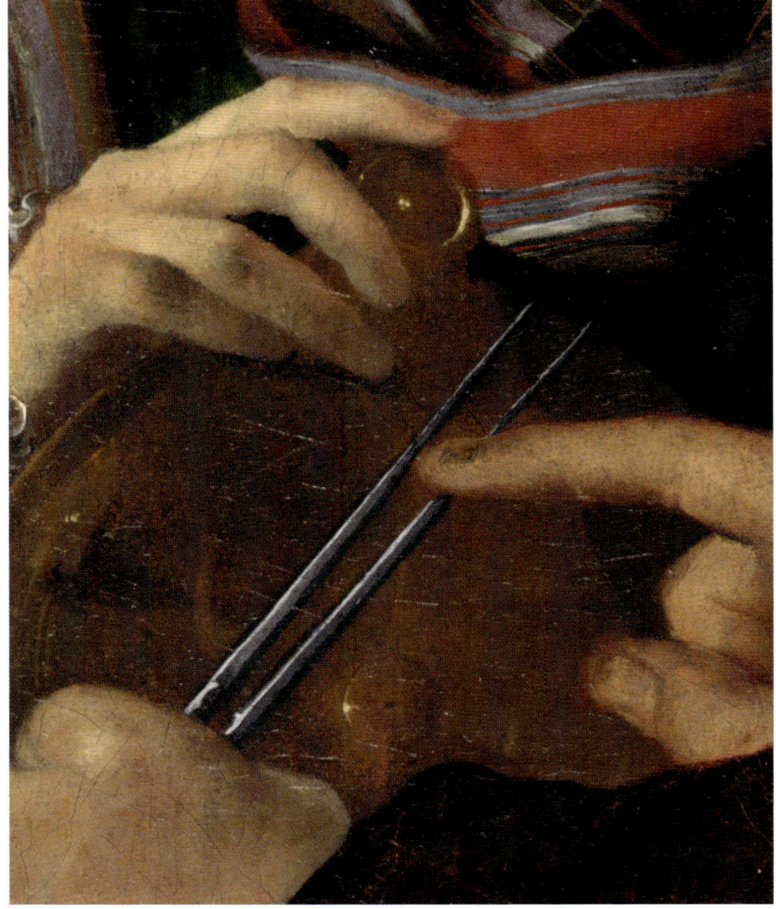

Fig. 10 Cat. 43 (detail)

resinate). The psychological and spatial dynamic is built through a complex structure: the master in the foreground, a truly "large head"[36], is in the midst of explaining, with his compass in one hand and the index finger of the other pointing at the astrolabe. He turns towards us, almost annoyed at being interrupted, while his pupil, slightly relegated to the foreground, looks at him, grateful but at the same time thirsty for more explanations. The powerful sense of realism seems highly comparable with the other Munich portrait (cat. 40) – which is, however, on panel, while this one is on canvas. The head of the boy and that of the master contain glimpses of elements that are also somehow Leonardesque (it should be pointed out that the painting was attributed to Leonardo in Duke Maximilian's 17th-century inventories), but filtered through Dürer – if we think, in particular, of the drawing of the *Young Christ* (c. 1506, Vienna, Albertina, inv. no. 3106), which is a study for the painting *Christ Among the Doctors* (dated 1506, and therefore during his stay in Venice; Madrid, Museum Nacional Thyssen-Bornemisza).[37] This comparison takes on even greater significance, as no better example can be found of a Dürer drawing that profoundly reinterprets the head of the Virgin in Leonardo's second version of the *Virgin of the Rocks*, now in London. To close the circle, it seems that this double portrait is also in a successful dialogue – not just in its composition, but also in the poses of the hands and the dimly lit architectural structures in the background – with the lost Grimani portrait immortalised by Federico Zuccari (fig. 7).

In the context of the ongoing interdisciplinary research project on Venetian Renaissance painting in the collection of the Alte Pinakothek, Johanna Pawis, as research associate, is carrying out in-depth and productive research on the painting; her focus includes the fascinating diagnostic investigations conducted by the project conservator

Anneliese Földes, which reveal various compositional stages and Giorgionesque elements that were concealed by the final layer of paint; but, for now, only a few suggestions shall be made.[38]

Klára Garas, the only scholar so far to have substantially published and discussed the work, rightly places it in the genre of "Unterweisungsbild", a type of double portrait ushered in by *Luca Pacioli with Guidubaldo da Montefeltro*, dated 1495 and with a still-disputed attribution (Naples, Museo Nazionale di Capodimonte).[39] With this in mind, the so-called *Portrait of a Teacher and His Pupil* should be mentioned, which has never seemed to contain the real qualities of Giorgione (c. 1510–1515 [?]; Washington, D.C., National Gallery of Art; see p. 140, fig. 10). Furthermore, its identification with the painting mentioned by Vasari as being in the Borgherini home is based mainly on a provenance reported in the 1932 catalogue of the Herbert Cook collection, which states: "purchased in 1923 from a gentleman in Milan whose great-grandfather received it from a great-nephew of Cavaliere Pier-Francisco Borgherini who [...] died in 1718".[40] This provenance seems very fragile, as it has nothing (no inventory or document) to confirm it, and therefore the unspecified "gentleman in Milan" could well have boasted about it on the basis of Vasari's famous passage to create a pedigree for the painting.

Instead, Vasari's description seems to fit very well (especially in terms of the pictorial qualities emphasised by the biographer from Arezzo) with the double portrait at the Munich Residenz: "In Florence, in the house of the sons of Giovanni Borgherini, there is a portrait by his [Giorgione's] hand of the said Giovanni, taken when he was a young man in Venice, and in the same picture is the master who was teaching him; and there are no two heads to be seen with better touches in the flesh-colours or with more beautiful tints in the shadows".[41] The Florentine Giovanni Borgherini was born in 1496 and, therefore, in 1506/07 – a plausible absolute chronology for the painting now in the Munich Residenz – would have been either ten or eleven years old, an age highly relevant to the pupil in the Munich painting. Moreover, in the literature on the Washington painting, a great early 16th-century humanist, man of letters, philosopher and astronomer in Venice has recently been mentioned as Giovanni's tutor: Trifone Gabriele (whom Carlo Dionisotti had identified as one of the members of the Compagnia degli Amici, an association of young Venetian patricians and intellectuals linked to Giorgione's portraiture).[42] As we try to shift the focus from the Washington painting to this one, why not imagine that Trifone is the figure looking "into the camera"? The only definite portrait of him is a medal (1530–1549) by Danese Cattaneo, in which the profile of a bald and rather plump man stands out on the recto, entirely compatible with our figure (see p. 138, fig. 8).[43] Born in 1470, it could be said that in the painting, in which he must have been either 36 or 37, time does not seem to have been kind to him. From today's perspective, however, figures from centuries ago often appear much older.[44]

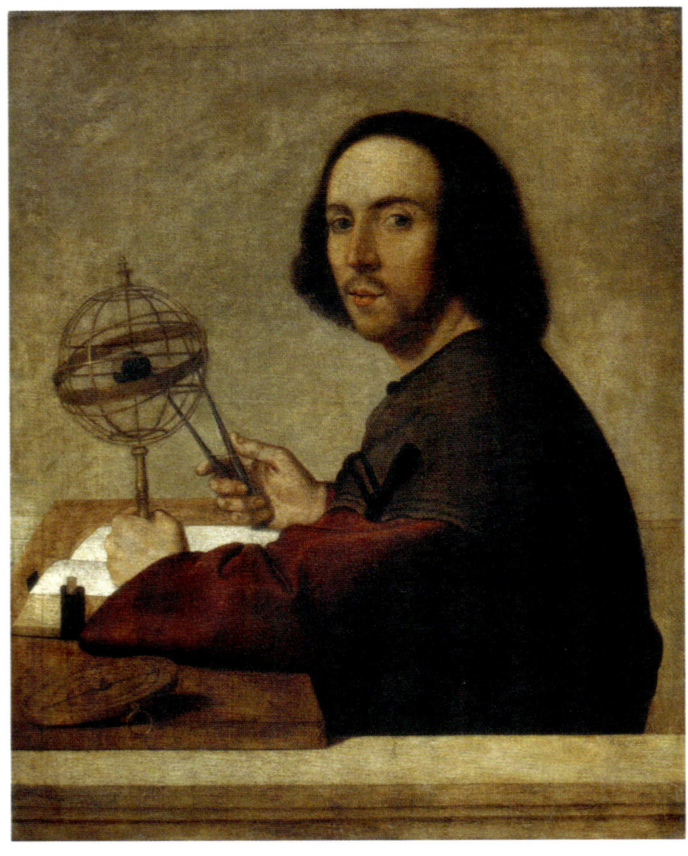

Fig. 11 Marco Basaiti, *Portrait of an Astronomer*, 1512, Lviv, Borys Voznytsky Lviv National Art Gallery

A few last thoughts: if the painting now at the Munich Residenz is the Borgherini picture and it "landed" in Florence in the 1510s, there is a certain value in comparing the figure of the master in the foreground with works produced in Florence during those years – characterised by a whiff of Giorgione and a "looking-over-the-shoulder" pose – such as the *Portrait of a Young Man* by Andrea del Sarto (c. 1517/18, London, The National Gallery), an artist who worked for the Borgherini on several occasions.[45] Finally, the unmistakable influence that the Munich Residenz painting has had in formal, typological and even stylistic respects on the *Portrait of an Astronomer* (fig. 11) found in Lviv – a "looking-over-the-shoulder" portrait by Marco Basaiti (c. 1470–rec. 1530), signed and dated 1512 – also serves as an additional argument for a very early dating of the Munich painting.

New discoveries

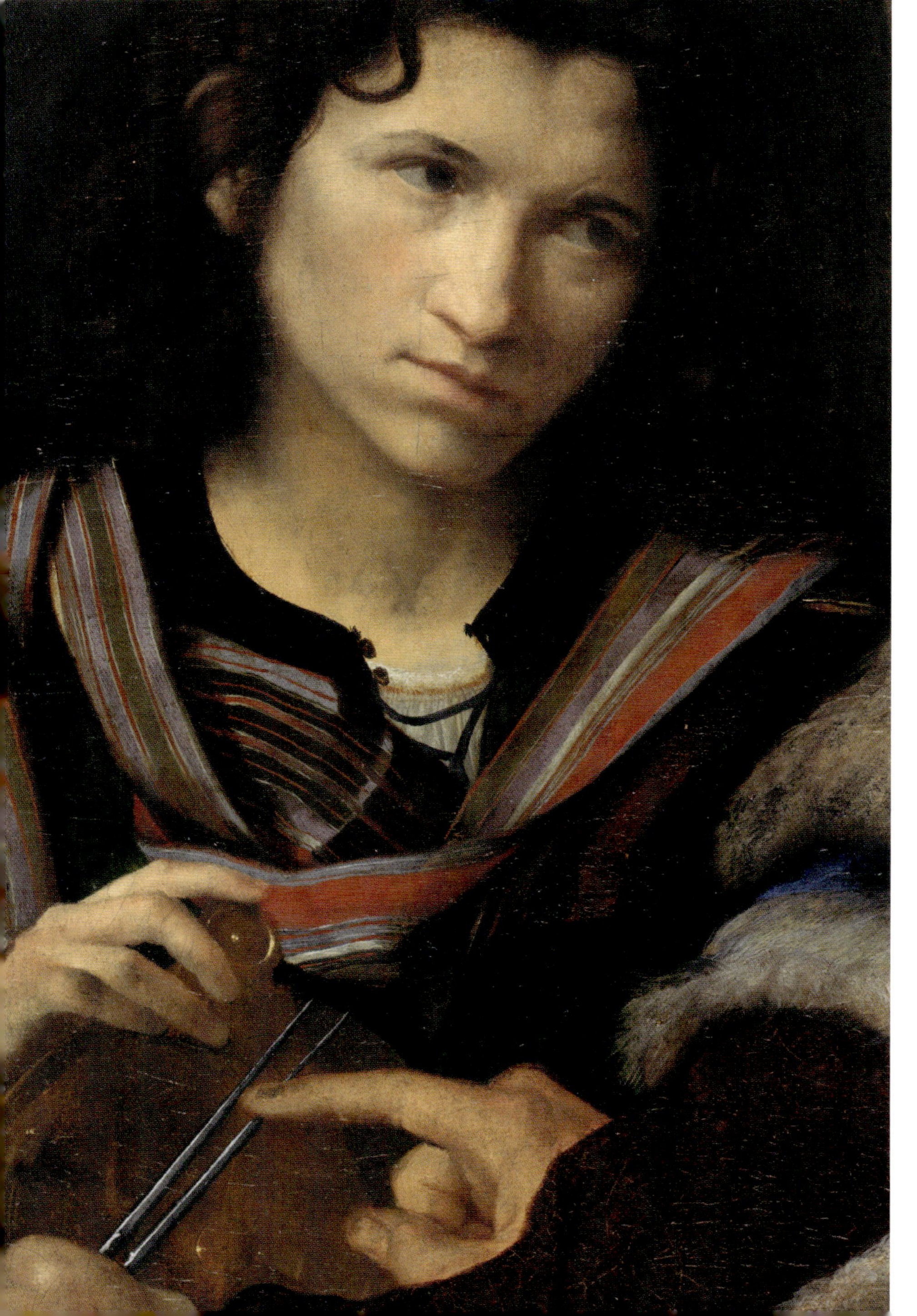

Insights into research on Veneto, Giorgione and Tintoretto at the Alte Pinakothek

JOHANNA PAWIS

Father and son? Jacopo Tintoretto and his workshop, *Portrait of the Maggi Family*, c. 1575

In 1793, Karl Theodor, Elector Palatine and Elector of Bavaria, who had been residing in Munich since 1778, acquired a painting titled "Self-portrait of the Painter Tintoretto with his Son before the Doge of Venice", which unites three generations of self-confident Venetians (cat. 48): a sedate, elderly gentleman whose silver hair and lynx fur coat lend him a sense of distinguished *grandezza;* a *gentiluomo* in his prime, elegantly dressed in black; and a small boy, about three or four years old, gazing out of the picture with wide eyes. Contrary to the illustrious title, which the art dealer Jérôme de Vigneux – who also served the Elector as a purveyor of tropical fruits to the court – certainly put to good use to promote sales,[1] the portrait met with little enthusiasm among art connoisseurs of the 19th century; in the mid-20th century, it disappeared into the depot of the Alte Pinakothek and thus fell out of scholarly view. For this very reason, the painting, which was last listed in the museum catalogue of 1971[2] as an anonymous *Family Portrait* by an unidentifiable Venetian painter, is one of those works that particularly benefit from the attention that a team of art historians, restorers and natural scientists has been devoting to Venetian Renaissance painting in the holdings of the Bayerische Staatsgemäldesammlungen since 2021. Funded by the Deutsche Forschungsgemeinschaft, the Ernst von Siemens Kunststiftung and the Hubert Burda Stiftung, the interdisciplinary research project will for the first time provide detailed insights into and analysis of the collection of Venetian painting from the 15th and 16th centuries, which comprises more than 200 paintings. The *Family Portrait* is an example of how the combination of technical and historical methods and research can lead to new insights: an observation by project conservator Anneliese Földes of a part of the background architecture that exhibits a divergent painting technique prompted an in-depth examination of the painting using imaging techniques (X-ray, infrared reflectography and macro-X-ray fluorescence scanning for insights into the structure of the paint layer and non-destructive colourant analysis), leading to surprising results: in the infrared reflectogram, an inscription painted with black paint on the grey wall was clearly legible in the centre of the picture, which had been covered over at a later time and can now be uncovered again: "ANT^{S}: MAG^{S}: / NOBİLİSSİM^{S}: / CİVİS VENET^{S}:" (fig. 1).[3] Latinised epigraphs are not uncommon, especially in portraits by Jacopo Tintoretto (1518/19–1594) and his workshop, though at first glance, this inscription seems to raise more questions than it clarifies: to whom does it refer? What name is denoted by "ANT^{S}: MAG^{S}:"? And what is the meaning of the two honorific titles that point in different directions within the social system of the Serenissima?[4] Researching Venetian genealogies revealed a whole series of family names that could possibly be used to resolve the abbreviation; however, only one of them had an Antonio in its family tree during the period in question: the *cittadino* Maggi family, named Mazzi in Venetian and Magius in Latin, which, originally hailing from Florence, had attained prestige and prosperity in Venice in the course of the 16th century.[5] The overpainted inscription, which by its position can be related to the piece of writing shown directly below it at the moment of delivery, refers to Antonio,[6] born in 1570/71, and thus the youngest of the three family members portrayed. Dressed in expensive silver brocade complete with fashionable lace collar, and with a flower and *fazzoletto* in his hands, entirely in keeping with the fashion illustrated in Cesare Vecellio's book of costumes of 1590,[7] little Antonio emerges not only as the protagonist of the painting but, as subsequent research in Venetian archives has shown, also as a key figure in a family feud, in light of which the painting turns from a decorative multigenerational portrait into a strategically deployed instrument for establishing the family's disputed line of inheritance. At his side, with a fatherly hand placed on the boy's shoulder, stands Carlo Antonio Maggi, who in turn is shown facing his father Giovanni Francesco. There is nothing in the simple restraint of his appearance to suggest that at the time the painting was created, around 1575, Carlo was already looking back on adventurous travels that had taken him as an agent of the Serenissima as far as the eastern Levant – a life far

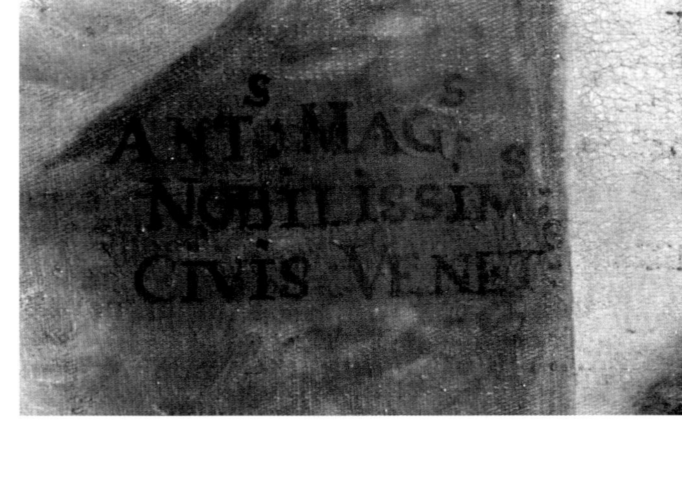

Fig. 1 Cat. 48, section from the infrared reflectogram

removed from the bourgeois civil service career pursued by his father and younger brother.[8] In order to share his exceptional personal history with posterity, he commissioned a richly illuminated manuscript in 1578 (cat. 49),[9] which, despite its historical and cultural source value as a travelogue and unique egodocument, has so far received little scholarly attention.[10] On its eight pages, each with ten individually inscribed and allegorically linked miniatures, the codex depicts an eventful hero's journey set between storms at sea and sightseeing by means of detailed *vedute* and small-figured narrative scenes. After a stopover in Jerusalem, where Carlo was accepted into the Order of the Holy Sepulchre, his fourth and last expedition takes a fateful turn in Cyprus: in the turmoil of the Ottoman–Venetian war, during which Famagusta, the last Christian stronghold in the eastern Mediterranean, was besieged from June 1570, Carlo Maggi is taken prisoner. The miniatures depict how he is stripped of his clothes by colourfully clad, turbaned men and offered in the slave market; how he follows a Christ-like path of suffering with barrels on his back; and how he is finally ransomed by Christian merchants on Chios.[11] Back in Venice, he is welcomed with open arms by his father and reports to the Signoria and the Doge Alvise Mocenigo.[12]

The masterfully illuminated 'picture book' – perhaps the work of "Francesco miniador" from the Calle dalle Acque, whose services Carlo had already used earlier[13] – was undoubtedly created with the intention of documenting and glorifying Maggi's eventful life. However, the actual reason for this commission is only revealed by the illustrations 'framing' the travelogue, which refer to Carlo's hardly less troubled family affairs: in a prelude preceding the chronicle, the Maggi family tree and coat of arms are followed by a full-page portrait of Carlo as a Knight of the Holy Sepulchre (fig. 2) and a portrait of young Antonio, who, according to the

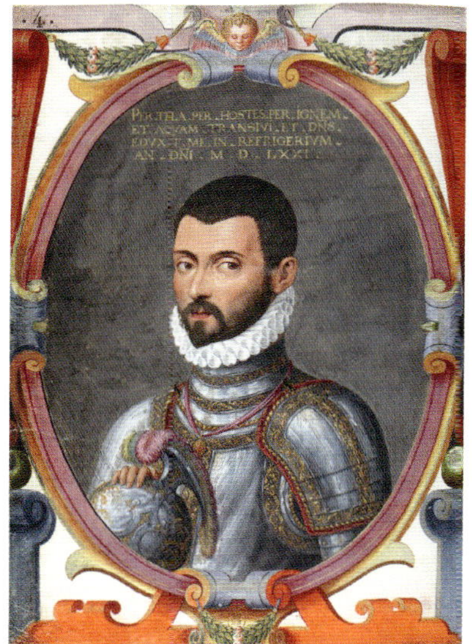

Fig. 2 Unknown miniaturist, *Portrait of Carlo Maggi*, from: Cat. 49, miniature 4

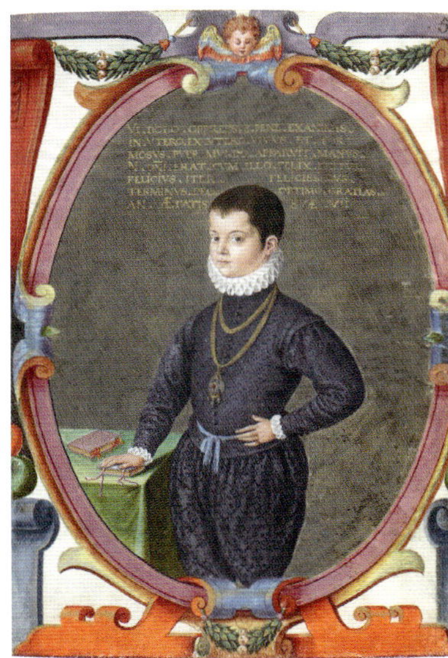

Fig. 3 Unknown miniaturist, *Portrait of Antonio Maggi*, from: Cat. 49, miniature 5

inscription accompanying his likeness, is depicted at the age of seven, and thus three to four years older than in the Munich painting (fig. 3); the two then return together in a double-page illustration at the end of the manuscript, which depicts a reunion of the Maggi family in the countryside – probably in a villa near Feltre[14] – that seems idyllic only at first glance (fig. 4). Once again placing his hand protectively on Antonio's shoulder and facing his father with an eloquent gesture, Carlo assumes the same role as in the Munich work. This time, however, the easily recognisable triad of Giovanni Francesco, Carlo and Antonio is joined by Carlo's brothers (Ottaviano, Girolamo and Camillo) and sisters (Diana and Modesta).[15] A banner unfurls from Carlo's hand over the head of Antonio, who is carelessly playing with his puppy. It addresses the visibly distanced siblings who have quite literally gone into opposition and epitomises the lack of domestic bliss in biblical terms: "VOS. COGITASTIS. DE. ME. MALVM. IN. BONVM. SED. DEVS. CONVERTIT. ILLVD." – freely adapted from Genesis 50:20: "You thought badly of me, but God turned it all into good." A similarly bad light is cast on the relatives by Carlo's will, which he wrote in great detail befitting his desire for self-promotion on 5 March 1587[16] – and which contains the resolution of the mystery surrounding the cause of the quarrel: bitter experiences with "quarrels and conflicts" ("lite e travagli") led him, as he writes, to fear that his envious "brothers, sisters and brother-in-law" ("fratt[elli], sorelle & cugnado") might oppose his last will and create "confusion and discord" ("garbugi e litigij") in order to deprive the sole heir of his, i.e. Carlo's, legacy: Antonio. Even though Antonio is dubbed by him as his "dearly beloved son" ("car.[issi]mo e diletiss.[imo] fig.[liuo]lo"), Antonio's legitimacy must have been anything but undisputed, since *Madonna* Giacomina, who was married to Carlo, gave birth to him in

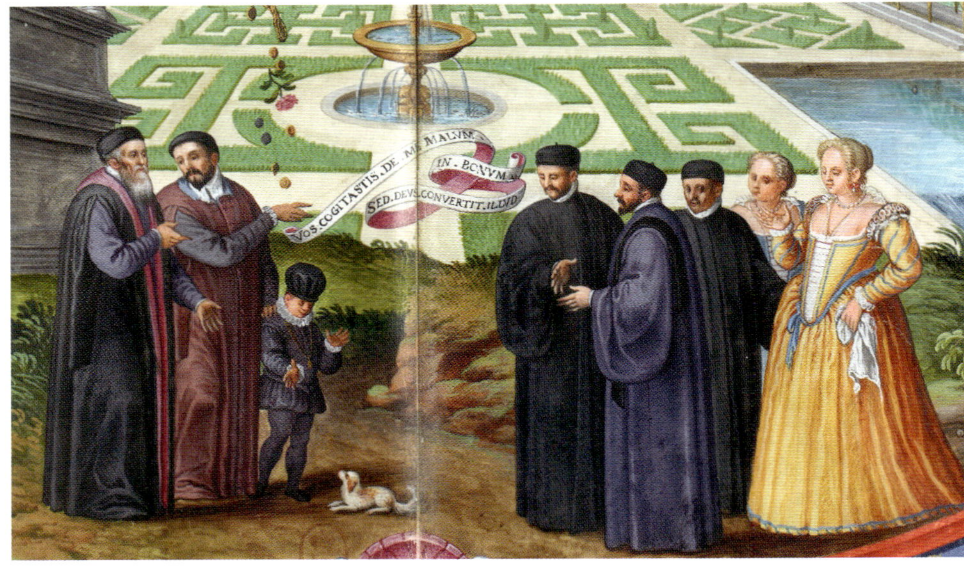

Fig. 4 Unknown miniaturist, *Reunion of the Maggi Family* (detail), 1578, from: Cat. 49, miniatures 16–17

1570/71[17], just at the time when Carlo was first on his travels, then in Ottoman captivity and possibly even presumed dead after the fall of Famagusta.[18] And indeed, the term commonly used to designate illegitimate offspring, "sia o non sia mio figlio" ("be he my son or not"), which follows Antonio's name in the will, reveals that Carlo at least had doubts about his paternity; in view of the involuntary course of his journey, which kept him away from Venice and his wife far longer than planned, it is only reasonable to assume that Antonio, who was born in the meantime, was in fact Carlo's stepson, whom he nevertheless accepted, as he makes unequivocally clear, as his own son.[19] This also explains the inscription of Antonio's portrait in the Codex Maggi (fig. 3), which celebrates the birth of the boy, symbolically depicted with a pelican pendant, in a panegyric epigraph that is as messianic in tone as it is explicit: weighed down by the burden of injustice (probably meaning: his illegitimate descent), Antonio almost died in his mother's womb before he, thanks to divine grace, appeared to the world alive and well "ex utero".[20]

Both with the manuscript, on the last page of which the father and the stepson jointly gaze at the ladder to heaven in a kind of apotheosis of the patchwork family, and with the commissioning of the family portrait now in Munich, Carlo Maggi thus pursued a strategy of legitimation qua representation: by handing over the document in the portrait – a pictorial motif also used by Titian (c. 1488/90–1576) to represent the transfer of hereditary rights[21] – Giovanni Francesco confirms Carlo's family model with his authority as *pater familias* and, at the same time, vouches for the genealogy recorded in the medium of painting for generations to come.[22] It seems that Antonio was indeed graced with the happy ending – "felicissimus terminus"[23] – that Carlo had wished for him, as the former pursued a career as secretary to the Venetian ambassador to France, thus following in the latter's international footsteps.[24] The comprehensive publication that will conclude the research project shall provide a detailed discussion of the Munich painting's attribution; at this point, it should only be noted that both art historical and technological indications leave no doubt that it is a painting from the workshop of Jacopo Tintoretto, whose *bottega* was located in the immediate vicinity of Carlo Maggi's home *alla corte vecchia*[25] in the Contrada S. Marcilian.

Rank and dignity: Bartolomeo Veneto, *Portrait of a Young Man from the Zane Family*, c. 1505

"The little picture here imputed to Giambellini [...] is in no case by the Venetian old master, nor by any master at all, but by a professional dabbler [...] The name of Giambellini is a sacred name in art-history, and really ought not to be so flagrantly abused",[26] Giovanni Morelli commented in 1883, expressing his indignation about a painting that had been acquired by Ludwig I from a Viennese art dealer in 1842 under the title of a "Self-portrait of Giovanni Bellini"[27] and had since been presented as such (cat. 47). Morelli's harsh judgement was certainly due not least to the condition of the painting, which in the 1930s made it necessary to transfer it to a new support. In fact, its early association with Giovanni Bellini (c. 1435–1516) is quite understandable insofar as the painting is formally close to the creations from his workshop: as a bust in three-quarter profile against a neutral background, it corresponds to a specifically Venetian portrait type, comparable to the *Portrait of a Young Senator* from Padua (cat. 71), in which the sitter, restrained in appearance and with an unmoving facial expression, takes a back seat to his function as a member of the social and political elite. Unlike his contemporaries portrayed by Bellini, however, the young Venetian with the bright blue eyes returns our gaze, which lends the portrait an immediacy that Marcantonio Michiel had already pointed out in 1533 as being characteristic of the portraits Antonello da Messina had created in Venice in the mid-1470s (see p. 194, fig. 5).[28] Through the striking inclusion of the hand, which adds a scenic element to the austerity of the bust format typical of both Antonello and Bellini, the painter also draws on a northern innovation known in Venice through imports such as Hans Memling's (c. 1430/40–1494) *Portrait of Bernardo Bembo* (cat. 70). Last but not least, the choice of the dark-green background, reminiscent of works such as Albrecht Dürer's *Portrait of a Young Man*, created in the lagoon city in 1506 (Genoa, Palazzo Rosso), reveals an artist with a keen eye for inspiration from beyond the Alps. Bartolomeo Veneto (active 1502–1531), a portrait specialist, belongs to a young generation of painters from the Venetian countryside who, like Lorenzo Lotto or Andrea Previtali,[29] are characterised precisely by their mobility and openness to new ideas. Probably trained by Gentile Bellini, as whose pupil he identifies himself in a signature,[30] he appears for the first time as an independent painter in 1502 and presumably remains in

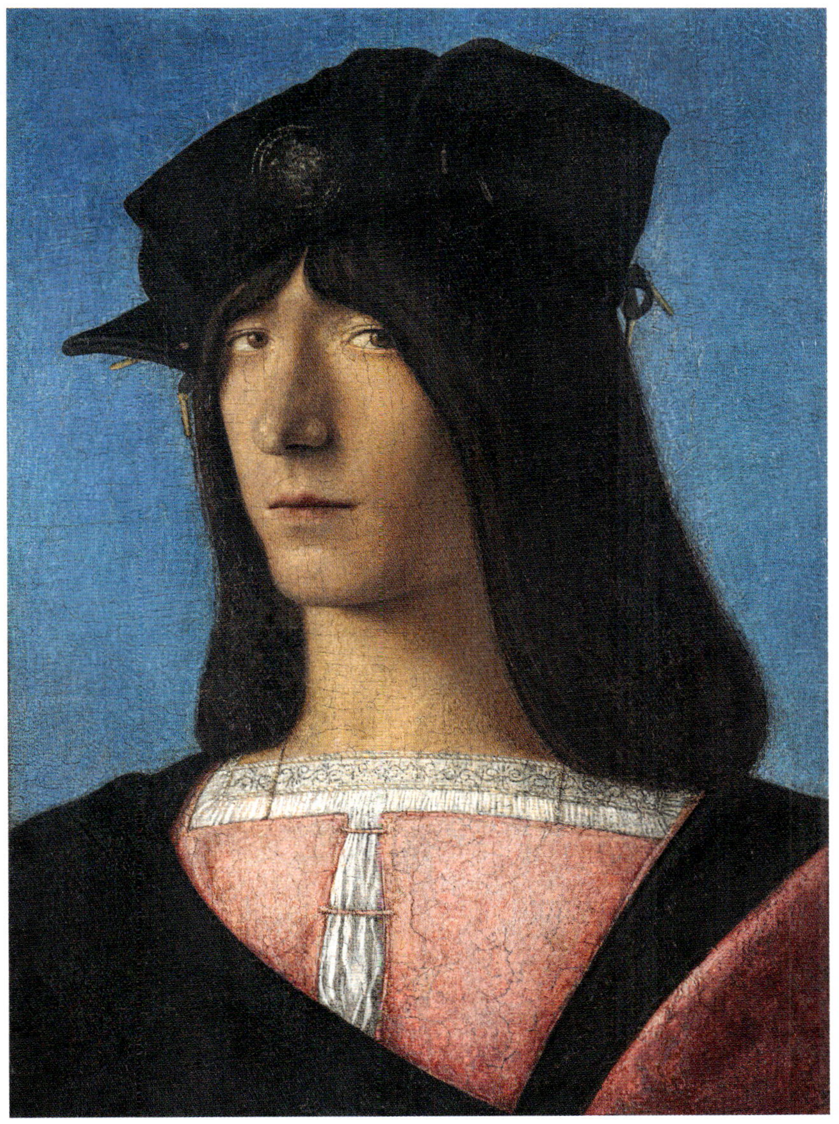

Fig. 5 Bartolomeo Veneto, *Portrait of a Young Man*, after 1510, Cleveland, The Cleveland Museum of Art

Venice until 1506/07, before going to Ferrara and Milan, where he makes painterly refinement in rendering precious garments his trademark.[31] If one accepts the proposal put forward by Laura Pagnotta in 1997, following a number of unconvincing hypotheses on the authorship of the Munich painting, to include the work as an early creation in Veneto's oeuvre[32] – an attribution that has not yet found its way into research discourse and will be taken up here – the portrait of this young man is the earliest surviving portrait by the artist, from whose Venetian period otherwise only sacred compositions are known. The arguments in favour of this attribution can only be briefly mentioned here: the delicacy of the painterly execution as well as motivic and stylistic characteristics, such as the sideways glance enlivened by the slight asymmetry of the eyes or the nuanced play of light and shadow on the sharply rendered facial features, find their counterparts in Veneto's early works,[33] to which the painting can be coherently assigned with a date of c. 1505 (cf. also the *Portrait of a Man* in Cleveland, which was painted after 1510 and probably in Milan, but in its austerity still corresponds entirely to the early style; fig. 5). The artist took particular care in rendering the signet ring, which is adorned with a coat of arms set in gilded *pastiglia*, identifying the sitter as a member of the Zane family, which belonged to the distinguished *case vecchie*. In this way, it refers to the function of the portrait as a painted testimony of family genealogy, which Giorgio Vasari (1511–1574)[34] already characterised as specifically Venetian and which becomes concretely palpable in the numerous family *ritratti* recorded in unpublished inventories of the Zane family's estate.[35]

At around 20 years of age, and thus not yet of marriageable age according to Venetian customs, the self-confident young man is on the verge of adulthood, which for Venetian *nobili* is synonymous with assuming political responsibility.[36] As the registers of the *Balla d'Oro*, the state lottery for early admission to the Maggior Consiglio, the most important political body of the Serenissima, show,[37] in the first decade of the cinquecento a total of ten young men from different branches of the Zane family applied at the age of 20 for the chance of gaining a head start to an official career, which was regularly only open from the age of 25. Any one of them could have been portrayed in the Munich portrait, so attempts at identification must remain hypothetical. Regardless of this, however, the Venetian coming-of-age ritual of the *Balla d'Oro* points to a possible occasion for the commissioning of the painting: with their entry into the Great Council, patrician-born Venetians took their place in the state structure of the Serenissima, identifying themselves as its members by the formal garb of the black toga with a stole (Venetian *becchetto*)[38], among other things. Although it is precisely this accessory that the young Zane lacks at first glance, the art historical hypothesis suggests that the clumsy posture of his hand clenched into a fist for no apparent reason can be explained if interpreted as grasping a stole, which may now be absorbed by the black of the toga, possibly due to ageing effects, thus representing a gesture of sociopolitical affiliation. Presumably to resolve the irritating isolation of the hand in the overall composition, a stick was freely added to the portrait in the middle of the 19th century,[39] which is still visible in photographs from the beginning of the 20th century and was subsequently interpreted as an original attribute – a restoration-related as well as art historical misunderstanding that was finally resolved in the course of the technological analysis of the painting carried out by project conservator Ronja Emmerich by means of an X-ray fluorescence analysis: in the lead distribution image (fig. 6), the *becchetto* is undoubtedly recognisable. Its differentiated rendering reveals the original quality of the painting, which has been affected not least by experimental restoration measures over the past 200 years.[40]

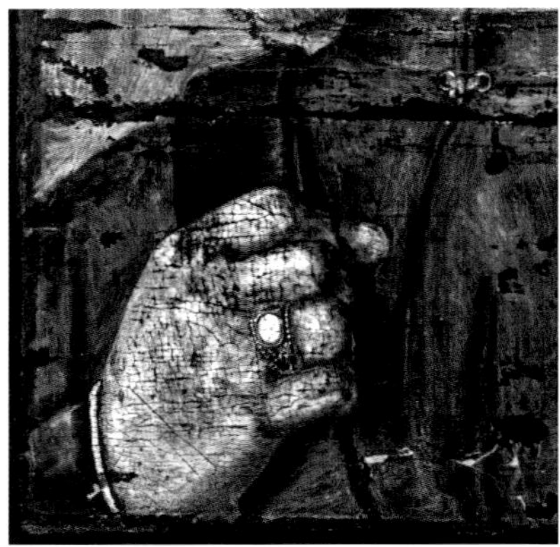

Fig. 6 Cat. 47 (detail), macro X-ray fluorescence scan, lead distribution image

Teacher and pupil: Giorgione (?), *Portrait of Giovanni Borgherini and Trifone Gabriele*, 1509/10

"Painted so diligently by Leonardo de Vinci", reads an entry in the inventory of the Old Schleißheim Palace from July 1637, describing a "mathematician in a blue, white-plumed coat, together with his disciple, who holds an astrolabe in his hand".[41] The unusual subject of the painting, which was first presented in the dressing room ("Abclaidzimmer") of Elector Maximilian I and then in the Kammergalerie of the Munich Residenz,[42] leaves no doubt that it is the double portrait exhibited since 2010 in a reconstruction of the historical hanging in the Grüne Galerie of the same residence (cat. 43). Dressed in a coat of luminous ultramarine blue with precious lynx fur, more like a *nobile* than an instructor of algebra, the mathematician fixes us with a penetrating gaze across his shoulder, conveying a correspondingly sharp intellect. The pupil at his side, with his soft brown curls, pale complexion and dark, serious eyes, corresponds entirely to the ideal of sensitive dreaminess characteristic of a *Giorgionismo* painting, which in turn emerged as the leitmotif of a new type of humanist painting on the topic of friendships such as the *Double Portrait* (1500–1502, Rome, Museo Nazionale del Palazzo di Venezia). He, too, is luxuriously dressed in a copper-green doublet under a stole that is draped around his shoulders with artful nonchalance in a display of painterly *sprezzatura*. The stole's rich spectrum of colours – from an orange-red that combines vibrant vermilion with glittering orpiment and the violet of a delicate red lake glaze to pale-blue indigo and olive-green *verderame*[43] – reflects the diverse palette of Venetian *vendecolori* (pigment merchants) and, at the same time, brings to mind the flamboyant fashion extravaganza of the Compagnie della Calza (associations of young *nobili* named after their colourful hosiery with a penchant for drama and spectacle). Oriental in appearance and sometimes associated in literature with the Jewish prayer shawl (tallit) in comparable cases,[44] here, however, it is most likely a kind of statement piece meant to emphasise the youthfulness of its wearer, since, as the chronicler Marin Sanudo (1466–1536) records,

Fig. 7 Cat. 43 (detail)

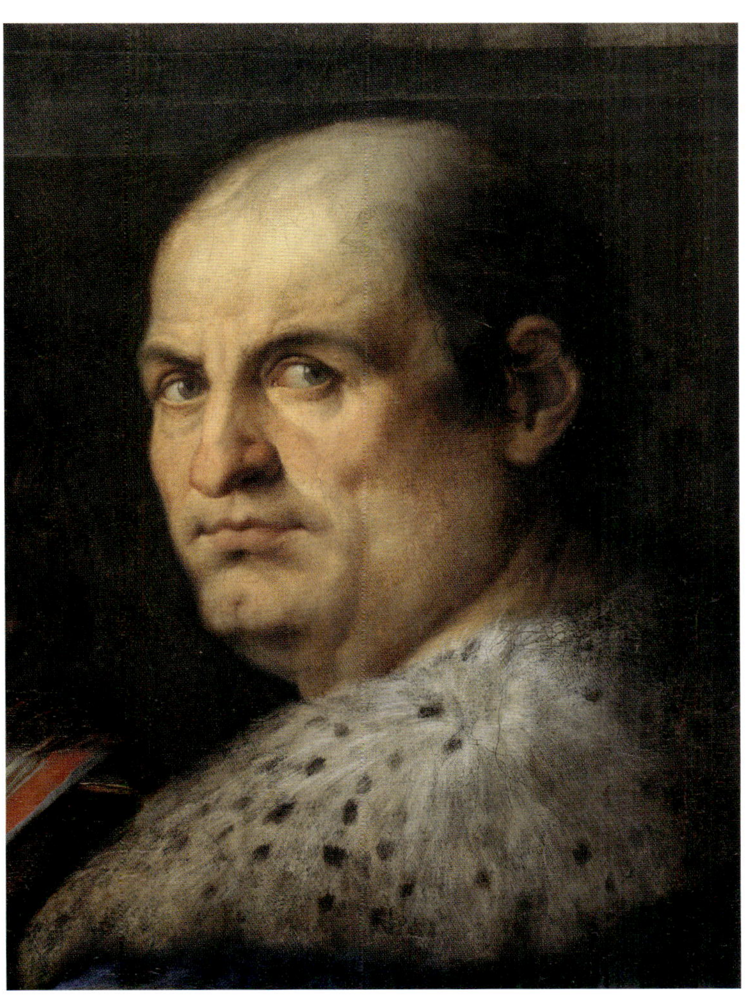

colourful striped clothing was considered a declared prerogative of adolescents ("da zovene") in Venice at that time.[45] Tilting his head to one side, the young *studioso* seems to have just been listening to the instructions of his teacher, who is shown demonstrating the possibilities of measuring heaven and earth with an astrolabe and a pair of compasses, attesting to the most fascinating discipline among the *artes liberales* of the period, whose appeal was reflected in the boom of astrological forecasts and cosmological theories in the early years of the 16th century, which artists such as Giorgione (1473/74–1510) and Giulio Campagnola (c. 1482–c. 1516) translated into a visual vocabulary for their humanist audience.

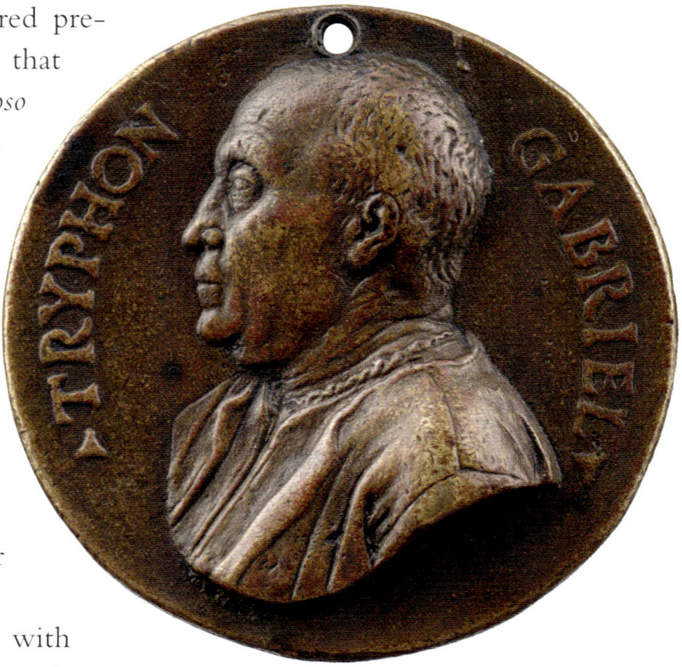

The historical association of the painting with Giorgione, or rather his circle or his successors, first documented in an inventory of 1745, has not stimulated any scholarly discussion until now.[46] It is all the more remarkable that the current studies and investigations within the framework of the Munich research project have led to new observations, which – like the arguments presented by Antonio Mazzotta in this catalogue[47] – in fact suggest an attribution to Giorgione.

The starting point for the following considerations is the proposal put forward here for discussion – namely, to recognise in the character of the mathematician (fig. 7),[48] devoid of any idealised rendering, the traits of the Venetian polymath Trifone Gabriele (1470–1549). Already stylised by his contemporaries as a "Nuovo Socrate", Trifone captivated an entire generation of young scholars, from Lodovico Ariosto and Pietro Aretino to Francesco Sansovino and Benedetto Varchi, in the contemplative seclusion of his villas in the Venetian countryside.[49] Among the publications of his students, which, in accordance with the classical concept of the oral transmission of knowledge, transmit Trifone's teaching activities, are a work on cosmology,[50] published by Giacomo Gabriele in 1545, and the treatise *La Spheretta del Clarissimo Messer Triphon Gabriele*,[51] a didactic discourse on the projection of the moving celestial sphere into a two-dimensional coordinate system – in short, on the principle of planispheric representation, which finds specific application precisely in the instrument of

Fig. 8 Danese Cattaneo, *Medal of Trifone Gabriele*, 1530–1549, New York, The Frick Collection

the astrolabe. However, it is not only the intellectual profile of the stargazing master that can be associated with the mathematician in the Munich painting; his striking features with a double chin and dimples, a prominent nose and a high, bald forehead are also consistent with his appearance as recorded in a portrait medal by Danese Cattaneo (c. 1510–1572; fig. 8).[52] Somewhat younger, but already with the unmistakable physiognomy, Trifone is also encountered in an engraving from Claude Pernet's *Illustrissimorum [...] virorum icones* (fig. 9)[53] – and in the role of the humanist man of letters perhaps even in the portrait of a laurel-wreathed poet with a muse, last attributed to Domenico Capriolo (c. 1520, Vienna, Kunsthistorisches Museum).

If one accepts this identification, it seems natural to associate the Munich painting with a work by Giorgione documented as early as 1568 by Vasari in his second edition of *The Lives*, which in art historical literature since 1926 has been repeatedly identified with a double portrait in the National Gallery of Art in Washington, D.C. (fig. 10), and whose attribution is, however, very controversial:[54] the portrait of the young Giovanni Borgherini with his teacher from Venice, which Vasari saw in the house of the sons of the very same Giovanni Borgherini in Florence.[55] In this point, the indications derived from the historical context discussed here meet the arguments of stylistic analysis and connoisseurship that lead Antonio Mazzotta along different lines to the same conclusion based on the Vasari passage. For Giovanni Borgherini,[56] born in 1496, was indeed one of Trifone Gabriele's pupils. In order to prove their contact, it is not necessary – as has been done time and again in literature on the painting in Washington – to point out a presumed stay in Venice by Giovanni from 1504 onwards, for which there is de facto no documentary evidence; instead, the Borgherini family's close ties to Venice are demonstrated not only by the business connections of the Florentine banking dynasty to the lagoon city, or the exchange of letters between the Borgherini brothers Giovanni and Pierfrancesco and the intellectual circle around Pietro Bembo,[57] but also by Donato Giannotti's *Libro de la Republica de Vinitiani*, written from 1526 onwards, which enacts a dialogue between Trifone as teacher and Giovanni as pupil in a literary form.[58] Assuming Giorgione's

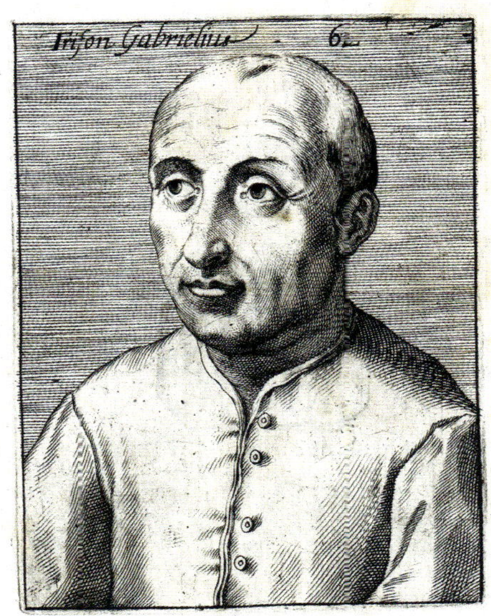

Fig. 9 Unknown engraver, *Bust of Trifone Gabriele* (from: Claude Pernet, *Illustrissimorum, omnique virtutis, et scientiarum laude praestantissimorv. virorum icones*, Rome, 1625, no. 62)

authorship as per Vasari, the *terminus ante quem* for the creation of the Borgherini painting is the year of the artist's death – 1510: if the painting were dated as late as possible, the adolescent Giovanni would thus be portrayed at the age of 14 to 15, and Trifone, who, according to the Pernet engraving (fig. 9), was already largely bald in his younger years, at the age of around 40. While the age and appearance of the young teacher portrayed in the painting in Washington contradict all attempts made so far to identify him with a personage in Borgherini's historical environment,[59] both these aspects can be readily reconciled in the Munich painting on the premise that it dates from 1509/10.[60]

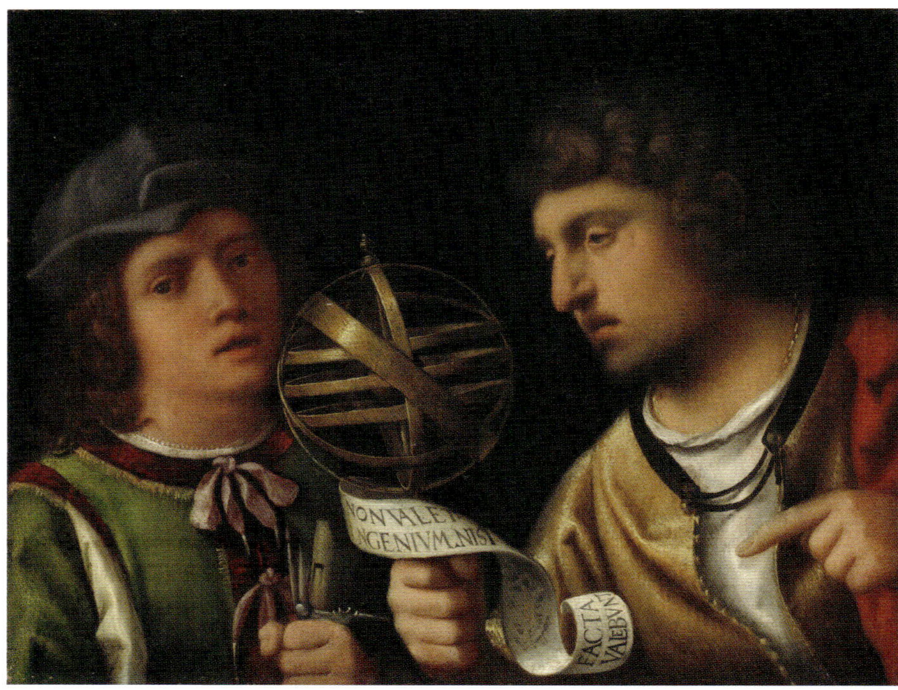

Fig. 10 Giorgione's circle, *Portrait of a Teacher and His Pupil*, c. 1510 (?), Washington, D.C., National Gallery of Art

The indications that the Munich painting could actually be the portrait of the young Giovanni Borgherini in the company of his famous teacher, mentioned by Vasari, can be further consolidated with a view to the patronage of Salvi Borgherini (1436–c. 1515) and his sons. For the representative decoration of their palazzo in the Borgo Santi Apostoli, the Borgherini family engaged artists such as Pontormo, Granacci, Bacchiacca and Andrea del Sarto (1486–1530). The latter in particular was not only one of the first Florentines to take up the innovative *ritratto di spalla*.[61] One of his portrait studies from around 1520 (fig. 11)[62] even begs the question as to whether he did, indeed, have Trifone's striking visage in mind here with the sanguine (red chalk) in hand. With the cursorily sketched shoulder section, he initially seems to adopt the postural motif from Giorgione's painting, only to deliberately vary it in the turn of the head, in keeping with his artistic practice: for, as his former pupil Vasari reports, del Sarto's own drawings served less for compositional preparation than "as memoranda of what he had seen",[63] while comparable studies based on known templates also prove that, when drawing, he was interested not in a detailed survey but in an artistic engagement with the object of study. In this sense, the portrait study can serve as another argument in favour of the Munich painting possibly being in Florence around 1520. Moreover, in view of the fact that Giovanni's sons (named by Vasari as the owners of the Borgherini painting) already removed individual works from the configurational context[64] for sale in the last decades of the 16th century,[65] a Florentine provenance for the double portrait is quite conceivable. The appreciation of the painting expressed in the Schleißheim inventory of 1637 reflects the efforts of the Wittelsbach dukes to expand their collection with high-calibre Italian masterpieces,[66] for which the transalpine art trade, stimulated in these years by the liquidation of estates and collections, offered the best conditions. The central players in this market were professional art agents such as Jacopo Strada (1507–1588; cf. cat. 84), whose expertise and negotiating skills were just as much in demand at the imperial courts of Maximilian II in Vienna and Rudolf II in Prague as at the residences of Dresden and Munich. From 1567 onwards, he advised the Bavarian Duke Albrecht V on the conception of the Antiquarium in the Munich Residenz, for which he was able to acquire Andrea Loredan's collection of antique sculptures and coins in Venice – a success he did not achieve for Gabriele Vendramin's prominent collection despite tough negotiations. At the same time, Strada repeatedly acquired works of art or entire collections without being commissioned to do so, for which he had offer lists drawn up in multiple copies in order to present them to his competing clients north of the Alps. Testimony to this strategy is a list of "delightful canvases by skilled painters from Venice and elsewhere in Italy, all painted in oil" ("gemalte[n] Lustigen Tiecher[n] vonn kunstreichen Mallern zu Venedig und sonst in Italia gemacht, alle von Oel Farbenn")[67] dating from the mid-1570s, which has been preserved in a loose volume of collection correspondence in Munich. In addition to 57 predominantly contemporary art objects, this list also includes "1 old painting made by Giorgon de Castel

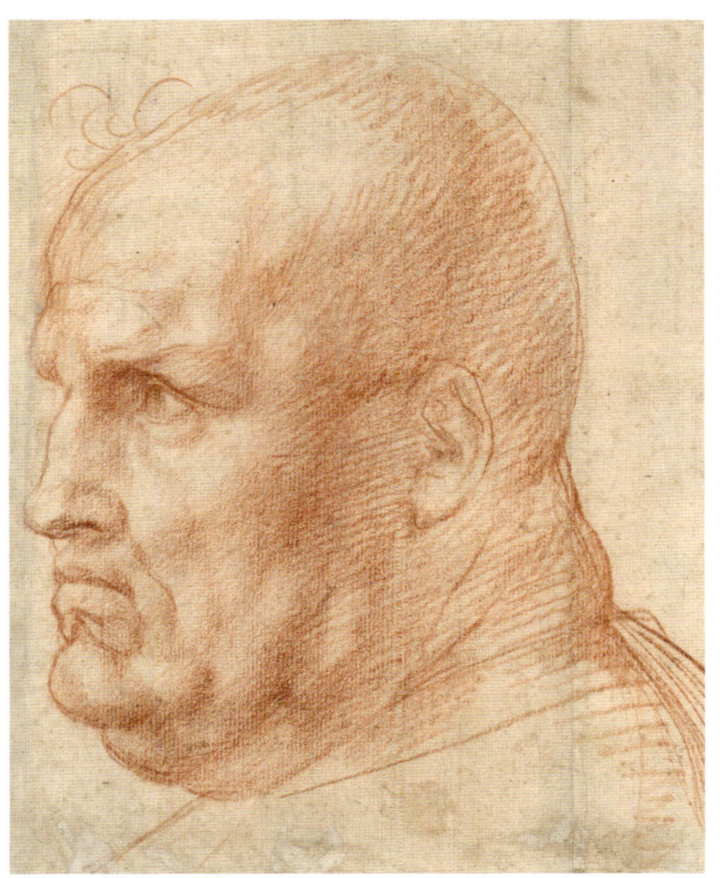

Fig. 11 Andrea del Sarto, *Study of Two Heads* (cetail), c. 1520, Berlin, Staatliche Museen, Kupferstichkabinett

Francho with two figures" ("1 alt Quatro von Giorgion de Castel Francho gemacht, mitt 2 figuren") – a description that undoubtedly applies to the Munich painting. By the hand of Jacopo Strada, and thus preceding the retrospective flood of attributions that began with the reception of Giorgione in the seicento, this document might provide further circumstantial evidence for the hypothesis put forward here. Last but not least, such an early transfer of the painting to Munich would also explain why the painting so prominently described by Vasari, unlike other Borgherini-owned works, is no longer mentioned in Florence from the late 16th century onwards.[68]

Since Vasari's knowledge of Giorgione's oeuvre was frequently second-hand and often derived from contradictory sources,[69] the identification of the Munich painting with the portrait of Giovanni Borgherini and his teacher, as thematised by him, does not necessarily permit the inverse conclusion that it is an authentic work by Giorgione. However, unlike in Venice, where Giorgione's paintings were mostly hidden behind the walls of private palazzi, Vasari in Florence had direct access to the Borgherini collection, about whose art and family affairs he shows himself to be well-informed in other biographies of the *Lives*, too (cf. for example, those of Bacchiacca, Pontormo and Baccio d'Angnolo). Indeed, the dapples of colour and the nuanced shading[70] he emphasises are strikingly matched by the colouristic brilliance and subtle *sfumato* of the Munich painting, but even quite independently of Vasari's testimony, the quality and characteristics of the painting are strong arguments for attributing it to Giorgione. In a direct juxtaposition with the *Portrait of a Young Man* (cat. 40) in particular, impressive parallels can be discerned beyond the formal exploration of the innovative shoulder view: both portraits combine the painterly care of detailed, yet softly nuanced rendering with a psychological presence that lends Giorgione's late *testoni*[71] their expressive power.

The stylistic arguments, which are per se controversial in any discussion about Giorgione, are decisively supported by the results of the technological analysis, on the basis of which project conservator Anneliese Földes was able to reconstruct the genesis of the painting from the Munich Residenz, which is multilayered in the literal sense of the word. Underneath the depiction visible today are at least two completely different earlier compositions: a portrait of a young man, visible in the X-ray image, who casts his gaze over his shoulder in a posture comparable to that in the controversial Giorgionesque *Giovinetto* from the Hermitage in St Petersburg (1512); and below this, rotated by 90 degrees and made visible by means of X-ray fluorescence analysis taken from the reverse, an Arcadian assemblage with a female nude and a figure presumably playing music in a landscape interspersed with foliage and architectural fragments in a horizontal format – motifs that correspond directly to Giorgione's pastoral pictorial inventions documented in the illustrated inventory of the Venetian collector Andrea Vendramin (1627).[72] The complexity of the paint layer structure attests to an experimental working process in which new ideas developed from and over old *invenzioni*. On the one hand, Giorgione reused forms created at an earlier time for new compositions and, on the other hand, even sections worked out in great painterly detail were open to revision at any time: for example, a sleeve pattern reminiscent of Islamic textiles, whose opulence may not have suited a scholar like Trifone Gabriele,[73] praised by contemporaries for his modesty, and which was perhaps therefore covered with the plain brown of a scholar's robe.[74] Even if the multiple use of painting supports was a widespread practice in Venetian painting of the cinquecento, this method of working is typical for Giorgione in its otherwise rare extent of radical intransigence. To what degree the material and technical parallels to secure works by his hand are further substantiated will be shown by the currently ongoing technological analyses and scientific investigations, the results of which will be presented in a separate publication and will also find their way into the aforementioned final publication of the research project.

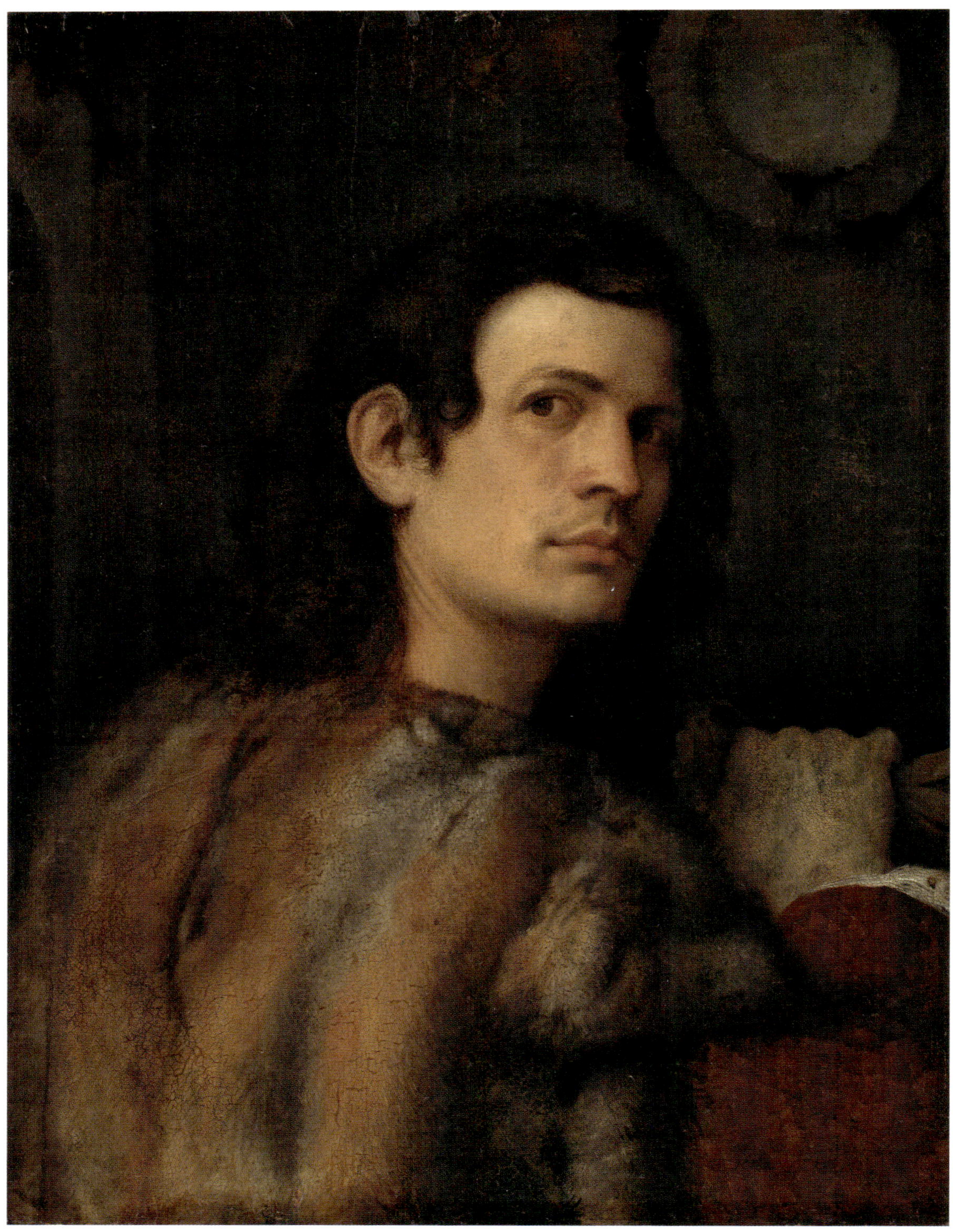

40 Giorgione, *Portrait of a Young Man*, c. 1505/10, Munich, Bayerische Staatsgemäldesammlungen, Alte Pinakothek

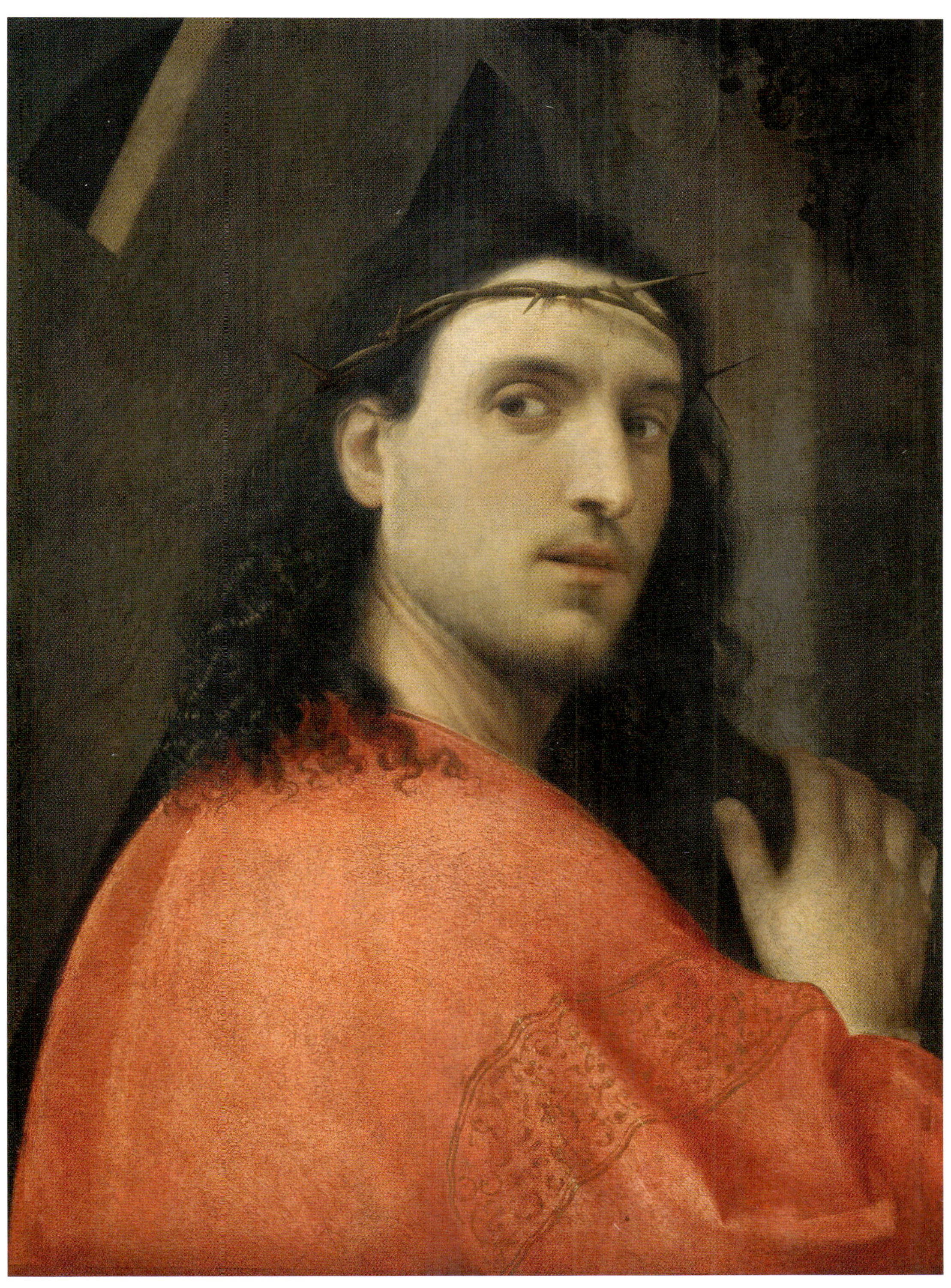

41 Venetian, *Christ Carrying the Cross*, c. 1515, Vienna, Kunsthistorisches Museum

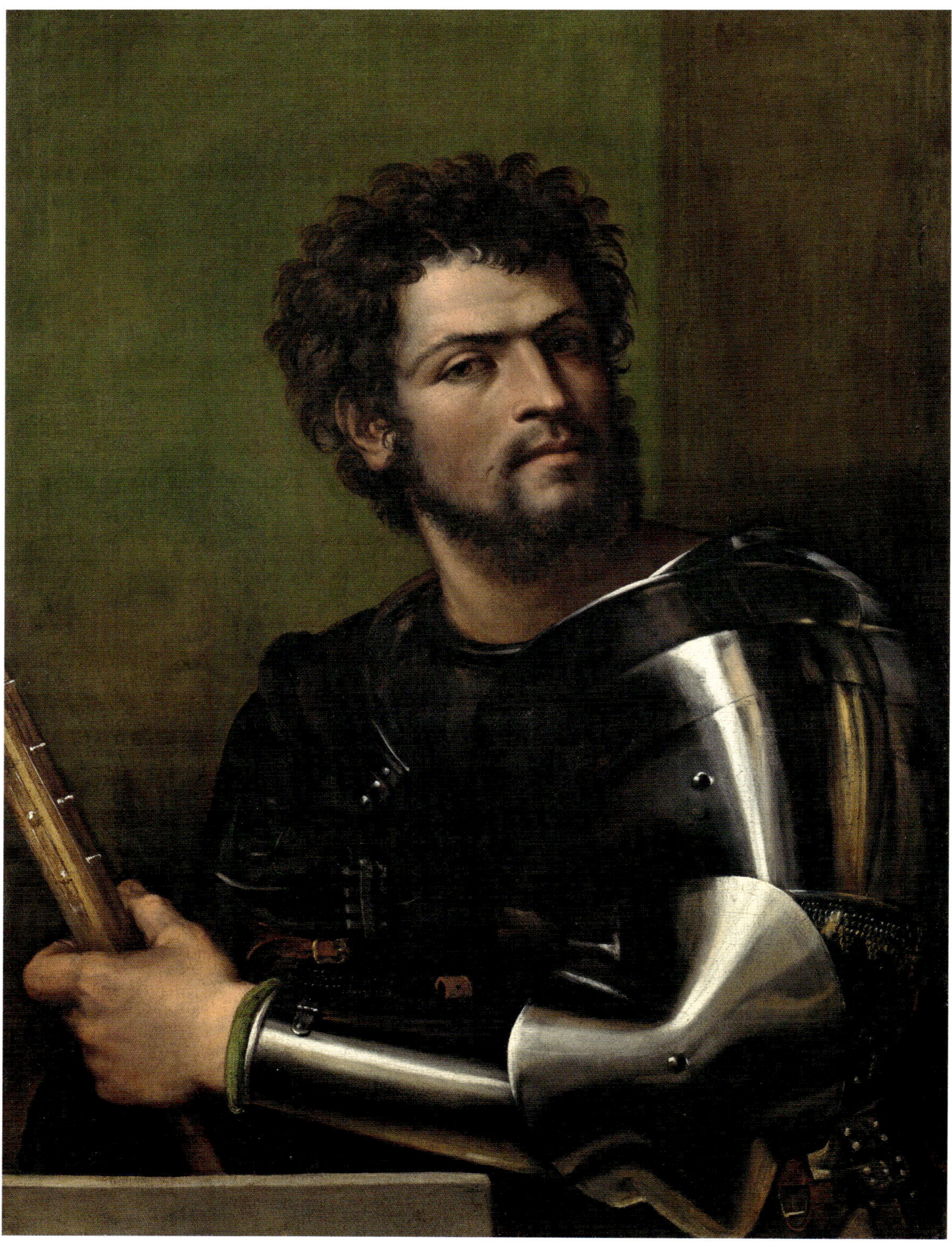

42 Sebastiano del Piombo, *Portrait of a Man in Armour*, c. 1512, Hartford, CT, Wadsworth Atheneum Museum of Art

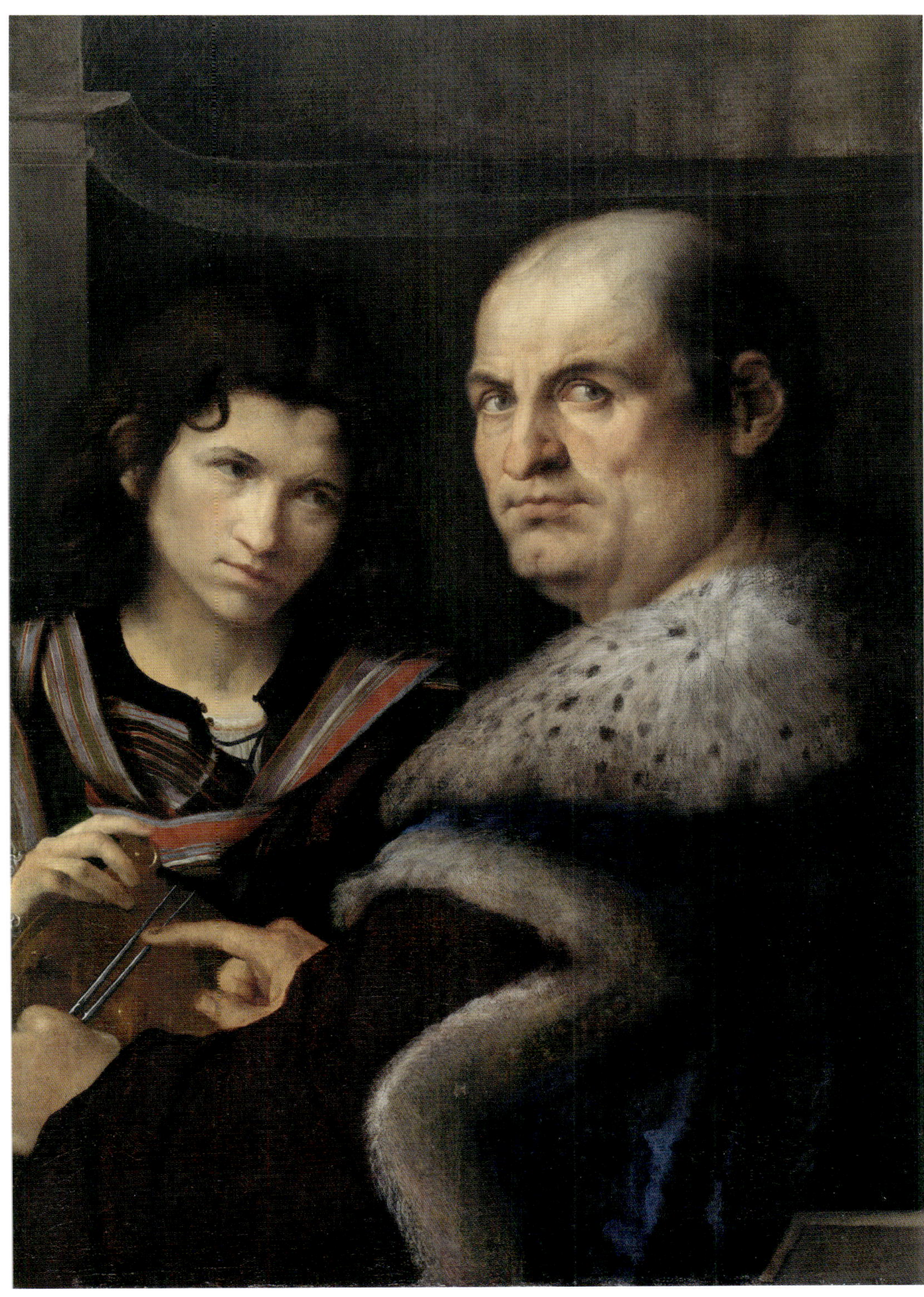

43 Giorgione (?), *Portrait of Giovanni Borgherini and Trifone Gabriele*, 1509/10, Munich, Bayerische Staatsgemäldesammlungen, Alte Pinakothek

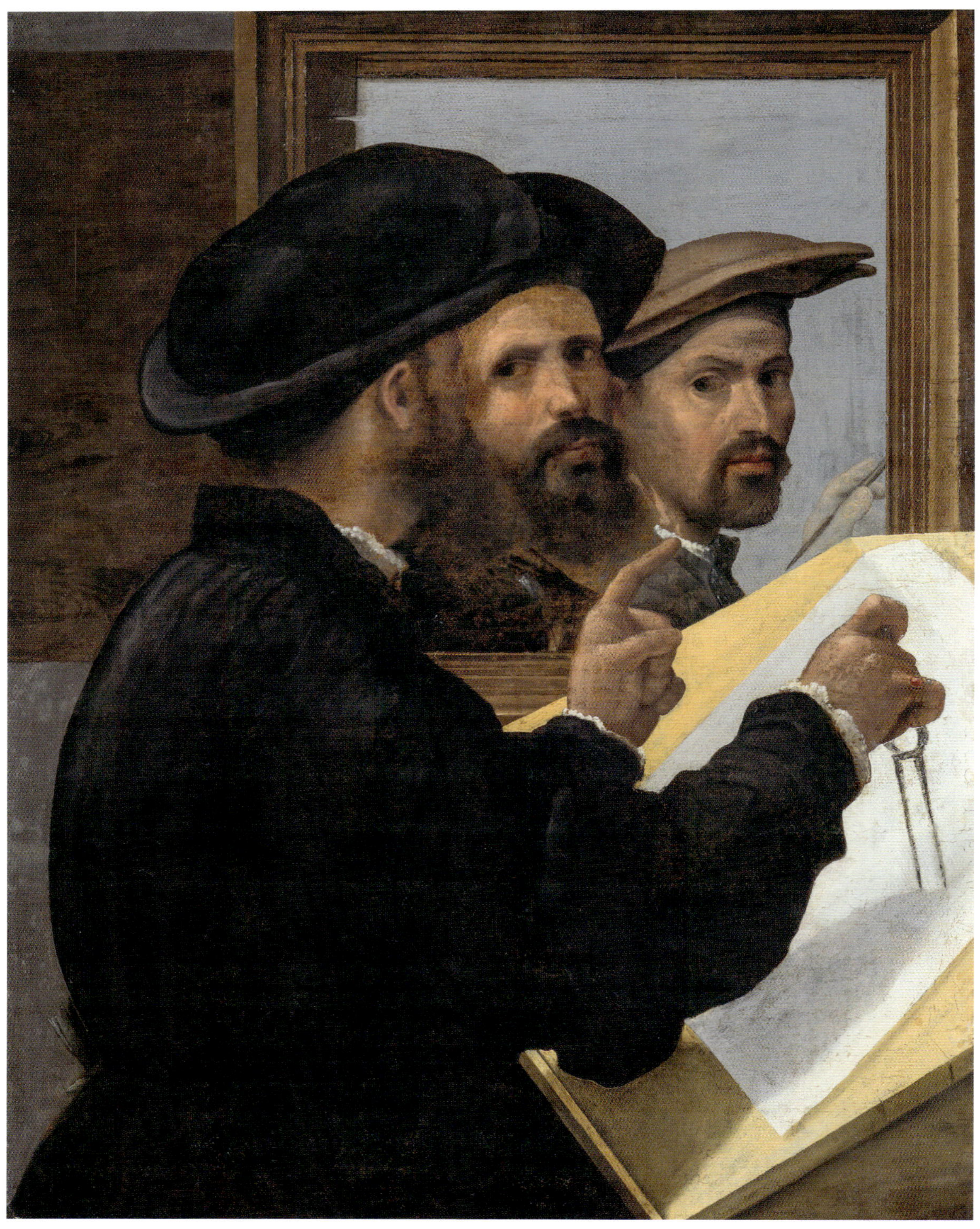

44 Bernardino Licinio, attribution, *Artist Friends in the Mirror (Self-Portrait with Sebastiano Serlio)*, c. 1530, Würzburg, Martin von Wagner-Museum

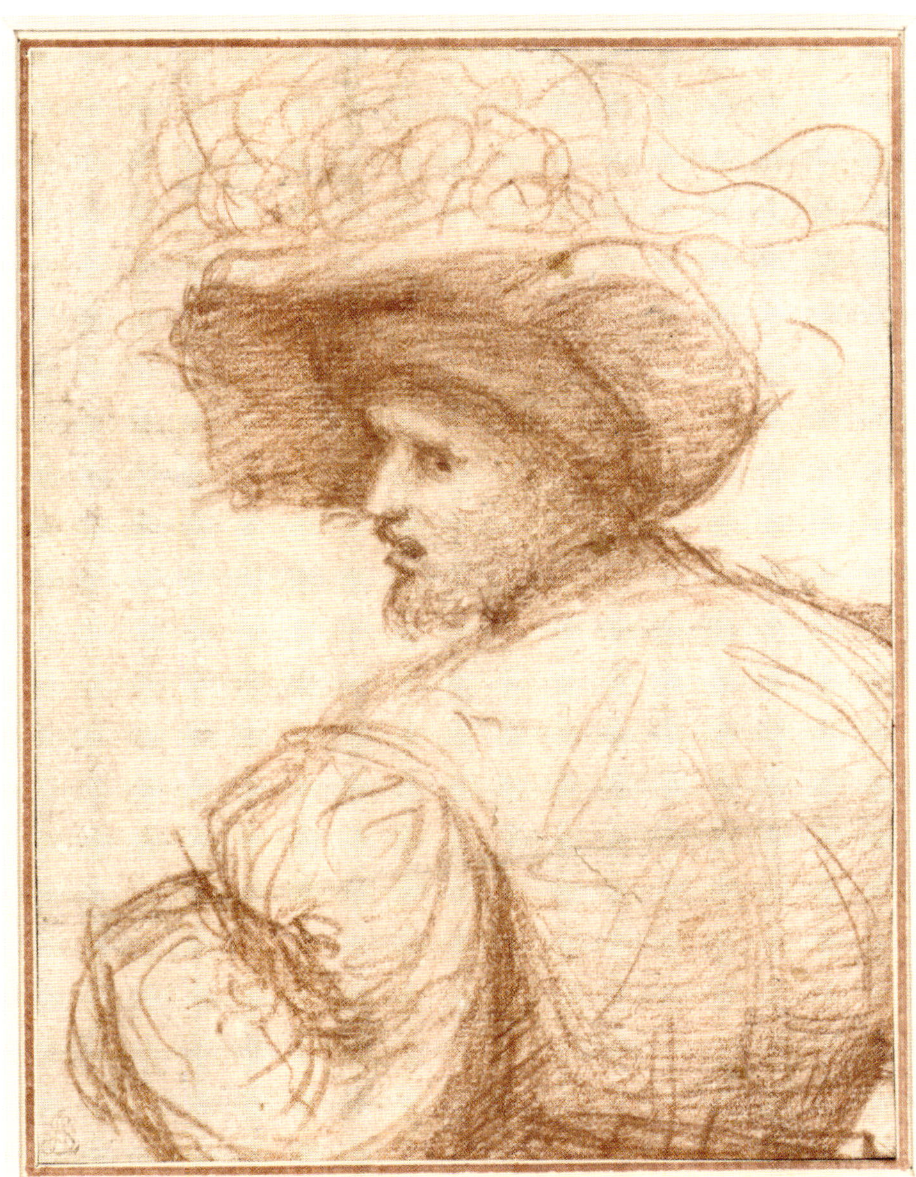

45 Pordenone, *Half Figure of a Man with Feather Hat*, 1520/21, Vienna, Albertina

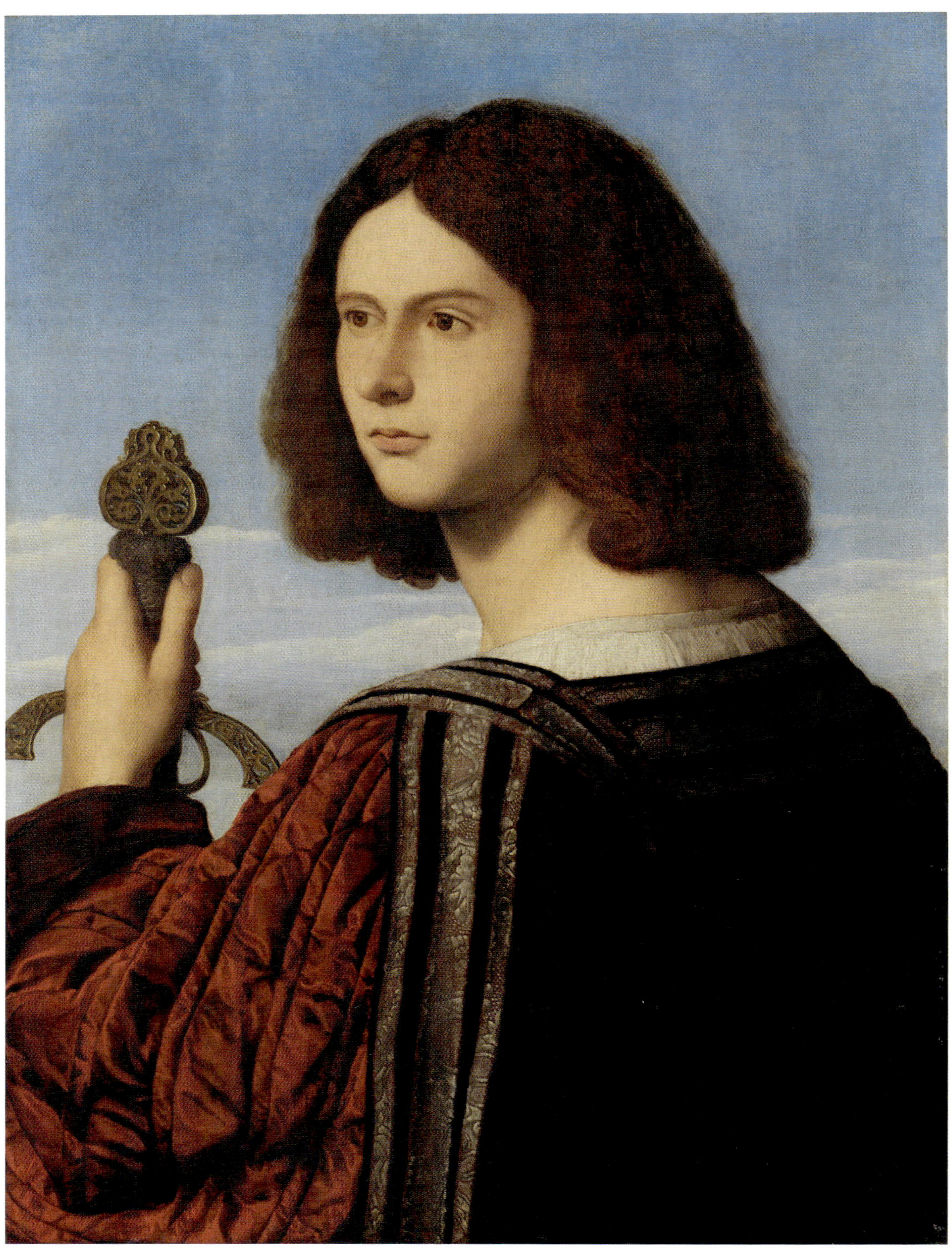

46 Vincenzo Catena, attribution, *Portrait of Francesco Maria della Rovere*, c. 1518, Bergamo, Accademia Carrara

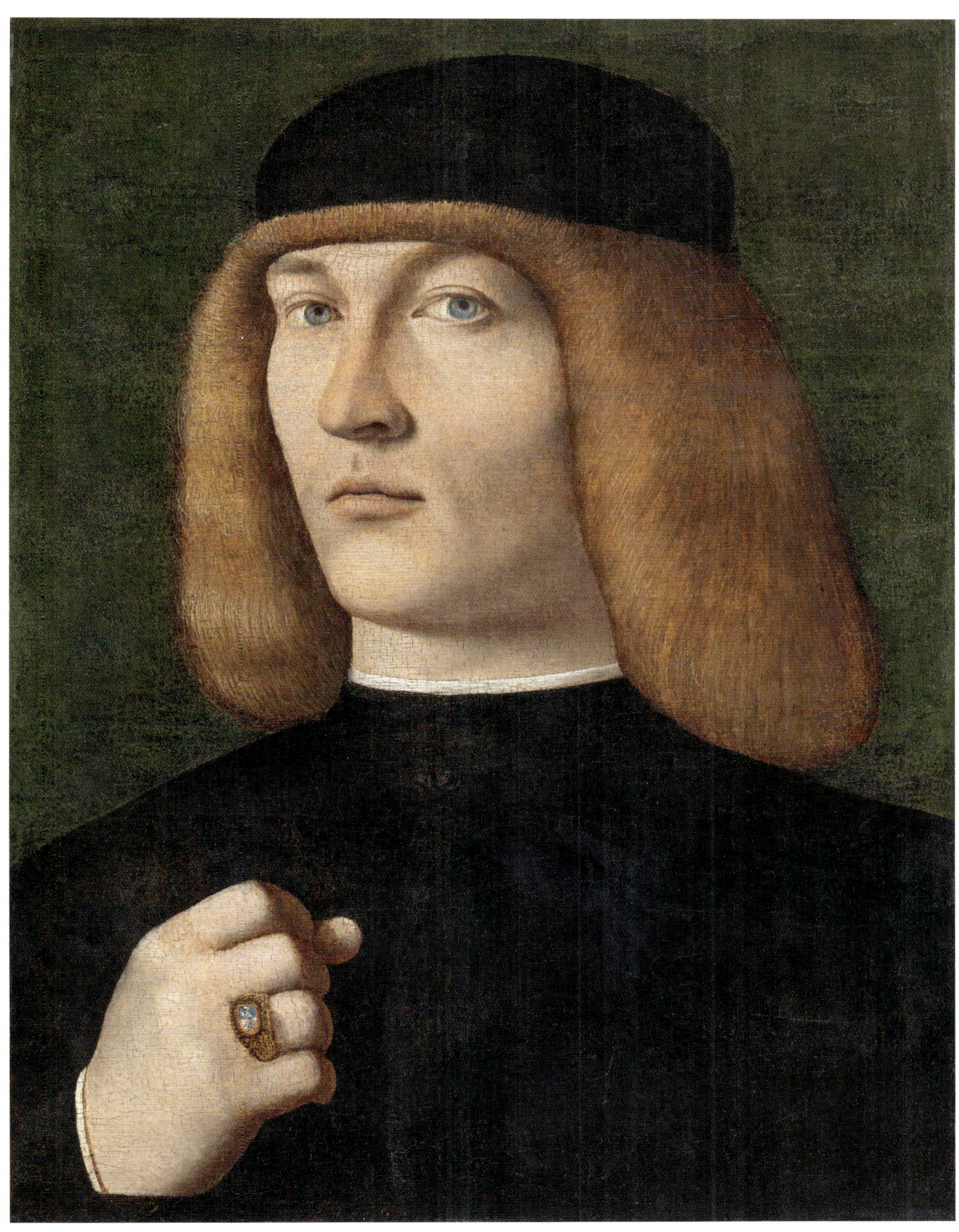

47 Bartolomeo Veneto, *Portrait of a Young Man from the Zane Family*, c. 1505, Munich, Bayerische Staatsgemäldesammlungen, Alte Pinakothek

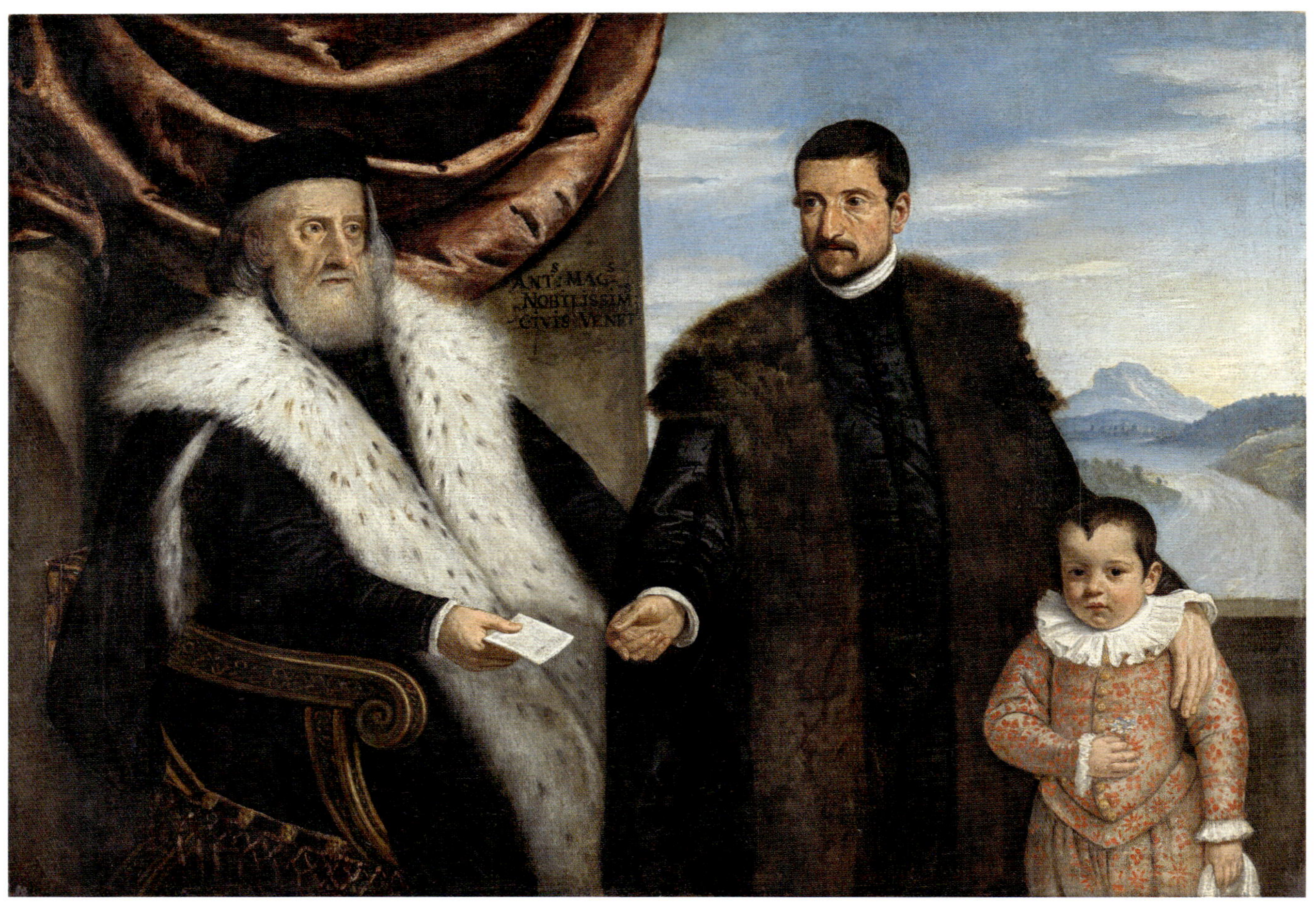

48 Jacopo Tintoretto and Workshop, *Portrait of the Maggi Family*, c. 1575, Munich, Bayerische Staatsgemäldesammlungen, Alte Pinakothek

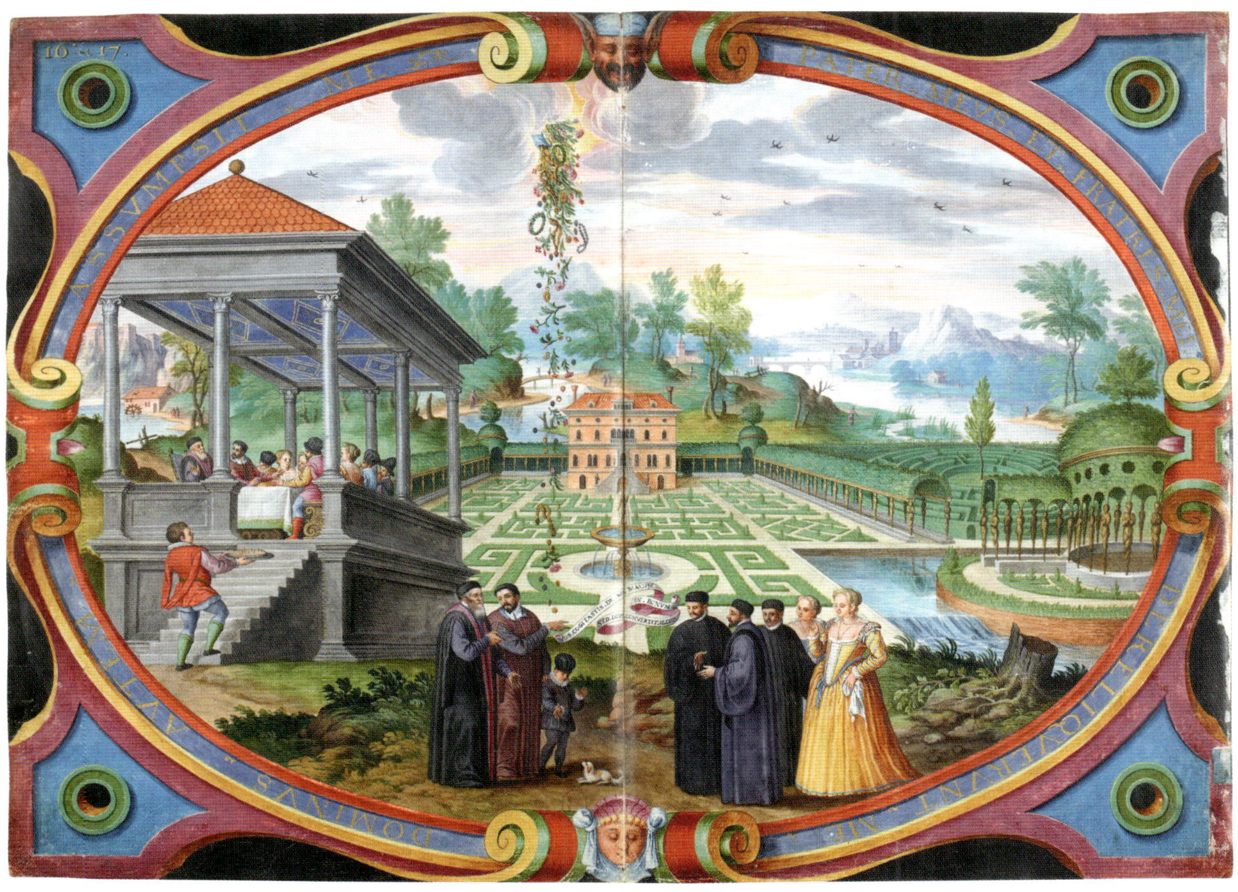

49 Unknown miniaturist, *Reunion of the Maggi Family*, from: *Les voyages de Charles Magius* (Codex Maggi), Venice, 1578, Paris, Bibliothèque nationale de France, Département estampes et photographie, miniatures 16–17

Eros and vaghezza

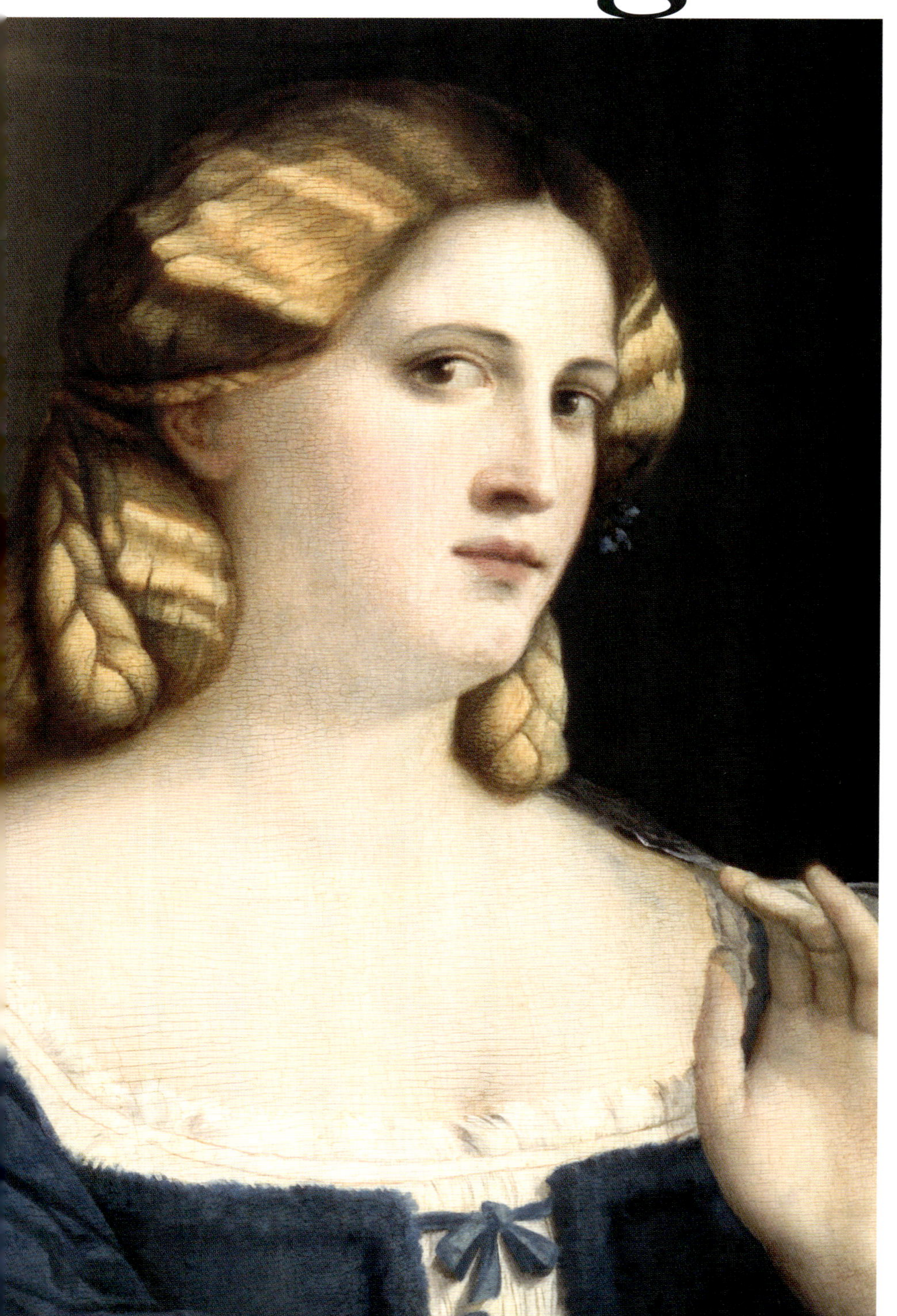

Female portraits and the lyrical image of man in Venetian *Giorgionismo*

THERESA GATARSKI

Tilting her head to one side, she looks out of the picture with dark, alert eyes (cat. 51). Her gaze is expressive yet difficult to decipher. Is it sceptical or flirtatious? Pensive or expectant? Her neatly parted black hair is covered and kept in place by a sweeping hairnet. In contrast to this rather restrained rendition, her wide-cut bodice is decorated with opulent gold embroidery, revealing the shoulders and cleavage. The heavy silk fabric and the elaborately draped, voluminous sleeves juxtapose charmingly with the smooth skin of her décolleté. Her left-hand fingers rest on an open music book, while her right-hand fingers elegantly spread to touch her breast and point towards the heart. The haptic representation of the textures gives the portrayed figure a vivid presence, while the intimacy suggested by the narrow crop of the image and the dark background make the young woman seem close enough to touch. The depiction appeals to our senses as viewers on several levels: the fingers on the dress and the musical score stimulate the sense of touch, while the open music book gives the impression of the protagonist just having interrupted her singing, which still reverberates in our imagination, thus also addressing our sense of hearing.

In contrast to the blonde *belle donne* by Titian (c. 1488/90–1576), Palma il Vecchio (c. 1480–1528) or Paris Bordone (1500–1571), which are always idealised according to a similar pattern, the young lady portrayed by Bernardino Licinio (c. 1485–after 1565/before 1565) evokes the impression of facing an actual personage. In fact, however, her identity cannot be determined. Single representations of individual women are comparatively rare in Serenissima portrait painting. Instead, the female portrait in the cinquecento is in its idealisation, much more than its male counterpart, a product of wishful imagination and stands in clear contrast to the historical reality of women's lives in the patriarchal Venetian society of the time, which was characterised by stereotypical role attributions. The epitome of Venetian portraits of women are the already mentioned *belle donne*: erotic half-length portraits of young women who correspond to the ideal of beauty of the 16th century but whose individuality is largely negated. Lorenzo Lotto's (c. 1480–1556) *Portrait of a Woman* from Dijon (cat. 50) is one of the exceptions. Even if the portrayed woman cannot be clearly identified, the non-idealised features unquestionably belong to a real person. She wears a black bodice with attached sleeves, whose slits allow the *camicia* (vest) to bulge out voluminously. Her wide neckline is covered by a *fazzuolo* and her blond hair overlaid by a delicate bonnet. The family portraits, too, such as the *Portrait of Giovanni della Volta with his Wife and Children* (cat. 69), also by Lotto, or Licinio's *Portrait of the Family of the Artist's Brother Arrigo Licinio* (cat. 68), also paint a different image of women, depicting the sitters not as representatives of an idealised femininity, but as socially established wives whose self-confident pose indicates their dominance in the sphere of domestic family life assigned to them.

Fig. 1 Giorgione, *Laura*, 1506, Vienna, Kunsthistorisches Museum

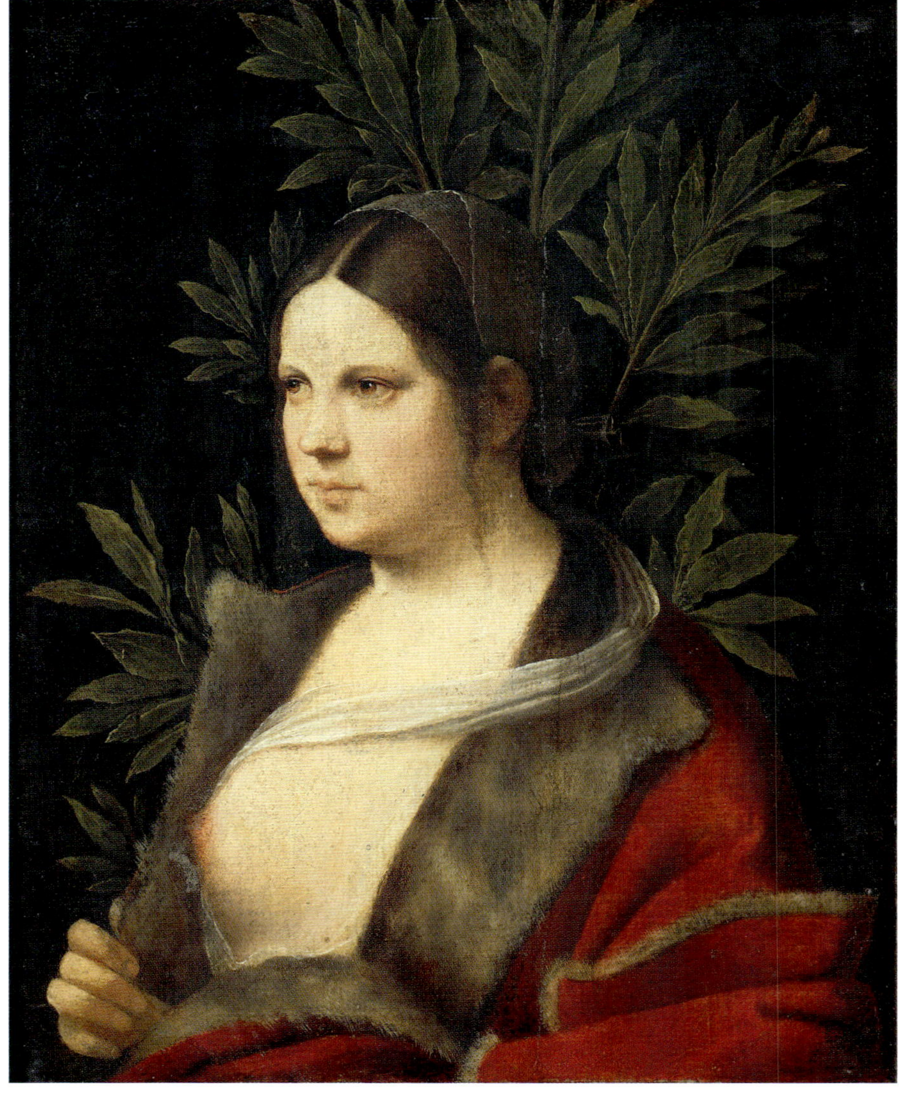

When compared with Lotto's portrait from Dijon (cat. 50), it is striking how strongly even Palma il Vecchio's *Portrait of a Young Woman in Blue Dress with Fan* (cat. 52) is idealised, resembling the lifelike image of a young Venetian woman on account of her alert gaze, the elaborately braided hairstyle and the detailed, colourful gown. In her right hand she holds a fan, while her left hand lifts the delicate veil that lies over her shoulders. Whether the sitter is a 'product' of the artist's imagination or a real person, albeit strongly idealised, must remain open. The twin rings on her right hand, used as an engagement ring, in conjunction with her fingers elegantly splayed in a V-shape, which together with the violet in her hair can be read as a sign of virginity, suggest that the sitter is a young Venetian bride. The V-gesture appears in a large number of ideal female portraits from this period, including Licinio's work mentioned at the beginning (cat. 51). Depending on the context, it refers not only to virginity, but also to *virtus* (virtue) or Venus, the goddess of love, and in this context can also indicate the loss of virginity. In any case, the gesture serves as a reference to the sitter's inner beauty which is matched by her outward pulchritude, according to the common poetic topos of *virtutem forma decorat* ("beauty adorns virtue").

Belle donne in painting and literature

The countless half-length *belle donne* portraits represent a genre of painting that emerged in the first decade of the 16th century and quickly became a speciality of Venetian painting. As in other genres, it was Giorgione (1473/74–1510) who provided the template with his *Laura* (fig. 1). Titian and Palma il Vecchio then standardised the appearance of the *belle* and spread the theme of the ideally beautiful, erotic woman in many variations. Although idealised female portraits are not an exclusively Venetian phenomenon, the supposed individuality and closeness to life of the *belle veneziane* is unique. Sometimes they are opulently dressed and elaborately coiffed like wealthy Venetian women (cat. 51, 52, 59), at other times shown in undergarments with their hair down and more or less undressed (cat. 53, 57, 58, 60, 63), giving them the appearance of nymphs from ancient mythology. The question of their identity is much discussed and has not yet been clarified. Are we looking at idealised portraits of real women or creations of pure artistic imagination? Are they courtesan portraits or bridal images? Or is the general discourse on ideal beauty thematised here using the example of the female portrait?

The growing reception of ancient Platonism in the course of the 15th century was accompanied by an increasing interest in beauty – a quality that was attributed first and foremost to women, along with young men. Questions about the nature and qualities of beauty are frequently raised in the discourses of the 16th century, as is evident by writings such as Agnolo Firenzuola's successful and widely received *Dialogo delle bellezze delle donne* (1548). It draws up a catalogue of criteria for the evaluation of the female body, defining the ideal proportionality of individual body parts on the basis of vase forms and discussing the essence of beauty, which – from a Neoplatonic perspective – could guide the soul to contemplation and, through the latter, awaken the longing for heavenly things, since the beauty of the woman is ultimately a reflection of divine beauty. In doing so, Firenzuola adopts a stance that Marsilio Ficino had already advocated in *De amore* (1484). In the fifth book of his work, conceived as a commentary on Plato's *Symposium* dialogue, the Florentine humanist explains how inner beauty as an expression of divine truth and how goodness also affects the outer form of the body. Conversely, the sight of beauty can also lead to the cognition of the good and the divine. According to Ficino, the driving force in this process is Eros, which, in accordance with the Platonic theory, is attracted to beauty and initially kindled by the sensual, while subsequently devoting itself, in a steady ascent, to the world of the spiritual and finally turning to the divine.

According to this model, it is Eros – which in the Platonic understanding goes beyond the sexualised Eros principle of psychoanalysis and stands for yearning desire per se – that determines the dynamics of all human existence. Based on this, Ficino even defines thinking as an erotic process. In Renaissance humanism, this holistic concept of Eros, in interaction with comparable ideas from Christian mysticism, led to a conception of man that could be defined as an erotic anthropology. A similar image of man as a yearning creature can also be found in Petrarchism. This stylistic form of love poetry, which goes back to Francesco Petrarch (1304–1374), dominated the lyrical culture of the early cinquecento. Petrarchism's basic condition is a yearning for the lost: a lost beloved or the lost paradise. In Petrarch's poetry, the painful experience of longing (*desio*) leads to a sublimation in the medium of art and, in this way, finally to the experience of the divine. This new dimension of the perception of the self as a desiring subject, combined with a rediscovery of ancient sensuality, led to an eroticisation of all pictorial themes in the course of the 16th century. A new, central quality criterion for painting was derived from the *paragone* (competition) with poetry: its ability to trigger the affects of love, longing and desire in the viewer. Beauty, too, was therefore primarily defined by its erotic potential.

The ideal woman

In his *Dialogo*, Firenzuola enacts the female body as an object of male contemplation, eroticises individual body parts such as the mouth and breasts and, in addition to perfect proportions, also provides criteria for the ideal shape and colouring of the female body parts: white and red for the cheeks, black for the eyelashes, red for the lips and blond for the hair, with a smooth forehead, gently curved brows, shapely cheeks and starry eyes. With these particulars, he adopts the canon of beauty that goes back to Petrarch's love poetry and also underlies the Venetian *belle donne*. The women of the lagoon city invested a great deal to conform to this aesthetic dictate. In the 16th century, countless "books of secrets" circulated with various recipes to enhance natural beauty and, for example, to bleach the hair or improve the colour of the face. The procedure of bleaching the hair, which Cesare Vecellio documented and described in detail in his costume book *De gli habiti antichi, et moderni di diverse parti del mondo libri due* (1590), became particularly well known.

In the face of the transience and inevitable imperfection of earthly beauty, Firenzuola concludes that the ideal image he has drawn cannot ultimately correspond to a natural body, but only to an artfully created composite body ("chimera"), which is to be assembled from the most beautiful body parts of various women. According to him, an ideally beautiful woman can thus only be a product of creative imagination, which was already thematised in ancient artists' anecdotes such as the legend of Zeuxis and the maidens of Croton handed down by Pliny the Elder (*Naturalis historia*, vol. XXXV, section 64). It can therefore be assumed that the Venetian *belle* are in most cases not faithful depictions of real women but composite images of the characteristics of ideal beauty, and were created as a contribution to an explicit *paragone* between painting and poetry centred around the creation of the most ideal images of desirable women.

Desirable portraits

Facing the unmistakable individuality and diversity of the Venetian *belle*, it must nevertheless be assumed that this type of portrait is based on real female models that were overlaid with idealising features and varied anew. Titian's *belle donne* in particular appear to be a perfect fusion of individuality and the beauty ideal. Thus, the theory persists that specific women served as models for him, such as the educated and respected Venetian courtesan Angela del Moro. It is said that she lent her face to his *La Bella* from Florence (fig. 2) as well as to the erotic,

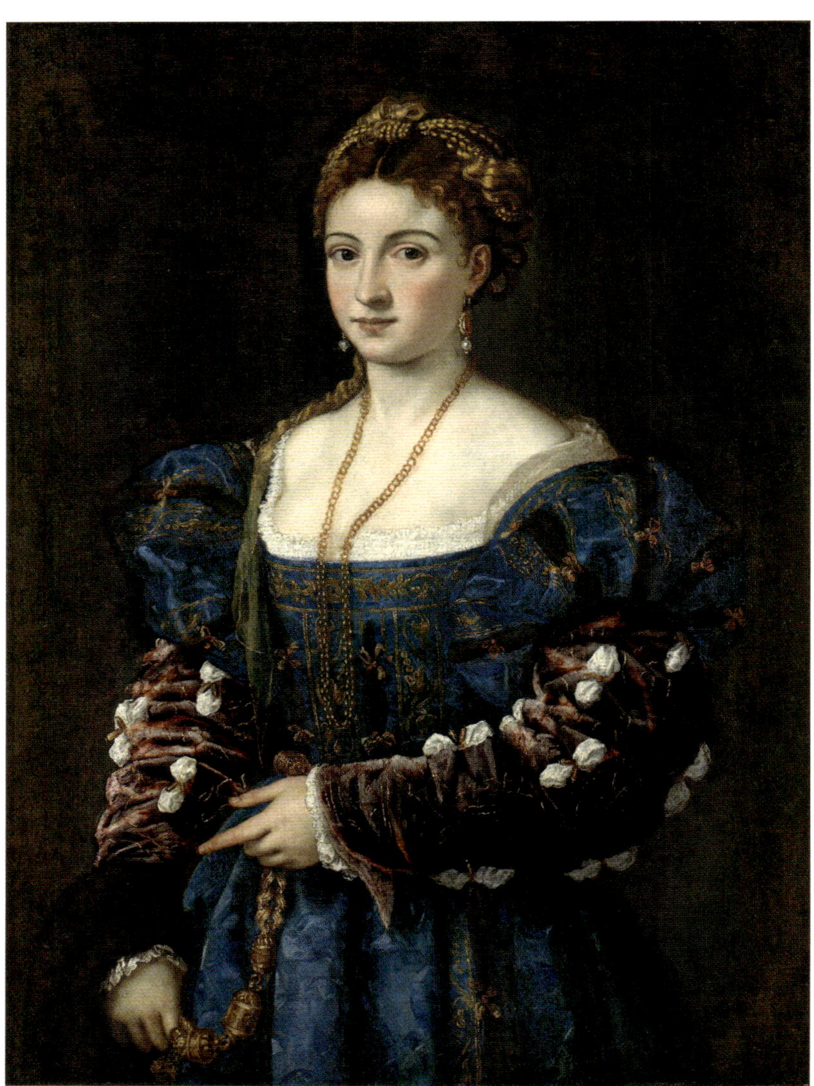

Fig. 2 Titian, *La Bella*, c. 1536, Florence, Palazzo Pitti, Galleria Palatina

permissive variants derived from it, including *Girl in a Fur* (c. 1536, Vienna, Kunsthistorisches Museum), *Young Woman with Feather Hat* (c. 1536, St Petersburg, Hermitage) and *Venus of Urbino* (c. 1538, Florence, Galleria degli Uffizi), although there is no reliable evidence for this. The only female portrait study by Titian that has survived is an expressive chalk drawing of a young woman with her head turned slightly to the right in the Uffizi (cat. 55). While her facial features are finely worked out, her garment with its puffy sleeves and open hair falling over her shoulder are sketched in quick strokes. The bust portrait cannot be associated with any specific work, although it shows formal parallels to the artist's idealised *belle donne*. It is not unlikely that the drawing repeatedly served Titian as an inspiration.

The gaze to the right, the implied double chin, the high forehead and the even brows bear resemblance to a *bella* type that Titian developed in his *Vanity* (cat. 57) and subsequently varied several times. A young woman is shown, looking pensively to the right out of the corner of her eye. Her robe has slipped carelessly over her shoulder and her braided hairstyle is unfinished. She rests her hand on an oval mirror with an octagonal box frame – it is possible that the painting was originally intended to depict a lady grooming herself. The references to the transience of all earthly things visible in the mirror (coins, jewels, pearls and an old woman with a distaff and a spindle), which make the *bella* an allegory of *vanitas*, are, according to conservation science examinations, later additions, as is the candle in the woman's right hand. The changes, visible in X-ray images, which Titian himself already made during the painting process, have led to the assumption that the Munich painting helped the master develop an experimental matrix, from which he then derived further compositional variants such as *Young Woman at Her Toilet* (cat. 58) in Paris. Titian's tendency to vary a successful pictorial composition is also attested by the aforementioned painting triad of the *belle* in Florence (fig. 2), Vienna and St Petersburg, which shows the same type of woman in different garments.

Since hardly anything is known about the circumstances of the *belle* commissions, scholars working on Titian's oeuvre now assume that at least some of them are pictorial inventions without an associated commission, which the artist produced in advance – perhaps with a view to very specific recipients – and knew how to place strategically when the corresponding customer came to his studio, as has been handed down in several cases. Probably the most famous example is that of the Duke of Urbino, Francesco Maria I della Rovere (1490–1538), who after visiting the workshop is said to have made every effort to bring Titian's *La Bella* (fig. 2) into his possession. Regardless of whether these accounts are accurate or merely serve the common topoi of artists' panegyric, they express what was essentially the recipe for success of Titian's *belle*: they were capable of arousing desire. However, since women such as Bianca Cappello (1548–1587), wife of Francesco de' Medici, Grand Duke of Tuscany, also acquired and commissioned ideal female portraits, this form of portraiture obviously involves more than a purely erotic display of the female body for the male gaze (also see Henry Kaap's essay in this catalogue).

Suggestiveness and ambiguity

The question as to which conception of women the *belle donne* represent and for which context they were created remains controversial among scholars. This can be traced particularly well in the different hypotheses on the interpretation of one of the paintings that show a *bella donna* in a narrative context – namely, Licinio's *Portrait of a Young Lady and Her Suitor* (cat. 60). The red curtain and the antique interior design create the impression of a theatre scene. We witness an intimate encounter: a fashionably dressed young nobleman approaches a half-exposed blonde beauty. With his right hand he grasps her wrist, while his left hand is placed against his chest in a gesture of deep emotional involvement, as he gazes at his beloved with a dreamy, transfigured gaze. She, in turn, is leaning on a parapet with her right arm. Her open *camicia* has slipped down far, revealing her right breast, which forms the brightly lit centre of the composition. Her head is slightly tilted and her opened blonde hair falls in silky strands on her bare shoulders. Out of the corner of her eye, she looks at her admirer. Her expression is indecipherable. Does it reflect scepticism, even rejection? Or, on the contrary, shy affection, perhaps even flirtatiousness? The enigmatic juxtaposition of gazes between the two offers plenty of scope for speculation.

This scene has been interpreted in different ways. For example, the permissive portrayal of the young woman has led Chriscinda Henry to believe that she is a courtesan and that the man must be her suitor. According to this hypothesis, Licinio is adopting character types and plots from the contemporary burlesque or the vernacular genre of the novella here. In the latter case, the scene would be reminiscent of dramatic fates described by Matteo Bandello (c. 1485–c. 1561) in one of his novellas, such as the unhappy love of a young Lombard nobleman. He falls under the spell of a Venetian courtesan, courts her and loses his entire fortune without being heard, which is why he finally takes his own life in desperation. The interplay of erotic promise and unattainability, which lends Licinio's *bella* an enigmatic aura, certainly permits such an interpretation. However, it also allows for an entirely opposite hypothesis. Although the exposure of the breast can, from today's perspective, hardly be read as anything other than sexualised objectification, in the perception of the 16th-century viewer, it does not necessarily identify the young woman as a courtesan. In combination with the antique-looking white *camicia*, the motif is rather reminiscent of the iconography of the goddess Flora, who in Roman mythology was worshipped as the companion of the fertility goddess Ceres and as the embodiment of spring. This reading makes it possible to interpret the depiction of the young woman as a promise of fertility. The naked breast also appears in the iconography of Mary in the form of the Madonna lactans, the milk-giving Mother of God. The exposed breast thus also refers to the ability to breastfeed children, which again addresses the theme of female fertility. Moreover, the breast was conceived as a gateway to the heart and a metaphorical place of interiority: in early modern treatises on the variety and expressiveness of gestures such as Giovanni Bonifacio's *L'arte de' cenni* (1616), the gesture of 'exposing the breast' stands for the willingness to lovingly receive someone in one's heart – in this case, the male counterpart. Alongside the possibility of a purely erotic reading, the visibility of the naked female breast thus referred to a whole range of contexts in the perception of the time.

Against this background, Anouck Samyn's analysis of further details of the work, which also takes into account the historical framework, suggests an interpretation of the painting as an engagement portrait. In Venetian society, marriage sealed the social, financial and political alliance of two families, forming the foundation of personal and family identity, and was seen as one of the guarantors of political stability. Especially in the circles of the *nobili*, fertility (more precisely: the ability to produce sons) was considered one of the most important elements of a marriage. With the fingers of her right hand, the young woman forms the already familiar V-gesture, which in this context may also allude to the future consummation of the marriage. The golden chain wrapped around her wrist, a so-called *laccio d'oro*, can be interpreted as a sign of affection between the lovers. The rings on their hands, together with the young man's grasp of the *bella*'s hand, complete the marital dimension of the painting. This variety of possible scenarios also casts a different light on the individual depictions of the *belle donne*. In some cases, there are plausible reasons to believe that these are also idealised portraits of Venetian marriage candidates, which is why the bride hypothesis is meanwhile established as another possible interpretation. Nevertheless, due to their interpretative openness, something mysterious about the depictions always remains. It can be assumed that their suggestive ambiguity was intended by the artists, which – then as now – contributes to the special charm of this genre.

Lyrical images of man

Irrespective of the question of whether Licinio's work is to be read as an engagement painting or as the meeting of a courtesan with her suitor, the relationship of desire between the woman and the man is enacted as a courtly love scene and is thus an expression of the lyrical conception of man in the early cinquecento, which was shaped by love poetry in the tradition of Petrarch. In contrast to his poetry – which remains a chaste adoration of the unattainable beloved, which, sublimated by art, is ultimately transcended to a metaphysical love of God – both Licinio's courtly love scene and the Venetian *belle donne* place much greater emphasis on the earthly erotic fulfilment of the desire for love and, in doing so, play with the affective, erotic power of the pictorial medium. According to Marianne Koos, the expressive glance that the young woman in Licinio's painting casts at her admirer from the corner of her eye visualises a central motif of Petrarchan love poetry, where the sparkling eyes of the beloved are compared to the stars in the sky, to which the lover looks up longingly. The young man's scarf, too, decorated with stars, refers to this metaphor. The materially conceived 'rays' from the eyes of the beloved penetrate the lover's chest like arrows and wound the heart. The painting is dedicated to that very moment of wounding through the "arrow-like" gaze that ignites love in the heart. The man's hand placed against his chest comments on the painfully sweet wound.

According to Koos, the metaphor of the gaze as an arrow of love underlies numerous paintings of the period, not only in connection the iconography of the *belle donne* – it is also a popular motif in erotic depictions of ideally beautiful, feminine-looking male youths, which were created as a counterpart to the *belle* and were equally in demand. A particularly eloquent example of this is Giorgione's *Boy with Arrow* (cat. 62). The soft *sfumato* and the ideal beauty of the protagonist, including his magnificent curls, delicate pale skin and red lips, evoke erotic associations. The attribute of the arrow can be read as a metaphor for his "arrow-like" gaze, echoing the theme of bittersweet love pains – the very affect that the young man's gaze and beauty aim to arouse in the viewer. Eroticisation in portrait culture is consequently a phenomenon that does not only affect the ideal female portrait. Francesco Torbido's (c. 1482/85–1562) *Portrait of a Young Man* (cat. 61) also shows such a youth, now with blond hair. The depiction is comparable to the type of the *belle donne* in several respects. The sitter holds a rose in his right hand and leans on a stone slab whose inscription refers to his erotic attractiveness: "Why should you be astonished at the beautiful figure? The rose of Paphos [the rose of Venus] is fragrant when plucked early in the morning, but, by sunset, it is withered and smells less [intense]."

The ambiguous mysteriousness and suggestive eroticism of the portraits of young men and *belle donne* find their counterpart in the so-called lyrical male portraits of the *Giorgionismo* style inspired by Giorgione, which were painted at the same time. The admirer in

Licinio's scene, too, is depicted in the lyrical mode of portraiture in terms of his dress and affect. This specific typology creates a striking counter-model to the Venetian Republic's ideal of masculinity, although it is a relatively short-lived phenomenon whose high points are limited to the period between the first and third decades of the cinquecento. Instead of being prime examples of sovereign strength, the protagonists are shown as devoted, melancholic and sentimental individuals who thus give the appearance of closeness and authenticity. The term "lyrical portrait" introduced by Marianne Koos captures, on the one hand, the emotional mood of those portrayed and, on the other hand, alludes to the parallels between the image of man conveyed here and the understanding of the subject in the Petrarchist poetry of the early cinquecento. For the latter, as we have seen, the unfulfillable nature of desire and the pleasure in the pain caused by unfulfilled longing are elementary. This can, in turn, be directed towards various objects: a beloved person, the golden age or the lost paradise. Characteristic emotions of Petrarchist poetry are the wistful longing and sad hope of the lyrical ego and its musings on death and transience. This connects the Petrarchist conception of man with the lyrical mode of portraiture of *Giorgionismo*, which also depicts the sitters as affective, yearning subjects. Just as in the poetry of the era, both the lyrical portraits of men as well as the depictions of beautiful women and handsome male youths are as much about longing and desire as about the affective power of beauty. For this reason, the designation "lyrical portraits" can also be applied to the latter two groups of works.

Vaghezza, the longing for Arcadia and the Venetian culture of reception

Thanks to their indeterminacy, the lyrical portraits provide a projection surface for one's own imagination and reflection. None of the presented interpretative approaches is fully satisfactory; the ambiguity remains. To this effect, these works ideally represent the quality of *vaghezza*. The term *vaghezza* is one of the central aesthetic terms of early modern art theory. On the one hand, it designates charm and attraction and, on the other hand, it stands for an interpretative openness in the sense of 'vagueness', corresponding to precisely the criterion that is so characteristic of the lyrical portraits. A painting that is characterised by *vaghezza* thus enables the gaze to wander longingly in several respects:

firstly, on account of the attractive beauty of the depiction and, secondly, the mysteriousness of the contradictory details, which always animate the viewer to find new meaning. The wandering gaze exemplifies a specifically Venetian mode of reception, which Johannes Grave describes as "thoughtful beholding" (see his essay in this catalogue). The lyrical qualities of *Giorgionismo* painting reflect this understanding of the image in a special way by stimulating free, associative movements of thought, which manifested itself in an intensively cultivated culture of discussion in front of pictures.

In addition to the lyrical portraits, the Arcadian landscapes, which were another great innovation in Venetian painting in the early cinquecento, also invite associative reception. A passage from Leonardo da Vinci's (1452–1519) treatise on painting illustrates how close the connection is between Arcadian landscapes and the ambiguous *belle donne* and youth portrayals. In this text, Leonardo describes the association that the viewer conjures up when faced with a painted *locus amoenus*, imagining himself to be there with his beloved, and thus stylises charming nature as a place of sensual pleasures and loving intimacy. A painting that unites all the above-mentioned motifs of longing is Titian's *Concert Champêtre* (fig. 3). Embedded in an Arcadian landscape, each of the three types of the lyrical portrait makes its appearance here: a fashionably dressed nobleman, reminiscent of the lyrical portraits of men; a young shepherd as a representative of the lyrical portraits of young men; and two women whose beauty and casual nudity recall lightly dressed *belle donne*. According to Dagmar Korbacher, the Arcadian landscape in 16th-century art and literature stands for a place of beauty almost equal to the lost paradise, where the experience of meaning, sensuality and connectedness provides the conditions for being truly human. In the medium of art, such Arcadian scenarios became accessible in the sense of an imaginary counterworld to real life in Venice with its social boundaries and constraints as well as the virulent political turmoil that accompanied the military conflicts between 1509 and 1517, and, as healing refuges, they invited the viewer to linger (see Andreas Schumacher's essay in this catalogue). In combination with a new culture of sentimentalism, which was accompanied by tendencies of withdrawal from active society, the context of the longing for Arcadia also allows the lyrical portraits – in and through which a contrary model to socially prescribed role models is developed – to appear in a different light. The lyrical male portraits visualise an

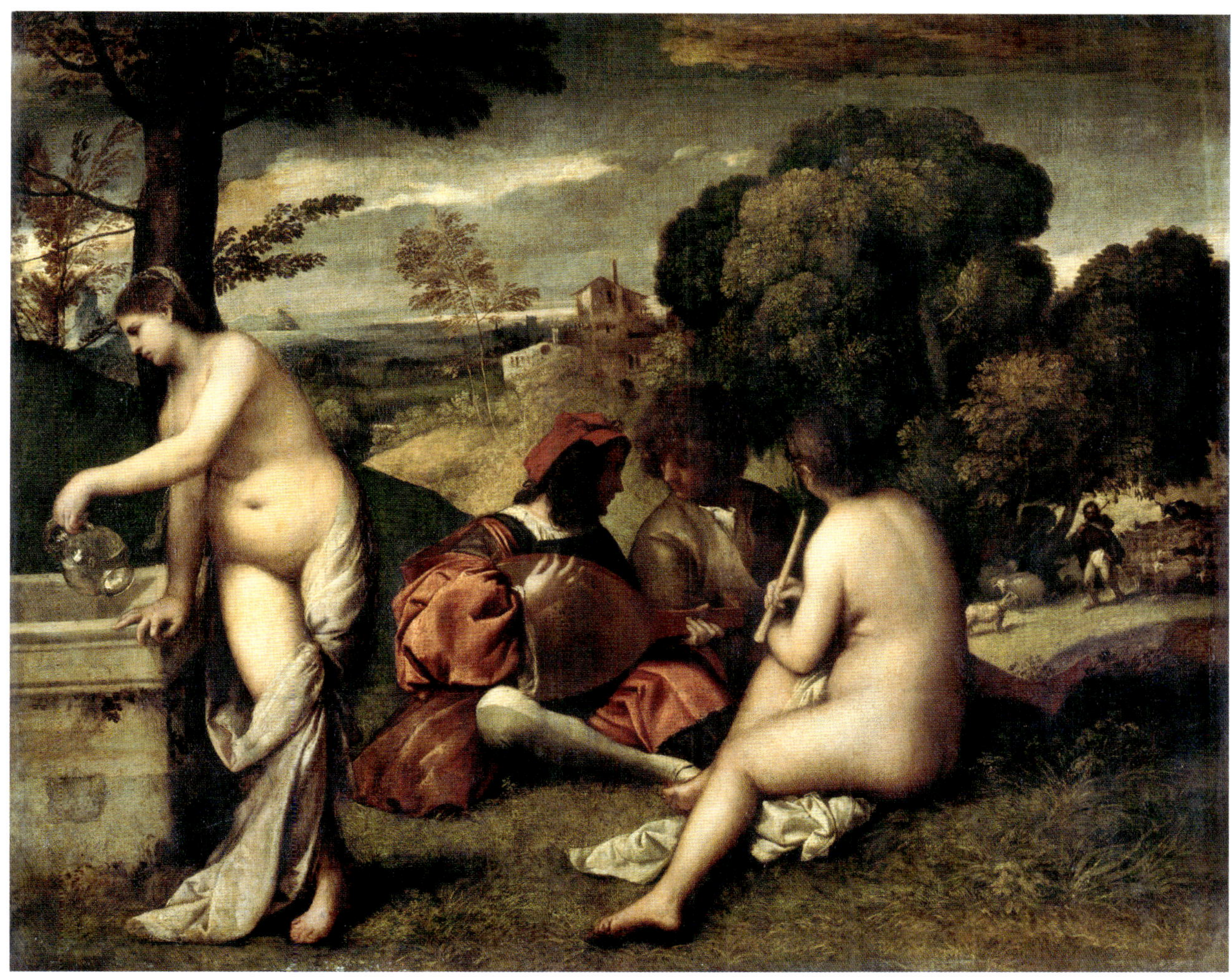

Fig. 3 Titian, *Concert Champêtre*, c. 1511, Paris, Musée du Louvre

approachable, vulnerable and devoted male ideal, whereas the *belle donne* represent self-confident and sensual women who, while remaining enigmatic in their emotional moods, nevertheless hold out the prospect of a fulfilment of the desire for mutual love and intimate belongingness. In times of crisis, the lyrical Arcadian pictorial themes of *Giorgionismo* gave rise to visionary designs of a counterworld of impressive imaginative power and great efficacy – an alternative world characterised by sensuality, belongingness and, above all, beauty.

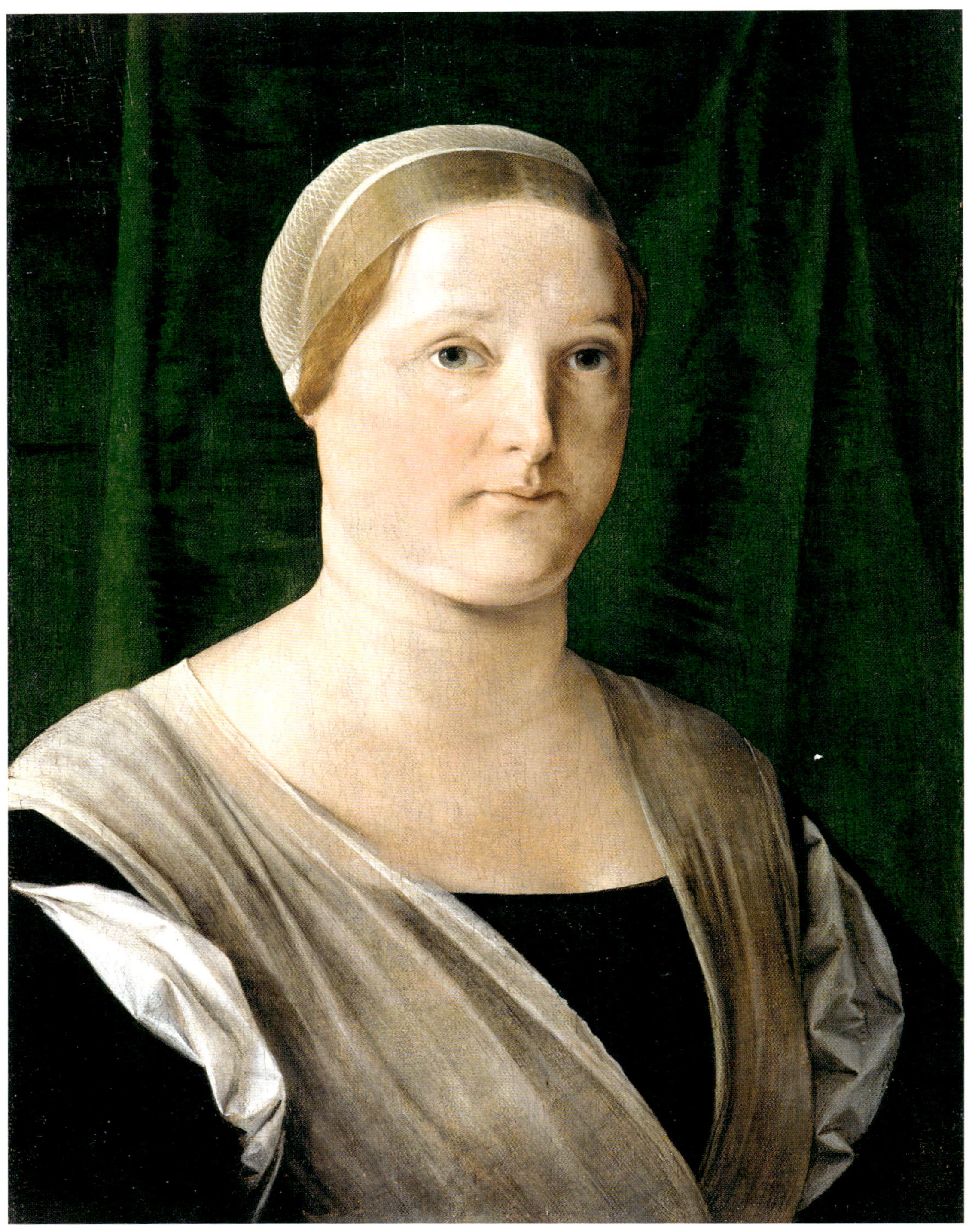

50 Lorenzo Lotto, *Portrait of a Woman*, c. 1505, Dijon, Musée des Beaux-Arts

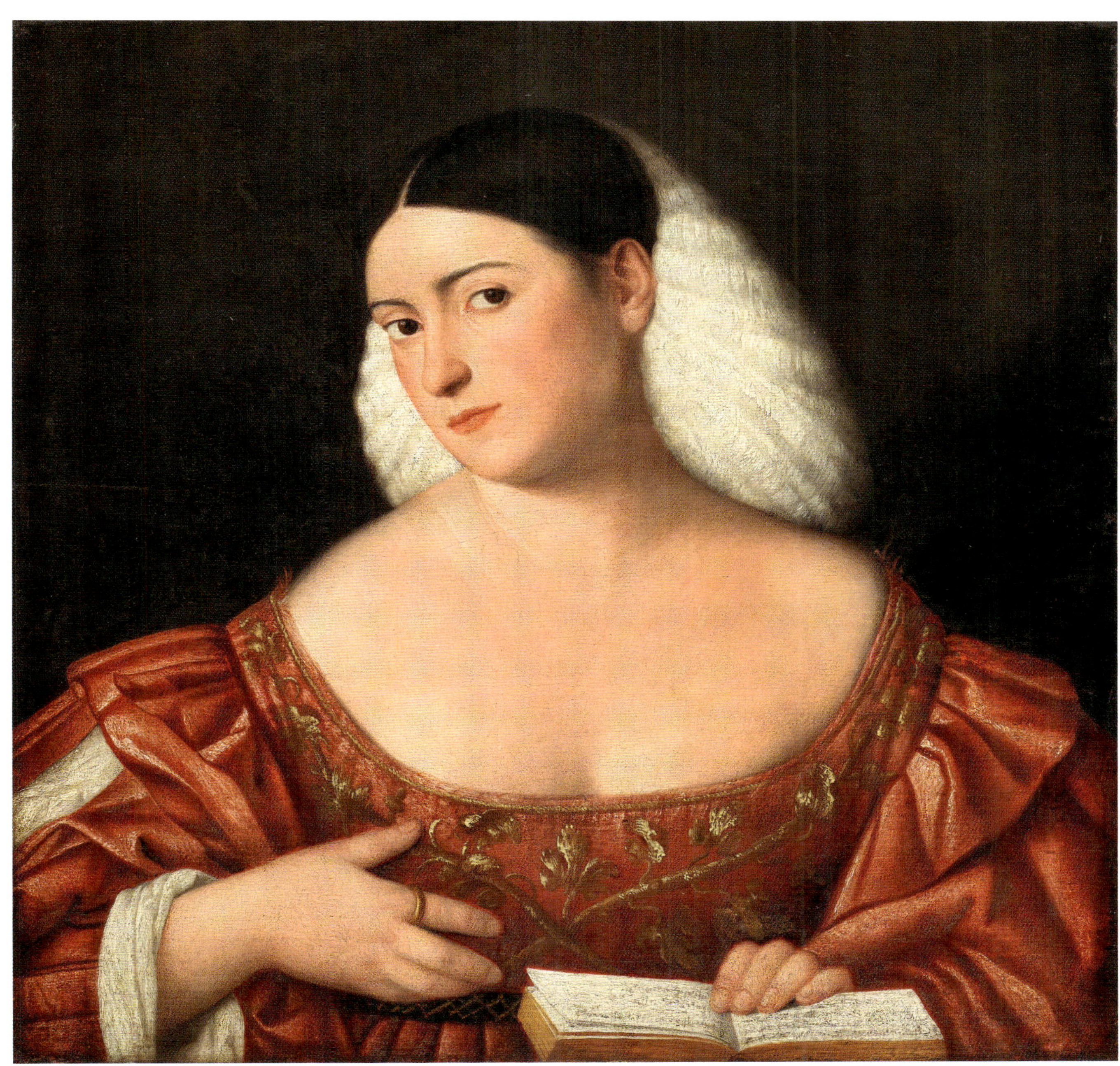

51 Bernardino Licinio, *Portrait of a Woman*, c. 1520, Munich, Bayerische Staatsgemäldesammlungen, Alte Pinakothek

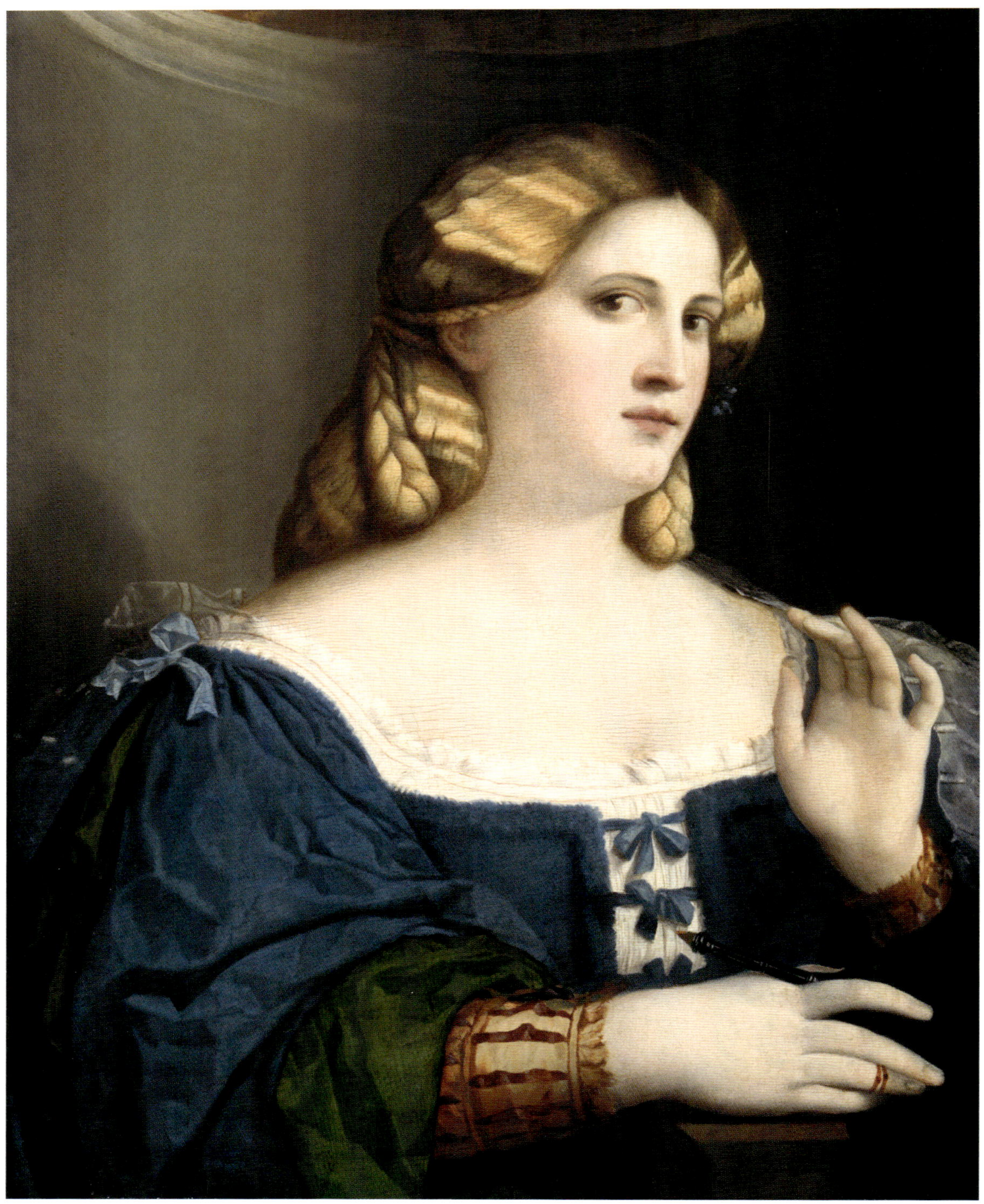

52 Palma il Vecchio, *Portrait of a Young Woman in Blue Dress with Fan*, after 1514, Vienna, Kunsthistorisches Museum

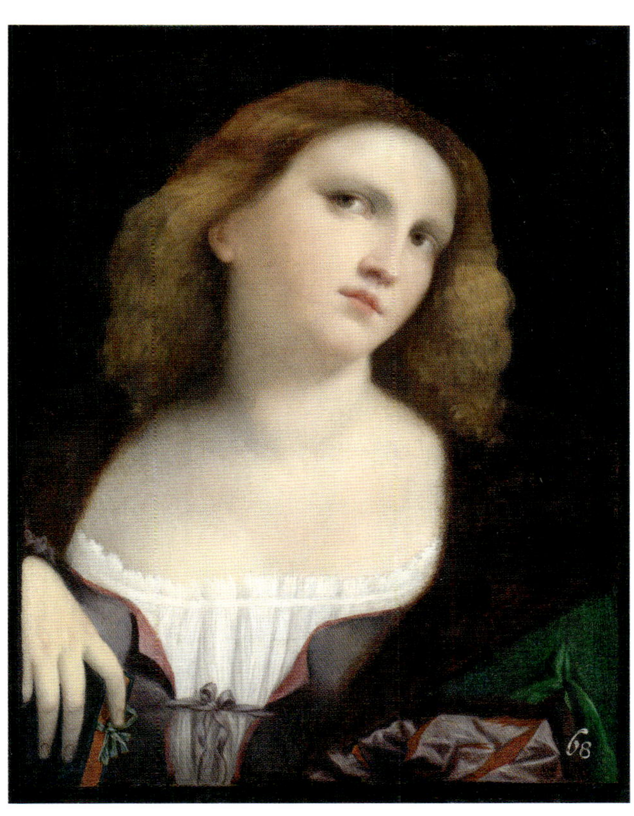

53 Palma il Vecchio, *Portrait of a Woman*, 1512/14, Lyon, Musée des Beaux-Arts

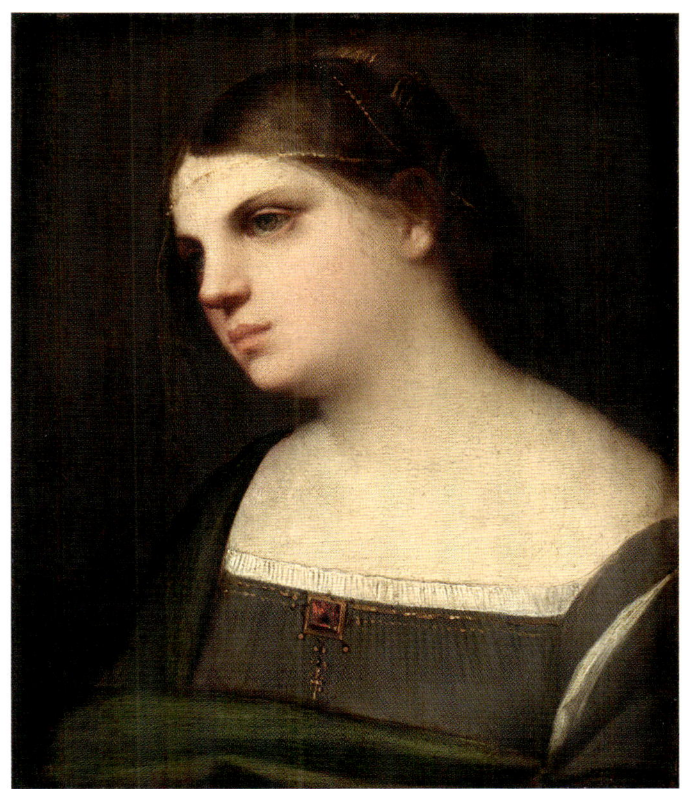

54 Sebastiano del Piombo, *Portrait of a Young Woman*, c. 1506/07, Buscot Park, The Faringdon Collection

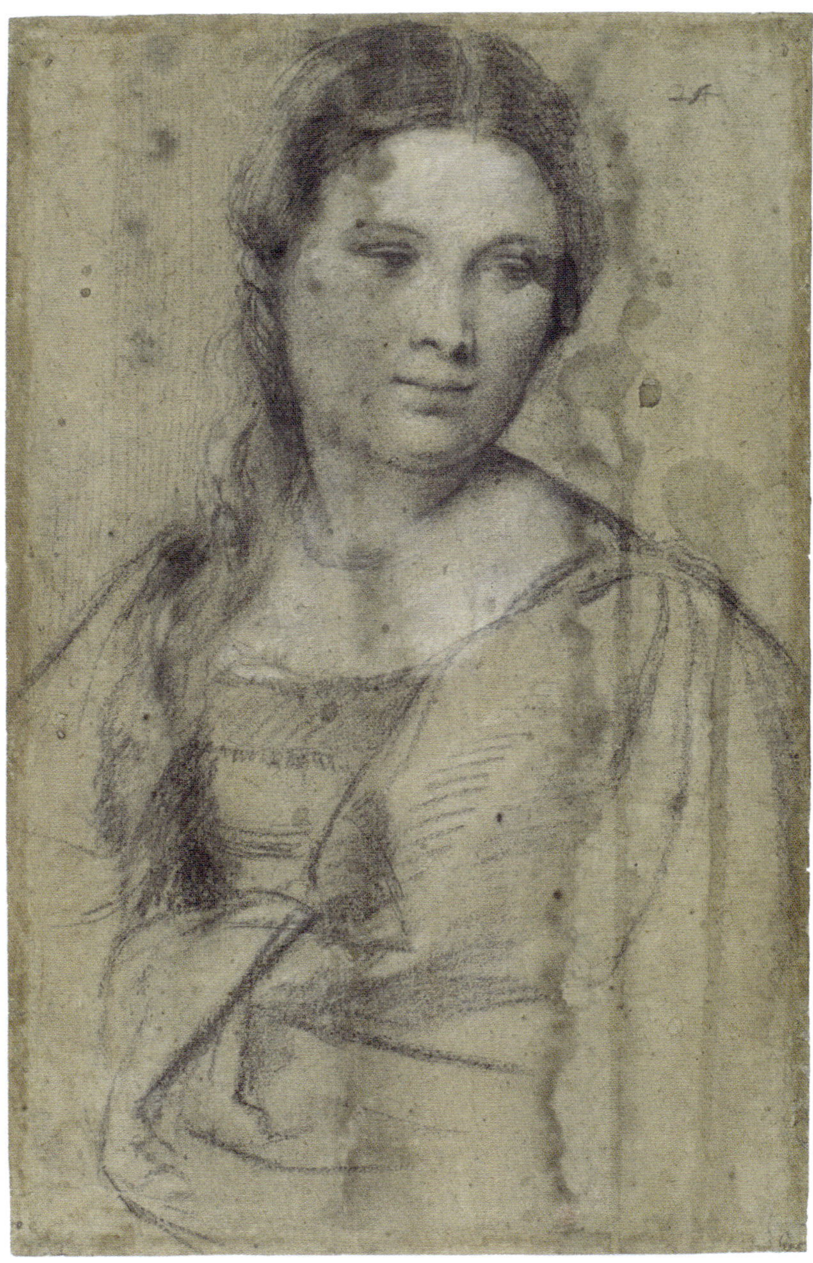

55 Titian, *Portrait of a Young Woman*, c. 1510/11, Florence, Galleria degli Uffizi, Gabinetto Disegni e Stampe

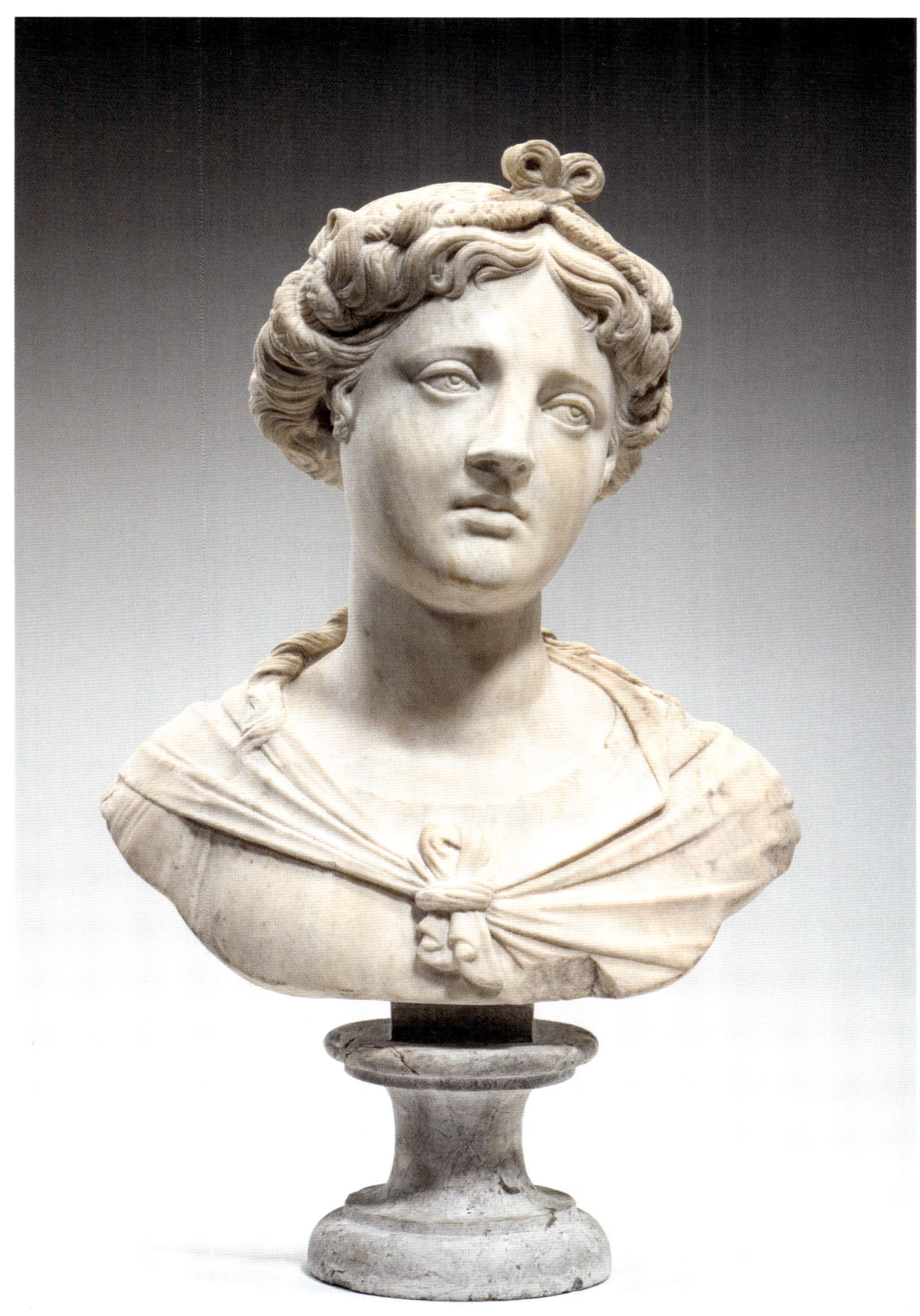

56 Simone Bianco, *Bust of a Roman Woman*, c. 1540, Munich, Bayerisches Nationalmuseum

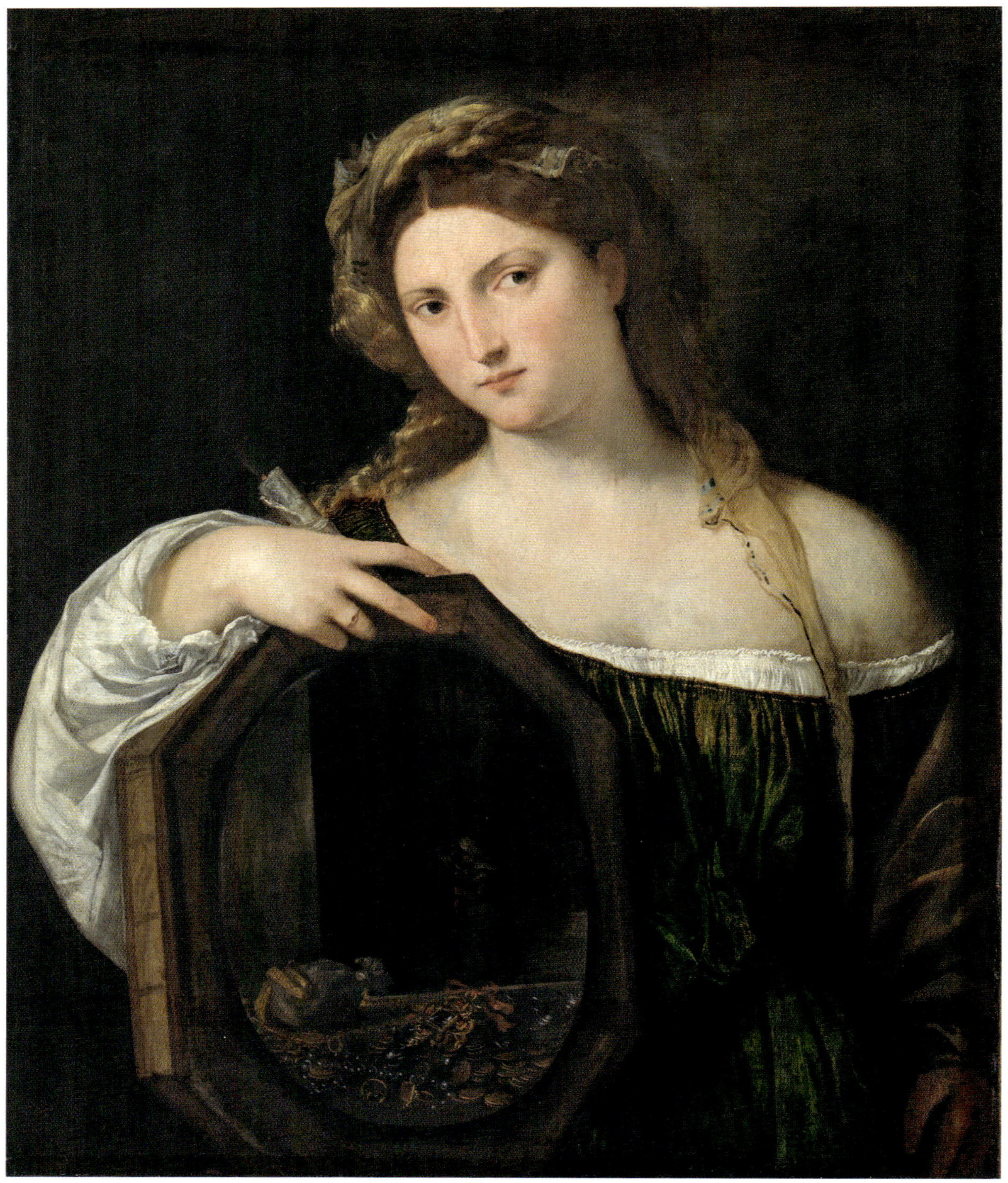

57 Titian, *Vanity*, c. 1515, Munich, Bayerische Staatsgemäldesammlungen, Alte Pinakothek

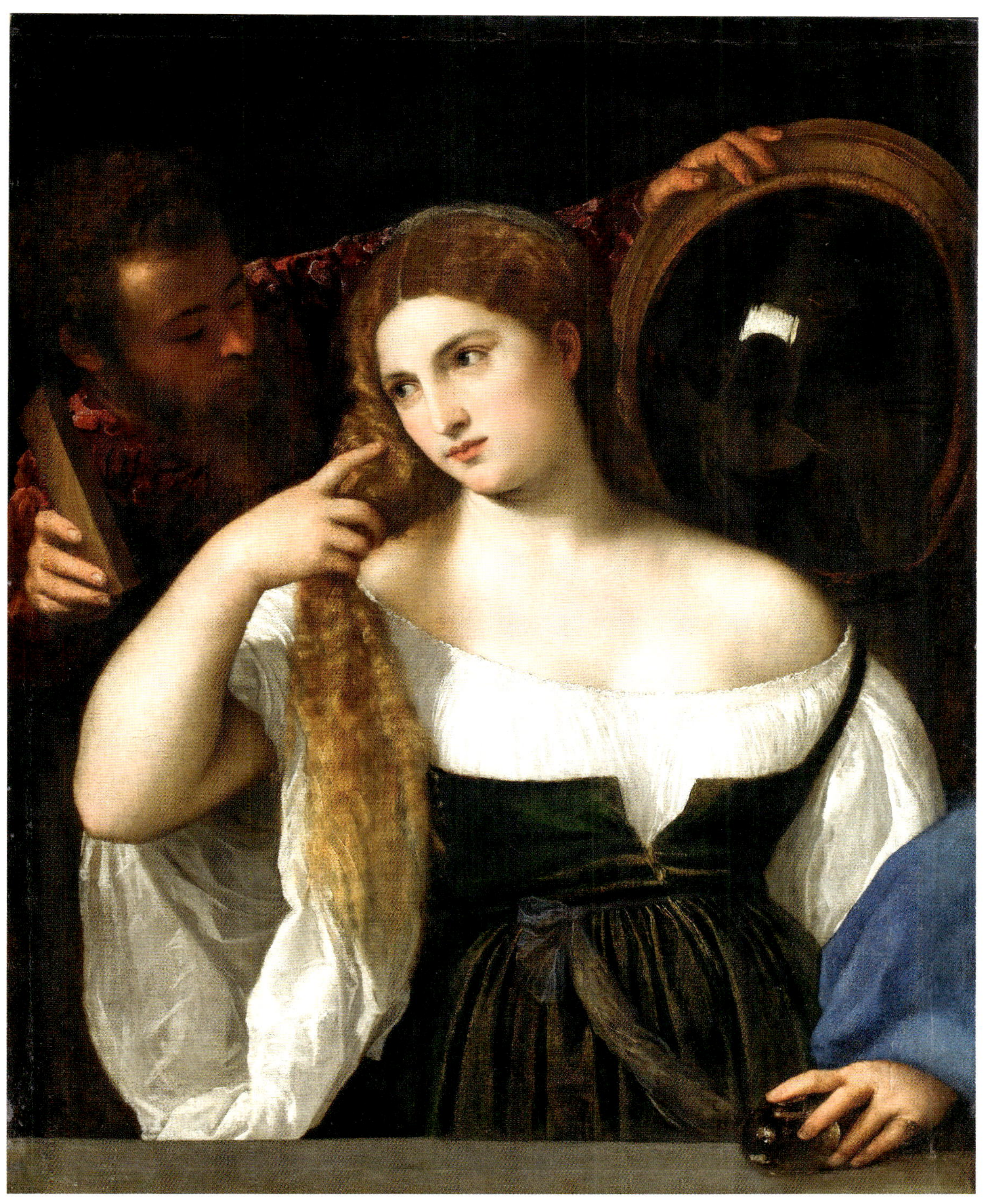

58 Titian, *Young Woman at Her Toilet*, c. 1515, Paris, Musée du Louvre

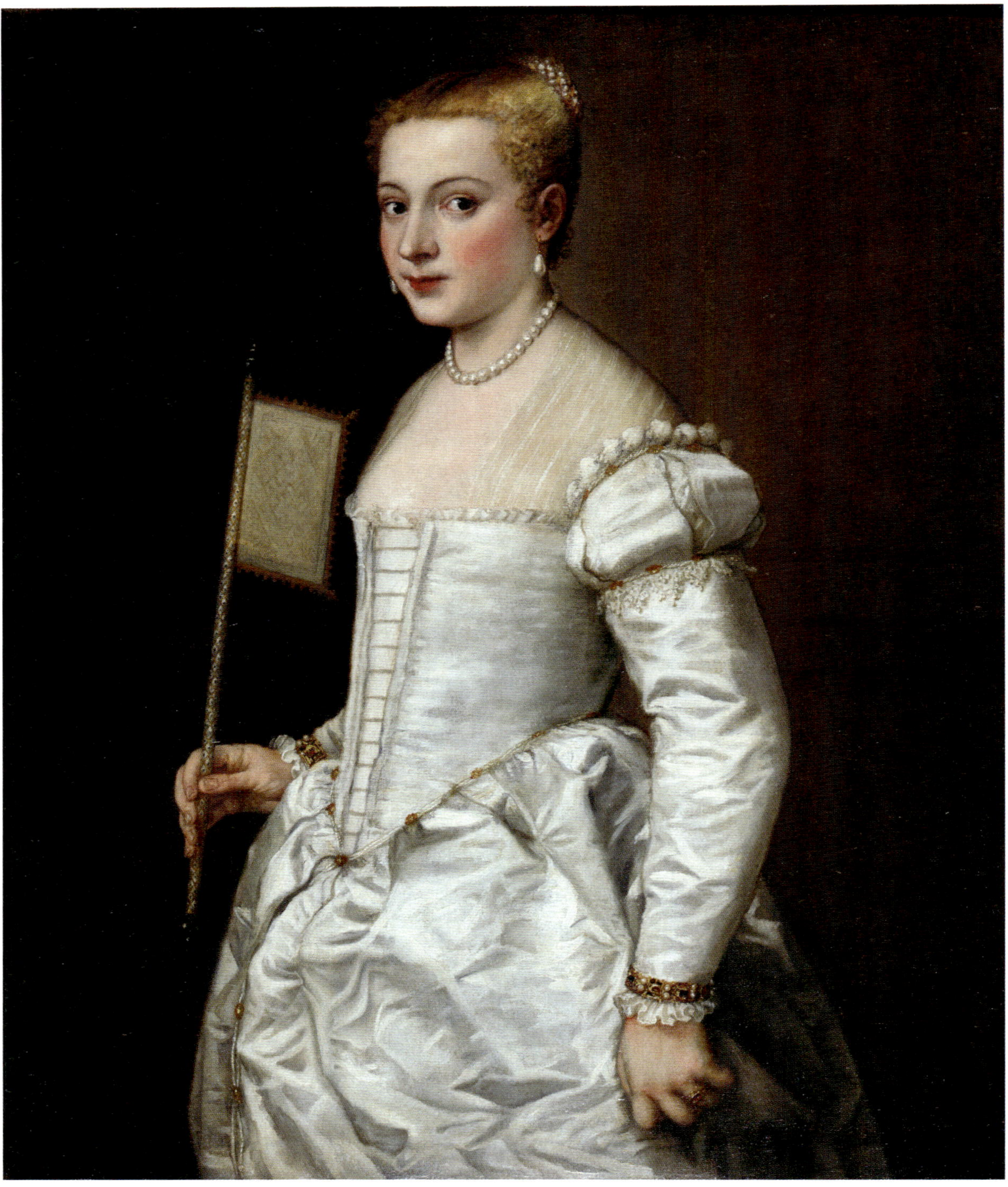

59 Titian, *Portrait of a Lady in White*, c. 1561, Dresden, Staatliche Kunstsammlungen, Gemäldegalerie Alte Meister

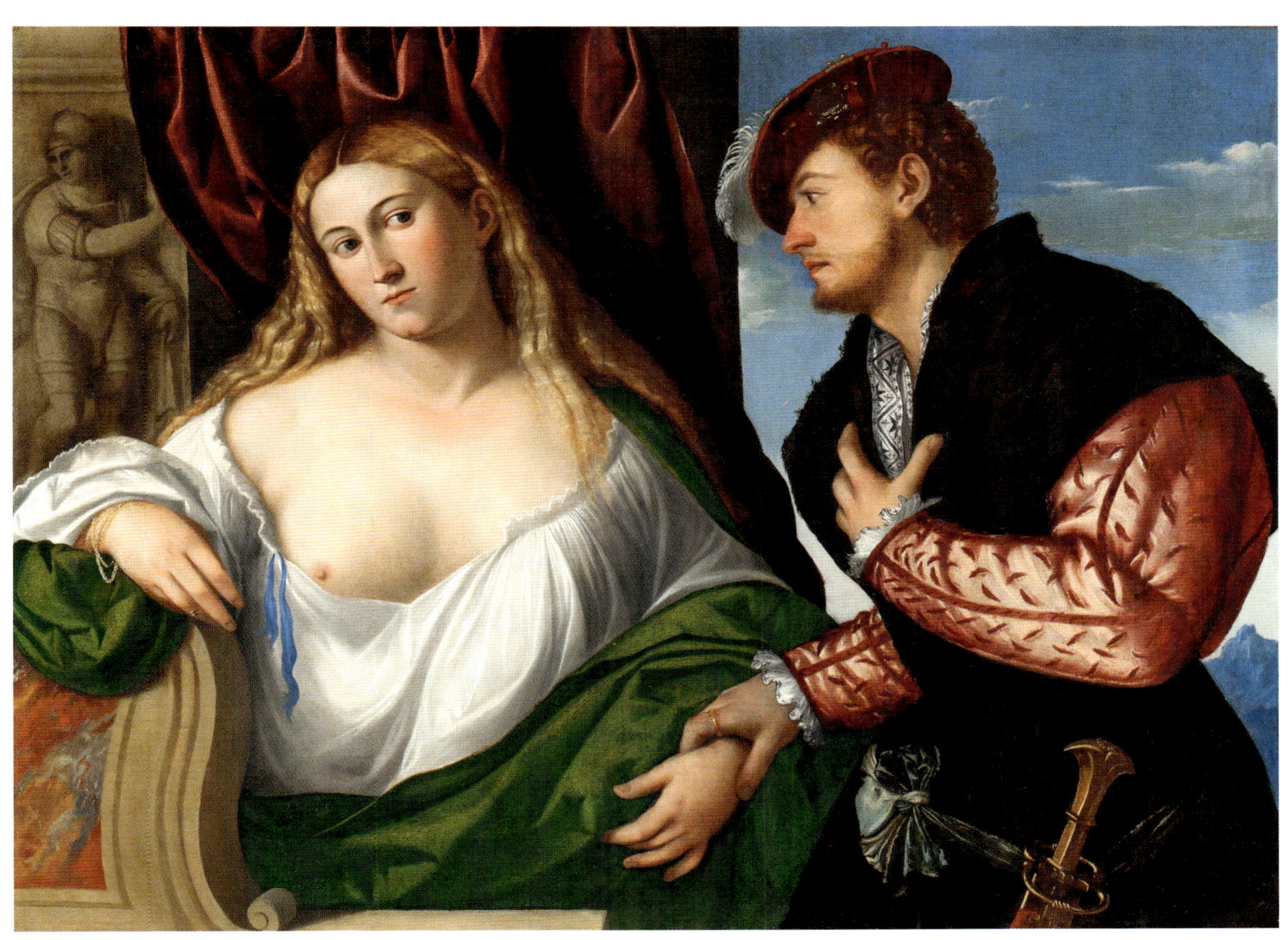

60 Bernardino Licinio, *Portrait of a Young Lady and Her Suitor*, c. 1520, Paris, Galerie Canesso

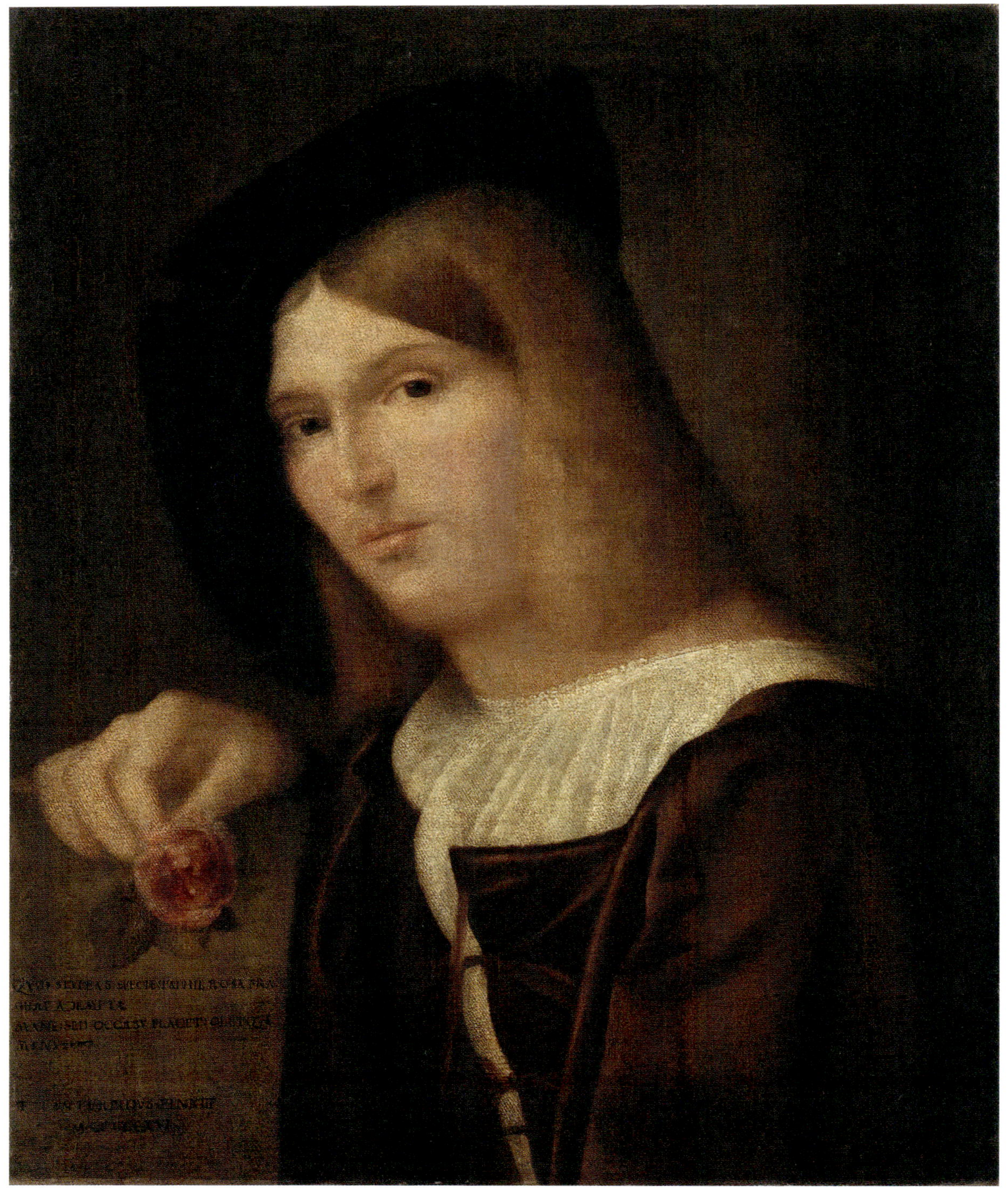

61 Francesco Torbido, *Portrait of a Young Man*, c. 1516, Munich, Bayerische Staatsgemäldesammlungen, Alte Pinakothek

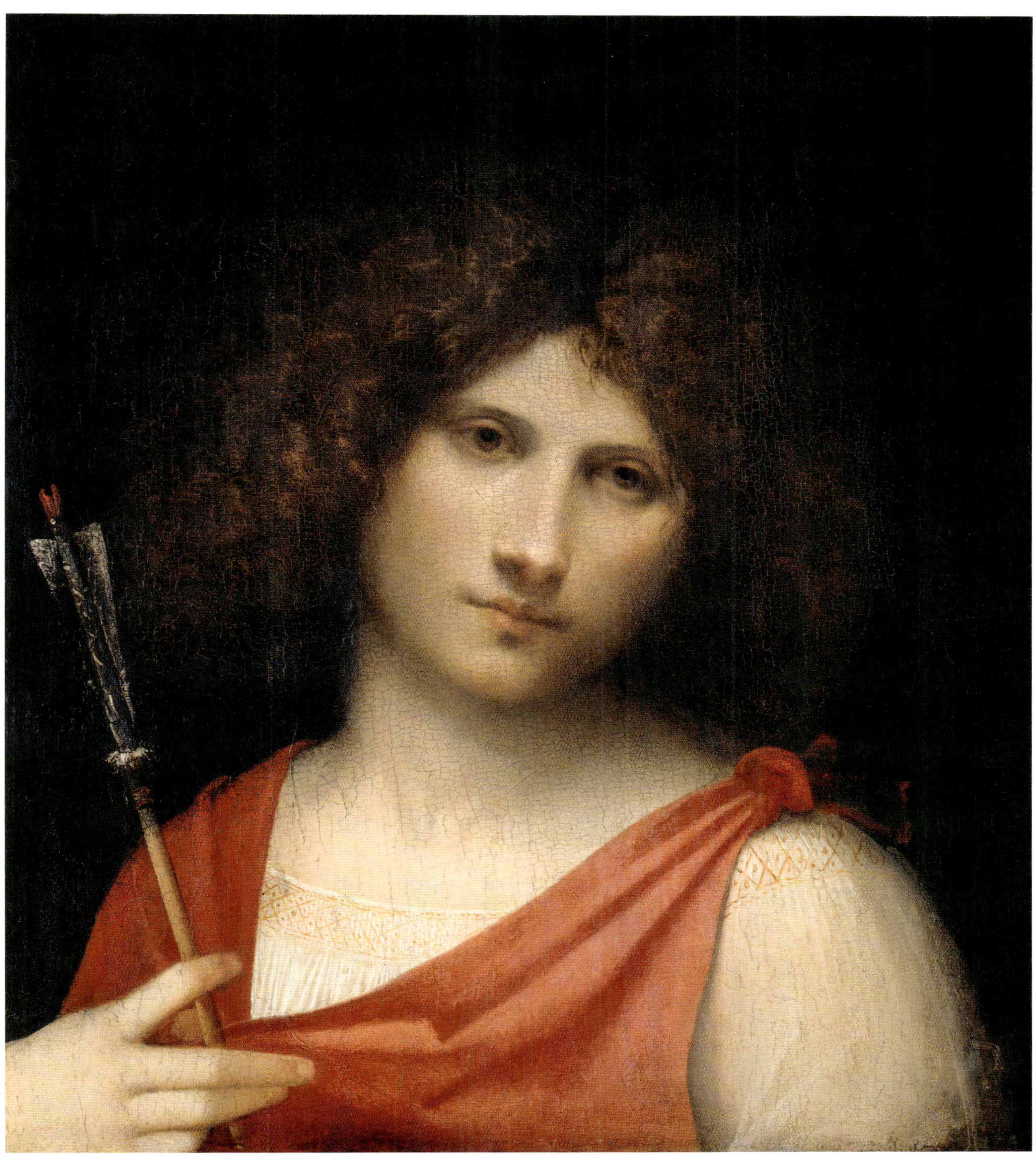

62 Giorgione, *Boy with Arrow*, c. 1505, Vienna, Kunsthistorisches Museum

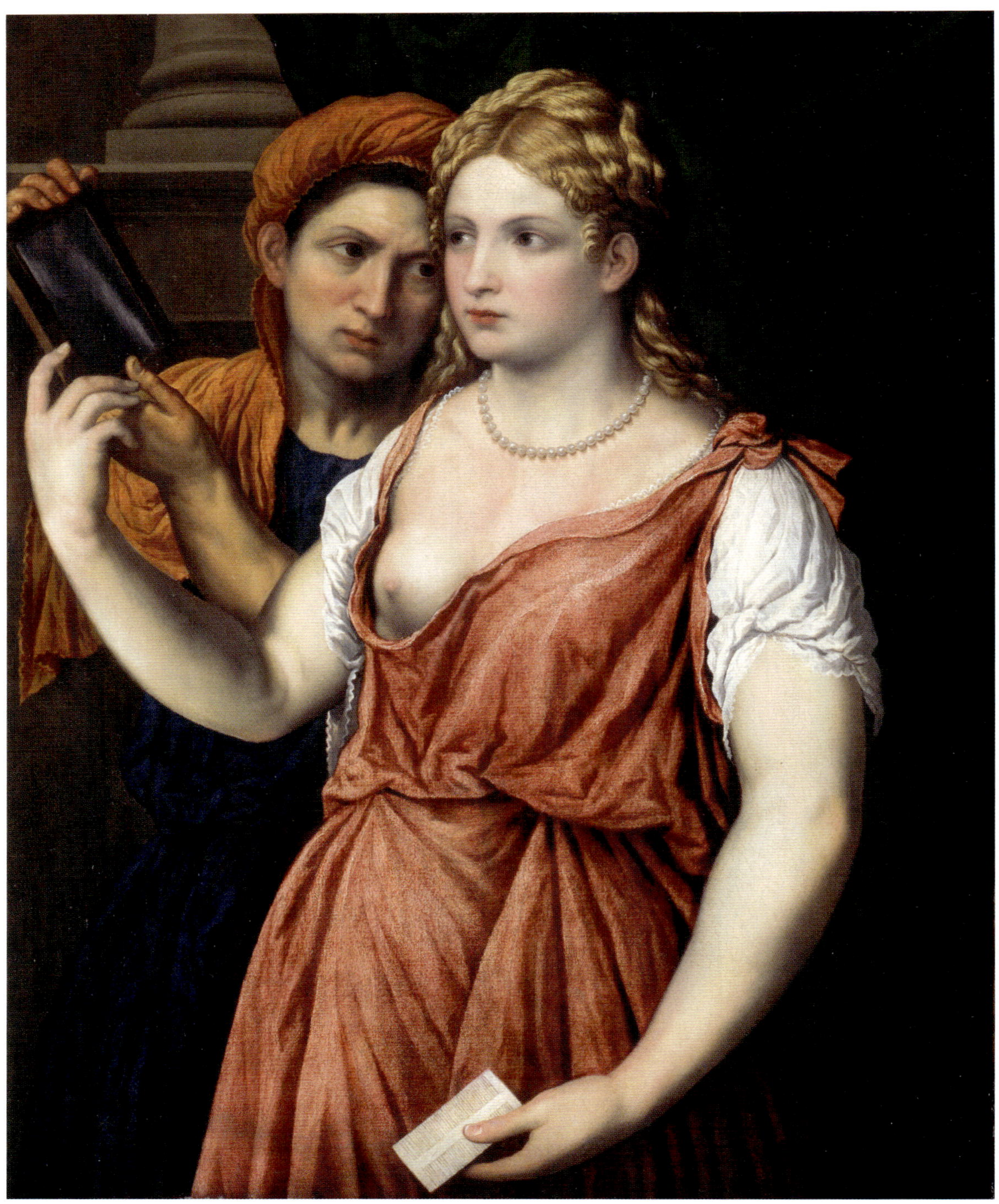

63 Par s Bordone, *A Young Woman Holding a Mirror with Her Servant*, c. 1535/40, Hamburg, Kunsthalle

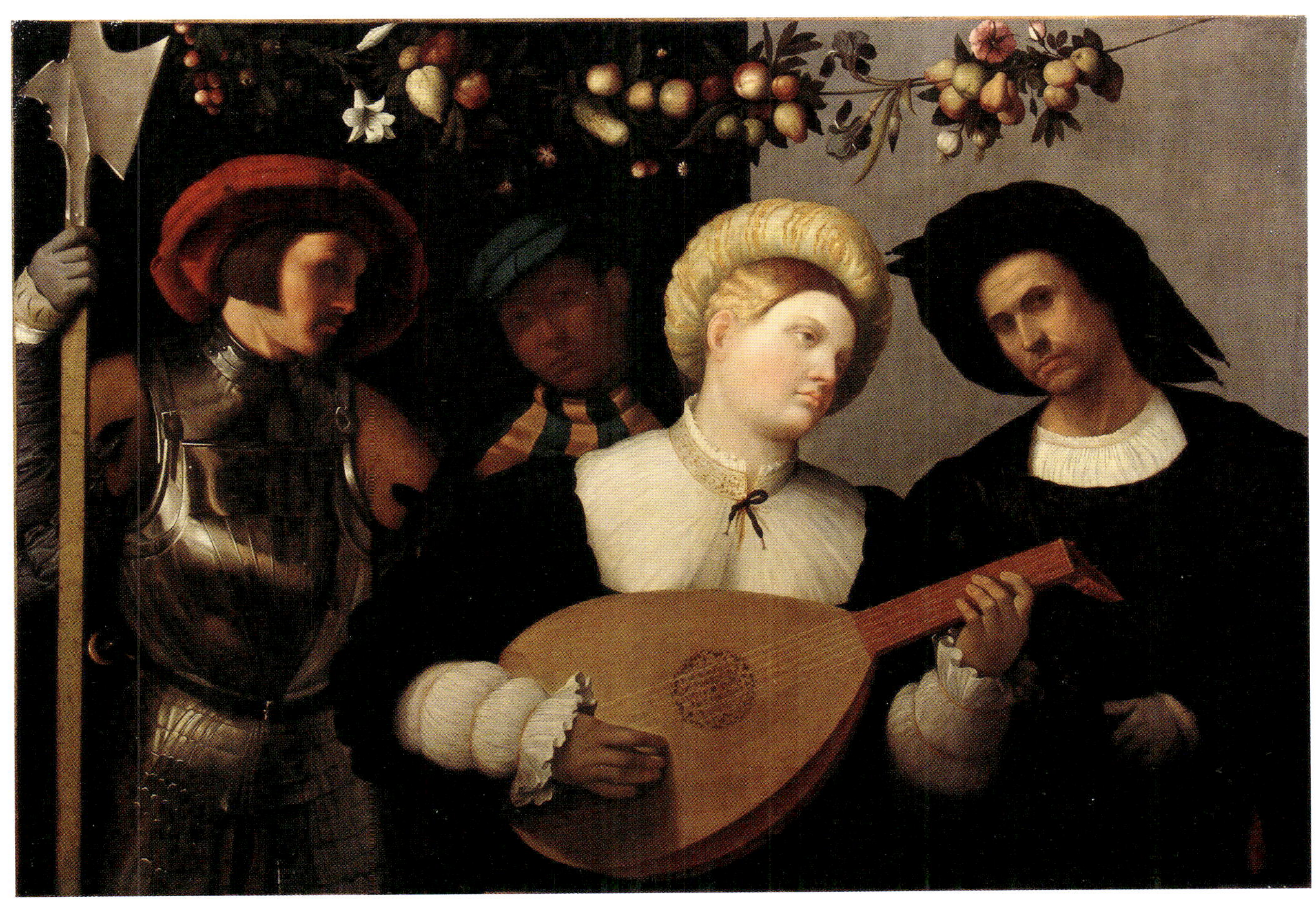

64 Bernardino Licinio, *The Concert*, 1518/20, Private collection

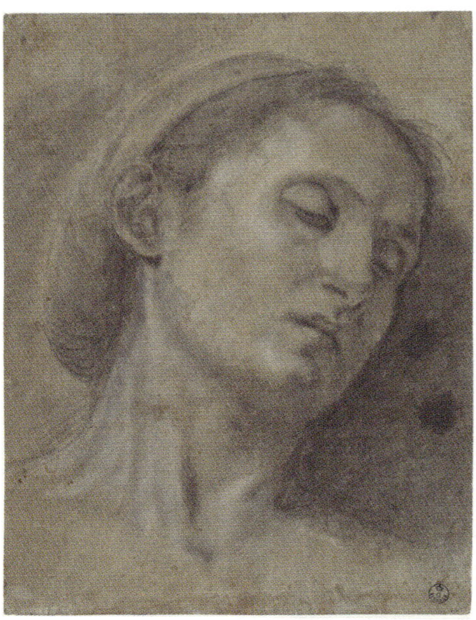

65 Giovanni Girolamo Savoldo, *Head of a Woman with Eyes Closed*, c. 1535/38, Florence, Galleria degli Uffizi, Gabinetto Disegni e Stampe

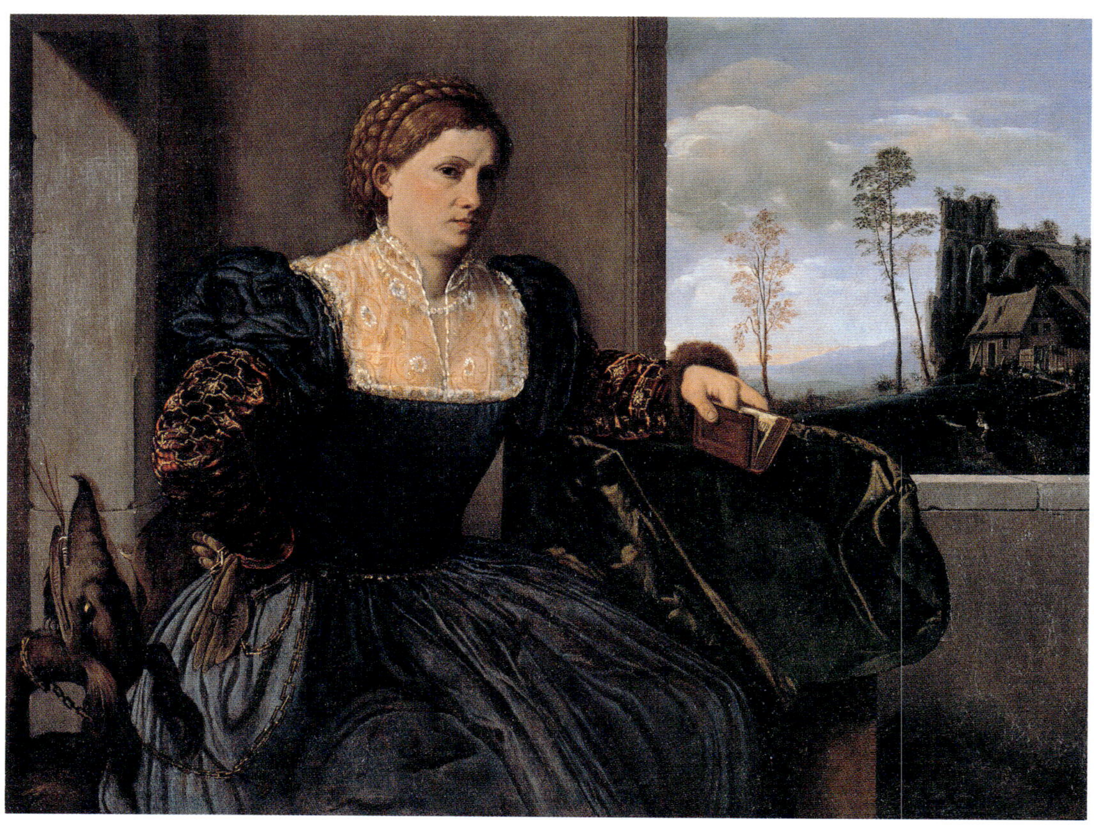

66 Giovanni Girolamo Savoldo, *Portrait of a Woman*, c. 1535, Rome, Musei Capitolini, Pinacoteca

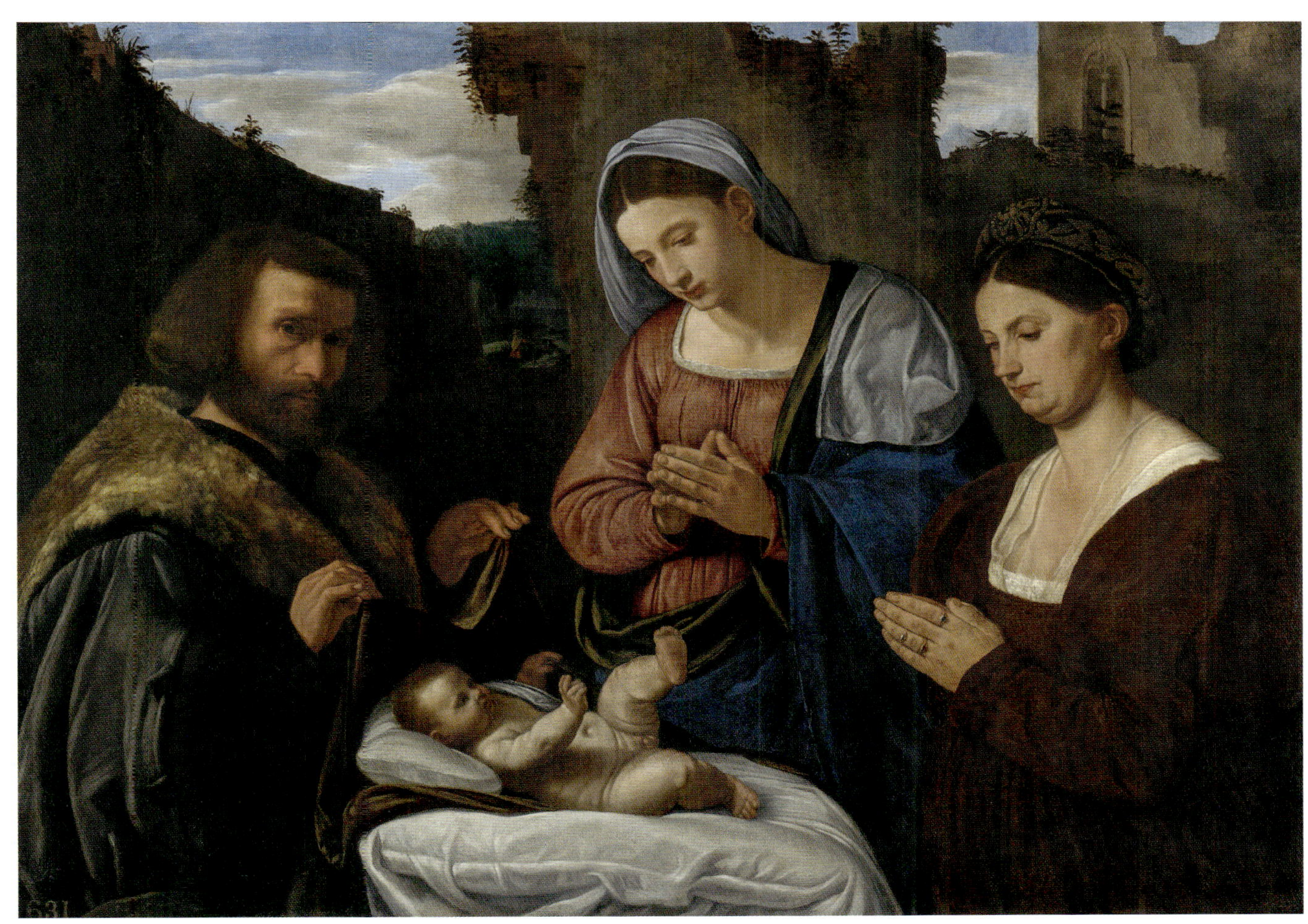

67 Giovanni Girolamo Savoldo, *The Virgin Adoring the Child with Two Donors*, c. 1527, London, The Royal Collection, HM King Charles III

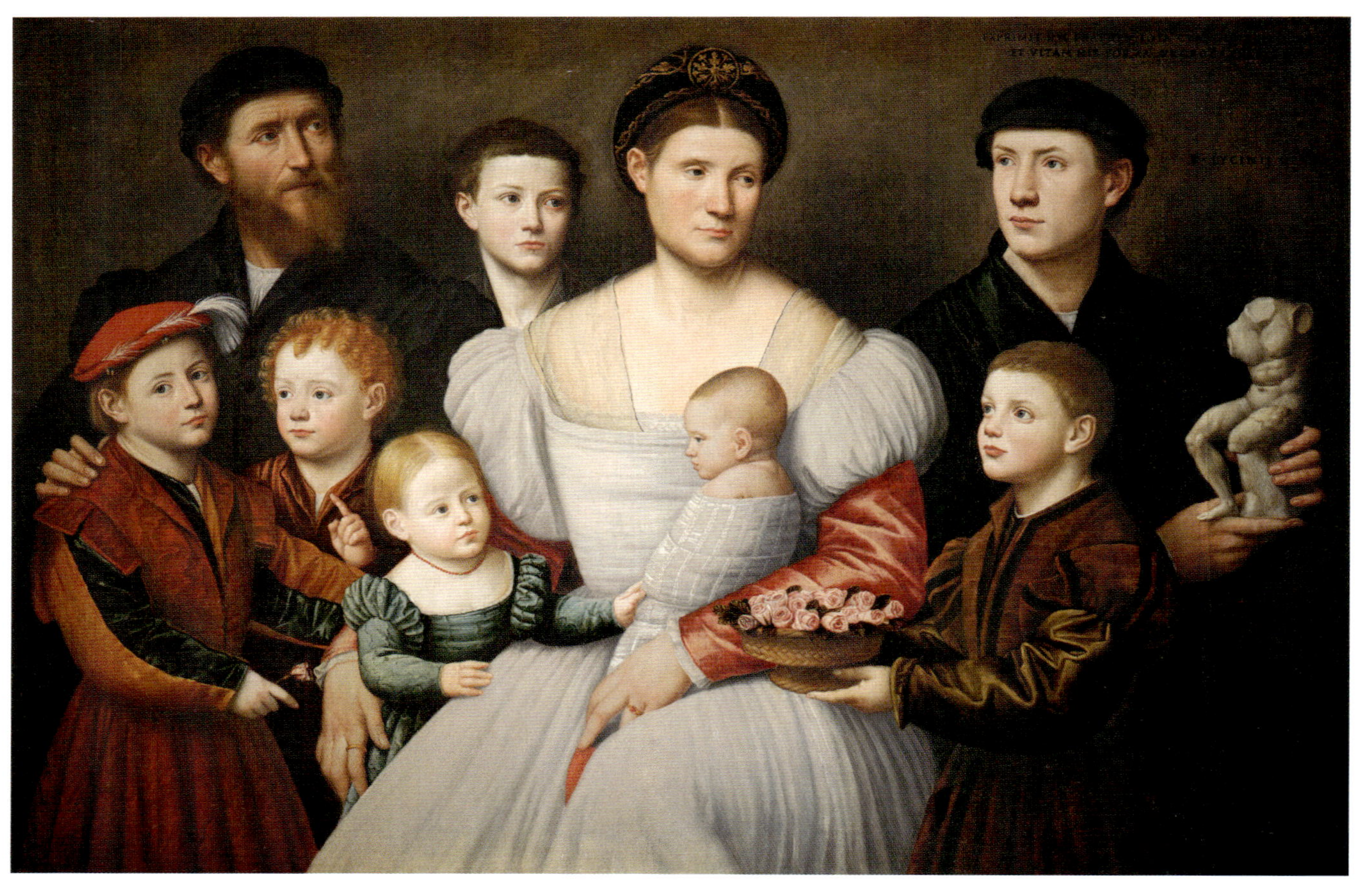

68 Bernardino Licinio, *Portrait of the Family of the Artist’s Brother Arrigo Licinio*, c. 1535, Rome, Galleria Borghese

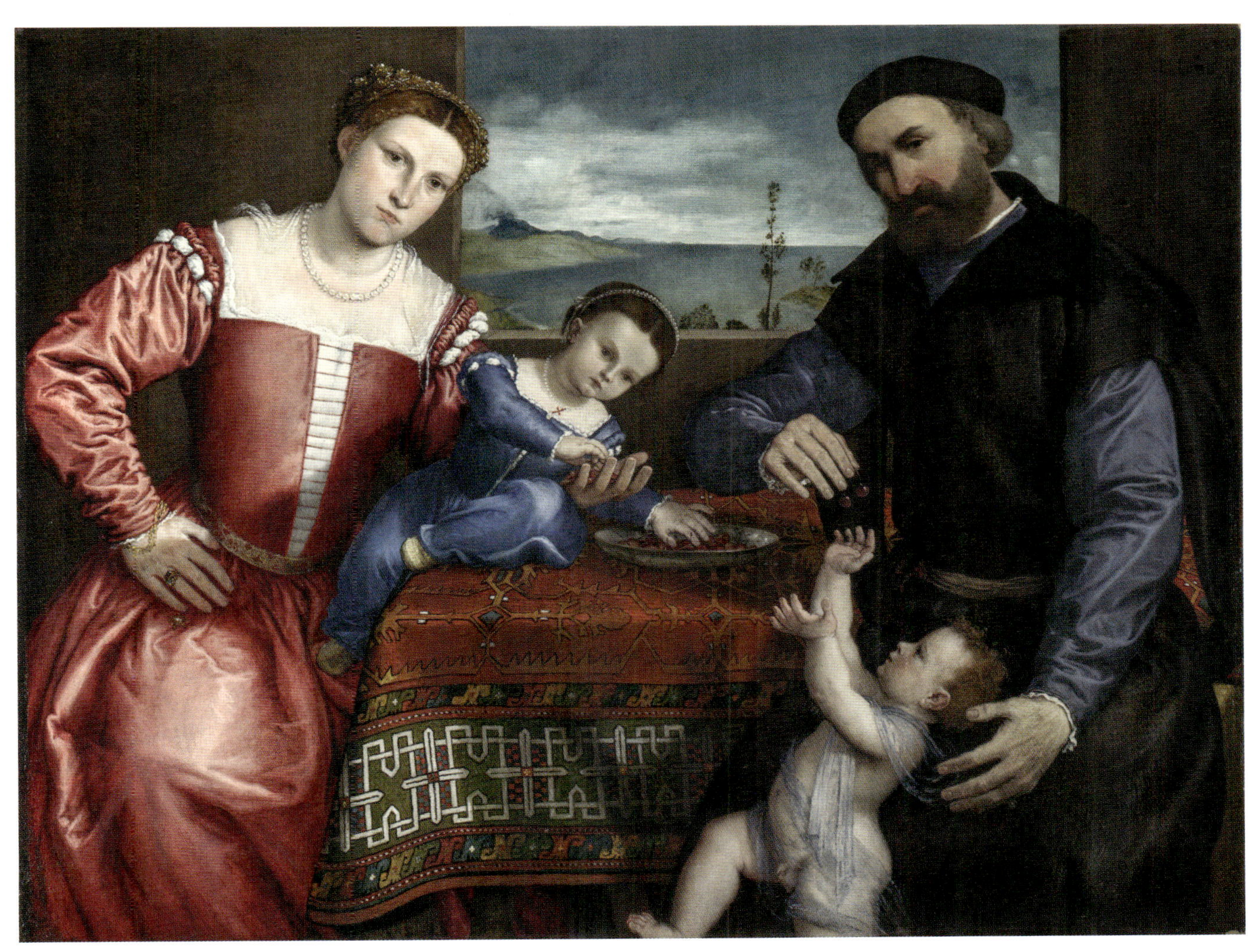

69 Lorenzo Lotto, *Portrait of Giovanni della Volta with His Wife and Children*, 1547, London, The National Gallery

Portrait painting in Venice

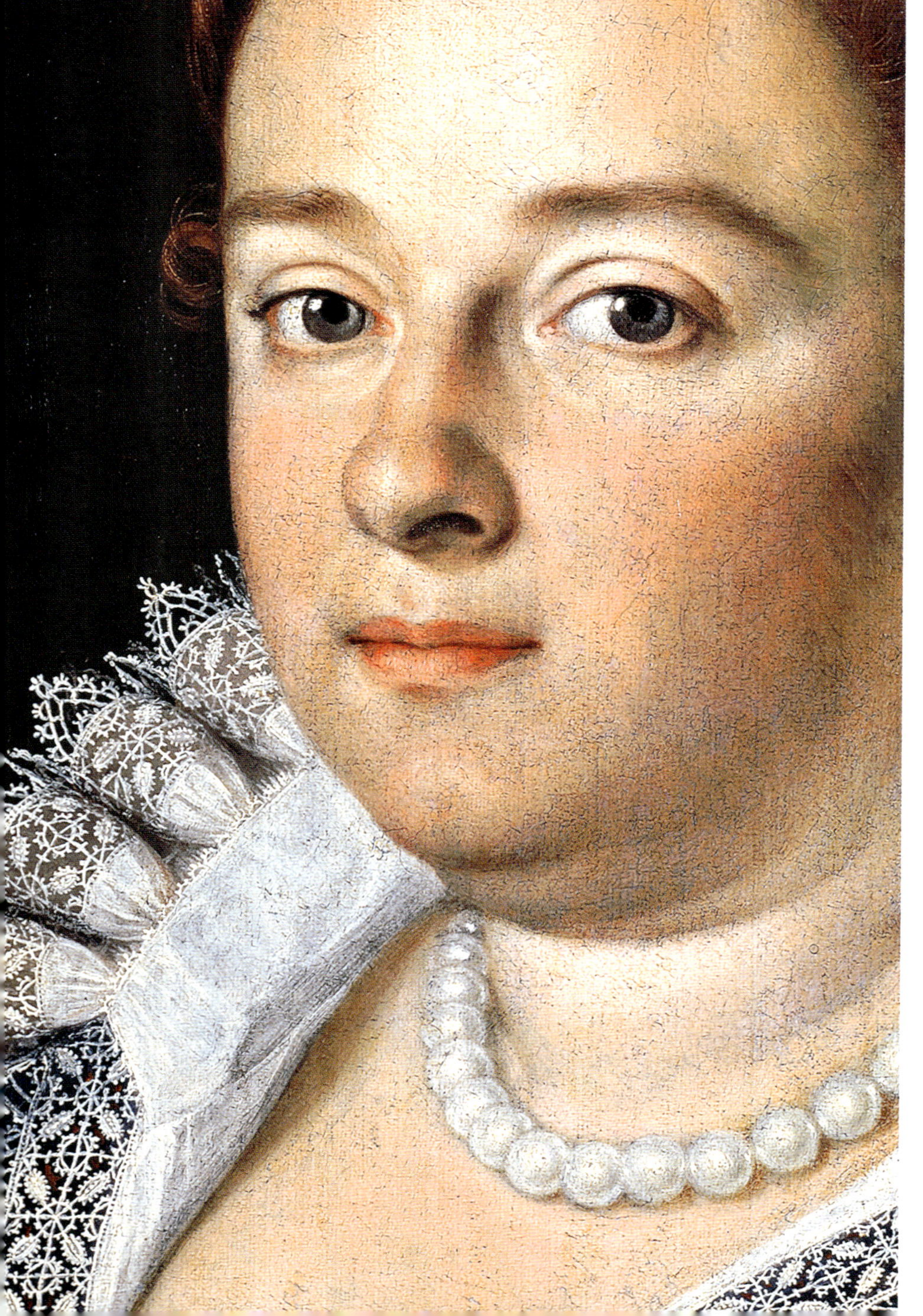

Love, art and politics

HENRY KAAP

In 1586, a portrait of Bianca Cappello (1548–1587) caused a sensation throughout Venice (fig. 1). The sitter, the daughter of a long-established Venetian patrician family, had – according to the myth-enshrouded tale – run away to Florence several years earlier as a 15-year-old with the accountant Pietro Bonaventuri. There, in Pietro's home town, they married, which prompted Bianca's father, Bartolomeo Cappello, to take legal action against the two. Meanwhile, in the Tuscan capital on the Arno, another liaison was in the offing for Bianca – this time it was none other than the grand ducal heir to the throne, Francesco de' Medici (1541–1587), whose interest she had aroused. While Bianca was now courted as his mistress, her husband Pietro died tragically in 1572. After the Medici's wife, Joanna of Austria, also died unexpectedly in childbirth in 1578, Francesco and Bianca married shortly afterwards, initially secretly. In 1579, their marriage was then publicly celebrated and Bianca henceforth bore the title Grand Duchess of Tuscany. Although she continued to have a latent bad reputation (*mala fama*) in Florence, she was henceforth regarded as a kind of early modern celebrity in Venice.

It seems that Bianca was well aware of this new status; at least she subsequently pursued a veritable image policy. Within the scope of this strategy, her portrait mentioned at the beginning, which was probably painted between 1584 and 1586 by the Rome-based painter Scipione Pulzone (c. 1542/44–1598), plays a central role. The finely painted picture shows the Grand Duchess as a bust in three-quarter profile and approximately life-size against a dark background. The precious blue dress, adorned with gold thread and elaborate lace trimmings, together with opulent pearl ornaments, show Bianca's Venetian origins. They give her appearance the presence of a princess befitting her status. From her round face, Bianca looks at the viewer with an unblinking eye. Her direct gaze and the red carnation tucked into her décolleté lend the portrait, which beyond that satisfies the rules of decency, "a little bit of innuendo", a characteristic that Agnolo Firenzuola demanded of women in his *Dialogo delle bellezze delle donne* (1548).

The painting in question travelled to Venice on behalf of Bianca where, in 1586, through the agency of a certain Francesco Bembo (1544–1599), himself the scion of a notable Venetian family, it enraptured the population of the lagoon city – an admiration that was to extend to the head of state of the Serenissima, the Doge. As Elsje van Kessel has recently been able to prove on the basis of a rich correspondence between Francesco Bembo and Bianca Cappello, this use of images must be seen as a calculated move. It probably emerged with an awareness of the history of portrait painting in Venice and made consistent use of the high social and political relevance attributed to portraits here. For this reason, Pulzone's Bianca portrait is particularly suitable for guiding us, cicerone-like, through the winding alleys of Venetian portrait painting with the aim of approaching its historical and artistic background.

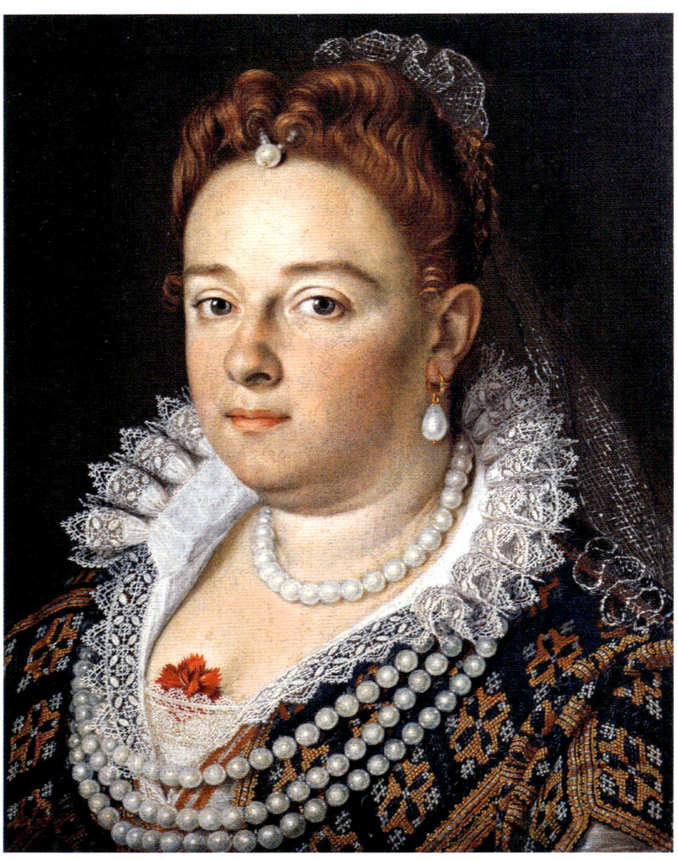

Fig. 1 Scipione Pulzone, *Portrait of Bianca Cappello*, between 1584 and 1586, Vienna, Kunsthistorisches Museum

The example of Bianca's portrait already hints at a condition on which the following is based: the historical city state of Venice was a strictly ordered and thus hermetic social structure, which, however, acted osmotically with regard to the production of cultural goods – in other words, Venice was open to imbibing external achievements into its own artistic production. In this way, social stability was to ensure the preservation of the city's existing prosperity, while innovations coming from outside ensured the growth of its own pecuniary as well as cultural wealth. This study of Venice's portrait painting between the 15th and 16th centuries is therefore based on two leitmotifs, which are referred to here as the politics of relatedness and the poetics of desire.

Genealogies

The politics of relatedness can be grasped in different forms. A connectivity that bridges time is expressed, for example, in genealogical references, regardless of whether we are talking about linear, hence real, or constructed relationships. Through her marriage to Francesco I de' Medici in 1578, Bianca Cappello not only received the title of Grand Duchess of Tuscany, but from then on she also occupied a key position in diplomatic relations between the Tuscan and Venetian states. Venice in particular recognised Bianca's political value, which is why the Senate named her the "true and exceptional daughter of our Signoria". This special distinction had previously only been bestowed on Catherine Cornaro (1454–1510). The daughter of the Venetian patrician family Corner had ruled over the island of Cyprus as queen from 1474 to 1489 after the death of her husband James II. As compensation for her abdication, which was forced upon her by the Venetian state, she was given the town of Asolo in Veneto, where she devoted herself intensively to patronage of the arts. Like Francesco Bembo, the poet, humanist and cardinal Pietro Bembo, who came from the Venetian family of the same name, created a literary memorial to her cultural patronage with *Gli Asolani* (1505), a philosophical dialogue on love and courtly life. Buoyed by the fame based on her cultural commitment, Catherine advanced over time to become the ideal image of a Venetian noblewoman, distinguished by the qualities of modesty, chastity and willingness to self-sacrifice that served the common good. Gentile Bellini (c. 1430–1507) created a portrait of Catherine around 1500, depicting her in three-quarter profile, crowned and wearing a noble robe richly decorated with pearls, against a neutral background (fig. 2). Bianca Cappello will have had herself presented in a similar manner by Scipione Pulzone in the 1580s. The collection of the Venetian senator and patron of the arts Jacopo Contarini, who had portraits of both regents mounted side by side, attests to the fact that this pictorial strategy worked wonderfully. Francesco Sansovino, in his chronicle of *Venetia, città nobilissima et singolare* (1581), dedicated to Bianca Cappello, also draws a direct comparison between the two 'daughters of the Republic'.

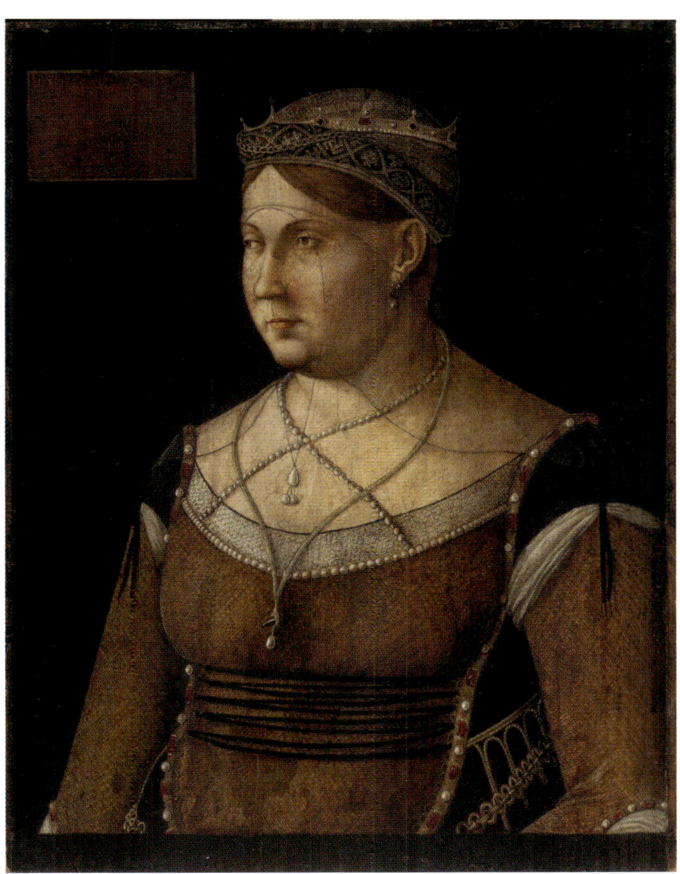

Fig. 2 Gentile Bellini, *Portrait of Catherine Cornaro*, c. 1500, Budapest, Szépművészeti Múzeum

The visual and rhetorical construct of an explicit connection between Bianca and Catherine, as a Venetian archetype of virtuous female rule, must be seen in the context of political relations between Florence and Venice in the period around 1580. At the same time, the fact that both women appear in their portraits as dignified, portly ladies opens up a reference to another political female figure in the Venetian state apparatus: the Dogaressa, the wife of the Doge. While it was necessary for the Tuscan regent Bianca Cappello to exhibit her fertility throughout her life, thus referring to her ability to produce (male) offspring in the genealogical thinking of a duchy, in the Republic of Venice, which determined its head of state by election, care had to be taken to avoid images that could convey the impression of dynastic claims. For this reason, there are only a few pictorial works in which the Dogaressa and the Doge appear together. It is therefore remarkable that the earliest surviving portrait of a doge depicts such a double portrait. The lunette painting created by Paolo Veneziano in 1339 in the Frari Church, which crowns the tomb of Doge Francesco Dandolo, shows the latter in profile on the left, looking up in an attitude of adoration at the Christ Child, who is sitting on the lap of the Madonna enthroned in the centre, who has turned towards the Dogaressa Elisabetta Contarini, who is likewise kneeling on the right. It is significant here that this is a pictorial programme in a sepulchral context, so a dynastic sequence is excluded.

Probably the first dogaressa portraits in the narrower sense are the portrait medals of Giovanna Dandolo (before 1400–1462) created around 1460 by the otherwise largely unknown artist Pietro da Fano (rec. 1452–1464). We still have several copies of these: Giovanna is placed on one side of the medal (fig. 3), while the other side depicts either the portrait of her husband, Doge Pasquale Malipiero (c. 1392–1462), or an allegory. The medals portraying Pasquale Malipiero and Giovanna Dandolo show both with facial features marked by age, thus paying tribute to their advanced age achieved in the service of Venetian society. The pictorial focus on the age of the ruling couple also communicates their 'harmlessness' with regard to possible genealogical successions.

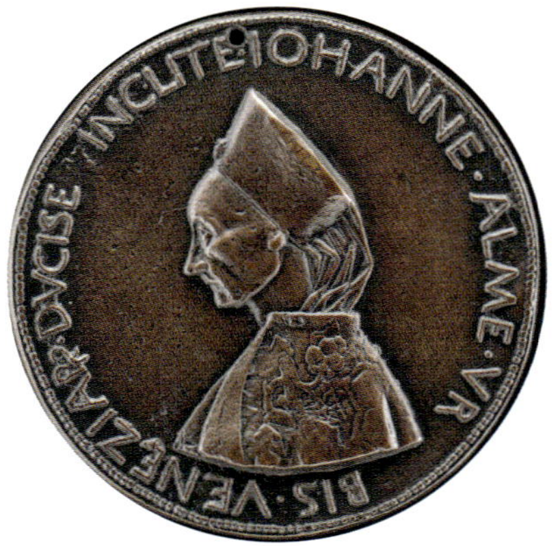

Fig. 3 Pietro da Fano, *Medal of Giovanna Dandolo* (reverse), c. 1460, Washington, D.C., National Gallery of Art

At approximately the same time as the medals mentioned above, Gentile Bellini produced a painted portrait of Malipiero (c. 1460/62, Boston, Museum of Fine Arts), which depicts the Doge in strict profile, as in medal or coin images. This mode of presentation, in which

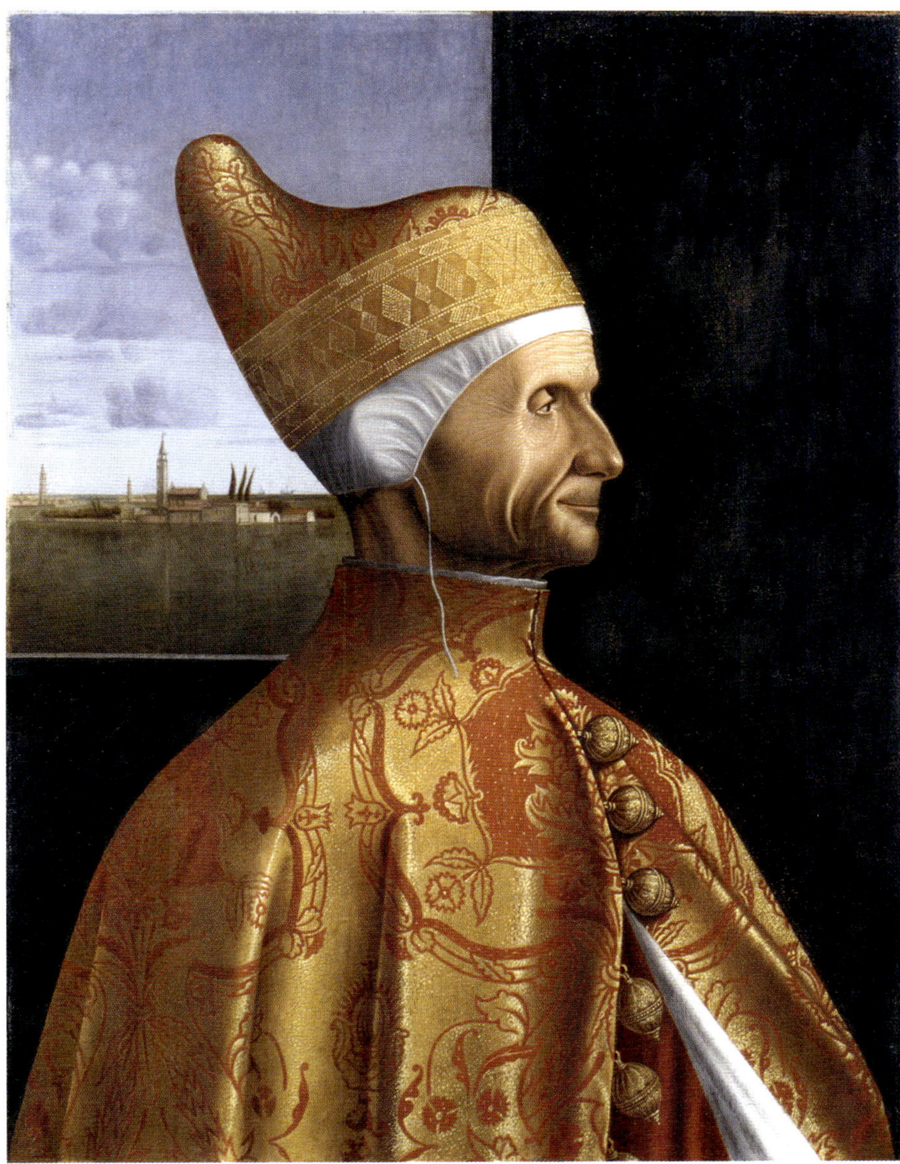

Fig. 4 Vittore Carpaccio, *Portrait of Doge Leonardo Loredan*, 1501–1505, Venice, Musei Civici, Museo Correr

the portrait does not occupy a pictorial space of its own and the person shown is not given the opportunity to look out of the picture or even to claim the fictitious space for themselves with the help of a self-referential gesture, was for a long time the most common form of portrait. Vittore Carpaccio's (c. 1465–1525/26) *Portrait of Doge Leonardo Loredan* (fig. 4), which depicts the head of the Serenissima dressed in his official insignia, the high-necked brocade coat with the pomegranate pattern and the horned, finely embroidered ceremonial cap (*corno ducale*), also attests to this traditional presentation scheme. The profile view is intended to emphasise the dignity of the person, but from a formal aesthetic perspective it already takes into account the function of remembrance after the demise of the sitter. Although Carpaccio, in an effort to give the panel painting spatial depth, opens up the background of the picture by means of a fictitious window view of two islands in the Venetian lagoon, his figuration of Leonardo Loredan (1436–1521) remains bound to the surface.

The triumph of the 'faciality' of the portrait, expressed in the detachment of the face from the pictorial plane and the turn towards the viewer, took place earlier in the Netherlands than in Italy, already in the 15th century, and is prominent in the paintings of Jan van Eyck or Hans Memling, for example. A work that clearly illustrates the process of detachment from the pictorial background and, through it, the 'facialisation' of the portrait is Hans Memling's (c. 1430/40–1494) *Portrait of Bernardo Bembo* (cat. 70). The Venetian envoy (1433–1519), father of the aforementioned Pietro Bembo, is depicted in three-quarter profile in front of an open landscape. In his left hand, Bernardo holds an antique coin with the profile of the Roman emperor Nero. Memling's portrait can be understood as a presentational piece with which the painter comprehensibly demonstrated his own skills in the profession of portrait painting. Contemporaries must have noticed the striking difference between the flatness of the coin's image, resulting in the binding of Nero's profile to the background, and the spatially rendered, three-quarter view of Bernardo's figure. By detaching his face from the pictorial plane, the sitter was given the necessary space to develop presence, in the sense of a person's presence in the picture, which is no longer merely the remembrance of a face.

Correspondences

Alongside the politics of relatedness, which focused on the factor of time, policies aimed at bridging spatial distance were also of importance; they are presented here under the heading "correspondences". Barely three months after Francesco Bembo received Bianca Cappello's portrait on 10 March 1586, he reported to her in a letter about the hundreds of people who visited his house every week to look at the portrait. This astonished crowd also included leading Venetian painters such as Tintoretto, Jacopo Bassano, Palma il Giovane and Veronese. They were all commissioned to copy Bianca's portrait. However, as

Francesco explains, Tintoretto's version is very dissimilar to the original and the sitter appears painted rather than alive as in Pulzone's work. Pulzone's fine painting, whose final result makes the brushstrokes barely visible to the naked eye and invites viewers to come very close to the painting, even so close that their own faces almost touch the painted one, seemed unusual in late 16th-century Venice, and Bianca's portrait attracted particular attention because of the way it was painted.

Unlike Pulzone, the generation of Venetian painters of the time continued to be influenced by the working method of the late Titian (c. 1488/90–1576), although he had already died ten years earlier. Titian's successors were accustomed to broad and spontaneous brushstrokes that were clearly visible, so that a great distance from the painting is necessary to perceive what is depicted. In Titian's vita, which the artist and biographer Giorgio Vasari published as part of the second edition of his famous *Vite de' più eccellenti pittori, scultori e architettori* (1568), he describes Titian's late style as roughly executed "patches of colour" that were unsuitable for close-up viewing but perfect from a distance. Vasari also draws a comparison with Titian's painting of his youth. His early works are, according to Vasari, characterised by a certain delicacy and were finished with incredible care, so that the paintings could be viewed from near and far. Pulzone's method of painting can therefore be compared to a certain extent with that of the young Titian, or rather his style, which aims for great plasticity and uniformity, equivalent to older painting methods, as they had once been cultivated in Venice. Having the Rome-based Pulzone paint a portrait of the Grand Duchess of Tuscany, who hailed from Venice, therefore appears to be a deliberate calculation. The special style of her portrait was not only striking because it was different from the painting that was common in the Serenissima at the time, but it also drew a link back to the generation of Venetian portrait painters of the time around 1500.

The fact that Bianca's portrait, coming from outside, provided new impulses in the lagoon is hardly surprising. The mobility of works of art and artists has always been the driving force of innovation. This is especially true for Venice in the late 15th and early 16th centuries. As the example of Memling's portrait of Bernardo Bembo (cat. 70) proves, Italian envoys in Flanders not only had their portraits painted, but they also brought them back to their homeland. We must assume a high degree of mobility of persons and works of art, which can only be rudimentarily reconstructed today. However, an important figure in terms of mobility-related innovations in the field of portrait painting is certainly Antonello da Messina (probably before 1430–1479).

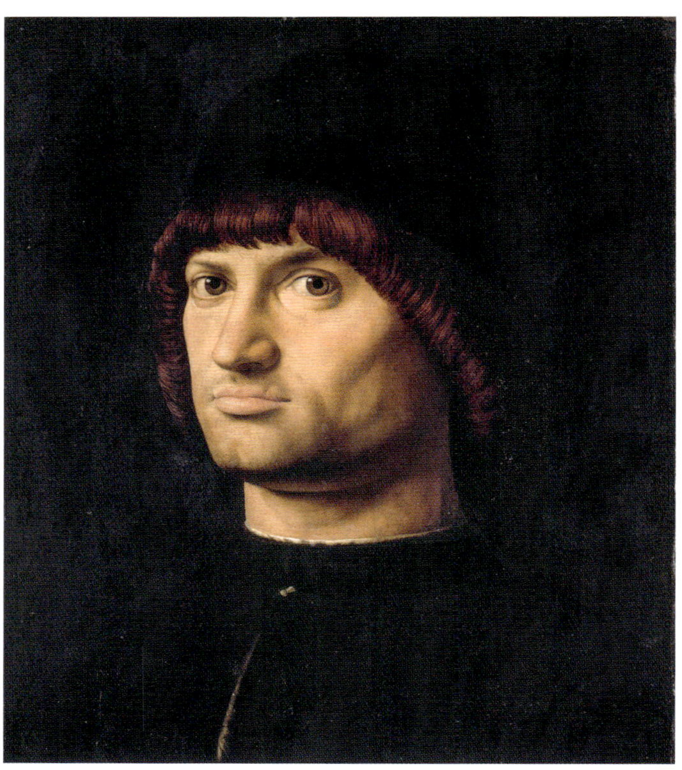

Fig. 5 Antonello da Messina, *Portrait of a Man*, 1475, Paris, Musée du Louvre

Antonello, who left Sicily in the mid-15th century and was trained in painting in Naples, may have found inspiration at the Aragonese court in the Dutch paintings that were preferably collected there, such as those of the likes of Jan van Eyck or Robert Campin. His oeuvre includes a large number of small-format portraits that occupy an intermediary position between Flemish and Italian art. Alongside compositional innovations in the profession of portrait painting, which contributed to the fame that preceded Antonello and made him attractive as an artist to various courts and city states in Italy, the desirability of his works may have played a significant role in the popularisation of oil painting. Since they can be modelled, oil paints are particularly suitable for portraits. In the mid-1470s, Antonello finally also travelled to Venice, where his paintings enjoyed extraordinary popularity and provided new inspiration for local portrait art.

Although portraits by Dutch artists had already been collected in Veneto before, leading to familiarisation with their aesthetic peculiarities, the Paris *Portrait of a Man* of 1475 (fig. 5), however, shows that Antonello's approach goes beyond a mere amalgamation of the various portrait types. Like the Dutch painters, in his portraits he also presents the depicted person in three-quarter profile, detached from contexts of action and mostly in front of a neutral background. Due to the narrow crop of the image and the focus on the face, these bust portraits give the impression of closeness. Antonello reinforces this impression of a communicative exchange in many of his works by the great importance he attaches to the direct gaze from the picture, which seeks a virtual counterpart. The majority of the people he portrayed conduct a silent dialogue with their viewers through eye contact – the spatial proximity between the painted person and the viewer resulting from the narrow crop of the picture is extended by a temporal and emotional dimension of closeness in the exchange of their gazes. In contrast to the aforementioned official portraits of the doges, which are intended to suggest everlasting permanence (figs 3, 4), Antonello's 'private' portraits focus on eye contact as a dynamic visual event that is made permanent in the picture.

In doing so, he was able to build on the fact that his contemporaries were accustomed to empathising with their painted counterparts. Not only did Leon Battista Alberti demand in his treatise on painting *Della pittura* (1435/36) that artists evoke feelings of empathy in the viewer through their works of art, but such an action was also practised almost daily in the submissive contemplation of devotional pictures. Especially the Ecce Homo representations, which are conceived as a bust and direct the focus to the tear-covered face of the suffering Christ, were made by Antonello himself in several copies in Venice and evoke associations with his portraits. While these pictures aim at the viewer's sympathy and thus at emotional proximity, they close, quite in the Dutch tradition, at the lower edge with a painted parapet (*parapetto*), with which the painter illusionistically creates spatial distance and on which a small label (*cartellino*) presents his signature. These parapets are also frequently found in Antonello's portraits, whose proportions are similar to those of his devotional paintings. In both cases, the size of the panel, the crop of the image, the framing and the facial expression presented thus give rise to an ambivalent play of a relationship of proximity and distance between the painted and the viewing person, which constitutes the aesthetic appeal of the respective painting.

Instead of a pitiful Christ in close-up, Antonello's Louvre portrait (fig. 5) shows a plainly dressed man with a confident and determined gaze. This reveals another of the painter's innovations: in contrast to the Dutch portraits of the time, whose sitters displayed indifferent facial expressions, the Italian's portraits attest to an increasing 'psychologisation'. Antonello vitalises the face he has captured by adding a minimal play of facial expressions – for instance, in the form of slightly bulging lips and raised eyebrows, or by hinting at particularities of the skin's surface, such as the small scar on the upper lip of the man in the Paris painting, who has therefore been interpreted as a mercenary leader (*condottiere*).

While Antonello's models send silent signals through the fixation of their eyes on a virtual counterpart and their fine facial expressions, the portraits produced by Gentile Bellini's younger brother Giovanni Bellini (c. 1435–1516) appear rather conventional in their formalised three-quarter profile without direct contact with the viewer. In the case of the *Portrait of a Young Senator* (cat. 71), this corresponds with the social rank of the protagonist and the milieu from which he comes. In keeping with his social status, the aspect of representation is much more pronounced in his portrait. The staging of the dignity of office follows traditional representational schemes, as perhaps most impressively shown by Giovanni Bellini in his *Portrait of Doge Leonardo Loredan* (c. 1501/02, London, The National Gallery). The painter's task was first and foremost to render the office represented, to which the individuality of the office bearer was to be subordinated. Nevertheless, the portrayed person is not presented as an emotionless and insensitive character but is to be perceived as a stable personality, who only due to this very quality is able to have the well-being of society as a whole in mind as a political office bearer and to let his own feelings recede into the background. In Bellini's portrait of the young Venetian senator, his emotional impulses are thus only reflected metaphorically and detached from the integrity of his official body by the atmospheric element of fleeting clouds against a serene blue sky.

Rituals of relational associativity

The example of Pulzone's portrait of Bianca Cappello and its object biography as a mobile image allow us to understand early modern pragmatics in dealing with portraits and portrait culture itself in terms of a social practice. As can be seen in the aforementioned works by Memling and Antonello (cat. 70; fig. 5), modes of production and reception are, on the one hand, of primary importance here. On the other hand, the mobile image becomes a political medium with regard to the diplomatic exchange of gifts. Sending Bianca's portrait was a political act, which, as Francesco Bembo's letters explain, was aimed at initiating social negotiations along the Florence–Venice axis. In 1586, during his stay in the lagoon city, this portrait crossed various social strata to finally even reach the Doge's Palace. According to Bembo, Doge Pasquale Cicogna was so enchanted by the work that he took it into his private chambers and placed it on a table next to a crucifix and his ceremonial hat. The portrait of Bianca thus joined these insignia of spiritual and secular power in the 'heart of the Republic' of Venice for one night. In Bembo's letters to Bianca Cappello, one can certainly assume a poetic exaggeration of the actual events. What they, however, hint at is the sense of an almost intimate closeness a portrait could

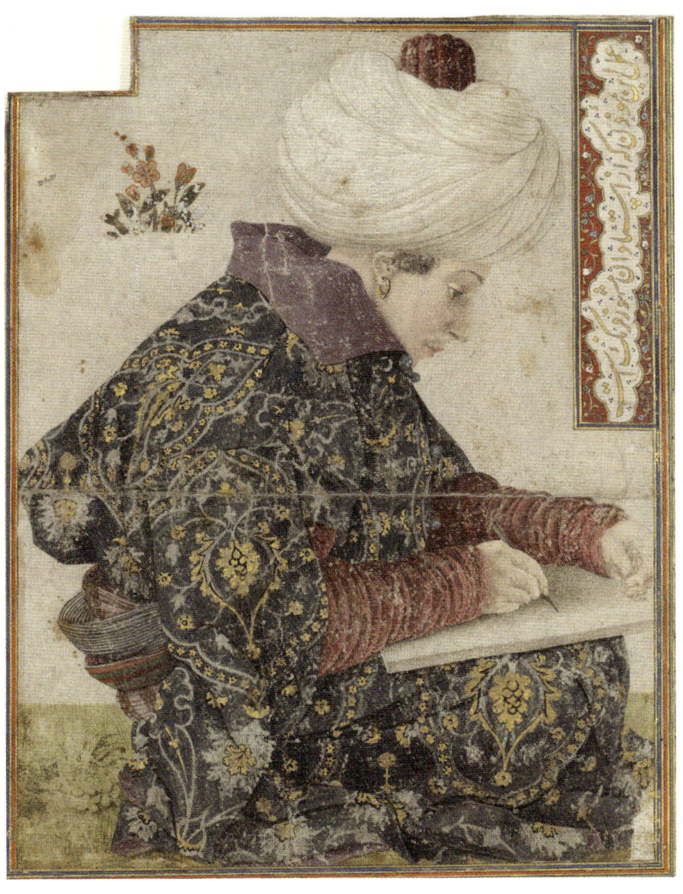

Fig. 6 Gentile Bellini, *Seated Scribe*, 1479–1481, Boston, Isabella Stewart Gardner Museum

achieve in the form of a diplomatic gift with respect to those in power. In the ritualised exchange of portraits between the courts, envoys and diplomats played the role of transmitters of works and messages. The envoys did not come as close as the portrait, which the respective ruler probably took into their own hands. Artists who acted as diplomats, however, might be an exception.

Perhaps the most famous example of early modern Venice in this respect is Gentile Bellini's journey to the Ottoman court of Mehmed II (1430–1481). After 16 years of war, the sultan made peace with Venice in January 1479. Six months later, he asked the Doge, Giovanni Mocenigo, to send him a good painter, a sculptor and a bronze caster. The Venetian state thereupon sent Gentile on this diplomatically important mission. Gentile's stay at the Ottoman court lasted from September 1479 to January 1481. Alongside several portrait medals of the sultan that were produced during this time, Gentile painted a portrait of Mehmed II, the quality of which the Ottoman ruler effusively praised in a letter accompanying the artist on his journey home. The work may be identical to Gentile's portrait of Mehmed II (1480) that is now in the National Gallery in London, where he appears as a bust behind a marble balustrade against a black background in keeping with the scheme of a ruler's portrait. In addition, there is a double portrait (between 1481 and c. 1500 [?]), possibly from the Bellini workshop, whose dating is disputed, which the city of Istanbul acquired at Christie's, London, in 2020. It shows the sultan together with a young man. The latter has a clean-shaven face, which emphasises his youthfulness, but seems unusual for an Ottoman official. The double portrait is reminiscent of a statement by Giovanni Maria Angiolello, who served as a slave at the court of Mehmed II from 1470. In the *Historia Turchesca*, which is attributed to him and covers the period from 1300 to 1515, Angiolello writes about the relationship between the sultan and the Venetian painter that the ruler liked to see the latter freely. In addition to making a drawing of Venice, Mehmed II asked Gentile to paint portraits of all the young men who were considered handsome.

A drawing in Boston attributed to Gentile (fig. 6) probably also belongs in this context. Its protagonist is a young man sitting cross-legged on a green meadow, who is about to write, draw or even paint. His richly decorated dark kaftan, belted with a silk sash, as well as the voluminous turban situate him in the Ottoman court. This type of turban was actually reserved for dignitaries, but the golden ring in his ear identifies the sitter as a court slave. Possibly he is a slave with a Christian background who had been trained for a position at the court of Mehmed II. The low social standing contrasted with the high degree of elaboration of the drawing, unusual in its refinement for Bellini's working practice, makes it unlikely that the artist produced a portrait after life here. It is more likely that Bellini's intention was to create the lyrically transfigured ideal portrait of a young man, who was presumably a poet or painter. The image of such an ideal artist fits in well with the new court school envisaged by Mehmed II.

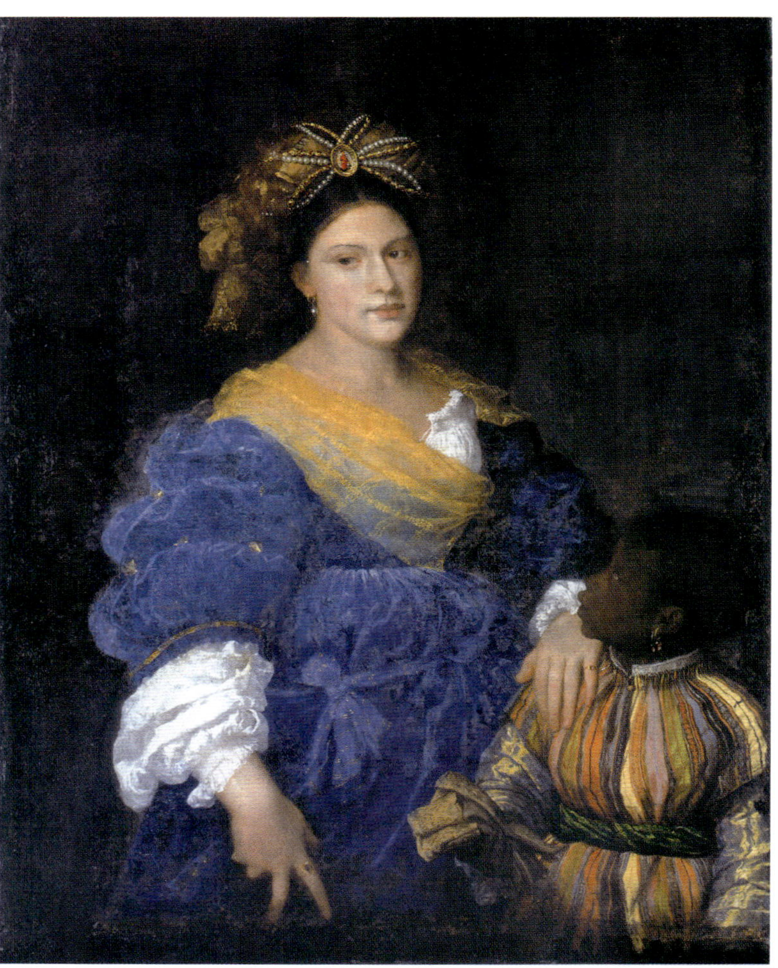

Fig. 7 Titian, *Portrait of Laura Dianti*, c. 1520/25, Kreuzlingen, Sammlung Heinz Kisters

At this point, we should take a look at Titian's *Portrait of Laura Dianti* (fig. 7). Painted a good 40 years after Gentile Bellini's journey to the Ottoman court and former aspirations of cultural exchange, this painting must be understood as an expression of a cultural disconnect. The sitter's turban does not reflect any actual knowledge of Ottoman dressing conventions, but is rather an oriental costume from Titian's artistic imagination. In an exotic misinterpretation, the sitter is frequently titled "Turk" or "Turkish woman" in later collection inventories, but in fact it is "Laura Dianti", who, born as the daughter of a hatter, was first the mistress and then probably also the wife of Alfonso I d'Este (1476–1534), Duke of Ferrara, Modena and Reggio. Her name, however, is an invention with which the duke sought to transfigure her lowly origins. Her portrait is the second individual portrait of a woman in Titian's oeuvre; however, since her name is a construct, her clothing a costume and her face comparatively heavily made-up, she acts as godmother for the many ideal Venetian portraits of women who have gone down in art history only as *La Bella*, *Flora* or similar names. Endeavouring to ennoble the portrayed "Laura", Titian placed a Black page with portrait-like features at her side in the picture, whereby "Black" here refers to the social construction of a skin colour. The child slave in a strikingly colourful robe looks up admiringly at his mistress. She ignores his gaze but confirms his presence by placing her hand on his shoulder and controlling his movements. With this painting, Titian coined a type of picture that in the baroque period many European painters would take up and modify: making use of a pointed contrast and hierarchic ordering of body images in terms of complexion and mentality, the inclusive exclusion of people of African origin is artistically thematised.

Poetics of desire

Let us take a final look at the portrait of Bianca Cappello (fig. 1): in addition to Pulzone's fine painting, which invites close-up viewing, Francesco Bembo's choreographed display of the painting contributed significantly to the portrait's resounding success with the Venetian public. As Bembo wrote to Bianca, he made the visitors who had come to see the portrait of the Grand Duchess wait in the basement of his house until the work, which was on the upper floor, had been 'dressed' with a gem-set frame and covered by a veil. Only after the visitors had gathered in front of the painting was the veil theatrically lifted. This act of staged unveiling triggered strong reactions among the viewers, who admired the portrait, some of whom even wanted to kiss it and humbly worshipped it.

Bembo's performative handling of Bianca's portrait, especially the withdrawal of its visibility through veiling and the subsequent event of unveiling, strives to produce in its magico-religious rituality an aesthetic experience of revelation. If we also consider the example of Giovanni Girolamo Savoldo's (c. 1480–after 1548) *The Virgin Adoring the Child with Two Donors* from 1527 (cat. 67), we can understand that the painters of the 16th century consciously drew on unveiling practices from religious cult. In Savoldo's case, this occurs on a content-based level, when the donor of the painting is himself assigned the role of the one who, in the act of lifting the veil, exposes the object worthy of adoration.

These effect-enhancing presentation practices have a rather long tradition, especially in relation to portraits. In the 15th and early 16th centuries, many of these works were provided with picture curtains or flexible picture covers. Only a few traces of these have survived over the centuries, but it is precisely those mobile portraits that were used as a gift to establish social relationships – for example, in a dynastic marriage initiation or as a gift between friends – that are likely to have had picture covers. On the one hand, these served to protect the portraits while, on the other hand, they also offered additional surfaces for coats of arms or allegorical heraldic badges, which, when painted on the covers, enriched the portraits underneath with an additional level of meaning. The early modern form of viewing portraits, which includes their unveiling, can be interpreted as a mode of viewing over the course of time, in which the meaning of the picture ensemble gradually emerges. Albrecht Dürer's *Portrait of Hieronymus Holzschuher* (1526, Berlin, Staatliche Museen, Gemäldegalerie) or Lorenzo Lotto's (c. 1480–1556) *Portrait of Bishop Bernardo de' Rossi* (1505, Naples, Museo Nazionale di Capodimonte) may be mentioned here as well-known examples of portraits whose covers still exist.

The way Francesco Bembo addresses Bianca Cappello in his letters and reports on her portrait must be seen against the background of the poetic transfiguration of friendship alliances popularised by Bernardo Bembo, for example. Francesco Bembo will most certainly have been familiar with the works of his distant relative. Bernardo Bembo is considered the main representative of Petrarchism – namely, those authors who imitated the poetry of the 14th-century poet Francesco Petrarch. Bembo's literary production in relation to the theme of love and friendship unfolds in many instances along the motifs of the image of the beloved and the image of the self. The former motif, based on Petrarch's literary veneration of a portrait of his beloved Laura, developed in the 16th century into the topos of a general veneration of portraits of beautiful women (*belle donne*). Such undertones are echoed in the veneration that Francesco Bembo bestowed on Pulzone's portrait of Bianca. It also, however, ties in with the latter motif: sending one's own portrait to good friends. The underlying idea here was that the friendship between the sender and the receiver reveals itself since the viewer may recognise their own self in the portrait of the other. This form of friendly, loving intimacy is expressed in the painting through direct eye contact, which is characteristic of both the Bianca portrait and the corresponding works by Antonello da Messina (fig. 5).

Leon Battista Alberti articulated the idea of a connection between painting (i.e. primarily portrait painting) and friendship in his aforementioned treatise on painting. He writes: "Painting contains a divine force which not only makes absent men present, as friendship is said to do, but moreover makes the dead seem almost alive. Even after many centuries they are recognized with great pleasure and with great admiration for the painter." According to Alberti, portrait painting thus enables its viewers to overcome two forms of absence of a beloved person: the spatial separation from a friend and the temporal separation from a deceased person. The former is accompanied by a longing desire for a possible reunion in this world, while the latter – if one does not want to wait for the hereafter – can only be overcome

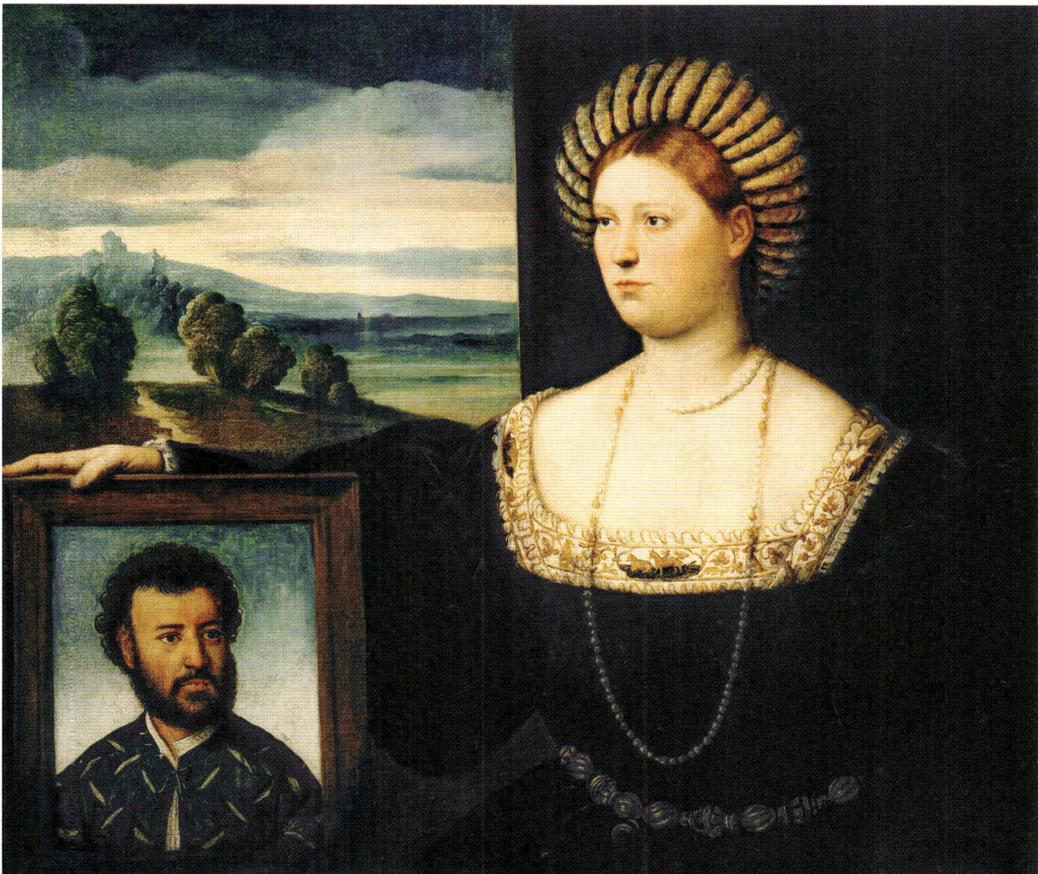

Fig. 8 Bernardino Licinio, *A Wife with Her Husband's Portrait*, c. 1525/28, Milan, Castello Sforzesco

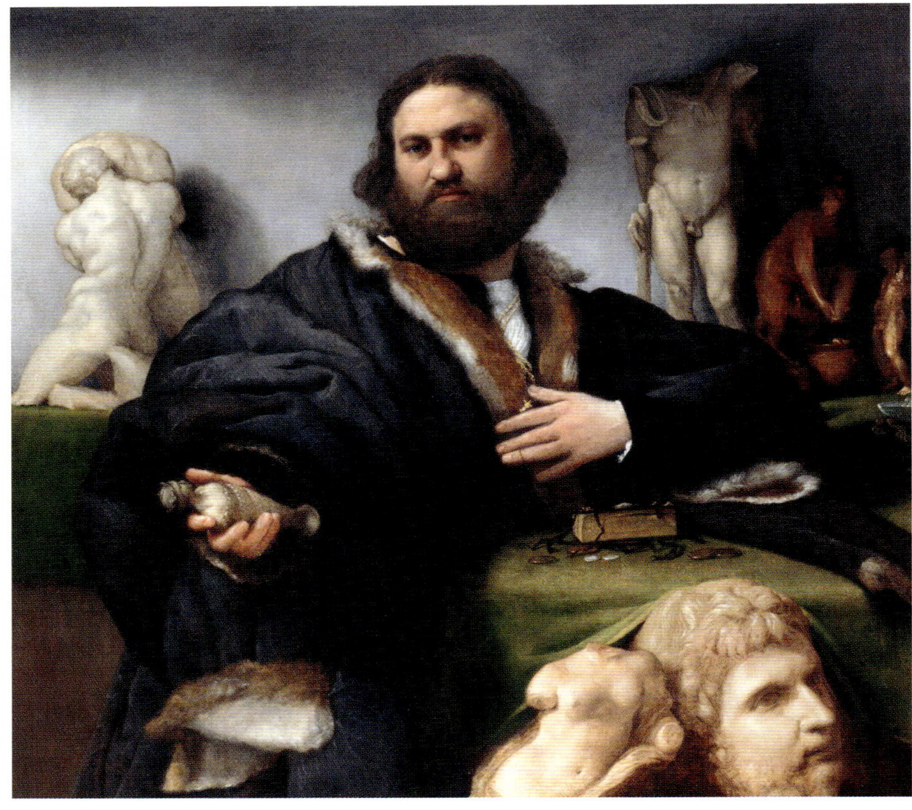

Fig. 9 Lorenzo Lotto, *Portrait of Andrea Odoni*, 1527, London, The Royal Collection, HM King Charles III

by means of art. Bernardino Licinio's (c. 1485–after 1549/before 1565) *A Wife with Her Husband's Portrait* (fig. 8) seems to be an attempt at such a reunion in the medium of painting – at any rate, Licinio's work has been interpreted as a portrait of a widow expressing the continuing emotional attachment to her departed husband by having the painter render her in the elegiac mode, holding the portrait of the deceased. Her hand holding the frame of his portrait signals togetherness, while the empty gaze marks the impossibility of direct contact. Only the window view of a stretch of land whose expanse is traversed by a path may be interpreted as a 'landscape of the soul' that poetically relegates a reunion to the realm of the imaginary.

Andrea Odoni (1488–1545) created for himself a charming place to stay (*locus amoenus*) on earth. In his palazzo on the Rio del Gaffaro, the commoner, who presumably became wealthy due to his high position in the Venetian tax authority, amassed an extensive art collection that was praised by the art critic Pietro Aretino. In Odoni's bedroom – in the heart of his well-thought-out, intellectually sophisticated 'art palace' – which highlighted aesthetic and sensual attractions and was only accessible to confidants, was his portrait painted by Lorenzo Lotto (fig. 9). Lotto increasingly chose the horizontal format for his portraits from the 1520s onwards, which enabled him to charge the sitter's surroundings with enigmatic, emblem-like allusions. In the London portrait, this was done concretely through the refined arrangement of the sculptures, which are pointedly staged by the action of light and shadow, as well as through Odoni's gestures, which refer to himself and simultaneously include a virtual counterpart. The result is a portrait full of suspenseful allusions that captivates the viewer with a high degree of psychological subtlety. In Odoni's bedroom, the portrait hung on the wall surrounded by other works of art, which in their overall appearance paralleled Christian-religious with pagan-erotic motifs and thus indirectly connected them with each other. In this way, the art collection as a whole became the site of a self-curated utopia that allowed Odoni and his private circle of friends to distance themselves from the business of everyday life and to experience moments of spiritual and sensual Arcadia that were out of time, as described by the poet Jacopo Sannazaro, who was very successful at the time.

Andrea Odoni represents only one prominent example of elaborate art collections. Bianca Cappello was also active as a collector; at her behest, a large number of Venetian objects, including portraits of Venetian women, were acquired for the so-called casino opposite San Marco in Florence. Bianca's local art agent in Venice was none other than Francesco Bembo, whom she commissioned in March 1587 to have two portraits painted: "[...] the one of Signora Labia, who I hear is very charming and beautiful, the other of one of the most beautiful noblewomen living in Venice, hoping that both are done by the best hand, as I want them to adorn my little room [...]". In one of his next letters, Francesco reports on his search for the most beautiful woman in Venice, whom he believes to have found in a certain Marina Marcello. Alongside the portrait of the Signora Labia, he sends Bianca Cappello a *Mary Magdalene* painted by Titian and a nude painting for the Grand Duke. What is remarkable about Bianca's commission to Bembo is the fact that by ordering portraits of Venetian *belle donne* she subverts common notions of a usually male patronage of the arts. This raises new questions in art historical research on the popular motif of the *belle donne*, which controversially discusses the idealised beauty and simultaneous anonymity of the sitter and assumes that these lyrically transfigured paintings are portraits of courtesans or young marriage candidates (also see Theresa Gatarski's essay in this catalogue). In Bianca Cappello's time, however, the pictorial politics described above were followed by realpolitik; the aforementioned portrait of the beautiful Marina probably never reached Bianca, as she and Francesco de' Medici died unexpectedly on 20 October 1587, possibly poisoned by Francesco's brother, Ferdinando, who subsequently rose to become Grand Duke of Tuscany as Ferdinando I de' Medici.

Viewed from the north

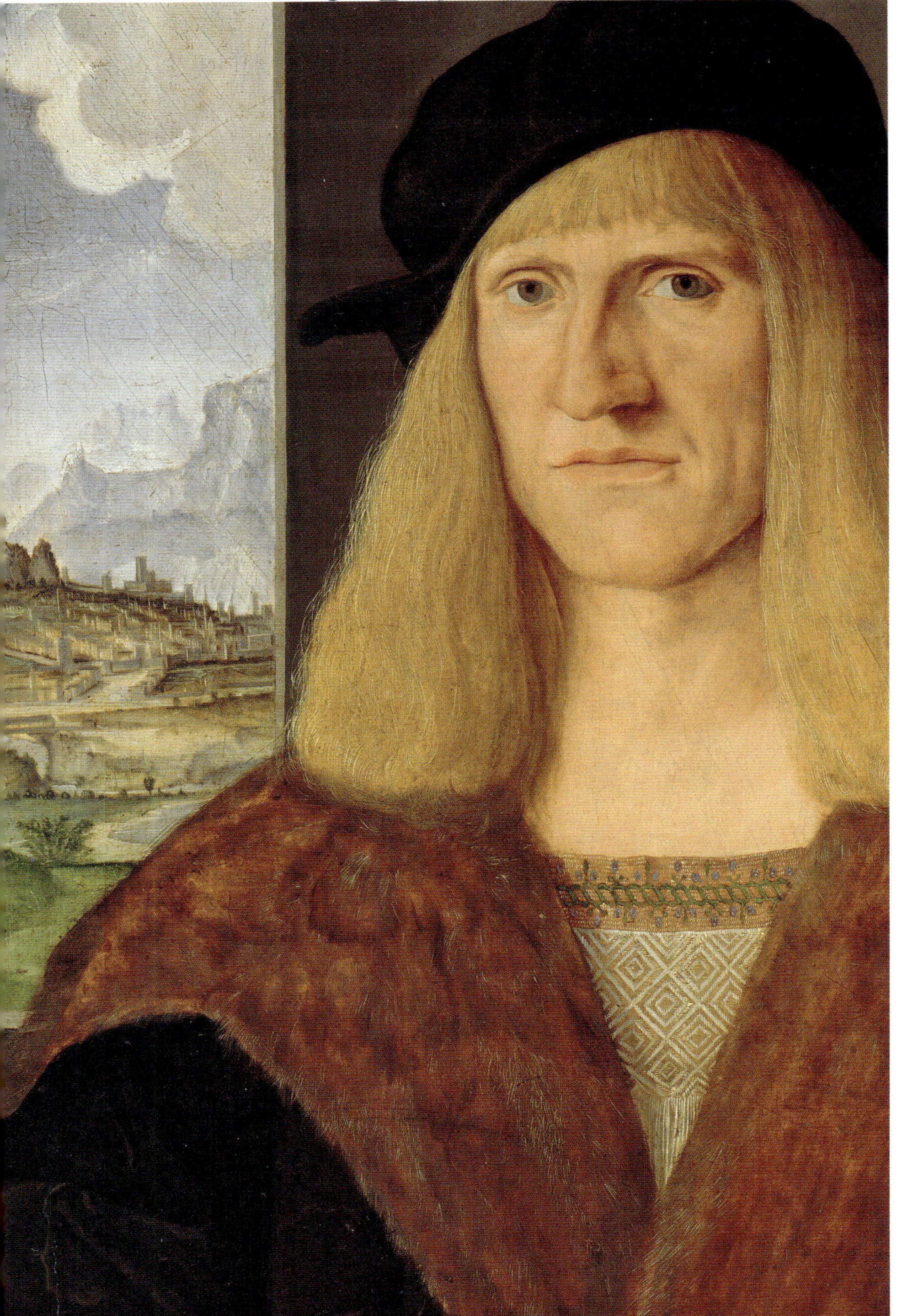

The fascination of Venetian portrait painting

ANNETTE KRANZ

The extraordinary appeal of Venetian painting during the Renaissance is, in retrospect, reflected not least in the observation that in the first half of the 16th century many artists north of the Alps temporarily went to the south. Albrecht Dürer, for example, stayed in the lagoon city twice – in 1494/95 and from late summer 1505 to early 1507. The fact that he was in contact with local artists there is documented, among other things, by his praise of Giovanni Bellini (c. 1435–1516) in a letter to his friend Willibald Pirckheimer from 1506: "He [Giovanni Bellini] is very old, but yet he is the best painter of them all."

Numerous German trading houses maintained a branch office in Venice, the nodal point of important long-distance trade routes in the Mediterranean; the lagoon city was also the central place for the transfer of money from north to south. The business hub was the Fondaco dei Tedeschi, the trading post of the Germans, on the Rialto Bridge, which not only served as a counting house and depot but was also the home of the German merchants for a long time, sometimes housing over a hundred people. Around 1500, Upper Germans represented the majority in the Fondaco. Many of them had already completed their training in Italy, where the innovative method of double-entry bookkeeping had developed in the field of commercial accounting.

In Venice, the German merchants also got to know the local art. As in Italy in general, it had broken away from the formal language of the Gothic in all areas – including architecture, sculpture and painting – earlier than north of the Alps. Evidence shows that the Germans sometimes already collected Venetian art objects during their stay in the Serenissima. Like other luxurious goods from the south (such as glass, jewellery, perfume, textiles, leather wallpaper, confectionery, wine, citrus fruits, spices as well as exports from the Levant), works of art were also traded northwards via the Fondaco. The fact that pieces from Venice were acquired in Augsburg, for example, was confirmed in 1565 by the collection theorist Samuel Quiccheberg, who had arranged and curated the Fugger art collections in the 1550s, in his writing *Inscriptiones vel Tituli*

Theatri Amplissimi. Although only a few of these objects have survived, their import becomes tangible through mentions in archival records and through artistic reflections. It is evident that the high quality of works with southern provenance was appreciated – and, due to a certain otherness, they were presumably even attractive status symbols in the north.

It is therefore not surprising that the Upper German merchants who often spent many months in Venice also commissioned their own portraits from the city's leading painters. Various portraits of tradesmen from Augsburg are, for instance, known. Although portrait painting flourished north of the Alps from the 15th century onwards, the evidence of Venetian works preserved or documented here suggest that Italian Renaissance portraiture exerted an enduring fascination. Interest was probably spurred not least by the phenomenon recorded by Giorgio Vasari (1511–1574) in his vita of Giovanni Bellini that numerous private households in the lagoon city were furnished with a conspicuously large number of portraits: "[…] he [Giovanni Bellini] introduced into Venice the fashion that everyone of a certain rank should have his portrait painted either by him or by some other master; wherefore in all the houses of Venice there are many portraits, and in many gentlemen's houses one may see their fathers and grandfathers, up to the fourth generation, and in some of the more noble they go still farther back." Marcantonio Michiel (1484–1552), himself an art collector, already referred to a large number of portraits of family members as well as friends and famous contemporaries in Venetian collections. In Venice, moreover, practical circumstances may have contributed to the fact that the merchants from north of the Alps oriented themselves towards Italian painting. For while the German tradesmen at the Steelyard in London, for example, could turn to Hans Holbein the Younger (1497/98–1543) for many years, who had lived there since 1532, no renowned German painter was permanently in Venice at the time. What, however, attracted the businessmen from the north to have their portraits painted in Venice? Or, to put it more aptly: what was special about portraiture in Venice at the time compared to that of Augsburg, for example?

Mediated by paintings from the southern Netherlands and 'translated' into Italian by Antonello da Messina (probably before 1430–1479; see p. 194, fig. 5), a turn away from the hitherto predominant depiction in pure profile took place in northern Italy in the 15th century, which had symbolised dignity and grandeur but had lacked liveliness.

In his *Portrait of Georg Fugger* from 1474 (fig. 1), Giovanni Bellini succeeds in detaching the sitter from the surface by means of the oblique view in three-quarter profile, through which the Augsburg merchant gains plasticity, although the background is still kept dark in a typical manner. At the same time, the painter was able to give Georg Fugger (1453–1506), who was only 21 years old, a stern but energetic and lively facial expression. The sitter's gaze, which seems to focus on a target in the distance, also contributes to this. The inscription on the reverse "Jeorg Fugger a di XX di Zugno MCCCCLXXIIII" attests to his name and the date of the painting's creation. Possibly the portrait was part of the new strategy of Georg Fugger and his brothers to make a stronger visual mark. After the death of their father Jakob Fugger the Elder in 1469 and with the grant of arms in June 1473, a new self-expression of the sons becomes discernible. While the decorative strings at the neckline of Georg Fugger can be explained by the current fashion north of the Alps, the delicate wreath with blue blossoms in his hair is a mystery in research. Such an attribute usually identifies the sitter as a poet and/or a friend of antiquity, as in the *Portrait of a Humanist* attributed to Giovanni Bellini from 1475/80 (Milan, Castello Sforzesco), which in the 19th century was, rather tellingly, believed to be a portrait of Andrea Mantegna (1430/31–1506). Nothing is known so far about Georg Fugger's relations to a learned, literary world, but his brother Marx had been working at the Curia in Rome since 1470, which may have brought him into contact with Roman antiquity – in the broad-est sense. The commission for the painting, which is considered to be Giovanni Bellini's earliest autonomous portrait, may have been given to the painter partly because in 1474 he had undertaken, together with his brother Gentile, the prestigious restoration of the old series of portraits of the Doge in the Sala del Maggior Consiglio in the Doge's Palace, as well as the renewal of the history paintings there,

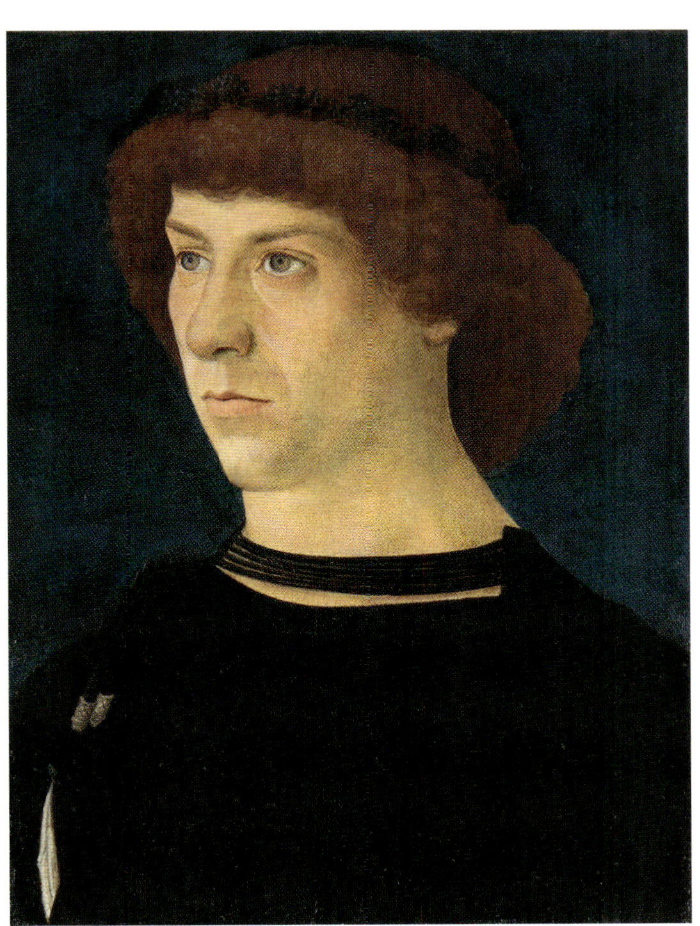

Fig. 1 Giovanni Bellini, *Portrait of Georg Fugger*, 1474, Pasadena, Norton Simon Museum

which also contained numerous portraits. Even if the small portrait (26 × 20 cm) may seem a little rigid and austere from today's perspective, comparably expressive, physiognomically individual portraits were not yet available by Augsburg artists in the mid-1470s, let alone as oil paintings. The situation did not change until the turn of the century, when artists experienced in portraiture appeared in the imperial city in the form of Hans Holbein the Elder (c. 1465–before 1524), Hans Burgkmair (1473–1531) and, from 1530, above all Christoph Amberger (c. 1500/05–1561). Nevertheless, the Upper German merchants continued to have portraits painted in Italy in the first half of the 16th century. After the end of their professional obligations, they took the paintings back to their homeland. As Vasari reports, even Giorgione (1473/74–1510), whose colouristic sensibility and poetic perception contributed significantly to the transformation of Venetian painting (cf. cat. 62), portrayed a member of the Fugger family: "There is in our book [Vasari's *Libro de' disegni*, a collection of drawings compiled by him] a head coloured in oil, the portrait of a German of the Fugger family, who was at that time one of the chief merchants in the Fondaco de' Tedeschi, which is an admirable work." Some of the research even related Vasari's reference to the much-discussed *Portrait of a Young Man* (cat. 40; see Antonio Mazzotta's essay in this catalogue), although this identification is unconvincing. Since Giorgione worked on

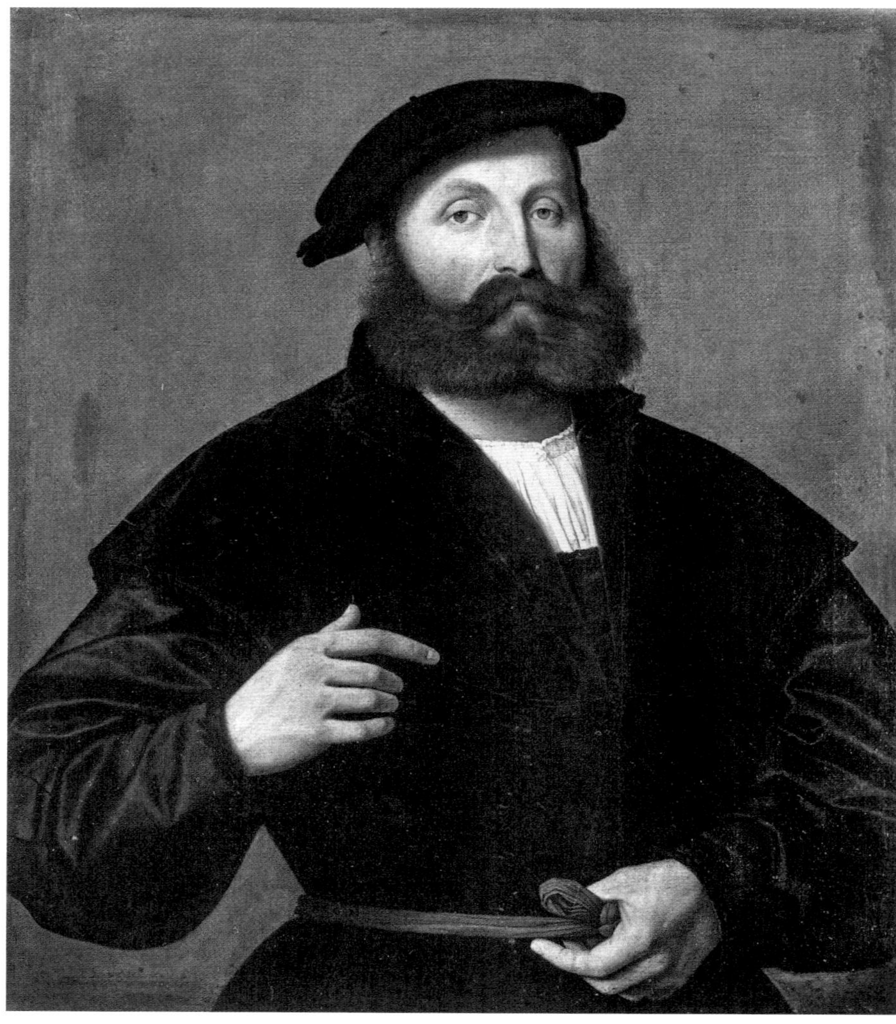

Fig. 2 Vincenzo Catena, *Portrait of Raymund Fugger*, c. 1525, formerly Berlin, Kaiser-Friedrich-Museum (probably burnt in May 1945 in the flak tower in Berlin-Friedrichshain)

the facade frescoes of the Fondaco around 1508, such a portrait commission is, nevertheless, entirely conceivable, especially since the Fuggers had contributed significant sums for the reconstruction of the building after the fire in 1505.

Almost 50 years later, his son Raymund (1489–1535) had himself portrayed in an entirely different way from Georg Fugger (fig. 2) – at the same time, the portrait, which was produced by Vincenzo Catena (c. 1470/80–1531), reflects the great innovations that had taken place in Venetian portrait painting in the first decades of the 16th century. Apart from the fundamental changes in format (75 × 63 cm) and the crop of the figure, the freedom and mobility of the sitter in space, which had been introduced by Giorgione, Palma Vecchio (c. 1480–1528) and Titian (c. 1488/90–1576), as well as a more psychologically motivated rendition, now dominate. The fact that Catena had direct contact with Giorgione, for example, is documented by the inscription on the reverse of the latter's *Laura* from 1506 (see p. 156, fig. 1), which, together with other indications, suggests that Giorgione shared a workshop with Catena for a time. In the *Portrait of Raymund Fugger*, which can be dated to around 1525 on the basis of the sitter's age, the darkly dressed, stately figure stands out clearly against the light, flat background, creating a latent spatial effect. With his face turned almost frontally into the plane and his gaze fixed on his counterpart, Raymund Fugger has noticeably gained in presence compared to his father in his portrait (fig. 1). The complex directional structure of the body axes and the staged, downright expressive appearance, with the right hand raised to chest level, gesticulating as if in conversation, and the left hand loosely hooked into the belt of the robe, underline the impression of spontaneity in the sense of an immediate snapshot, which Vasari had already emphasised: "[…] among others, that [portrait] of a German of the Fugger family, a man of rank and importance, who was then living in the Fondaco de' Tedeschi at Venice, was painted with great vivacity." Here, the interplay of the statuesque contrapposto posture, the lively gestures and the direct eye contact decisively shape the impression. A similar rendition, which seems like a visual equivalent to the nonchalance (*sprezzatura*) described by Baldassare Castiglione in his extremely successful *Libro del Cortegiano* (*The Book of the Courtier*; first edition 1528), is not to be found in the work of the Augsburg portrait painters of the same period. It corresponds to a courtly ideal that Titian, for example, also realised in a group of early portraits from around 1520/25

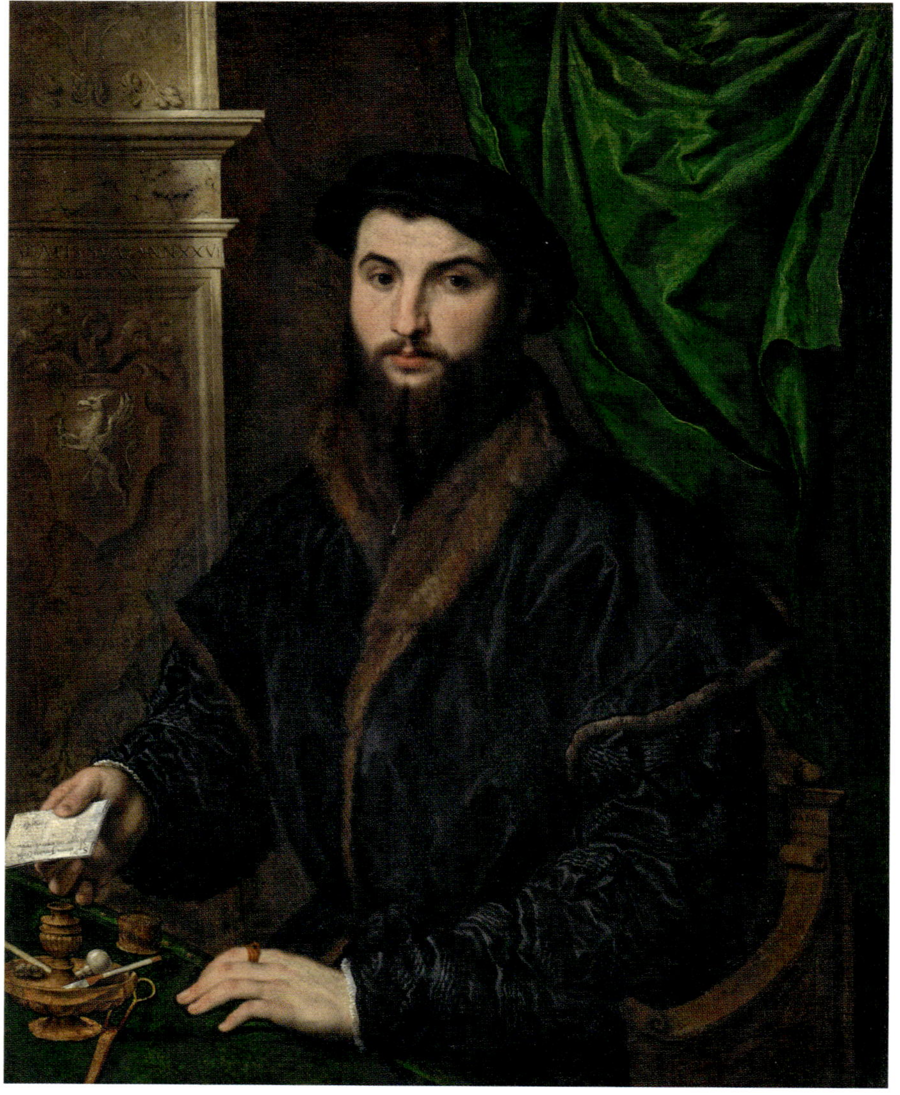

Fig. 3 Paris Bordone, *Portrait of Thomas Stahel*, 1540, Paris, Musée du Louvre

(cf. cat. 15). These works show related formal principles such as the reduced use of colour, the neutral background that does not evoke a definite pictorial space, the extension to a half-length portrait with the inclusion of the hands, the abandonment of a parapet and personalised attributes – the sitters are instead rendered in selected casualness, seemingly unpretentiously. Raymund Fugger, a representative of the family rather than an actual businessman, was demonstrably very interested in art and antiquities; he cultivated contacts with humanists and scholars, and compiled an extensive library and a large art collection. After the humanist Beatus Rhenanus had visited Raymund's Augsburg estate, he reported in 1531 on numerous Italian paintings there: "Here we saw everywhere quite excellent paintings that came from Italy [...]" ("Hic passim vidimus exquisitissimas picturas ex Italia advectas [...]"). If Fugger thus had a decided inclination to surround himself with Italian art in his own surroundings, it seems obvious that he also commissioned a portrait during one of his many journeys to the south; perhaps his elevation to the rank of count in 1526 formed a fitting occasion, and according to Vasari, Catena was a proven specialist in the field of portrait painting: "Another passing good painter in the time of these masters was Vincenzio [sic!] Catena, who occupied himself much more with making portraits from the life than with any other sort of painting; and, in truth, some that are to be seen by his hand are marvellous [...]." The instant appeal of the staging of the lively figure had to appear new and modern in Augsburg, and the differentiated painterly rendering of light also went beyond local standards – even a cursory glance at the *Portrait of Raymund Fugger* by Martin Schaffner from around 1530 (private collection) proves how significant the differences between the north and the south were in portrait art. The assumption that certain parts of the Augsburg upper class extensively owned Italian art as early as the beginning of the 16th century can only be corroborated in an exemplary manner by the Fugger family, which has been well researched in the archives, since other source material has not yet been made accessible in a comparably systematic way.

Thomas Stahel (c. 1513/14–1565), also a merchant from Augsburg, had himself in turn portrayed by Paris Bordone (1500–1571) in 1540 (fig. 3). The typology of the half-length figure in a seated position, whose inventor is considered to be Raphael with his *Portrait of Pope Julius II* of 1511/12 (London, The National Gallery), was already established in Upper Italy at the time and occurs, for example, in the work of Moretto da Brescia (c. 1498–1554) and Lorenzo Lotto (c. 1480–1556) since the 1520s (see p. 202, fig. 9). In Titian's oeuvre, seated figures appear in an architecturally defined interior space, with a table inserted at the side, in the second half of the 1530s. In the *Portrait of Thomas Stahel*, Bordone combines the seated figure turned strongly to the side with a pictorial space that suggests depth. The sitter is framed by a draped silk curtain in the background on the right and a richly ornamented pillar on the left, which records Stahel's age and the year in which the picture was painted in an inscription at the top: "[AE]TATIS SVAE ANN. XXVII / MDXXXX". The griffin crest of the Stahel family sits in the face of the pillar, with the initials "TS" appearing above it. While the numerous writing utensils on the table already suggest that this is a merchant's portrait, the label on the letter held by Stahel actually names the Augsburg entrepreneur Hieronymus Kraffter as the addressee: "To the honourable gentleman Hieronymus Kraffter the Elder, always highly esteemed. Augsburg" ("Sp.le domino Jeronimo Craft[er] / Magior suo semper observans / Augusta"). The address written in Latin, in which Augsburg is to be understood as the destination, proves that Stahel did not have himself portrayed in the imperial city. The imposing interior is echoed in the picture's format (107 × 86 cm), which is even larger than that of the *Portrait of Raymund Fugger* (fig. 2). Nobilitating set pieces and props such as pillars and curtains originally derive from imperial portrait iconography, symbolising wealth, power and permanence. In Venice, the idea of setting figures against an architecturally structured background had been circulating since Palma Vecchio. In his portraits of later years, Bordone would even expand on the architectural motifs and perfect their perspective arrangement, so that they sometimes become monumental architectural backdrops and describe a pictorial space opening up into great depth. The light incarnate parts are the dominant expressive elements in the *Portrait of Thomas Stahel*; within the elegant dark palette, the lighting and colours draw attention to the area of the table, hands and face. The merchant has turned his head off the axis of his body and is depicted with an alert, calm gaze. A comparably comprehensive organisation of the interior through a spatialised interior architecture was not yet common in southern German painting. Elaborate presentations of seated figures by Amberger in Augsburg – but also by Georg Pencz (c. 1500/02–1550) in Nuremberg – are not to be found until the 1540s. Stahel therefore ordered a portrait from Bordone whose modern compositional scheme had a definite Italian connotation and was certainly received as such.

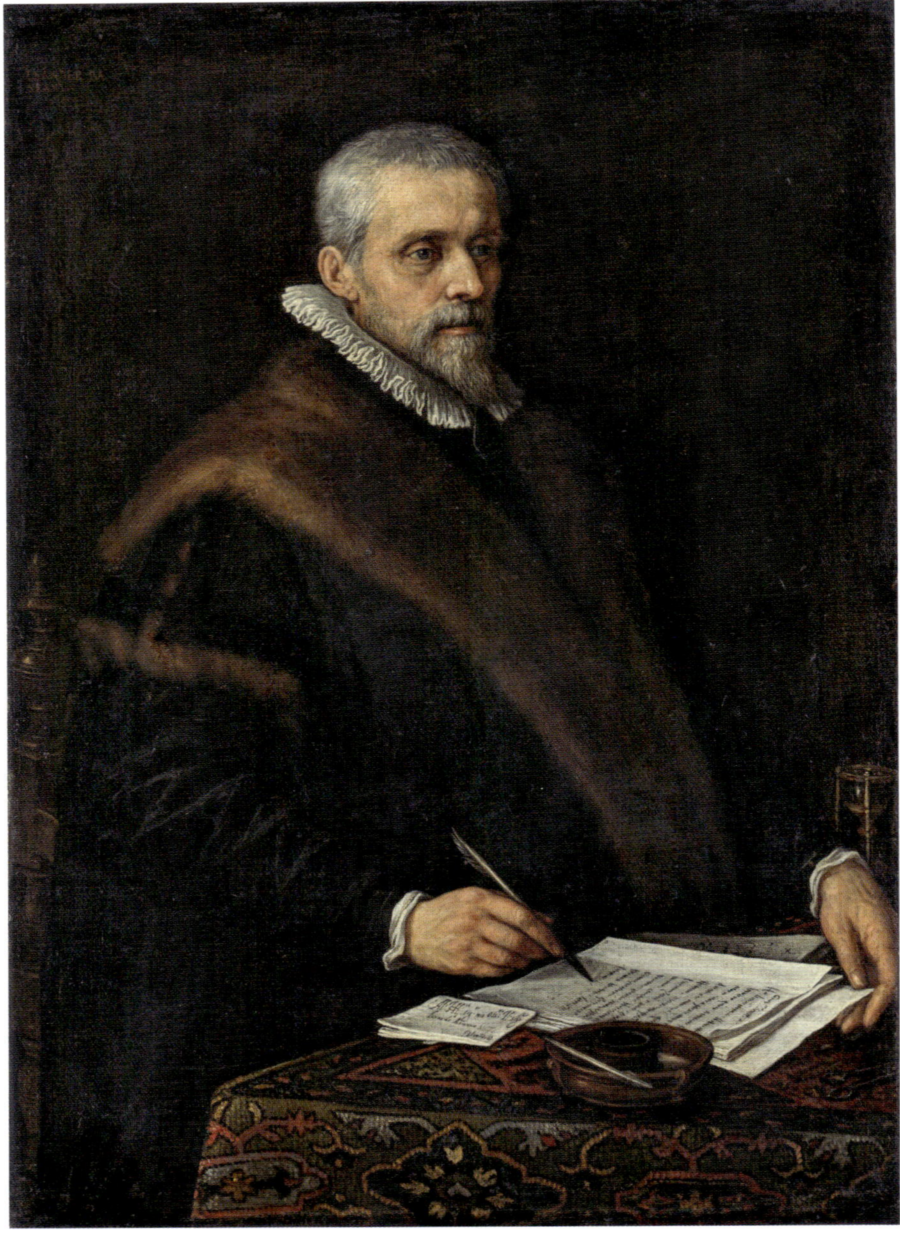

Fig. 4 Leandro Bassano, *Portrait of Leonhard Hermann von Wimpfen*, c. 1595, Würzburg, Staatsgalerie in der Residenz

The fact that the appreciation of Venetian painting within the German merchant community in the lagoon city continued unabated in the second half of the 16th century is impressively documented by the *Portrait of Leonhard Hermann von Wimpfen* from around 1595 (fig. 4).

Leandro Bassano (1557–1622) shows the tradesman, whose grandfather had already settled permanently in Venice in 1504, as a voluminous figure standing at a table on which business correspondence is spread out. Leonhard Hermann (c. 1525/35–after 1595) seems to have just paused in his writing, as the quill pen in his hand is still touching the top sheet of paper. Instead of seeking visual contact with the viewer as his counterpart, however, his gaze wanders off into the distance. An hourglass standing on the table at the back alludes to the merchant's advanced age as a memento mori symbol. The large picture format (133.4 × 95.5 cm) and the monumental conception of the figure are characteristic of many portraits by Bassano at the turn of the 17th century. In conjunction with the valuable carpet which attests to Hermann's luxurious taste and pecuniary wealth, his "Schaube" (overcoat) with its broad fur collar – the representative garment of the southern German upper class par excellence – demonstrates the merchant's high sense of status, who evidently still defines himself as German. Since the portrait type of the almost life-size figure in three-quarter profile was neither new nor unusual at the end of the 16th century – with Jacopo Tintoretto (1518/19–1594) and Paolo Veronese (1528–1588) in particular having contributed to its widespread use – Hermann may have been persuaded to choose Bassano, on the one hand, because of his high artistic quality, as is evident, for example, in his naturalistic depiction of different materials and their light reflections. On the other hand, Bassano's high reputation may also have played a role: the artist was considered the best portrait painter in the lagoon city – Carlo Ridolfi already praised him as such ("particolarmente eccellente ne' ritratti") in his artists' biographies (1648). For his portrait of Doge Marino Grimani of 1595/96 (Dresden, Gemäldegalerie Alte Meister), he was even appointed "Cavaliere di San Marco" by the latter a little later and was henceforth allowed to use the title "Eques". However, in the case of the Hermann portrait, the context of the commission differs categorically from the circumstances in which the aforementioned portraits were created, as Venice was the permanent domicile of the German and his family.

While Venetian portrait painting became the international standard in the first half of the 16th century, this development was also promoted by the taste of the clientele, which was generally oriented towards Italy. A central role in the cultural transfer was played by transalpine trade, which was the essential prerequisite for exchange. The various portrait commissions by southern German merchants in northern Italy, of which some examples have been presented here, prove that the stylistic gradient that existed in comparison with painting in the North was immediately recognised. Although contemporaneous Augsburg art itself also increasingly approached the Italian-influenced portrait style, seeking solutions such as those offered by the prevailing southern formulations, orders were evidently still readily placed directly with Italians. Thus, Pietro Aretino reported as late as 1545 that the Venetian Gian Paolo Pace, who had stayed in Augsburg in November and December 1543, had painted portraits of Anton Fugger and his nephews Hans Jakob and Georg in the imperial city.

Just how close the connection and exchange between Venice and southern Germany were in artistic terms is exemplified by two portraits that, significantly, are both the subject of controversial debate among researchers. One is the *Portrait of Anton Welser the Younger* from 1527 (fig. 5), which is predominantly assumed to be the work of Christoph Amberger. However, the architectural background design and the positioning of the hand on the balustrade show very close parallels to *Portrait of a Man* (Bordeaux, Musée des Beaux-Arts) from around 1515/25, which is attributed to Palma Vecchio's circle. The impressive format (85 × 67 cm) also follows rather northern Italian conventions of the time. While it is unlikely that such an Italianate portrait as that of Anton Welser the Younger (1486–1557) would have been painted in Augsburg already in the second half of the 1520s (especially since Amberger did not yet have the right to work as a craftsman there), the alternative proposition – namely, that the internationally active merchant could have commissioned the portrait during a stay in Italy from an as yet unestablished journeyman (again Amberger), who may have been travelling in the south – seems entirely unlikely.

Fig. 5 *Portrait of Anton Welser the Younger*, 1527, Freiherrlich von Welsersche Familienstiftung

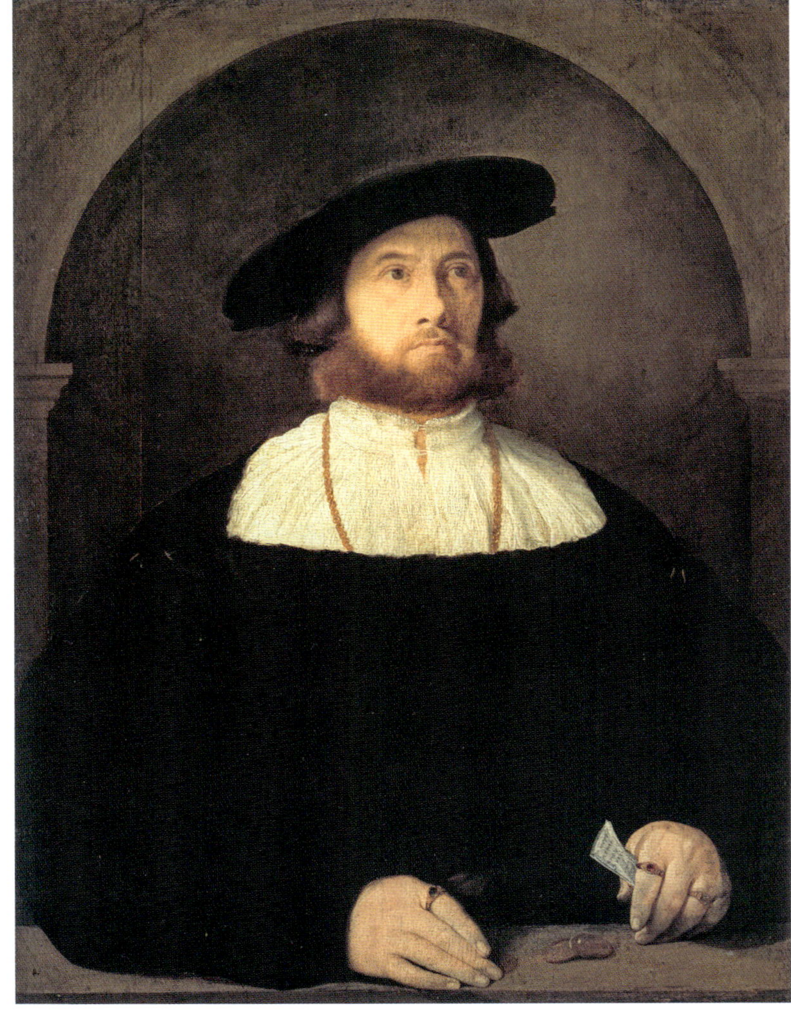

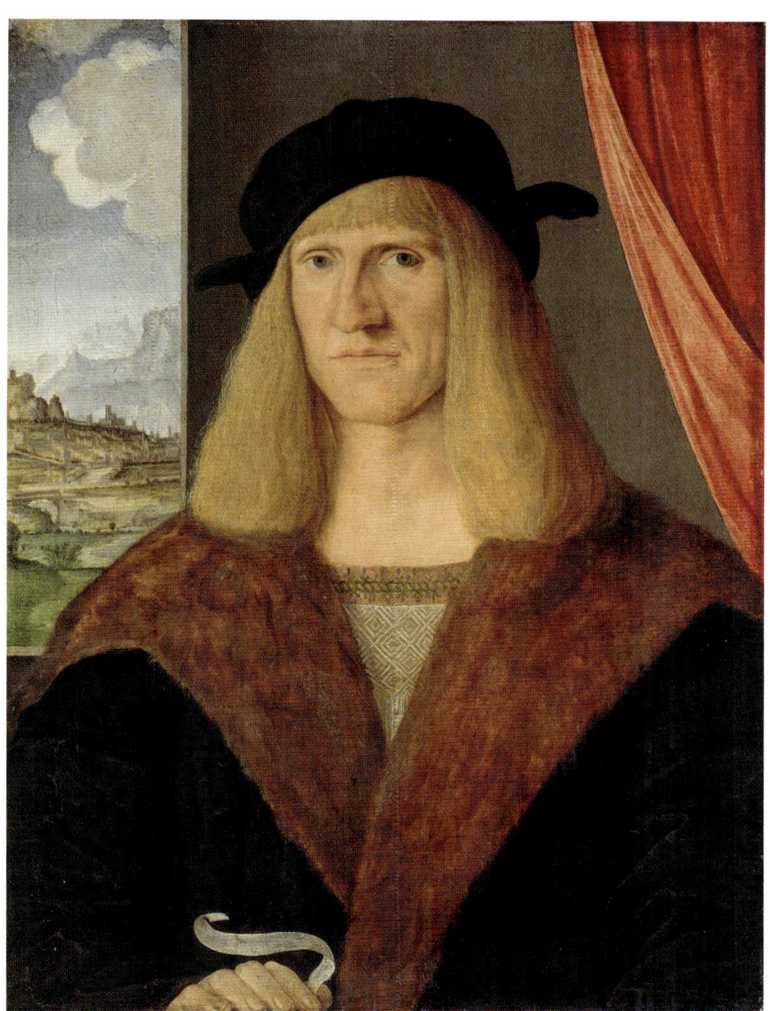

Fig. 6 *Portrait of a Man*, c. 1497/1500, Berlin, Staatliche Museen, Gemäldegalerie

Another case is the *Portrait of a Man* in the Gemäldegalerie in Berlin (fig. 6), last dated to around 1497/1500, which researchers initially attributed for a long time to an unknown German painter but more recently consider to be the work of Jacopo de' Barbari (1440/50 or around 1470–before 1516). The man with long blond hair is depicted frontally and is clearly characterised as a member of the southern German upper class by his "Schaube" with a broad fur collar. The vivid physiognomy with the striking facial features and the psychological immediacy evoked by the monumental rendition and the direct gaze may still be considered features of northern Italian painting at the turn of the century, while the format (60.5 × 45.5 cm) would also be rather large for a southern German work of this comparatively early period. However, the portrait type, with its lateral window view and the hand seemingly resting on the frame, come from the art north of the Alps. Perhaps precisely such 'Nordic' aspects were also the reason why Dürer, in the aforementioned letter to Pirckheimer in 1506, rated the skill of Jacopo de' Barbari, who had lived in Nuremberg for a few years from April 1500, less highly than that of many other Venetian painters whose works he saw in the lagoon city: "[...] also be it known to you that there are many better painters within this city than Master Jacob is without it [...]."

Venetian painting was thus perceived, appreciated and acquired as such in the north – and those who had the opportunity sometimes even commissioned their own portrait in the Serenissima, which not only allowed them to present themselves, but also to demonstrate their taste and connoisseurship at the same time.

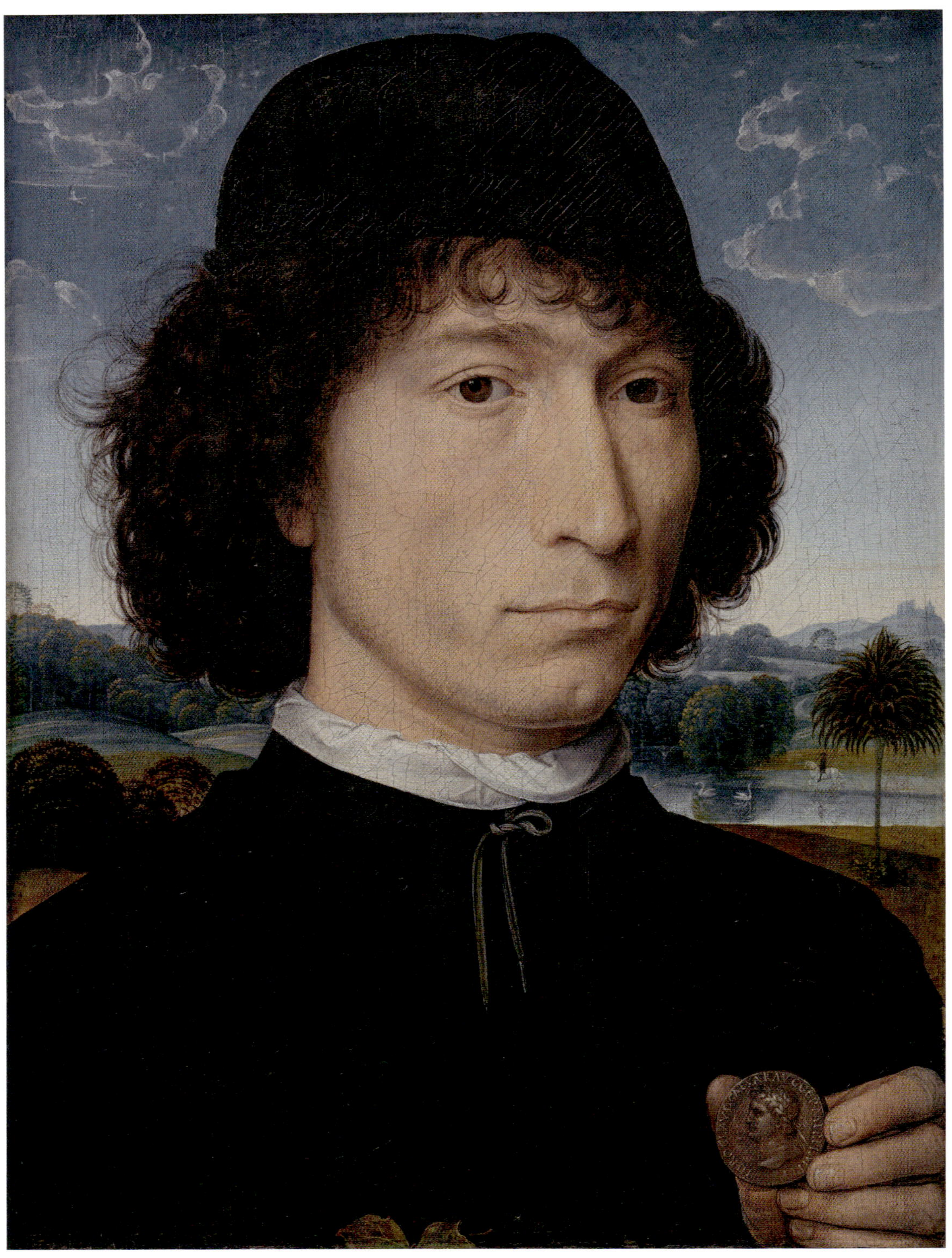

70 Hans Memling, *Portrait of Bernardo Bembo*, c. 1474, Antwerp, Koninklijk Museum voor Schone Kunsten

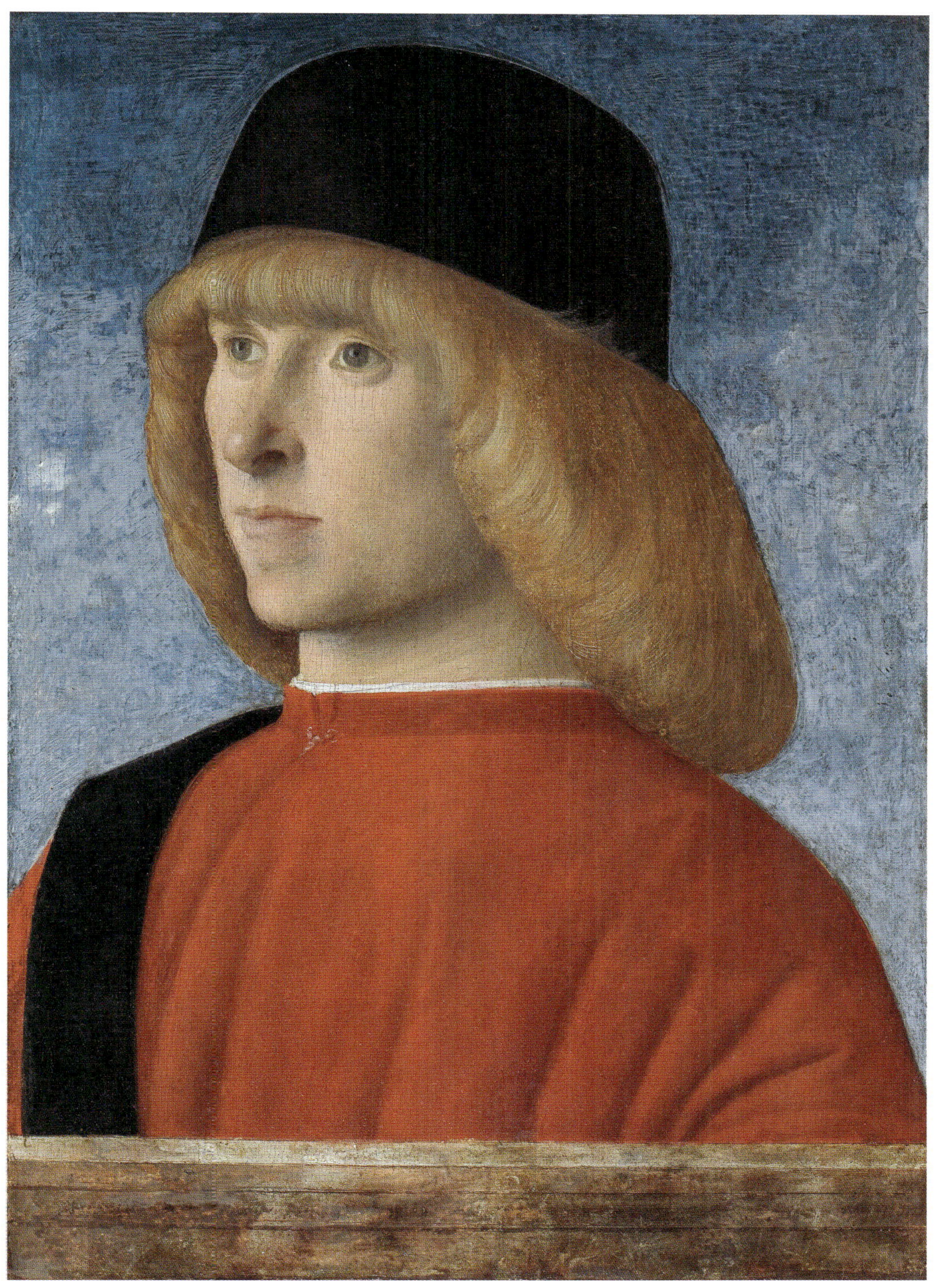

71 Giovanni Bellini, *Portrait of a Young Senator*, c. 1480/1510, Padua, Musei Civici, Museo d'Arte Medioevale e Moderna

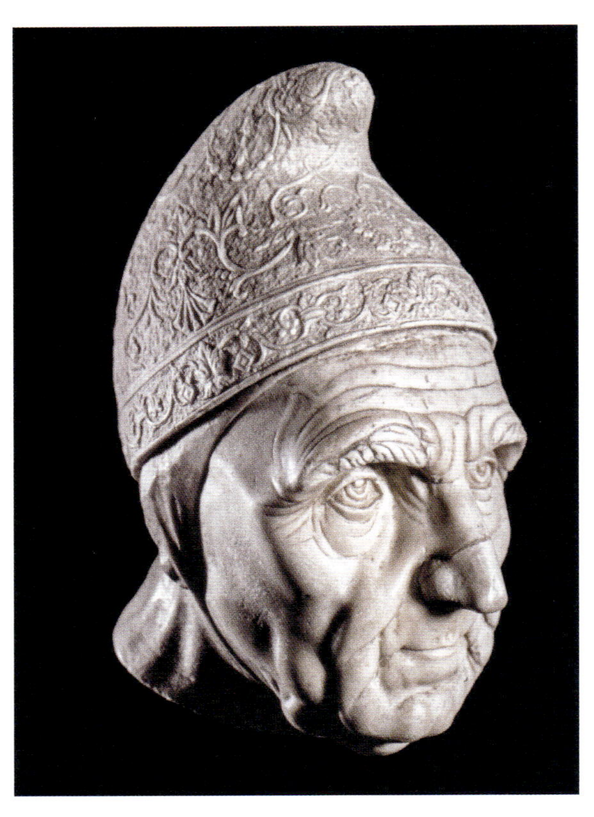

72 Antonio Rizzo, *Portrait of Doge Cristoforo Moro*, c. 1462/64, Venice, Musei Civici, Museo di Palazzo Ducale

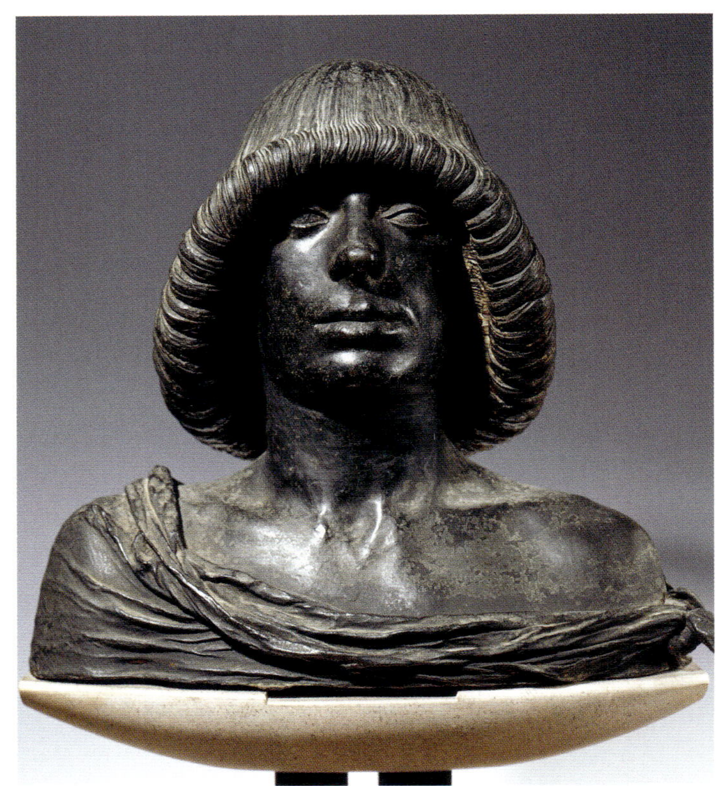

73 Andrea Riccio, *Portrait of a Young Man*, c. 1490/91, Venice, Musei Civici, Museo Correr

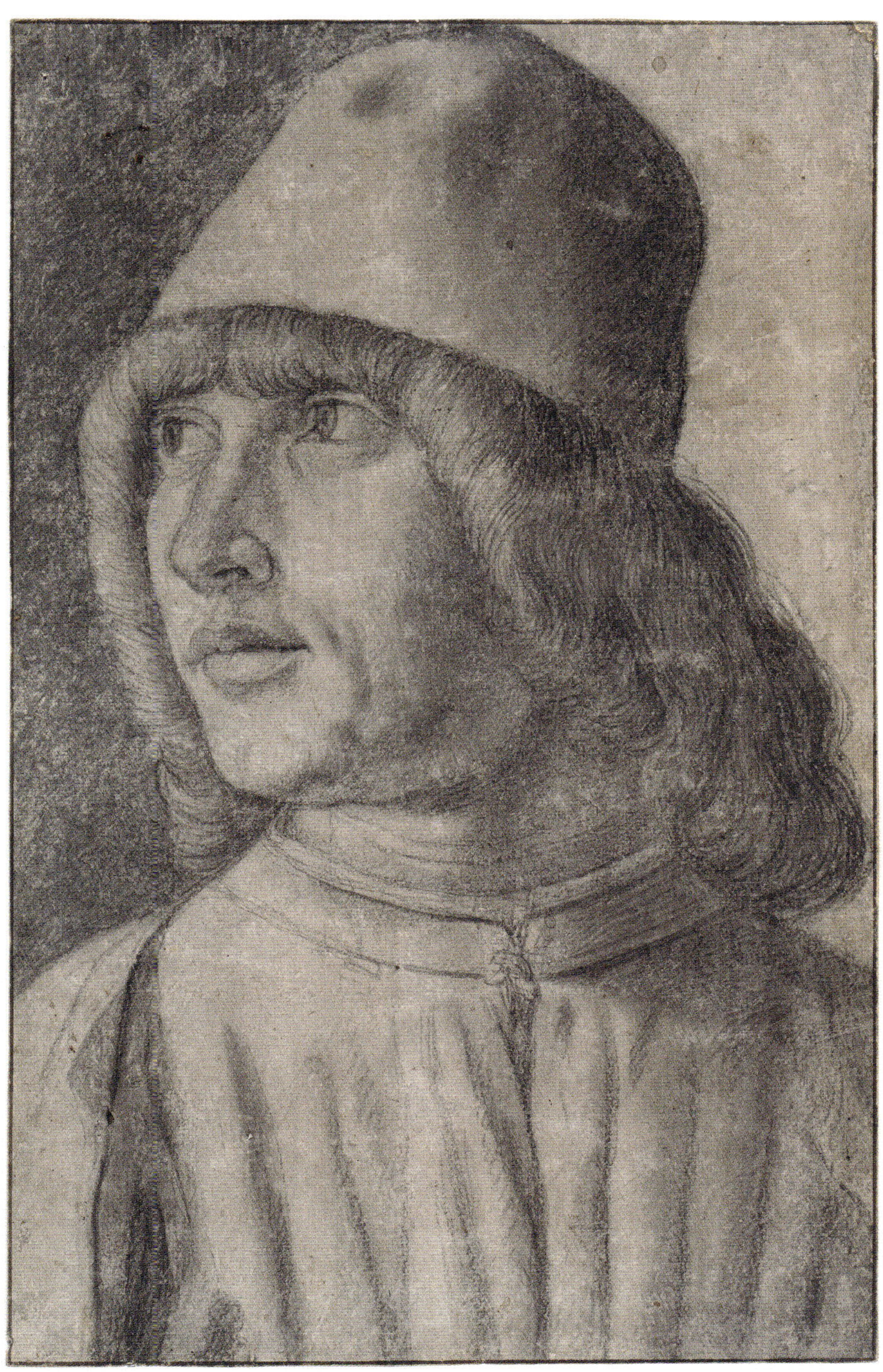

74 Alvise Vivarini, *Portrait of a Young Man*, c. 1490/1500, Berlin, Staatliche Museen, Kupferstichkabinett

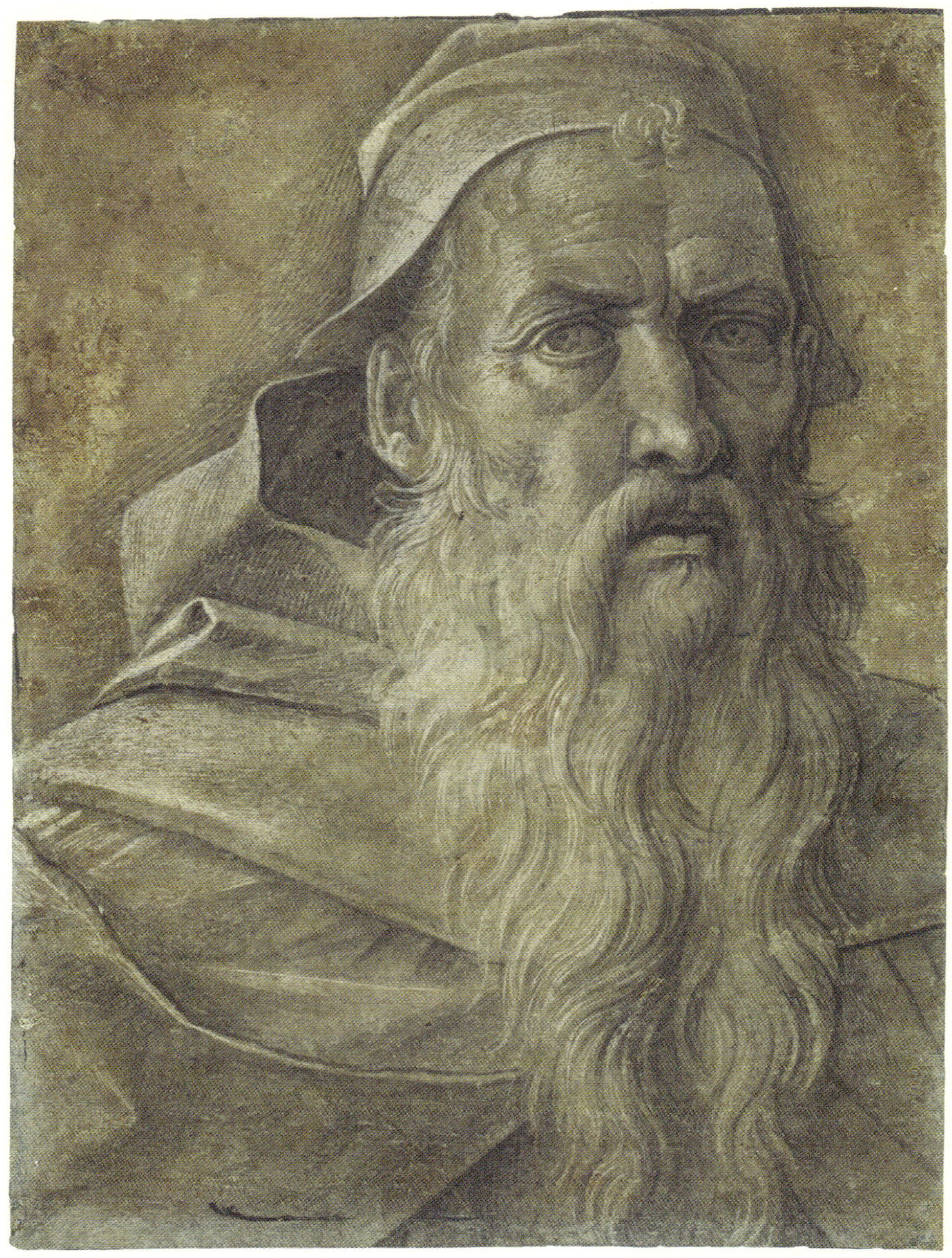

75 Giovanni Bellini, *Head of an Old Bearded Man*, 1460–1470, Windsor, The Royal Collection, HM King Charles III

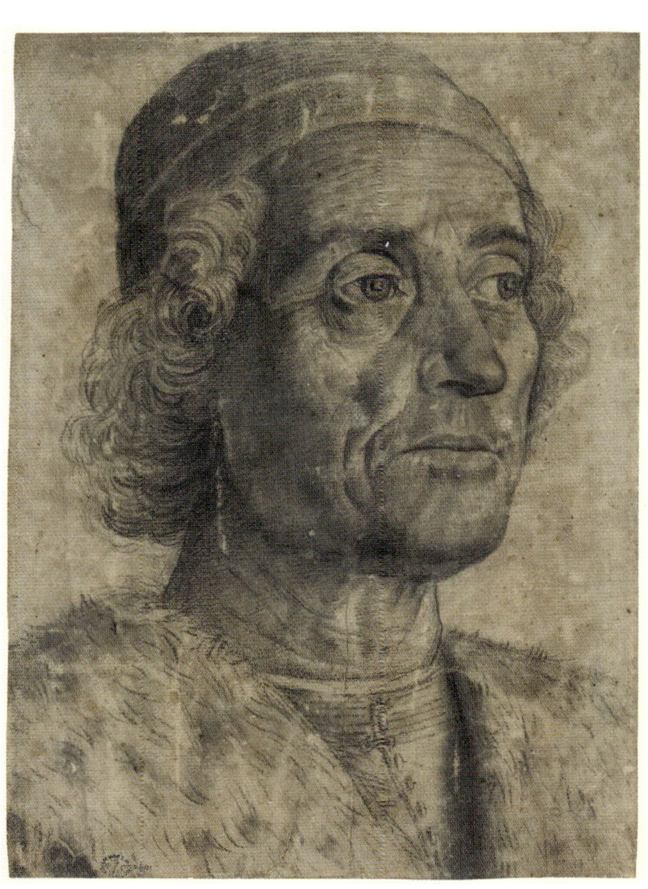

76 Andrea Mantegna, *Portrait of a Man*, 1470–1475, Besançon, Musée des Beaux-Arts et d'Archéologie, Collection d'arts graphiques

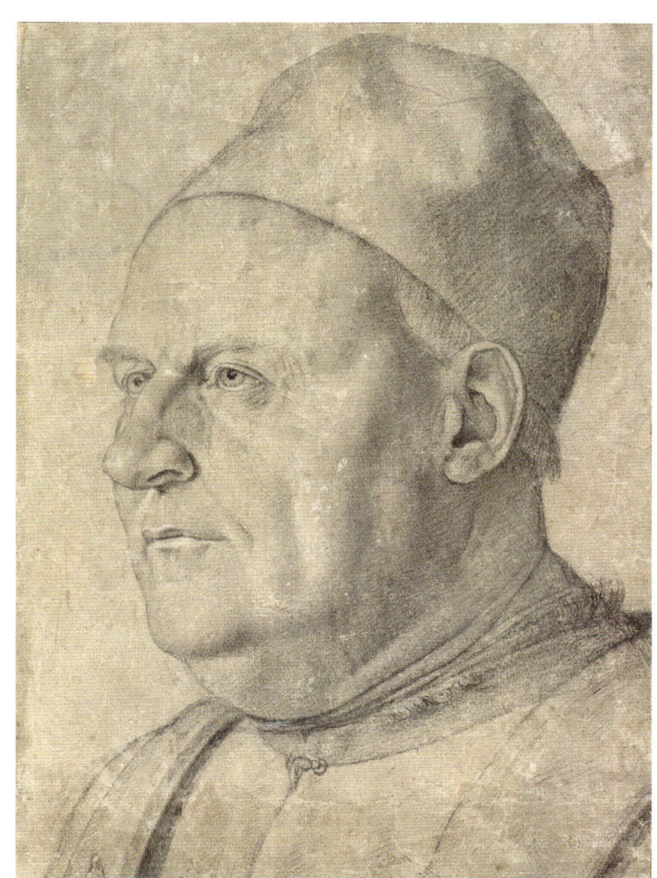

77 Francesco Bonsignori, *Portrait of a Venetian Senator*, 1487, Vienna, Albertina

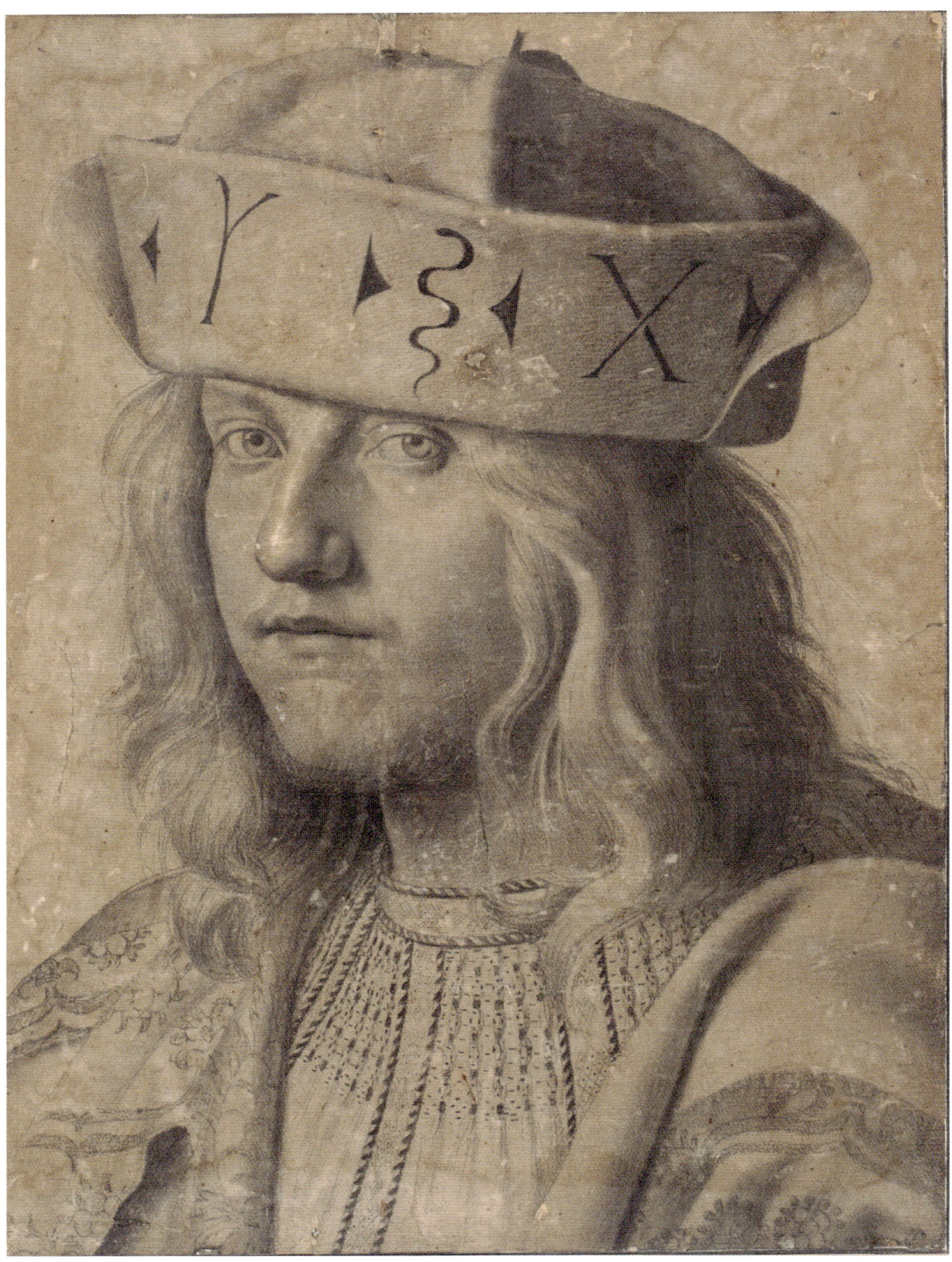

78 Bartolomeo Veneto, *Portrait of a Young Man with a Beret*, 1515–1525, Vienna, Albertina

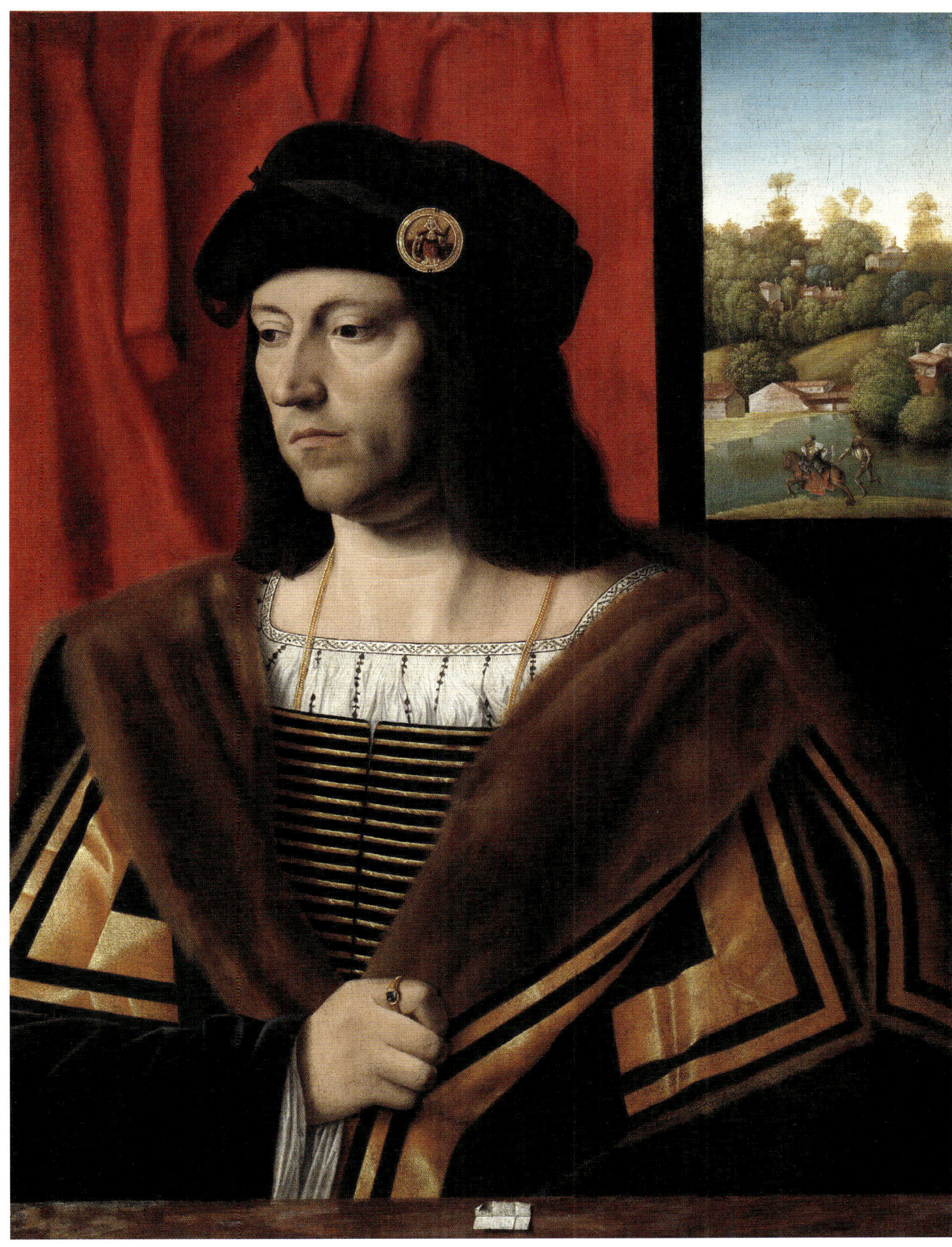

79 Bartolomeo Veneto, *Portrait of a Gentleman*, c. 1520, Washington, D.C., National Gallery of Art

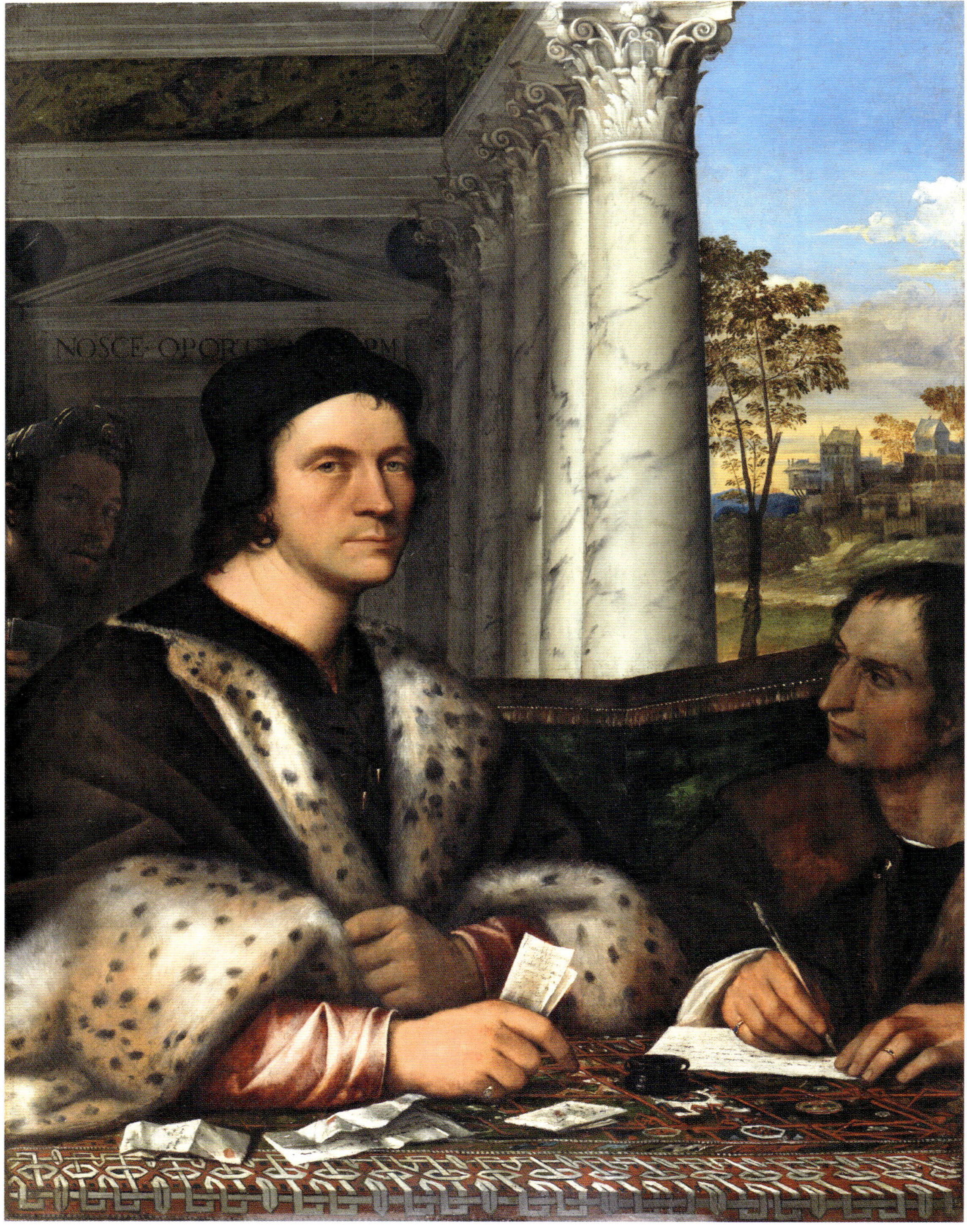

80 Sebastiano del Piombo, *Portrait of Ferry Carondelet with His Secretaries*, c. 1510/12, Madrid, Museo Nacional Thyssen-Bornemisza

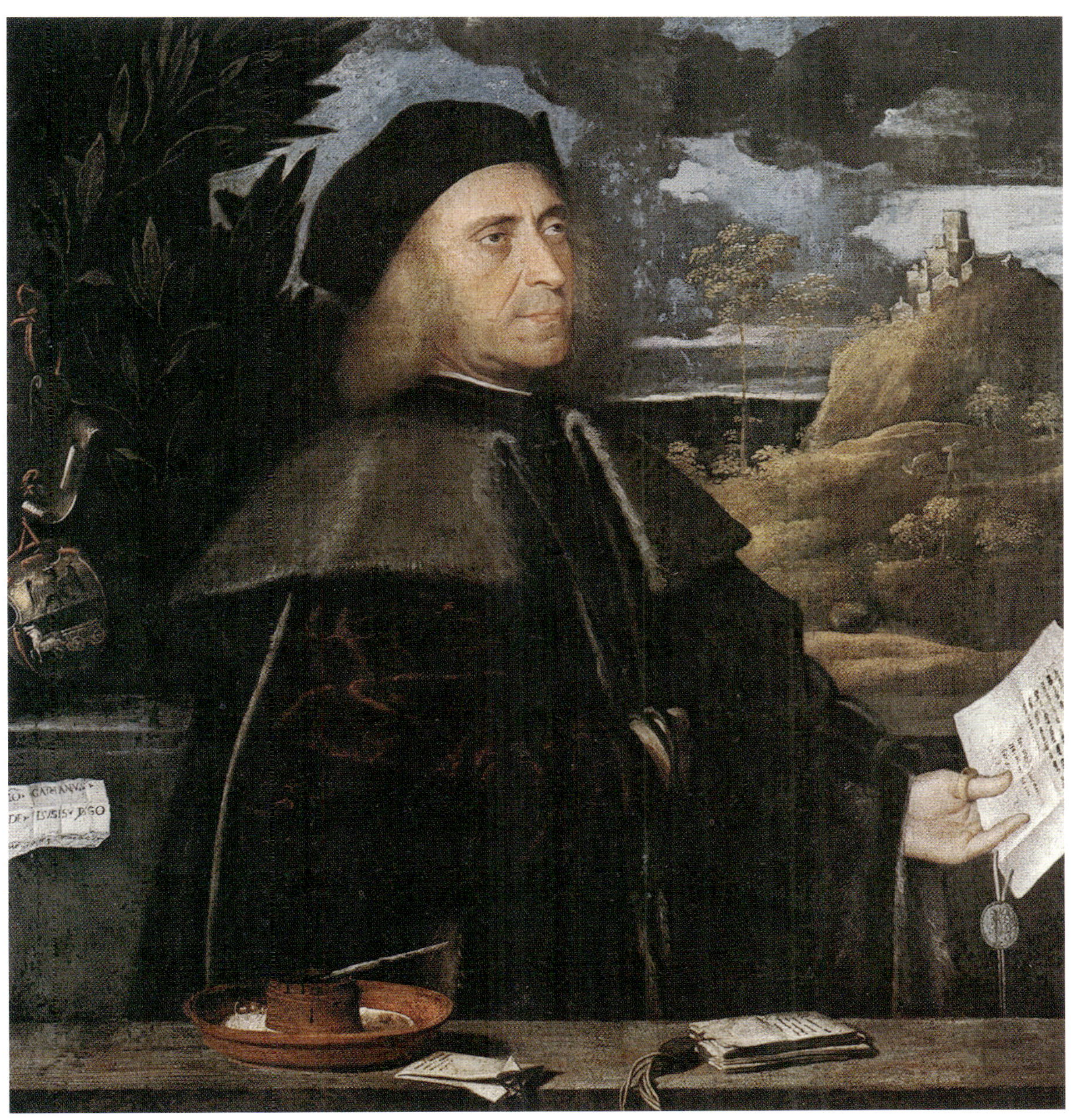

81 Giovanni Cariani, *Portrait of Giovan Antonio Caravaggi*, c. 1520/30, Ottawa, National Gallery of Canada

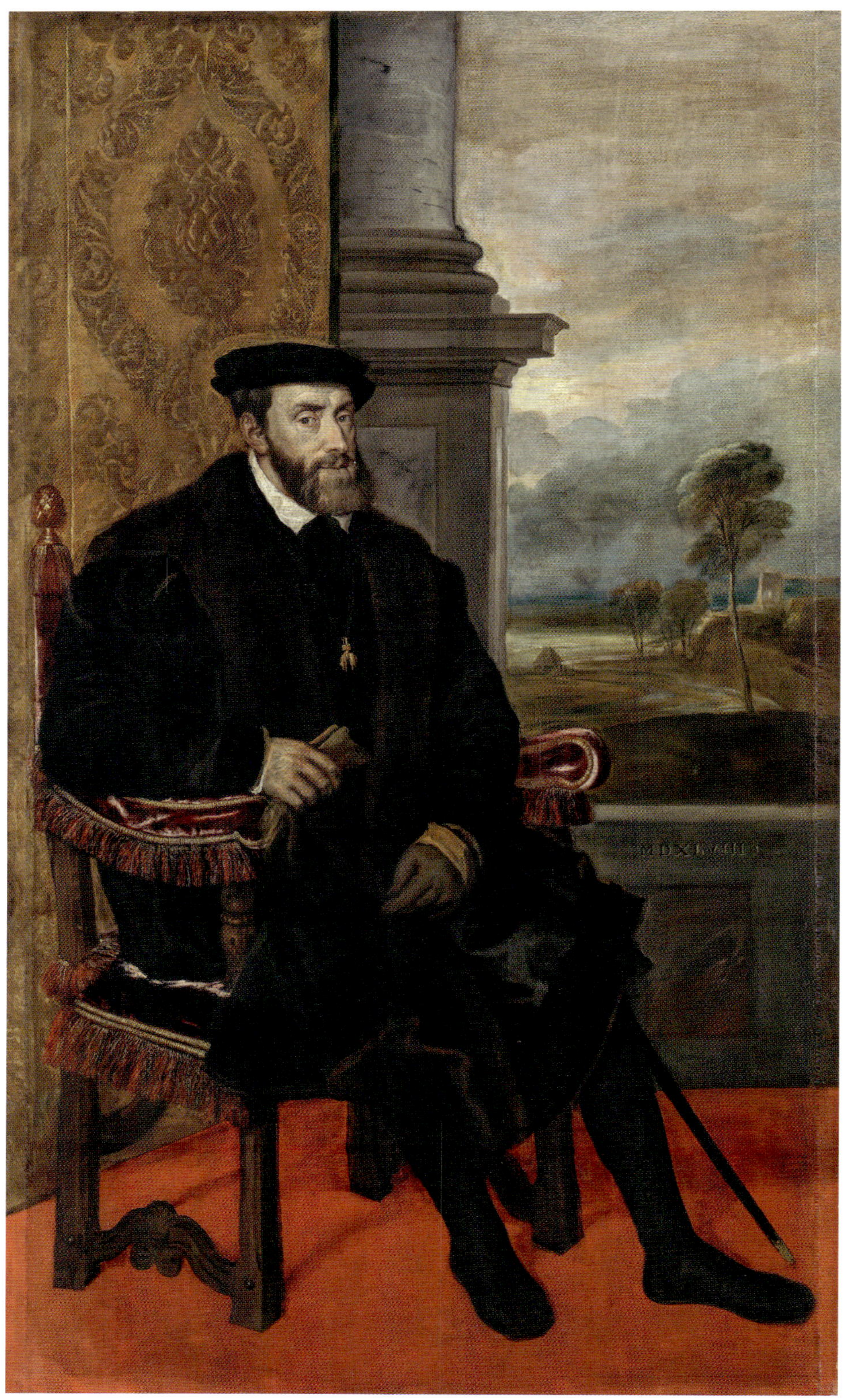

82 Titian, *Portrait of Charles V*, 1548, Munich, Bayerische Staatsgemäldesammlungen, Alte Pinakothek

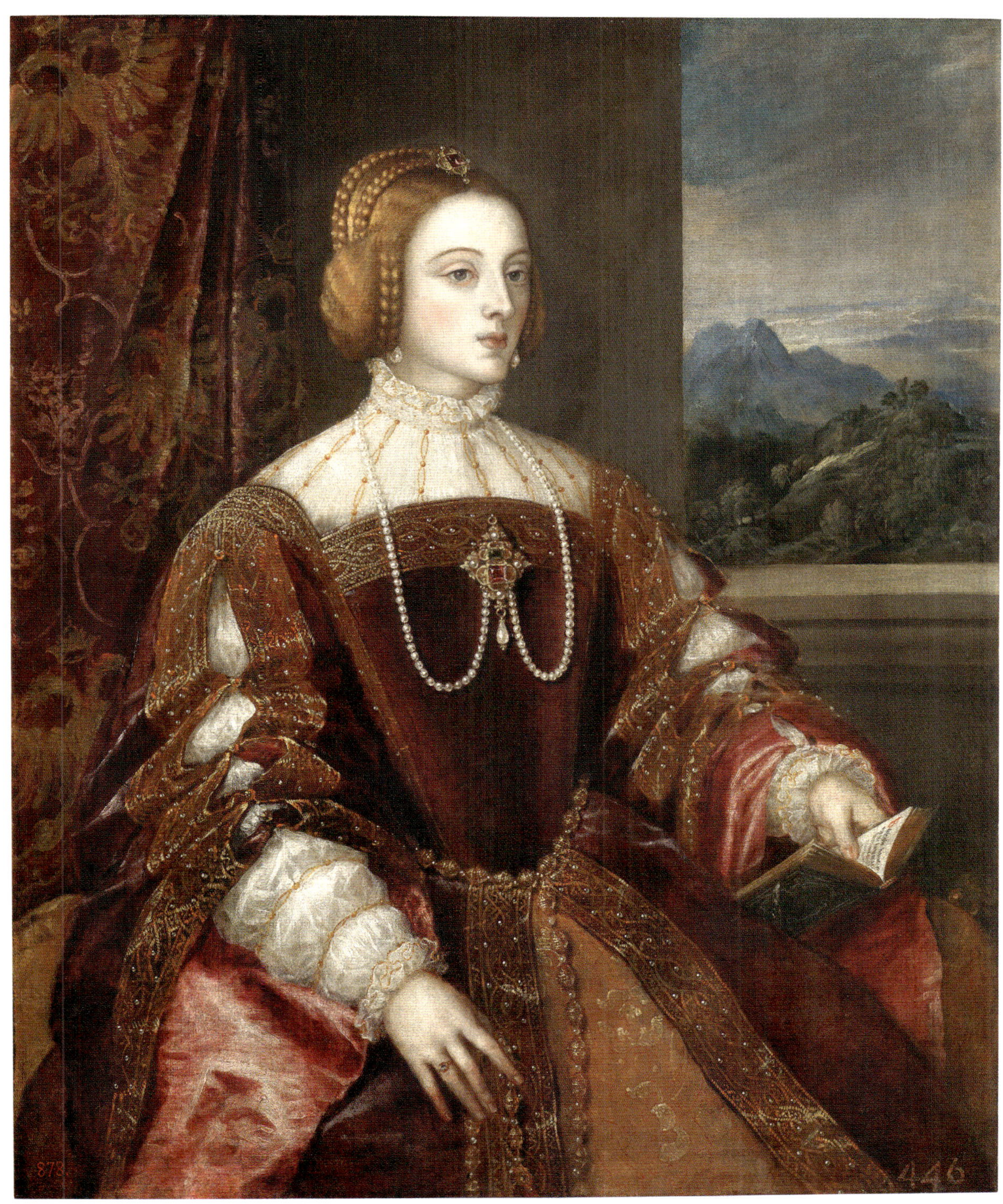

83 Titian, *Portrait of Isabella of Portugal*, 1548, Madrid, Museo Nacional del Prado

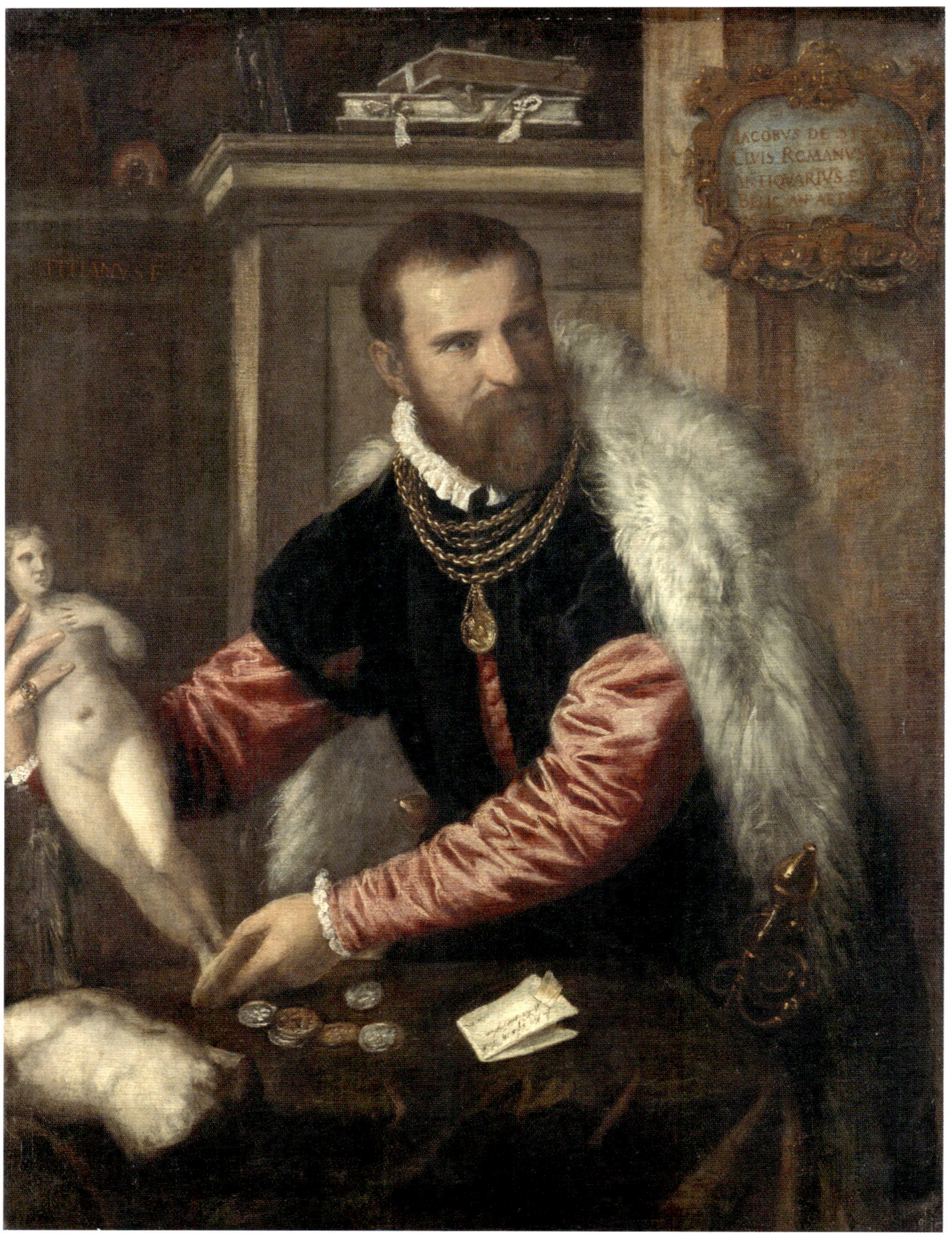

84 Titian, *Portrait of Jacopo Strada*, c. 1567/68, Vienna, Kunsthistorisches Museum

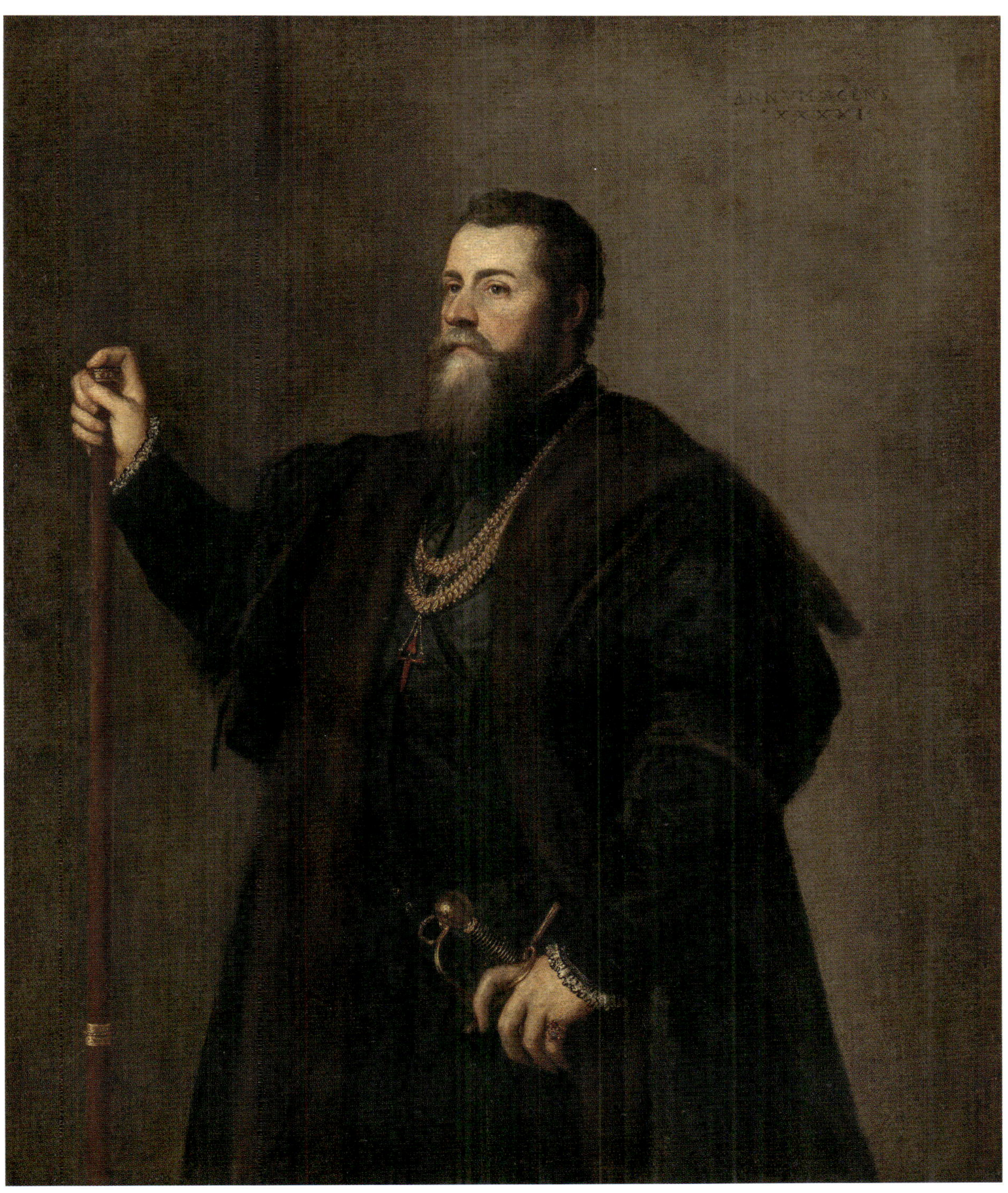

85 Titian and Workshop, *Portrait of Don Pedro Álvarez de Toledo*, c. 1540/45, Munich, Bayerische Staatsgemäldesammlungen, Alte Pinakothek

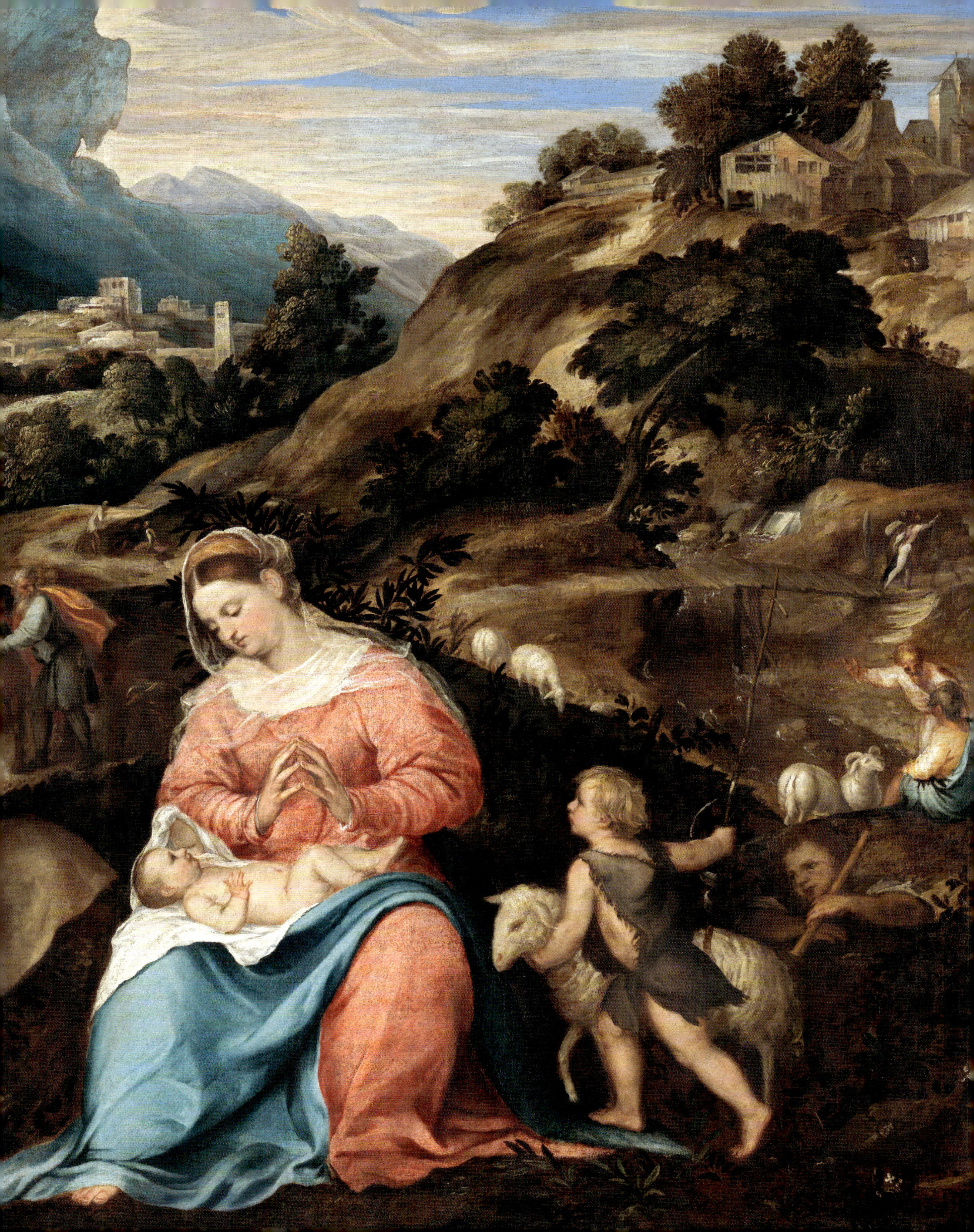

Works

1
Giovanni Bellini (c. 1435–1516)
St Jerome Reading in a Landscape, c. 1480/85
Panel, 46.8 × 33.8 cm
London, The National Gallery,
inv. no. NG 281

2
Giovanni Battista Cima da Conegliano
(1459/60–1517/18)
St Jerome in the Wilderness, c. 1500/05
Canvas transferred from panel, 48 × 40 cm
Washington, D.C., National Gallery of Art,
Samuel H. Kress Collection,
inv. no. 1939.1.168

3
Bartolomeo Cincani (Bartolomeo
Montagna) (c. 1450–1523)
St Jerome in the Desert, c. 1500/02
Panel, 51 × 58 cm
Milan, Pinacoteca di Brera, inv. no. 2188

4
Giovanni di Niccolò Mansueti (before
1485–c. 1526/27)
St Jerome in a Landscape, 1505–1520
Canvas, 50.8 × 71.1 cm
Bristol, Museum and Art Gallery,
inv. no. K 1657

5
Giovanni Bellini (c. 1435–1516)
Four Allegories, c. 1485/95
a) *Malinconia*
Panel, 34 × 22 cm
b) *Vanitas*
Panel, 34 × 22 cm
c) *Invidia*
Panel, 34 × 22 cm
d) *Bacchus*
Panel, 32 × 22 cm
Venice, Gallerie dell'Accademia,
inv. no. 595

6
Andrea Previtali (c. 1470/80 [1476?]–
1528 [?])
Allegory of Fortune, c. 1490
Panel, 27 × 18.5 cm
Venice, Gallerie dell'Accademia,
inv. no. 595

7
Sebastiano Luciani (Sebastiano del Piombo)
(c. 1485–1547)
Scenes from the Life of Adonis, c. 1505
a) *Birth of Adonis*
Panel, 40 × 48.5 cm
b) *Death of Adonis*
Panel, 40 × 48.5 cm
La Spezia, Museo Civico Amedeo Lia,
inv. nos 164, 165

8
Lorenzo Lotto (c. 1480–1556)
Sleeping Apollo with Fame and the Muses,
c. 1549
Canvas, 44.5 × 74 cm
Budapest, Szépművészeti Múzeum,
inv. no. 947

9
Domenico Campagnola (c. 1500–1564)
Resting Venus in a Landscape, 1517
Copper engraving and dry-point etching,
100 × 138 mm
Berlin, Staatliche Museen, Kupferstich-
kabinett, inv. no. 13-24

10
Giulio Campagnola (c. 1482–c. 1516)
Young Shepherd, c. 1509/12
Copper engraving, 132 × 78 mm
Munich, Staatliche Graphische Sammlung,
inv. no. 7629 D

11
Domenico Campagnola (c. 1500–1564)
Concert by a Brook, c. 1516/17
Copper engraving, 134 × 258 mm
Berlin, Staatliche Museen, Kupferstich-
kabinett, inv. no. 12-24

12
Jacopo Negretti (Palma il Vecchio)
(c. 1480–1528)
Shepherd with Panpipe, c. 1525
Panel, 43.5 × 37 cm
Private collection, courtesy of Eckart
Lingenauber

13
Jacopo Negretti (Palma il Vecchio)
(c. 1480–1528), attribution
Daphnis, c. 1513/15
Poplar panel, 19.6 × 16.4 cm
Munich, Bayerische Staatsgemälde-
sammlungen, Alte Pinakothek, inv. no. 76

14
Tiziano Vecellio (Titian) (c. 1488/90–1576)
Portrait of Giovanni Bellini, c. 1511/12
Canvas, 80 × 66 cm
Copenhagen, National Gallery of
Denmark, inv. no. DEP 15

15
Tiziano Vecellio (Titian) (c. 1488/90–1576)
Portrait of a Man, c. 1520/22
Canvas, mounted on oak panel,
89.3 × 74.2 cm
Munich, Bayerische Staatsgemälde-
sammlungen, Alte Pinakothek, inv. no. 517

16
Paris Bordone (1500–1571)
Portrait of Giulio Manfron, 1523
Canvas, 77.8 × 66 cm
Munich, Bayerische Staatsgemälde-
sammlungen, Alte Pinakothek, inv. no. 512

17
Paris Bordone (1500–1571)
Jeweller with a Lady, c. 1530/35
Canvas, 99.5 × 88.3 cm
Munich, Bayerische Staatsgemälde-
sammlungen, Alte Pinakothek, inv. no. 925

18
Lorenzo Lotto (c. 1480–1556)
Portrait of a Young Man, c. 1509/10
Panel, 29 × 23 cm
Florence, Galleria degli Uffizi,
inv. 1890 n. 1481

19
Lorenzo Lotto (c. 1480–1556)
Portrait of a Young Man, c. 1534/35
Canvas, 50.5 × 43.6 cm
Berlin, Staatliche Museen, Gemäldegalerie,
inv. no. 320

20
Lorenzo Lotto (c. 1480–1556)
Portrait of a Dominican Friar (Marcantonio Luciani?), 1526
Canvas, 78 × 67 cm
Treviso, Musei Civici, Palazzo Mazzolari Mosca, inv. no. P 88

21
Lorenzo Lotto (c. 1480–1556)
Portrait of a Gentleman (Mercurio Bua?), c. 1535
Canvas, 118 × 105 cm
Rome, Galleria Borghese, inv. no. 185

22
Giovanni Bellini (c. 1435–1516)
Virgin and Child with St John the Baptist and an Unknown Saint, 1500–1505
Panel, 55 × 77 cm
Venice, Gallerie dell'Accademia, inv. no. 881

23
Giovanni Bellini (c. 1435–1516)
Virgin and Child in a Landscape, c. 1508
Panel, 65.8 × 48.2 cm
Munich, Bayerische Staatsgemäldesammlungen, Alte Pinakothek, inv. no. L 2863

24
Bartolomeo Veneto (rec. 1502–1531)
Virgin and Child, c. 1505
Panel, 47.3 × 38 cm
Bergamo, Accademia Carrara, inv. no. 81LC 00127

25
Andrea Previtali (c. 1470/80 [1476?]–1528 [?])
Virgin and Child, c. 1502
Panel, 62 × 50 cm
Munich, Bayerische Staatsgemäldesammlungen, Alte Pinakothek, inv. no. 15284

26
Alvise Vivarini (1442/53–1503/05)
Crucifixion with the Virgin Mary, Mary Magdalene and St John, c. 1470
Panel, 83.4 × 62.5 cm
Pesaro, Museo Civico, inv. no. 3914

27
Giovanni Battista Cima da Conegliano (1459/60–1517/18)
St Helena, c. 1495
Panel, 40.2 × 32.2 cm
Washington, D.C, National Gallery of Art, Samuel H. Kress Collection, inv. no. 1961.9.12

28
Marco Basaiti (c. 1470–rec. 1530)
Lamentation of Christ, c. 1506
Panel, 124.1 × 91 cm
Munich, Bayerische Staatsgemäldesammlungen, Alte Pinakothek, inv. no. WAF 48

29
Marco Basaiti (c. 1470–rec. 1530), attribution
Rocky Shoreline, c. 1500/10
Watercolour, 203 × 274 mm
Florence, Galleria degli Uffizi, Gabinetto Disegni e Stampe, inv. no. 1700 F

30
Tiziano Vecellio (Titian) (c. 1488/90–1576)
Group of Trees, c. 1514
Pen and brown ink on beige paper, 218 × 319 mm
New York, The Metropolitan Museum of Art, Department of Drawings and Prints (Rogers Fund, 1908), inv. no. 08.227.38

31
Jacopo de' Barbari (1440/50 or c. 1470–before 1516)
The Virgin Nursing the Christ Child at the Foot of a Tree, end of 15th/beginning of 16th century
Copper engraving, 177 × 237 mm
Vienna, Albertina, inv. no. DG 1952/426

32
Domenico Campagnola (c. 1500–1564), attribution
St Jerome in the Wilderness, 1540–1560
Pen and brown ink, 278 × 440 mm
Windsor, The Royal Collection, HM King Charles III, inv. no. RCIN 904774

33
Giorgio da Castelfranco (Giorgione) (1473/74–1510)
Architectural Ensemble by a River, c. 1500
Brush in brown and white on light-brown tinted paper, 264 × 228 mm
Munich, Sammlung Bernd und Verena Klüser, inv. no. SK-9210

34
Domenico Campagnola (c. 1500–1564)
Two Kneeling Youths in a Landscape, 2nd quarter 16th century
Pen and brown ink, 236 × 213 mm
Vienna, Albertina, inv. no. 24364

35
Domenico Campagnola (c. 1500–1564)
Mountainous River Landscape with a Farmstead, 2nd quarter 16th century
Pen and brown ink, 235 × 367 mm
Vienna, Albertina, inv. no. 1505

36
Giulio Campagnola (c. 1482–c. 1516)
River Landscape with Buildings and a Bridge, 1st quarter 16th century
Pen and grey and brown ink, 130 × 197 mm
Munich, Sammlung Bernd und Verena Klüser, inv. no. SK-9087

37
Jacopo Negretti (Palma il Vecchio) (c. 1480–1528)
Virgin and Child with St Roch and Lucia, 1513/15
Panel, 67.6 × 92.6 cm
Munich, Bayerische Staatsgemäldesammlungen, Alte Pinakothek, inv. no. 505

38
Lorenzo Lotto (c. 1480–1556)
Mystical Marriage of St Catherine, c. 1506
Panel, 71.3 × 91.2 cm
Munich, Bayerische Staatsgemäldesammlungen, Alte Pinakothek, inv. no. 32

39
Giovanni Cariani (c. 1485/90–1547), attribution
Virgin and Child with St Anthony the Abbot and John the Baptist as a Boy, c. 1540
Canvas, 163.8 × 199.7 cm
Munich, Bayerische Staatsgemäldesammlungen, Alte Pinakothek, inv. no. 9210

40
Giorgio da Castelfranco (Giorgione) (1473/74–1510)
Portrait of a Young Man, c. 1505/10
Poplar panel, 69.4 × 53.6 cm
Munich, Bayerische Staatsgemäldesammlungen, Alte Pinakothek, inv. no. 524

41
Venetian
Christ Carrying the Cross, c. 1515
Panel, 63 × 46.3 cm
Vienna, Kunsthistorisches Museum, inv. no. GG 280

42
Sebastiano Luciani (Sebastiano del Piombo) (c. 1485–1547)
Portrait of a Man in Armour, c. 1512
Canvas, 87.5 × 67.3 cm
Hartford, CT, Wadsworth Atheneum Museum of Art, inv. no. 1960.119

43
Giorgio da Castelfranco (Giorgione) (1473/74–1510) (?)
Portrait of Giovanni Borgherini and Trifone Gabriele, 1509/10
Canvas, 91.5 × 67 cm
Munich, Bayerische Staatsgemäldesammlungen, Alte Pinakothek, inv. no. 7452

44
Bernardino Licinio (c. 1485–after 1549/before 1565), attribution
Artist Friends in the Mirror (Self-Portrait with Sebastiano Serlio), c. 1530
Panel, 82 × 62 cm
Würzburg, Martin von Wagner-Museum, inv. no. F 64

45
Giovanni Antonio de Lodesanis Pordenone (il Pordenone) (c. 1483/84–1539)
Half Figure of a Man with Feather Hat, 1520/21
Red chalk, 156 × 118 mm
Vienna, Albertina, inv. no. 2408

46
Vincenzo Catena (c. 1470/80–1531), attribution
Portrait of Francesco Maria della Rovere, c. 1518
Panel, 75.4 × 56.5 cm
Bergamo, Accademia Carrara, inv. no. 58AC 00439

47
Bartolomeo Veneto (rec. 1502–1531)
Portrait of a Young Man from the Zane Family, c. 1505
Plywood panel, transferred from wood, 40.4 × 32 cm
Munich, Bayerische Staatsgemäldesammlungen, Alte Pinakothek, inv. no. WAF 1151

48
Jacopo Tintoretto (1518/19–1594) and Workshop
Portrait of the Maggi Family, c. 1575
Canvas, 115.3 × 166 cm
Munich, Bayerische Staatsgemäldesammlungen, Alte Pinakothek, inv. no. 931

49
Les voyages de Charles Magius (Codex Maggi), Venice, 1578
Illuminated parchment manuscript, 18 fols, rebound and integrated in *Description historique d'un volume composé de tableaux peints en miniature* [...], Paris, 1761, print and manuscript, 66 fols, 33.2 × 25.2 × 2 cm (binding)
Paris, Bibliothèque nationale de France, Département estampes et photographie, Reserve 4-AD-134

50
Lorenzo Lotto (c. 1480–1556)
Portrait of a Woman, c. 1505
Panel, 36 × 28 cm
Dijon, Musée des Beaux-Arts, inv. no. CA T 52

51
Bernardino Licinio (c. 1485–after 1549/before 1565)
Portrait of a Woman, c. 1520
Poplar panel, 57.2 × 59.7 cm
Munich, Bayerische Staatsgemäldesammlungen, Alte Pinakothek, inv. no. 5093

52
Jacopo Negretti (Palma il Vecchio) (c. 1480–1528)
Portrait of a Young Woman in Blue Dress with Fan, after 1514
Poplar panel, 63.5 × 51 cm
Vienna, Kunsthistorisches Museum, inv. no. GG 63

53
Jacopo Negretti (Palma il Vecchio) (c. 1480–1528)
Portrait of a Woman, 1512/14
Panel, 48.5 × 39 cm
Lyon, Musée des Beaux-Arts, inv. no. A 195

54
Sebastiano Luciani (Sebastiano del Piombo) (c. 1485–1547)
Portrait of a Young Woman, c. 1506/07
Panel, 33.6 × 28.6 cm
Buscot Park, The Faringdon Collection Trust, inv. no. 48

55
Tiziano Vecellio (Titian) (c. 1488/90–1576)
Portrait of a Young Woman, c. 1510/11
Black and white chalk on discoloured, originally blue paper, 418 × 265 mm
Florence, Galleria degli Uffizi, Gabinetto Disegni e Stampe, inv. no. 718 E r.

56
Simone Bianco (rec. 1512–1553)
Bust of a Roman Woman, c. 1540
Marble, 54 × 35 × 24 cm
Munich, Bayerisches Nationalmuseum, inv. no. R 3224

57
Tiziano Vecellio (Titian) (c. 1488/90–1576)
Vanity, c. 1515
Canvas, 97 × 81.2 cm
Munich, Bayerische Staatsgemäldesammlungen, Alte Pinakothek, inv. no. 483

58
Tiziano Vecellio (Titian) (c. 1488/90–1576)
Young Woman at Her Toilet, c. 1515
Canvas, 99 × 76 cm
Paris, Musée du Louvre, inv. no. 755

59
Tiziano Vecellio (Titian) (c. 1488/90–1576)
Portrait of a Lady in White, c. 1561
Canvas, 102 × 86 cm
Dresden, Staatliche Kunstsammlungen, Gemäldegalerie Alte Meister, inv. no. 170

60
Bernardino Licinio (c. 1485–after 1549/before 1565)
Portrait of a Young Lady and Her Suitor, c. 1520
Panel, 81.3 × 114.3 cm
Paris, Galerie Canesso

61
Francesco Torbido (c. 1482/85–1562)
Portrait of a Young Man, c. 1516
Canvas, 62.3 × 52 cm
Munich, Bayerische Staatsgemäldesammlungen, Alte Pinakothek, inv. no. 1013

62
Giorgio da Castelfranco (Giorgione) (1473/74–1510)
Boy with Arrow, c. 1505
Poplar panel, 48 × 41.8 cm
Vienna, Kunsthistorisches Museum, inv. no. GG 323

63
Paris Bordone (1500–1571)
A Young Woman Holding a Mirror with Her Servant, c. 1535/40
Canvas, 87 × 72 cm
Hamburg, Kunsthalle, inv. no. HK-5736

64
Bernardino Licinio (c. 1485–after 1549/ before 1565)
The Concert, 1518/20
Canvas, 114 × 172 cm
Private collection, courtesy of Eckart Lingenauber

65
Giovanni Girolamo Savoldo (c. 1480–after 1548)
Head of a Woman with Eyes Closed, c. 1535/38
Black pen and white chalk on discoloured, originally blue paper, 255 × 197 mm
Florence, Galleria degli Uffizi, Gabinetto Disegni e Stampe, inv. no. 12806 F

66
Giovanni Girolamo Savoldo (c. 1480–after 1548)
Portrait of a Woman, c. 1535
Canvas, 92 × 123 cm
Rome, Musei Capitolini, Pinacoteca, inv. no. PC 49

67
Giovanni Girolamo Savoldo (c. 1480–after 1548)
The Virgin Adoring the Child with Two Donors, c. 1527
Canvas, 102.2 × 139.7 cm
London, The Royal Collection, HM King Charles III, inv. no. RCIN 405755

68
Bernardino Licinio (c. 1485–after 1549/ before 1565)
Portrait of the Family of the Artist's Brother Arrigo Licinio, c. 1535
Canvas, 107 × 163 cm
Rome, Galleria Borghese, inv. no. 115

69
Lorenzo Lotto (c. 1480–1556)
Portrait of Giovanni della Volta with His Wife and Children, 1547
Canvas, 104.5 × 138 cm
London, The National Gallery, inv. no. NG 1047

70
Hans Memling (c. 1430/40–1494)
Portrait of Bernardo Bembo, c. 1474
Panel, 30 × 22 cm
Antwerp, Koninklijk Museum voor Schone Kunsten, inv. no. 5

71
Giovanni Bellini (c. 1435–1516)
Portrait of a Young Senator, c. 1480/1510
Panel, 35.7 × 26.4 cm
Padua, Musei Civici, Museo d'Arte Medioevale e Moderna, inv. no. 43

72
Antonio Rizzo (before 1441–1499)
Portrait of Doge Cristoforo Moro, c. 1462/64
Marble, 31 × 20 × 25 cm
Venice, Musei Civici, Museo di Palazzo Ducale

73
Andrea Riccio (1470–1532)
Portrait of a Young Man, c. 1490/91
Bronze, 43 × 41 × 26 cm
Venice, Musei Civici, Museo Correr, inv. no. Cl. Xl n. 0023

74
Alvise Vivarini (1442/53–1503/05)
Portrait of a Young Man, c. 1490/1500
Black pen (charcoal?), partly rubbed off, on grey-brown paper, 402 × 263 mm
Berlin, Staatliche Museen, Kupferstichkabinett, KdZ 5050

75
Giovanni Bellini (c. 1435–1516)
Head of an Old Bearded Man, 1460–1470
Brown brush and ink, heightened with white over black chalk on discoloured, originally blue paper, 260 × 190 mm
Windsor, The Royal Collection, HM King Charles III, inv. no. RCIN 912800

76
Andrea Mantegna (1430/31–1506)
Portrait of a Man, 1470–1475
Black chalk on paper, 331 × 206 mm
Besançon, Musée des Beaux-Arts et d'Archéologie, Collection d'arts graphiques, inv. no. D 3101

77
Francesco Bonsignori (c. 1460–1519)
Portrait of a Venetian Senator, 1487
Black chalk, heightened with white, on brown paper, 359 × 262 mm
Vienna, Albertina, inv. no. 17672

78
Bartolomeo Veneto (rec. 1502–1531)
Portrait of a Young Man with a Beret, 1515–1525
Black chalk, heightened with white, on paper, 380 × 287 mm
Vienna, Albertina, inv. no. 1452

79
Bartolomeo Veneto (rec. 1502–1531)
Portrait of a Gentleman, c. 1520
Oil on panel transferred to canvas, 76.8 × 58.4 cm
Washington, D.C., National Gallery of Art, Samuel H. Kress Collection, inv. no. 1939.1.257

80
Sebastiano Luciani (Sebastiano del Piombo) (c.1485–1547)
Portrait of Ferry Carondelet with His Secretaries, c. 1510/12
Oil on panel, 112.5 × 87 cm
Madrid, Museo Nacional Thyssen-Bornemisza, inv. no. 369 (1934.20)

81
Giovanni Cariani (c. 1485/90–1547)
Portrait of Giovan Antonio Caravaggi, c. 1520/30
Canvas, 93.5 × 93.7 cm
Ottawa, National Gallery of Canada, inv. no. 3568

82
Tiziano Vecellio (Titian) (c. 1488/90–1576)
Portrait of Charles V, 1548
Canvas, 204.5 × 122 cm
Munich, Bayerische Staatsgemäldesammlungen, Alte Pinakothek, inv. no. 632

83
Tiziano Vecellio (Titian) (c. 1488/90–1576)
Portrait of Isabella of Portugal, 1548
Canvas, 117 × 98 cm
Madrid, Museo Nacional del Prado,
inv. no. P 000415

84
Tiziano Vecellio (Titian) (c. 1488/90–1576)
Portrait of Jacopo Strada, c. 1567/68
Canvas, 126 × 95.5 cm
Vienna, Kunsthistorisches Museum,
inv. no. GG 81

85
Tiziano Vecellio (Titian) (c. 1488/90–1576)
and Workshop
Portrait of Don Pedro Álvarez de Toledo,
c. 1540/45
Canvas, 140.3 × 117.6 cm
Munich, Bayerische Staatsgemäldesammlungen, Alte Pinakothek, inv. no. WAF 1085

Notes / Select bibliography

Bernhard Maaz: Foreword

1 *"es gibt im Moment keine besseren Künstler als uns in Deutschland" HP Zimmer, Tagebuch 1957–1965*, Nina Zimmer, Matthias Mühling and Barbara Hess (eds). Munich: Hatje Cantz, 2023, p. 49. All translations into English provided in this foreword are by Julian Jain.

2 *Max Beckmann. Tagebücher 1940–1950*, 2nd edition, Mathilde Q. Beckmann and Erhard Göpel (eds). Munich: Piper, 1987, p. 377.

3 *Max Beckmann. Briefe*, 3 vols, Klaus Gallwitz et al. (eds). Munich/Zurich: Piper, 1993–1996, 1993, vol. 1, p. 29.

4 Paula Modersohn-Becker, *Briefe und Aufzeichnungen*, Beate Jahn (ed.). Leipzig/Weimar: Gustav Kiepenhauser, 1982, p. 112.

5 Max Liebermann, *Die Phantasie in der Malerei*, Karl Hermann Roehricht and Günter Busch (eds). Berlin: Buchverlag Der Morgen, 1983, p. 136.

6 *Als Mensch unter Menschen. Vincent van Gogh in seinen Briefen an den Bruder Theo*, 2 vols, Fritz Erpel (ed.). Berlin: Henschelverlag, 1963, vol. 2, p. 98 (emphasis in original).

7 Eugène Delacroix, *Dem Auge ein Fest. Aus den Tagebüchern des Malers*, Kuno Mittelstädt (ed.). Berlin: Henschelverlag, 1979, p. 29.

8 Delacroix – Mittelstädt 1979 (see note 7), p. 90.

9 Delacroix – Mittelstädt 1979 (see note 7), pp. 234–235 (emphasis in original).

10 Delacroix – Mittelstädt 1979 (see note 7), p. 235.

Andreas Schumacher: Venice's longing for land

David Alan Brown and Sylvia Ferino-Pagden (eds), *Bellini, Giorgione, Titian, and the Renaissance of Venetian Painting*, exh. cat. National Gallery of Art, Washington, D.C. / Kunsthistorisches Museum, Vienna, New Haven/London: Yale University Press, 2006.

Stephen J. Campbell, "Giorgione's 'Tempest', 'Studiolo' Culture, and the Renaissance Lucretius", in: *Renaissance Quarterly*, vol. 56, no. 2, 2003, pp. 299–332.

Bastian Eclercy and Hans Aurenhammer (eds), *Titian and the Renaissance in Venice*, exh. cat. Städel Museum, Frankfurt am Main. Munich/London/New York: Prestel, 2019.

Davide Gasparotto (ed.), *Giovanni Bellini. Landscapes of Faith in Renaissance Venice*, exh. cat. J. Paul Getty Museum, Los Angeles. Los Angeles: Getty Trust Publications, 2017.

Rona Goffen, *Giovanni Bellini*. New York/London: Yale University Press, 1989.

Johannes Grave, *Giovanni Bellini, Venedig und die Kunst des Betrachtens*. Munich: Prestel, 2018.

Chriscinda Henry, *Playful Pictures. Art, Leisure, and Entertainment in the Venetian Renaissance Home*. University Park, PA: Pennsylvania State University Press, 2021.

Paul Hills, *Venetian Colour: Marble, Mosaic, Painting and Glass 1250–1550*, New Haven/London: Yale University Press, 1999.

Marianne Koos, *Bildnisse des Begehrens. Das lyrische Männerporträt in der venezianischen Malerei des frühen 16. Jahrhunderts – Giorgione, Tizian und ihr Umkreis*. Emsdetten: Edition Imorde, 2006.

Dagmar Korbacher (ed.), *Arkadien. Paradies auf Papier*, exh. cat., Kupferstichkabinett, Staatliche Museen, Berlin. Petersberg: Michael Imhof Verlag, 2014.

Antonio Mazzotta (ed.), *Titian. A Fresh Look at Nature*, exh. cat. The National Gallery, London. London: National Gallery Company, 2012.

Chriscinda Henry: The new golden age

1 Francesco Negri, *De moderanda venetorum aristocratia*, fol. 137, "Domus sanctij institutio". My translation is from the codex in the Biblioteca Nazionale Marciana (= BNMV) and is guided by King's partial translation, *Venetian Humanism*, 15. On Negri and the text, see Giovanni Mercati, *Ultimi contributi alla storia degli umanisti*, 2 vols. Vatican City: Biblioteca Apostolica Vaticana, 1939, vol 2, pp. 62, 80, 108 and, in the appendix, pp. 52 and 57. If not otherwise indicated, all translations into English provided in this essay are the author's own.

2 Negri's text is preserved in two codices: Vatican City, Biblioteca Apostolica Vaticana,Vat. lat. 4033 (autograph, the above-mentioned dedication exemplar for Agostino Barbarigo) Venice, Biblioteca Nazionale Marciana, Marciano lat. vi 6 (= 2753) (a dedication exemplar on parchment presented to Doge Leonardo Loredan between 1510 and 1512).

3 Giovanni Pontano's treatises, which were prepared for publication in 1498, exemplify this Renaissance humanist tradition. Giovanni Pontano, *I trattati delle virtù sociali*: "De liberalitate", "De beneficentia", "De magnificentia", "De splendore", "De conviventia", Francesco Tateo (ed.). Rome: Edizioni dell'Ateneo, 1965. On the values of *magnificentia* and *liberalitas* in relation to Renaissance domestic decoration, see Evelyn Welch, "Public Magnificence and Private Display: Giovanni Pontano's 'De splendore' (1498) and the Domestic Arts", in: *Journal of Design History*, vol. 15, no. 4, 2002, pp. 211–221; also

see Guido Guerzoni, "Liberalitas, Magnificentia, Splendor: The Classic Origins of Italian Renaissance Life-styles", in: Neil De Marchi and Craufurd D. W. Goodwin (eds), *Economic Engagements with Art* (History of Political Economy, Annual Supplement to Volume 31). Durham: Duke University Press, 1999, pp. 332–378

4 All citations are from the modern critical edition of the text: Theodor Frimmel (ed. and trans.), *Der Anonimo Morelliano (Marcanton Michiels "Notizia d'opere del disegno"). Text und Übersetzung* (Quellenschriften für Kunstgeschichte und Kunsttechnik des Mittelalters und der Neuzeit, new series, vol. 1). [Vienna, 1888] Vienna: Carl Graeser, 1896 (special issue).

5 For evidence of earlier private collections in Venice, Padua and the Veneto, including the key example of Petrarch, see Rosella Lauber, "Memoria, visione e attesa. Tempi e spazi del collezionismo artistico nel primo Rinascimento veneziano", in: Michel Hochmann, Rosella Lauber and Stefania Mason (eds), *Il collezionismo d'arte a Venezia. Dalle origini al Cinquecento.* Venice: Marsilio, 2008, pp. 41–81, here pp. 41–45.

6 Larry Silver attributes the origins of new pictorial "species" in Antwerp around 1500 to the rise of urbanism and capitalism; Larry Silver, *Peasant Scenes and Landscapes: The Rise of Pictorial Genres in the Antwerp Art Market.* Philadelphia: University of Pennsylvania Press, 2006. On artistic connections between Venice and the Netherlands in this period, see Bernard Aikema, "Tesori ponentini per la Serenissima: Il commercio d'arte fiamminga a Venezia e nel Veneto fra Quattro e Cinquecento", in: Enrico Maria dal Pozzolo and Leonida Tedoldi (eds), *Tra committenza e collezionismo: Studi sul mercato dell'arte nell'Italia settentrionale durante l'età moderna.* Vicenza: Terra Ferma, 2003, pp. 35–48; also see Bernard Aikema, "The Lure of the North: Netherlandish Art in Venetian Collections", in: *Renaissance Venice and the North: Crosscurrents in the Time of Bellini, Dürer, and Titian*, exh. cat. Palazzo Grassi, Venice, Bernard Aikema and Beverly Louise Brown (eds). New York: Rizzoli, 2000, pp. 83–89.

7 See Monika Schmitter, "The Dating of Marcantonio Michiel's 'Notizia' on Works of Art in Padua", in: *The Burlington Magazine*, vol. 145, 2003, pp. 564–571.

8 The incident is recorded in a pair of letters Isabella d'Este exchanged with her Venetian agent Taddeo Albani, which are transcribed in *I tempi di Giorgione*, Ruggero Maschio (ed.). Rome: Gangemi, 1994, p. 203; also see Alessandro Nova, "Giorgione's 'Inferno with Aeneas and Anchises' for Taddeo Contarini", in: Luisa Ciammitti, Steven F. Ostrow and Salvatore Settis (eds), *Dosso's Fate: Painting and Court Culture in Renaissance Italy* (Issues & Debates, vol. 5). Los Angeles: The Getty Research Center Publications, 1998, pp. 41–62.

9 Francesco Sansovino, "De i palazzi private et de loro ornamenti lib. IX", in: *Venetia, città nobilissima et singolare, descritta in XIII. libri.* Venice: Giacomo Sansovino, 1581, p. 387.

10 Giorgio Vasari, *Le vite de' più eccellenti pittori, scultori ed architettori*, Gaetano Milanesi (ed.), 9 vols. Florence: G. C. Sansoni, 1906, vol. 5, p. 136. For a close reading of Treviso's paintings for Odoni, see Monika Schmitter, "Odoni's Façade: The House as Portrait in Renaissance Venice", in: *Journal of the Society of Architectural Historians*, vol. 66, no. 3, 2007, pp. 294–315, here pp. 304–305.

11 On the home of the collector as a haven for virtuosi and "Teatro o albergo delle Muse" framed in terms of the cult of antiquity, see Lanfranco Franzoni, "Antiquari e collezionisti nel Cinquecento", in: *Storia della cultura veneta,* vol. 3, part 3, *Dal primo Quattrocento al Concilio di Trento.* Vicenza: Neri Pozza, 1981, pp. 207–266, here pp. 216–217.

12 Michiel saw the portrait in 1530 and describes it as "a half-length portrait of M. Gabriele [Vendramin] in oil, was by the hand of Zanin del Comandador [Giovanni Cariani], on canvas. The foliate ornament of powdered gold on the frame was by the hand of Pre Vido Celere [Guido Celere]." Michiel – Frimmel [1888] 1809 (see note 4), p. 106. Giovanni Cariani's father, originally from near Bergamo, was a *Comandador* (herald) for the Venetian government, thus Michiel refers to his son the painter as Zuan or Zanin del Comandador. Jaynie Anderson bases her identification of the portrait on descriptions and measurements given in the inventories of Vendramin's collection, taken after his death, in 1567 to 1569 and in 1601; see Jaynie Anderson, "A Further Inventory of Gabriele Vendramin's Collection", in: *The Burlington Magazine*, vol. 121, 1979, pp. 639–648, here pp. 642–643. The appearance of the man in the Fesch portrait with bulging eyes and long nose is close to that of the older Gabriele in Titian's votive portrait of the Vendramin family adoring the reliquary of the True Cross, which dates to the 1540s (London, The National Gallery). The attribution to Titian was, however, maintained in the exhibition in Frankfurt: *Titian and the Renaissance in Venice*, exh. cat. Städel Museum, Frankfurt am Main, Bastian Eclercy and Hans Aurenhammer (eds). Munich, London and New York: Prestel, 2019, pp. 152–155, cat. 52 (Daniela Bohde).

13 Baldassare Castiglione, *Il libro del cortegiano*, Walter Barberis (ed.). Turin: Giulio Einaudi, 1998, p. 127. On elite men turning towards dressing in black and away from bright and metallic colours in the 16th century, see "Black is the New Gold", in: Timothy McCall, *Brilliant Bodies: Fashioning Courtly Men in Early Renaissance Italy.* University Park, PA: Pennsylvania State University Press, 2022, pp. 151–159.

14 On the new "poetic" male portrait type that developed around the turn of the 16th century, see John Shearman, "Portraits and Poets", in: *Only Connect: Art and the Spectator in Renaissance Italy.* Princeton, NJ: Princeton University Press, 1992, pp. 108–147; on Venetian portraits specifically, see Marianne Koos, *Bildnisse des Begehrens: Das lyrische Männerporträt in der venezianischen Malerei des frühen 16. Jahrhunderts – Giorgione, Tizian und ihr Umkreis.* Emsdetten:

Edition Imorde, 2006, pp. 172–179 and pp. 279–282; also see David Alan Brown, "Portraits of Men", in: *Bellini, Giorgione, Titian, and the Renaissance of Venetian Painting*, exh. cat. National Gallery of Art, Washington, D.C. / Kunsthistorisches Museum, Vienna, David Alan Brown and Sylvia Ferino-Pagden (eds). New Haven/London: Yale University Press, 2006, pp. 237–245, esp. pp. 242–243.

15 Manlio Cortelazzo provides a useful, if limited, period definition of a virtuoso as an "artist, person expert in music, singing or dance" in *Dizionario veneziano della lingua e della cultura popolare nel XVI secolo* (Cultura popolare veneta, serie speciale). Limena (Padua): La Linea, 2007, p. 718.

16 On Giorgone, see Giorgio Vasari 1906, vol. 4, p. 92, and on Sebastiano's biography, see Giorgio Vasari 1906, vol. 5, pp. 565–566 (see note 10). On Venetian artists as musicians, see Tracy E. Cooper, "The Place of Music in the Artist's Home", in: Deborah Howard and Laura Moretti (eds), *The Music Room in Early Modern France and Italy: Sound, Space, and Object* (Proceedings of the British Academy, vol. 176). Oxford: Oxford University Press, 2012, pp. 51–75; also see Katherine A. McIver, "Maniera, Music, and Vasari", in: *The Sixteenth Century Journal*, vol. 28, no. 1, 1997, pp. 45–55; also see Chriscinda Henry, *Playful Pictures: Art, Leisure, and Entertainment in the Venetian Renaissance Home*. University Park, PA: Pennsylvania State University Press, 2021, pp. 83–93.

17 T. Sturge Moore, Albrecht Dürer. London: Duckworth and Co., 1905.

18 Heaton 1881 (see note 17), p. 96. Wolfgang Stechow, *Northern Renaissance Art, 1400–1600: Sources and Documents*. Evanston, IL: Northwestern University Press, 1989, p. 91.

19 See the note "A small portrait by Albrecht Dürer, his own self-portrait" by Aldo Ravà, "Il 'camerino delle antigaglie' di Gabriele Vendramin", in: *Nuovo archivio veneto*, vol. 39, 1920, nos 117–118, 1920, pp. 155–181, here p. 177. The supposed "self-portrait" is now identified as Dürer's 1506 *Portrait of a Young Man* in the Palazzo Rosso, Genoa, which does not represent the artist; see Anderson 1979 (see note 12), p. 644. On Vendramin's collection of Dürer prints, see Georg Gronau, "Venezianische Kunstsammlungen des 16. Jahrhunderts", in: *Jahrbuch für Kunstsammler*, vols 4/5, 1924/25, pp. 9–34, here pp. 29–30 and p. 34.

20 On the nature and early development of musical *ridotti* in Venice, see Rodolfo Baroncini, "Ridotti and Salons: Private Patronage", in: Katelijne Schiltz (ed.), *A Companion to Music in Sixteenth Century Venice* (Brill's Companions of the Musical Culture of Medieval and Early Modern Europe, vol. 2). Leiden: Brill, 2017, pp. 149–203, here pp. 182–186; also see Martha Feldman, *City Culture and the Madrigal at Venice*. Berkeley: University of California Press, 1995, pp. 19–23.

21 See Baroncini 2017 (see note 20), p. 182.

22 See Courtney Quaintance, *Textual Masculinity and the Exchange of Women in Renaissance Venice*. Toronto: University of Toronto Press, 2015; also see Shawn Marie Keener, "Virtue, Illusion, 'Venezianità': Vocal Bravura and the Early 'Cortigiana Onesta'", in: Thomasin LaMay (ed.), *Musical Voices of Early Modern Women: Many-Headed Melodies*. Burlington, VT: Ashgate, 2005, pp. 119–133.

23 See Flora Dennis, "Music", in: *At Home in Renaissance Italy: Art and Life in the Italian House, 1400–1600*, exh. cat. Victoria & Albert Museum, London, Marta Ajmar-Wollheim and Flora Dennis (eds). New York: Harry N. Abrams, 2006, p. 238; also see Flora Dennis, "When Is a Room a Music Room? Sounds, Spaces, and Objects in Non-Courtly Italian Interiors", in: *The Music Room* 2012 (see note 16), pp. 37–49, here p. 40; also see Kathleen Weil-Garris and John F. D'Amico, "The Renaissance Cardinal's Ideal Palace: A Chapter from Cortesi's 'De Cardinalatu'", in: Henry A. Millon (ed.), *Studies in Italian Art and Architecture, 15th through 18th Centuries* (Studies in Italian Art History, vol. 1 / Memoirs of the American Academy in Rome, vol. 35), Rome, 1980, pp. 45–123.

24 While such collectables were displayed throughout the Venetian home, they were often concentrated in a study (*studio, studiolo, scrittoio*) or dedicated display space (*camerino, gabinetto*) often attached to the study. See Dora Thornton, *The Scholar in his Study: Ownership and Experience in Renaissance Italy*. New Haven/London: Yale University Press, 1997.

25 For a discussion of Michiel's friendships with artists, see Rosella Lauber, "Una lucente linea d'ombra. Note per Giorgione nel collezionismo veneziano", in: *Giorgione*, exh. cat. Museo Casa Giorgione, Castelfranco Veneto, Enrico Maria Dal Pozzolo and Lionello Puppi (eds). Milan: Skira, 2009, pp. 189–206, here p. 190; also see Jennifer Fletcher, "Marcantonio Michiel: His Friends and Collection", in: *The Burlington Magazine*, vol. 123, 1981, pp. 453–467, and Jennifer Fletcher, "Marcantonio Michiel, 'che ha veduto assai'", in: *The Burlington Magazine*, vol. 123, 1981, pp. 602–609.

26 See *Il collezionismo d'arte a Venezia* 2008 (see note 5); also see Maria Ruvoldt, "Sacred to Secular, East to West: The Renaissance Study and Strategies of Display", in: *Renaissance Studies*, vol. 20, no. 5, 2006, pp. 640–657.

27 On the revival of the pastoral mode in Venetian and North Italian literature and art from the late 15th century onwards, see Dieter Blume, "Beseelte Natur und ländliche Idylle", in: *Natur und Antike in der Renaissance*, exh. cat. Liebighaus Museum Alter Plastik, Frankfurt am Main, Herbert Beck, Dieter Blume and Peter C. Bol (eds). Frankfurt am Main: Liebieghaus Museum Alter Plastik, 1985, pp. 173–197; David Rosand, "Giorgione, Venice, and the Pastoral Vision", in: *Places of Delight: The Pastoral Landscape*, exh. cat. National Gallery of Art, Washington, D.C. / The Phillips Collection, Washington, D.C., Robert C. Cafritz, Lawrence Gowing and David Rosand (eds). Washington, D.C.:

Phillips Collection in association with the National Gallery of Art, 1988, pp. 20–81; Jodi Cranston, *Green Worlds of Renaissance Venice*. University Park, PA: Pennsylvania State University Press, 2019. On Venetian festive and performance culture in relation to art, see Henry 2021 (see note 16), pp. 68–78 ("Pastoral and Musical Self-Fashioning").

28 See Giuseppe Gerbino, *Music and the Myth of Arcadia in Renaissance Italy* (New Perspectives in Music History and Criticism, vol. 18). Cambridge: Cambridge University Press, 2009; also see Nino Pirrotta, "Orpheus, Singer of 'Strambotti'", in: *Music and Theatre from Poliziano to Monteverdi*, by Nino Pirrotta and Elena Povoledo, trans. Karen Eales. Cambridge: Cambridge University Press, 1982, pp. 3–36.

29 See Emma T. K. Guest, "Virgil in Venice, 1470–1507: Illuminated Books from the Junius Spencer Morgan Collection", in: *The Princeton University Library Chronicle*, vol. 69, no. 1, 2007, pp. 71–101; also see Martin Lowry, *The World of Aldus Manutius: Business and Scholarship in Renaissance Venice*. Ithaca, NY: Cornell University Press, 1979; also see Martin Davies, *Aldus Manutius, Printer and Publisher of Renaissance Venice*. Tempe, AZ: Arizona Center for Medieval and Renaissance Studies, 1999. For links between Manutius and Venetian visual culture of the period, including the stunning and influential woodcut illustrations for the *Hypnerotomachia Poliphili* (1499), see *Aldo Manuzio: Il Rinascimento di Venezia*, exh. cat. Gallerie dell'Accademia, Venice, Guido Beltramini and Davide Gasparotto (eds). Venice: Marsilio, 2016.

30 On the Venetian reception of Sannazaro's *Arcadia*, see Angela Caracciolo Aricò, "Mito e bucolica nell''Arcadia' di Iacopo Sannazaro e la cultura figurativa del Quattrocento", in: Francesco Tateo (ed.), *La Serenissima e il regno: Nel V Centenario dell'"Arcadia" di Iacopo Sannazaro; Atti del convegno di studi*, Bari/Venice, 4–8 October 2004. Bari: Cacucci, 2006, pp. 65–96.

31 Tania Basile and Jean-Jacques Marchand (eds), *Antonio Tebaldeo, Rime*. Modena: Edizioni Panini, 1989.

32 Guest 2007 (see note 29); Helena K. Szépe, "Bordon, Dürer and Modes of Illuminating Aldines", in: David S Zeidberg (ed., with Fiorella Gioffredi Superbi), *Aldus Manutius and Renaissance Culture: Essays in Memory of Franklin D. Murphy*. Florence: L. S. Olschki, 1998, pp. 185–200; Carlo Vecce, "Arcadia at the Newberry", in: *I Tatti Studies in the Italian Renaissance*, vol. 17, no. 2, 2014, pp. 283–302.

33 On landscape as a subject of drawings and prints in Venice, see Catherine Whistler's essay in this catalogue.

34 On the market and collecting of antiquities in Renaissance Venice, see Patricia Fortini Brown, "Le antichità", in: Franco Franceschi, Richard Goldthwaite and Reinhold Müller (eds), *Il Rinascimento italiano e l'Europa*, vol. 4: *Commercio e cultura mercantile*. Treviso: Angelo Colla Editore, 2007, pp. 309–337; Irene Favaretto, *Arte antica e cultura antiquaria nelle collezioni venete al tempo della Serenissima* (*Studia archaeologica*, vol. 55), Rome: L'Erma di Bretschneider, 1990; Betrand Jestaz, "Porcelaine de Chine et bronze islamique à Venise. La collection Redaldi (1527)", in: *Annali della Scuola Normale Superiore di Pisa. Classe di Lettere e Filosofia*, series III, vol. 20, no. 1, 1990, pp. 23–60.

35 Cf. Rudolf Kultzen and Peter Eikemeier, *Venezianische Gemälde des 15. und 16. Jahrhunderts*, 2 vols (Gemäldekataloge Bayerische Staatsgemäldesammlungen, Munich, vol. 9). Munich: Hirmer, 1971, vol. 1, pp. 114–117, cat. 16; Cornelia Syre, *Alte Pinakothek – italienische Malerei*. Ostfildern: Hatje Cantz, 2007, p. 177; Irene Brooke, "New Evidence for the Life and Career of Giulio Campagnola," in: *Print Quarterly*, vol. 37, no. 4, 2020, pp. 371–382. Philip Rylands, author of an important monograph on Palma il Vecchio, rightly rejected the previous attribution to Giorgione and confirmed the attribution to Palma, placing the painting in a small group of autograph works with pastoral and mythological subjects; see Philip Rylands, *Palma Vecchio*. Cambridge: Cambridge University Press, 1992, pp. 130 and 158, cat. 14. More recently, David Alan Brown intriguingly proposed Giulio Campagnola, yet no extant painting has been universally attributed to his hand, and because Campagnola worked in a variety of media and emulated several artists over the course of his career – most notably Andrea Mantegna, Albrecht Dürer and Giorgione – those paintings that have been put forward differ significantly from each other in style and technique; see David Alan Brown, "Giulio Campagnola: The Printmaker as Painter", in: *Artibus et Historiae*, vol. 31, no. 61, 2010, pp. 83–97. Irene Brooke discusses the various candidates that have been proposed and finds Keith Christiansen's attribution of the *Venus and Mars* in the Brooklyn Museum, New York, the most convincing; see Irene Brooke, "Giulio Campagnola, Landscape, and Venetian Illumination", in: *Colnaghi Studies Journal*, vol. 3, 2018, pp. 137–154, here pp. 137–138; Brooke 2020 (see note 35), pp. 373–378.

36 The figure of Apollo in Cima da Conegliano's *The Judgement of Midas* of around 1506 (Parma, Galleria Nazionale) appears similarly nude, draped with a light blue cape, and playing a rebec.

37 Brown 2010 (see note 35), pp. 93–94.

38 Paul Joannides has shown that Longus's novella circulated in manuscript form in Padua by 1510, and he associates it with his interpretation of the young couple in Titian's *Three Ages of Man* (c. 1512/14, on loan by the Duke of Sutherland to the Scottish National Gallery, Edinburgh) as Daphnis and Chloe; see Paul Joannides, *Titian to 1518. The Assumption of Genius*. New Haven/London: Yale University Press, 2001, p. 199.

39 Virgil, eclogue V, lines 60–61, Paul Alpers, *The singer of the Eclogues: a study of Virgilian pastoral, with a new translation of the Eclogues*. Berkeley: University of California Press, 1979, p. 35.

40 For a detailed account of the statuette, see C. D. Dickerson III's entry in *Andrea Riccio: Renaissance Master of Bronze*, exh. cat. The Frick Collection, New York, Denise Allen and Peta Motture (eds). New York/London: The Frick Collection, 2008, pp. 234–239, cat. 22. On its resemblance to the Munich painting, see Jeremy Warren's entry on the closely related *Inkstand with a Faun* from Oxford in the same catalogue, pp. 240–245, cat. 23, here pp. 242–243.

41 Cf. Edgar Peters Bowron, *Renaissance Bronzes in the Walters Art Gallery.* Baltimore: The Walters Art Gallery, 1978, pp. 32–34.

42 The exhibition *Andrea Riccio: Renaissance Master of Bronze* from 2008 in the Frick Collection brought the two statuettes together. On the Louvre bronze, see Philippe Malgouyres's catalogue entry, in: exh. cat. New York 2008 (see note 40), pp. 228–233, cat. 21.

43 These are the *Inkstand with a Faun* in the Ashmolean Museum, Oxford, and the *Seated Faun with a Syrinx* in the Quentin Foundation; cf. Warren 2008 (see note 40) and exh. cat. New York 2008 (see note 40), pp. 246–251, cat. 24 (Denise Allen).

44 Michiel here documents the collection of Giovanni ("Zuan") Ram, a wealthy Catalan merchant who was a long-term resident in Venice, whose home Michiel visited in 1531; Michiel – Frimmel [1888] 1809 (see note 4), p. 106. Collectors who owned large numbers of modern bronze *figurette* also include Pietro Bembo and Andrea Odoni, the nephew of Francesco Zio (for the latter, continue reading our essay). The bronzes are often listed as made by the hand of "diverse masters". This is the case with the bronzes in the lawyer and professor Marco Mantova Benadvides's collection in Padua; see ibid., p. 28.

45 See Rylands 1992 (see note 35), p. 130; Warren 2008 (see note 40), pp. 242–243.

46 Michiel – Frimmel [1888] 1809 (see note 4), p. 94. Zio died in 1523. Michiel visited him in 1521 (erroneously transcribed in the original manuscript and in Frimmel as 1512). He first notes that the sculpture was previously owned by Pietro Contarini before striking this through upon realising it was a different sculpture from one that he must have previously seen in Contarini's home (for Contarini and this second figure, continue reading our essay); see Monika Schmitter, *The Display of Distinction: Art Collecting and Social Status in Early Sixteenth-Century Venice*. PhD dissertation, University of Michigan, Ann Arbor, 1997, p. 113.

47 Michiel – Frimmel [1888] 1809 (see note 4), p. 92. Michiel does not say how Foscarini acquired the sculpture from Zio, although it was likely by purchase; cf. Rosella Lauber, "Francesco Zio", in: *Il collezionismo d'arte a Venezia* 2008 (see note 5), pp. 326–328; Rosella Lauber, "Antonio Foscarini", in: *Il collezionismo d'arte a Venezia* 2008 (see note 5), pp. 282–283.

48 Michiel – Frimmel [1888] 1809 (see note 4), p. 110.

49 Michiel – Frimmel [1888] 1809 (see note 4), p. 110.

50 Cf. Rosella Lauber, "Michele Contarini", in: *Il collezionismo d'arte a Venezia* 2008 (see note 5), p. 262; Schmitter 1997 (see note 46), p. 113.

51 Philippe Malgouyres notes two mounting holes under the buttocks of the Louvre statuette, which reveal that it was originally attached to a low base; cf. exh. cat. New York 2008 (see note 40), p. 227. The right buttock of the Walters Art Musuem statuette was filed flat in a modern intervention, which makes it difficult to determine if it was originally mounted or not; cf. Dickerson III 2008 (see note 40), pp. 237–238.

52 The curly-haired faun plays a flute rather than a syrinx or double-reeded pipe and wears a chaplet of flowers, a detail not mentioned by Michiel; see Warren 2008 (see note 40), p. 243. On the Fitzwilliam marble, see Ludwig Budde and Richard Nicholls, *A Catalogue of the Greek and Roman Sculpture in the Fitzwilliam Museum, Cambridge*. Cambridge: Cambridge University Press, 1967, pp. 51–52, cat. 83.

53 Michiel – Frimmel [1888] 1809 (see note 4), p. 108. See Millard Meiss, "Sleep in Venice Ancient Myths and Renaissance Proclivities", in: *Proceedings of the American Philosophical Society*, vol. 110, no. 5, 1966, pp. 348–382, here p. 350. Irene Favaretto has identified this marble sculpture with the version of the famous *Sleeping Ariadne* once in the Borghese collection in Rome and now in the Louvre; Favaretto 1990 (see note 34), p. 80.

54 Michiel – Frimmel [1888] 1809 (see note 4), pp. 110 and 112.

55 On Vendramin's collection of antiquities, see Favaretto 1990 (see note 34), pp. 79–82. Of course, Vendramin was not alone in owning ancient works that may have been emulated by Renaissance artists; the phenomenon was widespread, with one of the most well-known examples being Isabella d'Este's juxtaposition in her *grotta* of modern and antique *Sleeping Cupids*, the former by Michelangelo and the latter attributed to Praxiteles. On the ideal of the half-figure portrait, see Theresa Gatarski's essay in this catalogue.

56 Stephen J. Campbell, *Andrea Mantegna: Humanist Aesthetics, Faith, and the Force of Images* (The Bettie Allison Rand Lectures in Art History). London: Harvey Miller Publishers, 2020, pp. 1–40; Stephen J. Campbell, "Naturalism and the Venetian 'Poesia': Grafting, Metaphor, and Embodiment in Giorgione, Titian, and the Campagnolas", in: Alexander Nagel and Lorenzo Pericolo (eds), *Subject as Aporia in Early Modern Art*. Farnham: Ashgate, 2010, pp. 115–142.

57 David Alan Brown describes the instrument and its carved ornamentation in Brown 2010 (see note 35), pp. 92–93, but mistakes the carved finial as an eagle's head rather than a grotesque skull.

58 The skull finial is reminiscent of Giorgio Vasari's report, in his biography of Leonardo da Vinci, that the artist owned a *lira da braccio* in the shape of a horse's skull; see Emanuela Vai, "Fantastic Finials: The Materiality, Decoration and Display of Renaissance Musical Instruments", in: Chriscinda Henry and Tim Shephard (eds), *Music and Visual Culture in Renaissance Italy*. New York/London: Routledge, 2023, pp. 295–322, here pp. 306–308.

59 Jacopo Sannazaro, *Arcadia*, Francesco Erspamer (ed.). Milan: Mursia, 1990, prologue 2; the English translation is from Jacopo Sannazaro, *Arcadia and Piscatorial Eclogues*, trans. and with an intro. by Ralph Nash. Detroit: Wayne State University Press, 1966, p. 29.

60 On figurations of this contrast in paintings such as Titian's *Concert Champêtre* (c. 1511; see p. 167, fig. 3), framed in terms of *discordia concors*, or the harmony of opposites, see Rosand 1988 (see note 27), pp. 38–39; Joanna Kilian Michieletti, "Tastar de corde: Musical Improvisation and the Aesthetics of Sprezzatura in Sixteenth-Century Venetian Painting", in: *Artibus et Historiae*, vol. 34, no. 68, 2013, pp. 219–235, here pp. 220–224.

61 See note 59.

62 *The Greek Bucolic Poets*, trans. John M. Edmonds (Loeb Classical Library, vol. 28). Cambridge, MA: Harvard University Press, 1912, p. 9.

63 On Vianello's exceptional painting collection, ownership of a wondrous organ with paper pipes coveted by Isabella d'Este and long-term hosting in his home of the renowned Pavia instrument maker Lorenzo Gusnasco, see William F Prizer, "Isabella d'Este and Lorenzo da Pavia, 'Master Instrument-Maker'", in: *Early Music History*, vol. 2, 1982, pp. 87–118 and pp. 120–127.

64 Palma painted several small paintings in oil on panel early in his career between 1510 and 1515, but the exceptionally small dimensions of the Munich panel are indicative of paintings for furniture (continue reading our essay), numerous examples of which have been gathered and systematically examined according to type by Susannah Rutherglen, *Ornamental Paintings of the Venetian Renaissance*. PhD dissertation, Princeton University, Princeton, 2012.

65 The dimensions of the single Munich panel closely match those of the individual London scenes, which measure about 19.8 × 18.5 cm each, and those of other similar panels that once decorated furniture, such as the set of four *Pastoral Scenes* now shared between the Museo d'Arte Medioevale e Moderna in Padua and the Phillips Collection in Washington, D.C., as well as the National Gallery of Art (Samuel H. Kress Collection) there. On the London panels, see most recently Rutherglen 2012 (see note 64), pp. 152–154 and pp. 281–283, cat. 5, and on the panels in Padua and Washington, ibid., pp. 326–327, cat. 20. Cima da Conegliano's *Endymion Asleep* and *Judgment of Midas* of around 1506–1508 (Parma, Galleria Nazionale) – panels that were made to ornament a chest – are also similar in subject, technique and size (although round in form); cf. Rutherglen 2012 (see note 64), pp. 301–304, cat. 12; also exh. cat. Washington/Vienna 2006 (see note 14), pp. 152–155, cat. 26–27 (Jaynie Anderson).

66 Nicholas Penny suggests a musical instrument case in Nicholas Penny, *The Sixteenth Century Italian Paintings*, vol. 1: *Paintings from Bergamo, Brescia and Cremona* (National Gallery Catalogues). London: National Gallery, 2004, vol. 1, p. 291.

67 Brown 2010 (see note 35), p. 93.

68 Part 2 of Antonfrancesco Doni's *Dialogo* transpires in Venice, where Doni moved to in 1544; see James Haar, "Notes on the 'Dialogo della musica' of Antonfrancesco Doni", in: *Music & Letters*, vol. 47, no. 3, 1966, pp. 198–224.

69 Antonfrancesco Doni, *Dialogo della musica*, G. Francesco Malipiero (ed.). Milan: Universal Edition, 1965, p. 8.

Johannes Grave: The wandering gaze

1 Salvatore Settis, *Deeper Thoughts. Beyond the Allegory of Bellini, Giorgione and Titian* (The Finbury Lecture at the National Gallery, 2020). London: National Gallery Company, 2021, p. 12.

2 The widespread assumption that early Renaissance painting (especially in Florence) was strongly oriented towards Alberti's specifications would have to be discussed critically. For some reflections on this, see Johannes Grave, *Architekturen des Sehens. Bauten in Bildern des Quattrocento*. Munich: Wilhelm Fink, 2015.

3 Cf. the tabular overviews in Salvatore Settis, *Giorgione's Tempest. Interpreting the Hidden Subject*. Chicago: University of Chicago Press, 1990, pp. 78–79; Ursula and Warren Kirkendale, *Hesiod's Theogony as Source of the Iconological Program of Giorgione's "Tempesta" – The Poet, Amalthea, the Infant Zeus and the Muses*. Florence: Olschki, 2015, pp. 79–80.

4 A selection of recent examples: Stephen J. Campbell, "Giorgione's 'Tempest', 'Studiolo' Culture, and the Renaissance Lucretius", in: *Renaissance Quarterly*, vol. 56, no. 2, 2003, pp. 299–332; Carlo Falciani, "La 'Tempesta' di Giorgione e un poemetto encomiastico dedicato ai Vendramin", in: *Studiolo. Revue d'histoire de l'art de l'Académie de France à Rome*, vol. 7, 2009, pp. 101–123; Kirkendale 2015 (see note 3); Sergio Alcamo, *La verità celata. Giorgione, la "Tempesta" e la salvezza*. Rome: Donzelli, 2019; Anthony Colantuono, "Giorgione's 'Tempesta' in Iconological Perspective. Pierio Valeriano, Giovanni Cotta and the 'Paduan Hypothesis'", in: *Zeitschrift für Kunstgeschichte*, vol. 83, 2020, pp. 173–212.

5 See, for example, Dan Lettieri, "Landscape and Lyricism in Giorgione's 'Tempesta'", in: *Artibus et historiae*, vol. 15, no. 30, 1994, pp. 55–70; Hans Belting, "Exil in Arkadien. Giorgiones 'Tempesta' in neuer Sicht", in: Reinhardt Brandt (ed.), *Meisterwerke der Malerei. Von Rogier van der Weyden bis*

Andy Warhol. Leipzig: Reclam, 2001, pp. 45–68; Hans Aurenhammer, "Berge in der Lagune. Die Entdeckung der Landschaft in der venezianischen Renaissancemalerei (1450–1520)", in: Barbara Kuhn (ed.), *Wie sonst nirgendwo … Venedig zwischen Topographie und Utopie*. Würzburg: Königshausen & Neumann, 2017, pp. 93–135, here pp. 125–130. On the fundamental question of the interpretability of the picture, also see Creighton Gilbert, "On Subject and Not-Subject in Italian Renaissance Pictures", in: *The Art Bulletin*, vol. 34, 1952, pp. 202–217; James Elkins, "On Monstrously Ambiguous Paintings", in: *History and Theory*, vol. 32, 1993, pp. 227–247.

6 Cf. Lettieri 1994 (see note 5).

7 On Vendramin, see Rosella Lauber, "Per un ritratto di Gabriele Vendramin. Nuovi contributi", in: Linda Borean and Stefania Mason (eds), *Figure di collezionisti a Venezia tra Cinque e Seicento* (Fonti e testi). Udine: Forum, 2002, pp. 25–75.

8 This idea is already tangible in the later 15th century – for example, in a poem by Giovanni Aurelio Augurello dedicated to the Venetian Bernardo Bembo, which states that the variety of different interpretations is even more beautiful than the painted images themselves ("Multi multa ferunt, eadem sententia nulli est: / Pulchrius est pictis istud imaginibus"; quoted after Arnaldo Della Torre, "La prima ambasceria di Bernardo Bembo a Firenze", in: *Giornale storico della letteratura italiana*, vol. 35, 1900, pp. 258–333, here p. 267). On the context, cf. among others Peter Lüdemann, *Virtus und Voluptas. Beobachtungen zur Ikonographie weiblicher Aktfiguren in der venezianischen Malerei des frühen Cinquecento* (Studi/Deutsches Studienzentrum in Venedig, new series, vol. 1). Berlin: Akademie, 2008, pp. 55–56; Wolfgang Brassat, *Das Bild als Gesprächsprogramm. Selbstreflexive Malerei und ihr kommunikativer Gebrauch in der Frühen Neuzeit*. Berlin/Boston: DeGruyter, 2021, pp. 101–102.

9 Theodor Frimmel (ed. and trans.), *Der Anonimo Morelliano (Marcanton Michiels "Notizia d'opere del disegno"). Text und Übersetzung* (Quellenschriften für Kunstgeschichte und Kunsttechnik des Mittelalters und der Neuzeit, new series, vol. 1). Vienna: Carl Graesner, 1888, pp. 106–107.

10 Cf. Brigit Blass-Simmen, "'Qualche lontani'. Distance and Transcendence in the Art of Giovanni Bellini", in: Carolyn C. Wilson (ed.), *Examining Giovanni Bellini. An Art "More Human and More Divine"*. Turnhout: Brepols, 2015, pp. 77–91, esp. pp. 79–81.

11 Michiel – Frimmel 1888 (see note 9), pp. 86–87. If not otherwise indicated, all translations into English provided in this contribution are by the translator of the essay (Julian Jain).

12 Michiel – Frimmel 1888 (see note 9), p. 89.

13 Michiel – Frimmel 1888 (see note 9), pp. 88–89. Also see Rosella Lauber, "'Finito et ricercato mirabilmente.' Per nuovi contributi sul 'San Francesco nel deserto' di Giovanni Bellini, ora nella Frick Collection di New York", in: Wilson 2015 (see note 10), pp. 93–112; Susannah Rutherglen, "The Desert and the City. Marcantonio Michiel and the Early History of 'St. Francis'", in: Susannah Rutherglen and Charlotte Hale (eds), *In a New Light. Giovanni Bellini's 'St. Francis in the Desert'*. New York: Giles, 2015, pp. 47–57, here pp. 47–49.

14 For example, cf. John V. Fleming, *From Bonaventure to Bellini. An Essay in Franciscan Exegesis*. Princeton: Princeton University Press, 1982; Willi Hirdt, "Giovanni Bellinis heiliger Franziskus (Frick Collection, New York)", in: Birgit Tappert and Willi Jung (eds), Willi Hirdt, *Lesen und Sehen. Aufsätze zu Literatur und Malerei in Italien und Frankreich. Festschrift zum 60. Geburtstag* (Stauffenburg-Festschriften, vol. 6). Tübingen: Stauffenberg, 1998, pp. 29–74; Emanuele Lugli, "Between Form and Representation. The Frick 'St Francis'", in: *Art History*, vol. 32, 2009, pp. 21–51; Michael F. Cusato, "The Formative Stimulus for Bellini's 'St. Francis in the Desert'. History and Literature of the Franciscan Movement in Late Medieval Italy", in: Rutherglen and Hale 2015 (see note 13), pp. 155–166; Marilyn Aronberg Lavin, "Bellini's Frick 'Saint Francis' and the Source of the Absent Side Wound", in: *Artibus et historiae*, vol. 43, no. 85, 2022, pp. 51–87. For an overview of previous research on the painting, see Johannes Grave, *Landschaften der Meditation. Giovanni Bellinis Assoziationsräume* (Rombach Wissenschaften, Reihe Quellen zur Kunst, vol. 23). Freiburg: Rombach, 2004, pp. 29–42; Rutherglen and Hale 2015 (see note 13); Johannes Grave, *Giovanni Bellini and the Art of Contemplation*. London/New York: Prestel, 2018, pp. 162–172; Mauro Lucco, Peter Humfrey and Giovanni Carlo Federico Villa, *Giovanni Bellini. Catalogo ragionato*. Treviso: ZeL Edizione, 2019, pp. 440–443, cat. 82 (Peter Humfrey).

15 Cf. Millard Meiss, *Giovanni Bellini's "St. Francis" in the Frick Collection*. Princeton: Princeton University Press, 1964.

16 Mauro Di Vito thus concludes that Bellini's painting depicts an autumnal morning and, in doing so, also refers to the stigmatisation that is said to have taken place shortly before dawn on 17 September 1224; cf. Mauro Di Vito, "'Per lo quale ennallumini la nocte.' Il verbasco fiorito del 'San Francesco che riceve le stimmate' di Giovanni Bellini alla Frick Collection ed altri appunti di storia naturale", in: Wilson 2015 (see note 10), pp. 113–125. The fact that several completely defoliated trees loom in the middle ground is, however, difficult to reconcile with this hypothesis.

17 Cf. Johannes Grave, "Ein neuer Blick auf Giovanni Bellinis Darstellung des heiligen Franziskus", in: *Bruckmanns Pantheon*, vol. 56, 1998, pp. 35–43; Grave 2004 (see note 14); Grave 2018 (see note 14), pp. 161–179. For similar assessments, see Keith Christiansen, "Bellini and the Meditational Poesia", in: *Artibus et historiae*, vol. 34, no. 67, 2013, pp. 9–20; Aurenhammer 2017 (see note 5), pp. 110–117; Davide Gasparotto, "Giovanni Bellini and Landscape", in: Davide Gasparotto (ed.), *Giovanni Bellini. Landscapes of Faith in Renaissance Venice*, exh. cat. J. Paul

Getty Museum, Los Angeles. Los Angeles: Getty Trust Publications, 2017, pp. 11–23, here pp. 18–21; Lars Zieke, *Natur und Mimesis. Visualisierungen des Atmosphärischen in der religiösen Malerei Venedigs und Mailands um 1500* (Studi/Deutsches Studienzentrum in Venedig, new series, vol. 19). Regensburg: Schnell & Steiner, 2020, pp. 76–91.

18 Bellini's painting is thus part of a development that leads to the emergence of decidedly atmospheric qualities in painting; cf. Zieke 2020 (see note 17).

19 Even the rocks and their cracks can be included in such considerations; cf. David Young Kim, *Groundwork. A History of the Renaissance Picture*. Princeton: Princeton University Press, 2022, pp. 83–127.

20 Cf. Friedrich Ohly, "Vom geistigen Sinn des Wortes im Mittelalter", in: Friedrich Ohly, *Schriften zur mittelalterlichen Bedeutungsforschung*. Darmstadt: Wissenschaftliche Buchgesellschaft, 1977, pp. 1–31, here p. 9.

21 Cf. Grave 2018 (see note 14), pp. 173–174. For the paintings mentioned, see Lucco, Humfrey and Villa 2019 (see note 14), pp. 503–504, cat. 140 (Fort Worth), pp. 547–548, cat. 166 (Washington), pp. 565–566, cat. 179 (Detroit).

22 Cf. Grave 2018 (see note 14), pp. 14–27 (on *Sacred Allegory*), pp. 200–205 (on *Madonna of the Meadow*); also see Lucco, Humfrey and Villa 2019 (see note 14), pp. 461–463, cat. 99 (Peter Humfrey), pp. 549–550, cat. 168 (Giovanni Carlo Federico Villa); on *Sacred Allegory*, also see most recently Antonio Mazzotta, *Con Giovanni Bellini. Dodici esercizi di lettura*. Rome: Officina Libraria, 2020, pp. 128–137.

23 Manuela Barausse, "Giovanni Bellini. I documenti", in: Mauro Lucco and Giovanni Carlo Federico Villa (eds), *Giovanni Bellini*, exh. cat. Scuderie del Quirinale, Rome. Milan: Silvana Editorale, 2008, pp. 327–359, here p. 352, cat. 99.

24 For general systematic reflections on the temporality of picture viewing, see Johannes Grave, *Bild und Zeit. Eine Theorie des Bildbetrachtens*. Munich: C.H. Beck, 2022.

Catherine Whistler: Innovation and experimentation

1 "The panel in oil of St Francis in the wilderness was the work of Giovanni Bellini [...] and it is filled into the foreground with a marvellously composed and detailed landscape" ("La tavola del San Francesco nel deserto a oglio fo opera de Zuan Bellino [...] et ha un paese propinquo finito e ricercato mirabilimente"); "The oil on canvas of three philosophers in a landscape observing the rays of the sun, two of them standing and one seated, with its marvellously represented rock [...]" ("La tela a oglio delli 3 phylosophi nel paese, due ritti ed uno sentado che contempla li raggi solari cun quel saxo finto cusì mirabilmente [...]"; Theodor Frimmel (ed. and trans.), *Der Anonimo Morelliano (Marcanton Michiels "Notizia d'opere del disegno"). Text und Übersetzung* (Quellenschriften für Kunstgeschichte und Kunsttechnik des Mittelalters und der Neuzeit, new series, vol. 1). [Vienna, 1888] Vienna: Carl Graeser, 1896 (special issue), p. 86 and p. 88. English translations are by the author of this essay.

2 See Genevieve Verdigel, "*Colore* in *Disegno*: A Reappraisal of the Use of Color in Fifteenth-century Draftsmanship in the Veneto", in: *Master Drawings*, vol. 58, no. 2, 2020, pp. 148–168.

3 See Francis Ames-Lewis, *Isabella D'Este and Leonardo. The artistic relationship between Isabella D'Este and Leonardo da Vinci 1500–1506*. New Haven/London: Yale University Press, 2012, pp. 32 and 246, note 55.

For detailed bibliographical references on this topic, see Whistler 2018 cited below. In addition, also see the following recent literature:

Bernard Aikema in collaboration with Andrew John Martin (eds), *Dürer e il Rinascimento tra Germania e Italia*, exh. cat, Palazzo Reale, Milan. Milan: 24 Ore Cultura, 2018.

Irene Brooke, "Tratta da Zorzi: Giulio Campagnola's Copies after other Artists and his Use of Models", in: Maddalena Bellavitis (ed.), *Making Copies in European Art 1400–1600*. Leiden: Brill, 2018, pp. 212–260.

Irene Brooke, "New Evidence for the Life and Career of Giulio Campagnola", in: *Print Quarterly*, vol. 37, 2020, pp. 371–382.

Irene Brooke, "A Poetic Prognostication by Giulio Campagnola and its Relationship to his *Astrologer*", in: *Print Quarterly*, vol. 39, 2022, pp. 251–263.

Andrea Caracausi, Marsel Grosso and Vittoria Romani (eds), *Il paesaggio veneto nel Rinascimento europeo. Linguaggio, rappresentazioni, scambi*. Milan: Officina libraria, 2019.

Jodi Cranston, *Green Worlds of Renaissance Venice*. University Park: Pennsylvania State University Press, 2019.

Karen Hope Goodchild, April Oettinger and Leopoldine Prosperetti (eds), *Green Worlds in Early Modern Italy: Art and the Earth* (Visual and Material Culture, 1300–1700, vol. 11) Amsterdam: Amsterdam University Press, 2019.

Paul Holberton, *A History of Arcadia in Art and Literature: The Quest for Secular Human Happiness Revealed in the Pastoral – fortunato in terra*, 2 vols. London: Ad Ilissum, 2021.

Dagmar Korbacher (ed.), *Arkadien. Paradies auf Papier*, exh. cat. Kupferstichkabinett, Staatliche Museen, Berlin. Petersberg: Michael Imhof Verlag, 2014.

Mauro Lucco, *Tiziano e la nascità del paesaggio moderno*. Florence: Giunti, 2012.

Leopoldine Prosperetti, "Trees: An Overlooked Topic in Renaissance Art", in: Laura de Fuccia and Christophe Brouard (eds), *"Di là dal fiume tra gli alberi": il paesaggio del Rinascimento a Venezia – nascita e fortuna di un genere artistico*. Ravenna: Pozzi, 2012, pp. 71–88.

Catherine Whistler, "*Disegni a stampa, Disegni a mano* and the Development of the Independent Landscape Drawing in Venice", in: Daniela Bohde and Alessandro Nova (eds), *Jenseits des Disegno: Die Entstehung selbstständiger Zeichnungen in Deutschland und Italien im*

15. und 16. Jahrhundert. Petersberg: Michael Imhof Verlag, 2018, pp. 128–145.

Antonio Mazzotta: Giorgione's *Portrait of a Young Man*

1 The term "coffee-coloured" for the eyes is inspired by a "chromatic" note by Giovan Battista Cavalcaselle (1819–1897) written on a sketch that immortalises the Munich painting (Venice, Biblioteca Nazionale Marciana, *Fondo Cavalcaselle*, inv. It. IV, 2033 (=12274) – Fascicolo II, f. 39v). The work is also immortalised in another densely annotated sketch (ibid., f. 37r).

2 On the sonnet and painting, see the catalogue entry by Luke Syson in Luke Syson (ed.), *Leonardo da Vinci. Painter at the Court of Milan*, exh. cat. The National Gallery, London. London: National Gallery of London Publications, 2011, pp. 110–113, cat. 10 (Luke Syson).

3 The famous letter from Isabella d'Este to her friend Cecilia Gallerani is discussed and contextualised by Giovanni Romano, "Verso la maniera moderna: da Mantegna a Raffaello", in: Giulio Bollati et al. (eds), *Storia dell'arte italiana*, Parte seconda: Dal Medioevo al Novecento, vol. 2: Dal Cinquecento all'Ottocento, 1. Cinquecento e Seicento (*Storia dell'arte italiana*; vol. 6, no. 1), Turin: Einaudi, 1981, pp. 3–85, here p. 26.

4 On the theme of Leonardo, Giorgione and the "shoulder portrait", see Carlo Pedretti, "Ancora sul rapporto Giorgione-Leonardo e l'origine del ritratto di spalla", in: *Giorgione, Atti del convegno internazionale di studio*, Castelfranco Veneto, 29–31 May 1978. Venice, 1979, pp. 181–185.

5 Bernard Berenson, *The Drawings of the Florentine Painters*. Amplified edition, 3 vols. Chicago: University of Chicago Press, 1938, vol. 1, p. 72.

6 Cf. Alessandro Ballarin, "Le due versioni della 'Vergine delle rocce'. Con una nota sul 'Ritratto di Cecilia Gallerani' ed una sugli studi di teste e di mani per il 'Cenacolo' (1996–2000)", in: *Leonardo a Milano. Problemi di leonardismo milanese tra Quattrocento e Cinquecento. Giovanni Antonio Boltraffio prima della Pala Casio*, 4 vols (Pittura del Rinascimento nell'Italia settentrionale, vol. 7). Verona: Grafiche Aurora, 2010, vol. 1, pp. 65–262, here pp. 206–209.

7 Cf. Pliny the Elder, *Naturalis Historia*, vol. XXXV, 79.

8 Cf. Alessandro Ballarin, "La ritrattistica degli anni 1500–1503 (1979)", in: *Giorgione e l'umanesimo veneziano*, 7 vols (Pittura del Rinascimento nell'Italia settentrionale, vol. 10). Verona: Grafiche Aurora, 2016, vol. 1: Una nuova prospettiva su Giorgione, pp. 83–111, here pp. 101–102.

9 Cf. Giorgio Vasari, *Le Vite de' più eccellenti pittori, scultori e architetti, nelle redazioni del 1550 e 1568*, Rosanna Bettarini and Paola Barocchi (eds), 6 vols. Florence: Sansoni, 1966–1987, vol. 4, 1976, pp. 42–43. It is no coincidence that, as has often been pointed out, in the structure of Vasari's *Lives*, the life of Giorgione appears immediately after that of Leonardo.

10 See the recent catalogue entry (with previous literature): Simone Facchinetti, Arturo Galansino and Per Rumberg (eds), *In the Age of Giorgione*, exh. cat. Royal Academy of Arts, London. London: Royal Academy of Arts, 2016, pp. 150–151, cat. 9 (Simone Facchinetti).

11 For an attribution to Giorgione, and its date shortly after 1500, for the Vienna *Christ Carrying the Cross*, cf. Alessandro Ballarin, "Nota alle tavole", in: *Giorgione e l'umanesimo veneziano*, 2016 (see note 8), vol. 4: Tavole. Giorgione (1500–1505), pp. XI–LXVI, here pp. XXI–XXII.

12 Its inclusion as a work by Pordenone at the recent exhibition on the painter (cf. Caterina Furlan and Vittorio Sgarbi (eds), *Il Rinascimento di Pordenone con Giorgione, Tiziano, Lotto, Correggio, Bassano, Tintoretto*, exh. cat. Galleria d'Arte Moderna/Parco Galvani, Museo Civico d'Arte, Milan. Milan: Skira, 2019, pp. 152–153, cat. 47 [Simone Facchinetti]) has definitively clarified, as far as I am concerned, that the work cannot be his.

13 Theodor Frimmel (ed. and transl.), *Der Anonimo Morelliano (Marcanton Michiels "Notizia d'opere del disegno"). Text und Übersetzung* (Quellenschriften für Kunstgeschichte und Kunsttechnik des Mittelalters und der Neuzeit, new series, vol. 1). [Vienna, 1888] Vienna: Carl Graeser, 1896 (special issue), p. 89. If not otherwise indicated, all translations into English provided in this contribution are by the translator of the essay (Laura Bennett).

14 It was not by chance that the work was put on display at the *Leonardo & Venezia* exhibition; cf. Giovanna Nepi Scirè and Pietro C. Marani (eds), *Leonardo & Venezia*, exh. cat. Palazzo Grassi, Venice. Milan: Bompiani, 1992, pp. 340–341, cat. 57 (David Alan Brown).

15 It appears, for example, among the works accepted in Philip Rylands's monograph on Palma; cf. Philip Rylands, *Palma il Vecchio. L'opera complete*. Milan: Mondadori, 1988, pp. 210–211, cat. 32. On Vasari's description, see Vasari – Bettarini/Barocchi 1966–1987 (see note 9), 1976, vol. 4, p. 55.

16 These objections are lined up very clearly by Ballarin (it was he who described it as "one of the masterpieces of the century"), who supports the attribution of the work to Giorgione, with a chronology around 1506; cf. Alessandro Ballarin, "Giorgione. Da 'Le siècle de Titien'" (1993), in: *Giorgione e l'umanesimo veneziano* 2016 (see note 8), vol. 1: Una nuova prospettiva su Giorgione, pp. 431–581, here pp. 559–564.

17 The most recent attributions of the Munich portrait to Sebastiano include: Paul Joannides, *Titian to 1518. The Assumption of Genius*. New Haven/London: Yale University Press, 2001, pp. 218–219; Claudio Strinati and Bernd Wolfgang Lindemann (eds), *Sebastiano del Piombo, 1485–1547*, exh.

cat. Palazzo di Venezia, Rome / Gemäldegalerie, Staatliche Museen, Berlin. Milan: Federico Motta, 2008, pp. 124–125, cat. 14 (Mauro Lucco); Simon P. Oakes, "The Attribution and Sitter of the Munich *Portrait of a Young Man in a Fur Coat*", in: *Renaissance Studies*, vol. 22, no. 2, 2008, pp. 143–153.

18 The signed painting was published some years ago as part of the Bragantini Collection, Verona; cf. Fritz Heinemann, *Giovanni Bellini e i Belliniani*, 2 vols (Saggi e studi di storia dell'arte, vol. 6), Venice: Neri Pozza, 1962, vol. 1, p. 118, cat. pp. 197–198, vol. 2, fig. 560.

19 Cf. Johannes Wilde, "Die Probleme um Domenico Mancini", in: *Jahrbuch der Kunsthistorischen Sammlungen in Wien*, new ed., 7, 1933, pp. 97–136, here pp. 113–127.

20 The attribution to Capriolo is by Giorgio Fossaluzza, "Pittura nella Marca trevigiana fra Quattro e Cinquecento", in: Enrico Maria Dal Pozzolo and Lionello Puppi (eds), *Giorgione*, exh. cat. Museo Casa Giorgione, Castelfranco Veneto. Milan: Skira, 2009, pp. 71–86, here p. 84, fig. 17, with p. 86, note 80.

21 For example, by Rodolfo Pallucchini, *Tiziano*, 2 vols. Florence: Sansoni, 1969, vol. 1, p. 26 and p. 242; Terisio Pignatti, *Giorgione. L'opera complete*. Venice: Alfieri, 1969, pp. 130–131, cat. A 33.

22 Cf. Vasari – Bettarini/Barocchi 1966–1987 (see note 9), vol. 6, 1987, p. 156. On the proposed identification as Gerolamo Barbarigo, cf. Antonio Mazzotta, "A 'gentiluomo da Ca' Barbarigo' by Titian in the National Gallery, London", in: *The Burlington Magazine*, vol. 154, 2012, pp. 12–19.

23 The well-known engraving is dated 1639, while the painting, dated 1640, is kept at the National Gallery in London.

24 The description, written on 17 March 1666, can be found in Pepys's diary, which is accessible online at: https://www.pepysdiary.com/diary/1666/03/17/ [accessed: 23 March 2023].

25 A comparison with Titian's Spada *Portrait*, also to demonstrate that the Munich *Portrait* is not by Titian, was proposed by Ballarin (1993) 2016 (see note 16), pp. 561–562. About 30 years ago, a drawing from a private collection with a "looking-over-the-shoulder" pose was published as a work by Titian (an attribution that does not convince me), also comparing it with the Munich *Portrait*; cf. Ugo Ruggeri, "Due nuovi disegni di Tiziano," in: *Studies in the History of Art*, vol. 45, 1993, pp. 84–99, here p. 88, fig. 3.

26 The writing "Giorgon de Castel Franco F / Maestro de Titiano" in black paint on the reverse of the panel looks 16th century (but not Venetian, otherwise the "G" would have been replaced by a "Z"). The numbers "120" and "N° 19", also in black paint, should refer to inventories as well.

27 Carlo Ridolfi, *Le maraviglie dell'arte. Ovvero Le vite degli illustri pittori veneti e dello Stato* (1648), Detlev Freiherr von Hadeln (ed.), 2 vols. Berlin, 1914–1924, 1914, vol. 1, pp. 105–106. On this phase of the history of the collections to which the painting has belonged, and on the Van Veerle brothers' collection, see Sarah Ferrari, "Una traccia per la fortuna europea di Giorgione e Tiziano. Da Venezia ad Anversa, seguendo le imprese di Giovanni e Giacomo van Veerle", in: Benedetta Crivelli and Marsel Grosso (eds), *Venezia e gli Asburgo. Pittura, collezionismo e circuiti commerciali nel tardo Rinascimento europeo* (Pittura del Rinascimento nell'Italia settentrionale. Quaderni, vol. 8). Padua: Padova University Press, 2018, pp. 103–121; Jeremy Wood, "Buying and Selling Art in Venice, London and Antwerp. The Collection of Bartolomeo Della Nave and the Dealings of James, Third Marquis of Hamilton, Anthony van Dyck, and Jan and Jacob van Veerle, c. 1637–50", in: *The Volume of the Walpole Society*, vol. 80, 2018, pp. 1–200, here pp. 32–36.

28 Giorgio Vasari, *Lives of the Most Eminent Painters, Sculptors and Architects*, 10 vols, trans. Gaston du C. de Vere. London: Macmillan and the Medici Society, 1912–1914, vol. IV, p. 114.; cf. Vasari – Bettarini/Barocchi 1966–1987 (see note 9), 1976, vol. 4, pp. 46–47.

29 A classic work on Buffalmacco – identified as the artist of the *Triumph of Death* in the Camposanto in Pisa – is still Luciano Bellosi, *Buffalmacco e il Trionfo della Morte* (Saggi, vol. 522). Turin: Einaudi, 1974.

30 For the identification as Ulrich (as painted by Giorgione in 1506), see Andrew John Martin, "I rapporti con i Paesi Bassi e la Germania. Pittori, agenti e mercanti, collezionisti", in: Michel Hochmann, Rosella Lauber and Stefania Mason (eds), *Il collezionismo d'arte a Venezia. Dalle origini al Cinquecento*. Venice: Marsilio, 2008, pp. 143–163, here p. 144, fig. 2a–b, pp. 146–147. (Martin also assumes, although without any real objective confirmation, that the sealing wax coat of arms on the reverse of the panel was that of the Van Veerle brothers). For the identification as Anton (as painted by Sebastiano del Piombo around 1511), see Oakes 2008 (see note 17).

31 Vasari 1912–1914 (see note 28), p. 111; cf. Vasari – Bettarini/Barocchi 1966–1987 (see note 9), 1976, vol. 4, p. 43. Also see Ridolfi – Hadeln 1914–1924 (see note 27), 1914, vol. 1, pp. 105–106.

32 He is identified for the first time in the Grimani portrait described by Vasari by Ballarin (1993) 2016 (see note 16), pp. 434–435.

33 The Grimani owned a total of three works by Giorgione (but not a painting that can be identified with the one now in Munich), including his lost self-portrait, which also ended up in the Van Veerle collections and was engraved by Hollar; cf. most recently Ferrari 2018 (see note 27), pp. 111–115 and 161, fig. 4.

34 Bologna, Fondazione Federico Zeri, inv. 35789.

35 The work was restored in 2010. In addition to information concerning the measurements in the 17th-/18th-century inventories that record a width greater by 8–10 cm, Johanna Pawis (also see her essay in this catalogue) has drawn my attention to a copy in a private Viennese collection clearly showing how much has been lost from the sides.

36 Cf. Vasari's description above, p. 122.

37 The first to establish that the painting now in the Munich Residenz corresponds to the one in the Munich Kammergalerie inventory of 1641/42 was Klára Garas, "Alcuni ritratti veneziani poco noti del Rinascimento", in: *Arte documento*, vol. 14, 2000, pp. 74–79, here pp. 77–79 with fig. 7. In the same publication (p. 79, note 19), she also refers to a painting modelled on the one in Munich – the work, which is in the Villa Camerini in Piazzola sul Brenta, was attributed to Cavazzola by George Martin Richter; cf. George Martin Richter, "An Unknown Portrait by Cavazzola", in: *The Burlington Magazine*, vol. 82, 1943, pp. 121, 123 and 124, here p. 124, fig. C.

38 For the detailed results of the investigations, see the essay by Johanna Pawis in this catalogue.

39 Cf. Garas 2000 (see note 37), pp. 77–79 with fig. 7. Fossaluzza 2009 (see note 20), p. 86, note 80, attributed the Munich painting to Domenico Capriolo, an artist who has never even remotely achieved this quality.

40 Maurice W. Brockwell, *Abridged Catalogue of the Pictures at Doughty House, Richmond, Surrey, in the Collection of Sir Herbert Cook*. London: William Heinemann, 1932, pp. 69–70.

41 Vasari 1912–1914 (see note 28), p. 111. Cf. Vasari – Bettarini/Barocchi 1966–1987 (see note 9), 1976, vol. 4, p. 43.

42 For the Washington painting, Trifone Gabriele has recently been mentioned by Sergio Alcamo, *La verità celata. Giorgione, la "Tempesta" e la salvezza*. Rome: Donzelli, 2019, pp. 43–49, figs 45–48. On the identification of Gabriele as one of the members of the "Compagnia degli Amici" ("Community of friends"), cf. Pietro Bembo, *Prose e rime*, Carlo Dionisotti (ed.). Turin: UTET, 1966, pp. 699–703. The links between this "Compagnia" and Giorgione are explored by Allessandro Ballarin, "Il Doppio ritratto Ludovisi" (1983), in: *Giorgione e l'umanesimo veneziano* 2016 (see note 8), vol. 2: Giorgione e la Compagnia degli Amici, pp. 999–1054; Ballarin resolves the initials "T. G." belonging to one of the members as those of "Tommaso Giustiniani").

43 This insight owes much to the research of Johanna Pawis (also see her essay in this catalogue). A copy of Danese Cattaneo's medal is kept, for instance, at the British Museum in London.

44 Nowadays, a 37-year-old is still called a "young man" (*ragazzo*), at least in Italy. But there are numerous examples of portrait sitters in the early 16th century who, by today's standards, look much older than their known ages. Such examples include *Portrait of a 37-Year-Old Man* by Lorenzo Lotto in Rome (c. 1530–1535, Galleria Doria Pamphilj) or, staying in Bavaria, the print by Barthel Beham of Ludwig X of Bavaria at 37 years old (1532; a copy is kept in the British Museum, London).

45 Interestingly, Andrea del Sarto's portrait is shown by Joannides 2001 (see note 17), p. 219, figs 195–196, next to the Munich *Portrait of a Young Man*. Del Sarto most probably painted the *Holy Family with the Young Saint John the Baptist* for Giovanni Borgherini (c. 1528, New York, The Metropolitan Museum of Art); he also executed – together with Pontormo, Granacci and Bacchiacca – some paintings for the nuptial bedroom of Giovanni's brother Pierfrancesco in around 1515; cf. Allan Braham, "The Bed of Pierfrancesco Borgherini", in: *The Burlington Magazine*, vol. 121, 1979, pp. 754–763.

Johanna Pawis: New discoveries

The research project of the Bayerische Staatsgemäldesammlungen and the Doerner Institut brings together the disciplines of art history (Andreas Schumacher, Annette Kranz, Johanna Pawis), conservation science and restoration (Eva Ortner, Jan Schmidt, Ronja Emmerich, Anneliese Földes) as well as the scientific examination of paintings (Heike Stege, Patrick Dietemann, Ursula Baumer, Carola Komar, Andrea Obermeier, Jens Wagner).

1 Munich, Bayerisches Hauptstaatsarchiv (BayHStA), IX A 1, Akt "Gemälde Erwerb 1784–1805", act of purchase: 1793.

2 Rolf Kultzen and Peter Eikemeier (eds), *Venezianische Gemälde des 15. und 16. Jahrhunderts*, complete catalogue, 2 vols (Munich: Gemäldekataloge Bayerische Staatsgemäldesammlungen, 1971), vol. 9, pp. 211–213 (Rolf Kultzen).

3 The restoration work begun in May 2023 reveals a different earlier version beneath the executed inscription, which had already been suggested by the technological investigations; the envisaged removal of the overpainting promises further results.

4 While "nobilissimus" suggests a member of the Venetian noble class, "civis venetus" formulaically refers to a *cittadino* as a member of the bourgeois middle class.

5 On the ennoblement of the *cittadino* family, cf. Girolamo Ruscelli's preface in Ottaviano Maggi, *De legato libri duo* (Venice, 1566).

6 For the derivation of Antonio's year of birth, see note 17.

7 See Cesare Vecellio, *De gli habiti antichi, et moderni di diverse parti del mondo libri due* (Venice, 1590, p. 160), with the matching illustration to the entry "Giovanetti" ("young [people]").

8 Giovanni Francesco and Camillo both held the office of *pesadori* of the Venetian trade supervision to control the sale of meat at the Rialto; see the will of Giovanni Francesco of 17 December 1567 in the Archivio di Stato di Venezia (ASV) (Notarile, Testamenti, 1187, no. 31, fol. 1r) and Camillo's will of 28 August 1628 (Notaio Giovanni Crivelli, BB 288–90, no. 185, fol. 1r), which was opened in the course of this research.

9 Paris, Bibliothèque nationale de France, Département estampes et photographie, Reserve 4-AD-134 (formerly inv. no. 2747; hereafter referred to as Codex Maggi).

10 With the exception of Ariane Isler-de Jongh and François Fossier, who

published the codex for the first time in *Le voyage de Charles Magius, 1568–1573*. Arcueil: Anthèse, 1992. The historical contextualisation supplementing the facsimile is, however, often erroneous with regard to sources and dates (e.g. regarding the duration of Carlo's travels given in the title).

11 The illustrations of the codex are confirmed by a *relazione* (embassy report) from Constantinople of 18 April 1571: Carlo is named here in an enumeration of prisoners of war who had fallen into the hands of Lala Kara Mustafa Pasha and his troops on Cyprus; a note following Carlo's name says that he had, in the meantime, become a slave on Chios (ASV, Collegio, Relazioni, 84, cited in: Wipertus Hugo Rudt de Collenberg, *Esclavage et rançons des chrétiens en Méditerranée 1570–1600: d'après les Litterae Hortatoriae de l'Archivio Segreto Vaticano*. Paris: Le Léopard d'Or, 1987, pp. 456–457, note 46, here p. 457).

12 The date of 6 March 1571 given in the caption of the full-page miniature in question cannot refer to the depicted hearing of the returned Carlo, since he was still in Ottoman captivity in April 1571 (see note 11). The date of 23 February 1572 (*more veneto*, 1571; on this yearly count, see note 17) can be considered a *terminus ante quem* for Carlo's return, since on that day he was elected *segretario* of the financial authority of the Ufficiali alle Rason Vecchie (ASV, Collegio, Notatori, Registri, 39, fol. 106r).

13 On 12 June 1573, the account books of the Rason Vecchie record expenses amounting to 27 *lire* and 5 *denari*, which Carlo Maggi paid to a "Francesco miniador in calle dale Acque"; the latter had produced an unspecified miniature painting intended for the ambassador of Constantinople (ASV, Ufficiali alle Rason Vecchie, Documenti della cassa grande, 279, edited by Ricciotti Bratti, "Notizie d'arte e d'artisti", in: *Nuovo archivio veneto*, vol. 30, 1915, pp. 435–485, here p. 459). For a briefly suggested proposal to attribute the miniatures of the Codex Maggi to the Flemish artist Lodewijk Toeput (called il Pozzoserrato), who worked in Italy, see Natsumi Nonaka, "Verdant Architecture and Tripartite Chronography. Toeput and the Italian Villa Tradition", in: Karen Hope Goodchild, April Oettinger and Leopoldine Prosperetti (eds), *Green Worlds in Early Modern Italy* (Visual and Material Culture 1300–1700, vol. 11). Amsterdam: Amsterdam University Press, 2019, pp. 131–152, here p. 133–134.

14 This villa is mentioned in Carlo Maggi's will of 5 March 1587 (ASV, Notarile, Testamenti, 840, no. 237, fol. 1v). In addition, he owned "terre e fabriche" in Taggi di Sotto near Padua and Limena as well as estates near Mira (ibid., fol. 1v, 2r).

15 The names of all the siblings appear from the will of the mother, Eleanora Maggi (ASV, Notarile, Testamenti, 1187, no. 918, fol. 1r).

16 Registered with notary Mario Renio on 17 December 1587 (ASV, Notarile, Testamenti, 840, no. 237).

17 Since Antonio's age is given as seven in the 1578 Codex (dated on the title page), he must have been born in 1570/71; if one assumes the *more veneto* calendar count used in Venice for official documents (with a delayed start of a new calendar year only on 1 March, which is why the deviation from the Gregorian calendar for the months of January and February must always be taken into account), this covers the period from 1 March 1570 to 28 February 1572.

18 The question arises here whether it is a coincidence that Antonio, in deviation from the family tree in the Codex Maggi, is listed in later genealogies as the son of Carlo's brother Camillo (Venice, Biblioteca Nazionale Marciana, Manoscritti, Miscellanea, It. Class VII, Cod. 90, fol. 60v; ASV, Miscellanea Codici, Storia Veneta, Cittadinanze Toderini, vol. 3, b. 6, p. 1160).

19 See the addition to the phrase "be he my son or not", reading "which I say not because I question that he is my son, but rather so as not to give anyone an excuse to bully him" ("sia o no[n] sia mio fig.[liuo]lo" with the addition "Ilch[e] dico no[n] p[er]ch[é] dubiti ch[e]l no[n] sia mio fig.[liuo]lo ma p[er] levar l'occ[asio]ne de ogniuno ch[e] le volese dar molestia"; ASV, Notarile, Testamenti, 840, no. 237, fol. 1v). On comparable cases of will-related legitimation of illegitimate and adopted children, see Anna Bellavitis, "Stepfamilies and Inclusive Families in Early Modern Venice", in: Lyndan Warner (ed.), *Stepfamilies in Europe, 1400–1800*. London: Routledge, 2018, pp. 56–72, here p. 64. Likewise significant for the question of succession in this context is the fact that Antonio remained without siblings even after Carlo's return to Venice.

20 "Vİ. DOLO. OPPRESSVS. PENE. EXANİMİS. İN. VTERO. EX. VTERO. VİVVS. ET. FOR:MOSVS. PVER. MVNDO. APPARVİT. MANVS. N. DÑİ. ERAT. CVM. İLLO. FELİX. EXİTVS. FELİCİVS. İTER. FELİCİSSİMVS. TERMİNVS. DEO OPTIMO. GRATİAS. AN. ÆTATİS. SVÆ. VİI." Sincere thanks to Marco Cavarzere, Università Ca' Foscari, Venice, for his help in interpreting legal terminology in Renaissance Latin.

21 Cf. Titian and Workshop, *Girolamo and Cardinal Marco Corner Investing Marco, Abbot of Carrara, with His Benefice*, c. 1520/25, Washington, D.C., National Gallery of Art, Timken Collection.

22 The importance of paintings for intergenerational family memorialisation is also illustrated by the aforementioned will of Carlo's brother Camillo of 28 August 1628, in which he decrees that "all the large paintings and the two large pictures of the Madonna and the medium-sized portraits of crowned rulers and the portraits of the knights of our house" ("li quadri grandi tutti, et le due madone grande, et li quadri mezzani de principi coronati de Re, et li quadri di Caual[e]ri di n[ost]ra casa"), should be brought to Treviso to his daughters in "a chest, well packed" ("un casson ben riposto") (ASV, Notaio Giovanni Crivelli, BB 288–90, no. 185, fol. 1v). In addition to a number of precious items, Carlo himself also owned several collectibles, which, significantly, he did not bequeath to the family, but to friends scattered as far as Greece, including a "small painted miniature of a Pietà next to the bed in my bedroom" ("quadreto di pieta miniato che tengo al leto d[el]la mia camera"; ASV, Notarile, Testamenti, 840, no. 237, fol. 1r).

23 Codex Maggi, miniature 5 (see note 20).

24 This information from a manuscript in the Venetian Biblioteca Nazionale Marciana (It. Class VII, Cod. 90, fol. 60v) is confirmed by letters signed by Antonio Maggi in this capacity, which are in the Bibliothèque nationale de France (Département des Manuscrits, Français 16084, e.g. fols 55, 504).

25 So recorded in Carlo's will of 5 March 1587 (ASV, Notarile, Testamenti, 840, no. 237, fol. 1r).

26 Ivan Lermolieff [Giovanni Morelli], *Italian Masters in German Galleries. A Critical Essay on the Italian Pictures in the Galleries of Munich, Dresden, Berlin.* London: George Bell and Sons, 1883, pp. 9–10.

27 Inventar über die Koeniglichen Bayerischen Staats-Gemälde-Sammlungen [...] neu angefertiget in Gemäßheit höchster Ministerial-Entschließung vom 17. Januar 1856, Munich, Bayerische Staatsgemäldesammlungen (BStGS), Inventory Department, inv. no. WAF 1151.

28 In Antonello's portraits, Michiel admired above all the "markedly lively expressiveness, especially the eyes" ("gran vivacità, et maxime in li occhi"); Marcantonio Michiel, *Notizia d'opere del disegno*, ed. by Theodor Frimmel, pref. by Cristina de Benedictis (Le voci del museo, vol. 4). Florence: Edifir, 2000, p. 51.

29 Cf. Previtali's portraits created around 1506, which are formally but not stylistically close to the Munich painting: *Portrait of a Young Man*, Toulouse, Fondation Bemberg; *Portrait of a Young Man*, Madrid, Museo Nacional Thyssen-Bornemisza (for attribution and dating, see Antonio Mazzotta, "Altri 'ritratti' veneziani per Antonello, Jacometto e Andrea Previtali", in: *Prospettiva*, no. 165/166, 2016, pp. 69–91, here pp. 82–83 and pp. 89–90).

30 This signature is found on a *Madonna and Child* from 1509 (Ajaccio, Palais Fesch – Musée des Beaux Arts). For a discussion of the inscription, cf. Laura Pagnotta, *Bartolomeo Veneto. L'opera completa.* Florence: Centro Di, 1997, p. 21.

31 For a reconstruction of Veneto's biography, based on fragmentary records, see Pagnotta 1997 (see note 30), pp. 21–122.

32 Cf. Pagnotta 1997 (see note 30), p. 33 and p. 168, cat. 7.

33 See, for example, *The Circumcision of Christ*, dated and signed "1506" (Paris, Musée du Louvre).

34 Giorgio Vasari, *Le Vite de' più eccellenti pittori, scultori e architetti, nelle redazioni del 1550 e 1568*, Rosanna Bettarini and Paola Barocchi (eds), 11 vols. Florence: Sansoni, 1966–1997, 1971, vol. 3, pp. 438–439.

35 Venice, Biblioteca del Museo Correr, MS PDc 1103, Archivio privato Zane; for the 16th century, see esp. inventory nos 1, 6, 7 and 8.

36 See fundamentally Stanley Chojnacki, "Political Adulthood in 15th-Century Venice", in: *American Historical Review,* vol. 91, 1986, pp. 791–810.

37 ASV, Avogaria di Comun, Balla d'Oro, Registro 165–IV (1414–1523), fols 391r–392v.

38 See Stella Mary Newton, *The Dress of the Venetians 1495–1525.* Aldershot: Scolar Press, 1988, p. 9 and p. 33.

39 The measure must have taken place before 1884, since in the *Katalog der Gemälde-Sammlung der Kgl. Älteren Pinakothek in München. Amtliche Ausgabe*, Munich, 1884, p. 203, cat. 1030, the stick is described as an attribute for the first time.

40 Already in the museum catalogue of 1872 (Rudolf Marggraff, *Die ältere königliche Pinakothek zu München. Verzeichniss und Beschreibung der in ihr aufgestellten Gemälde mit biographischen und kunstgeschichtlich-kritischen Erläuterungen*, 3rd extensively impr. and suppl. edition with new addenda (Munich, 1872), p. 236, no. 1196), its condition, described as desolate, was attributed to improper restoration measures; in 1936, the painting was transferred to a glued wood panel.

41 Inventarium yber Schleißhaim de anno 1637, BayHStA, HR II, fasc. 40, as facsimile in BStGS, Inventory Department, Schl/A 37, fol. 12v; if not otherwise indicated, all translations into English provided in this contribution are by the translator of the essay (Julian Jain). The fact that the painting is not listed either in the Kunstkammer inventory of 1598 or in the Kammergalerie inventories of 1607 and 1627 to 1630 does not necessarily mean that it could not have been in the possession of the House of Wittelsbach before or around 1600. At that time, it had not yet been included in the inventoried collection, but was part of the representative furnishings of the Schleißheim country chateau.

42 Inventar Schleißheim, 1637 (see note 41), fol. 12v, transfer note: "N^a^. Verdunckh hats seithero auf München abgeholt"; cf. Peter Diemer, "Materialien zu Entstehung und Ausbau der Kammergalerie Maximilians I.", in: Hubert Glaser (ed.), *Quellen und Studien zur Kunstpolitik der Wittelsbacher vom 16. bis zum 18. Jahrhundert.* Munich/Zurich: Hirmer/Piper, 1980, pp. 129–174, here p. 142 and p. 155, note 91a. Subsequently in the inventory of Maximilian I's Kammergalerie of 1641/42, fol. 89v; redacted by Monika Bachtler, Peter Diemer and Johannes Erichsen, "Die Bestände von Maximilians I. Kammergalerie. Das Inventar von 1641/1642", in: Hubert Glaser (ed.), *Quellen und Studien zur Kunstpolitik der Wittelsbacher vom 16. bis zum 18. Jahrhundert.* Munich/Zurich: Hirmer/Piper, 1980, pp. 191–252, here p. 239, no. XIII, 17. The dimensions of 97.3 × 80.3 cm recorded there document an originally wider format.

43 At this point, we can only refer to the results of the ongoing material and pigment analyses, which are to be published in a separate publication.

44 For a similar stole in *The Concert* controversially discussed in its attribution to Giorgione (c. 1507, Milan, Collezione Mattiolo), cf. Enrico Maria Dal Pozzolo and Lionello Puppi (eds), *Giorgione*, exh. cat. Museo Casa Giorgione, Castelfranco Veneto. Milan: Skira, 2009, pp. 439–442, cat. 50 (Giorgio Fossaluzza). On striped fabrics in the Venetian cinquecento, cf. also Sabine Engel, "Titian's 'Portrait of Laura Dianti'. Appropriation and Transformation between Orient and Occident", in: *Studi tizianeschi*, vol. 10, 2019, pp. 8–33, here pp. 12–16 and pp. 28–29. Although colourful striped fabrics are comparatively rare in contemporary portraits, it is striking that in the inventory published by Renata Segre of Giorgione's estate on 14 March 1511 (Renata Segre, "Una rilettura della vita di Giorgione. Nuovi documenti d'archivio", in: *Atti dell'Istituto Veneto di Scienze Lettere ed Arti*, vol. 171 (2013), pp. 69–114, here pp. 107–110), multiple striped ("vergà", "vergadi") textiles are listed as well as fabrics described with "tralixe", which can be understood, among others, as a "light, thin cloth interwoven with brightly coloured threads" (for a linguistic interpretation, see Segre 2013, p. 108, note 98).

45 Marin Sanudo, *Diarii (1496–1533)*, Rinaldo Fulin et al. (eds), 58 vols (Venice, 1879–1903), 1901, vol. 56, entry of 18 August 1532, column 774.

46 The attribution to Giorgione is first found in the "Schleißheimer Verlustliste", a list of paintings that were moved from Schleißheim to Munich in 1745 to furnish the Residenz: "Georgeon. Un philosophe [...]"; BayHStA, HR 209/8, p. 14, no. 297. For documentation of the collection history, see Amanda Ramm, *Die Grüne Galerie in der Münchner Residenz von 1737 bis 1836* (Forschungen zur Kunst- und Kulturgeschichte, vol. 10). Munich: Bayerische Schlösserverwaltung, 2009), p. 428, cat. 140. Without commiting herself to an attribution, Klára Garas first introduced the painting into the *Giorgionismo* discourse; see Klára Garas, "Alcuni ritratti veneziani poco noti del Rinascimento", in: *Arte documento*, no. 14, 2000, pp. 74–79, here pp. 77–79 with fig. 7; with the exception of Giorgio Fossaluzza and Paolo Ervas, who advocate an attribution to Domenico Capriolo, Garas's impulse was not taken up by further research; cf. Giorgio Fossaluzza, "Pittura nella Marca trevigiana fra Quattro e Cinquecento", in *Giorgione* 2009 (see note 44), pp. 71–86, here p. 86, note 80; Paolo Ervas, *Domenico Capriolo (Venezia? 1494 – Treviso 1528)* (I grandi minori, vol. 1). Saonara: Il Prato 2018, p. 76.

47 See Antonio Mazzotta's essay in this catalogue, who is thanked here for the exchange and discussion. Many thanks also to Jaynie Anderson for the stimulating joint examination of the painting, which encouraged us to locate the painting's genesis in early cinquecento Venice and to further pursue references to *Giorgionismo* painting even before conducting the art-technological analyses and the historical research presented here in the following.

48 The succinctly elaborated features can be seen as a reflection of Leonardo da Vinci's studies of heads drawn with a comparable interest in expressive physiognomy, without, however, sharing the latter's typological character.

49 Fundamental for Trifone's biography is still Emmanuele Antonio Cicogna, *Delle iscrizioni italiane*, 6 vols. Venice: A Forni, 1824–1853, 1830, vol. 3, pp. 208–223; cf. also Şirin Dadaş, "Sie nannten ihn Sokrates. Trifone Gabrieles schriftliches Schweigen und dessen beredtes Echo", in: Şirin Dadaş and Christian Vogel (eds), *Dynamiken der Negation. (Nicht)Wissen und negativer Transfer in vormodernen Kulturen* (Episteme in Bewegung, vol. 20). Wiesbaden: Harrassowitz, 2021, pp. 243–292.

50 Giacomo Gabriele, *Dialogo nel quale de la Sphera, et de gli orti et occasi de le stelle, minutamente si ragiona*. Venice: Giovanni de Farri, 1545.

51 Published as an appendix to Giasone de Nores, *Tavole del Mondo, et della Sphera*. Padua: Paolo Meietti, 1582.

52 In addition to the specimen illustrated here from the Frick Collection in New York, another one is preserved in the British Museum in London. The medal is not dated. However, Cattaneo stayed in the Veneto from 1530 onwards, where he came into contact with Trifone and became a "listener of his lessons" ("uditore de le sue lettioni"); in 1549, Trifone even appointed him as the witness to his will (will of Trifone Gabriele, ASV, Notarile, Testamenti, 1214, no. 993, redacted by Manuela Morresi, "Trifon Gabriele, Danese Cataneo e il monumento Bembo al Santo di Padova", in: Lorenzo Finnochi Ghersi (ed.), *Alessandro Vittoria e l'arte veneta della maniera* (Atti del convegno internazionale di studi), Udine, 26/27 October 2000. Udine: Editrice Universitaria Udinese, 2001, pp. 71–96 and pp. 95–96, here pp. 95–96). For the dating of the medal, therefore, a time span of 1530 to 1549 results.

53 Like the other illustrations in this collection of portraits, the engraving with Trifone's portrait probably goes back to a 16th-century original, which in this case has not survived.

54 Cf. most recently Carlo Piga, *Pierfrancesco Borgherini. Mecenatismo artistico di un banchiere fiorentino del Rinascimento alla corte dei papi* (Monografie di Horti Hesperidum, vol. 6). Rome, UniversItalia, 2018, pp. 32–34; Sergio Alcamo, *La verità celata. Giorgione, la "Tempesta" e la salvezza*. Rome: Donzielli, 2019, pp. 43–49. David Alan Brown (in: "Art and Espionage. Michael Straight's Giorgione", in: *Artibus et historiae*, vol. 34, no. 67, 2013, pp. 101–116, here p. 114, note 9), summarises the information on the provenance of this double portrait, brought to the art market in 1923 by an unidentifiable "Milanese Doctor" who in turn claimed to have obtained it from the Borgherini family estate. This account is based solely on the statements of the buyer, Sir Herbert Cook, who was, however, considerably less certain about the identification of the painting he had acquired when it was first published than subsequent literature suggests, readily taking up and expanding Cook's

still cautiously formulated thesis ("It is all very curious and puzzling and offers a problem difficult of solution"; Herbert Frederick Cook, "A Giorgione Problem", in: *The Burlington Magazine*, vol. 48, 1926, pp. 23–24, here p. 24). This weak point was already named by Paul Holberton in 1998 as a "lack of provenance" (Paul Holberton, review of: Jaynie Anderson, *Giorgione. Peintre de la "brièveté poétique": Catalogue raisonné*. Paris: Lagune, 1996, and Mauro Lucco, *Giorgione*. Milan: Electra, 1995, in: *The Burlington Magazine*, vol. 140, 1998, pp. 482–483, here p. 482); for further justified doubts, cf. Antonio Mazzotta's essay in this catalogue.

55 Cf. Giorgio Vasari, "Das Leben des Giorgione, Correggio, Palma il Vecchio und Lorenzo Lotto", ed., intro. and comm. by Sabine Feser and Hana Gründler (Edition Giorgio Vasari). Berlin: Wagenbach, 2008, pp. 19–20; cf. Vasari – Bettarini/Barocchi 1966–1997 (see note 34), 1976, vol. 4, p. 43.

56 Although no (pictorial) source survives that records Borgherini's appearance, two portraits of his elder brother Pierfrancesco (1517, London, The National Gallery; 1516–1520, San Diego, Museum of Art) plausibly identified in paintings by Sebastiano del Piombo do suggest a certain family resemblance with the dark curls, the finely curved brows and the angular facial features.

57 Thus, an exchange of letters with Bembo attests to Giovanni's talent for combining knowledge exchange with financial transactions; see, for example, Pietro Bembo, *Lettere*, Ernesto Travi (ed.), 4 vols. Bologna: Commissione per i Testi di Lingua, 1987–1993, 1989, vol. 2, p. 501, no. 863, 1992, vol. 3, p. 26–27, no. 947; also Hélène Soldini, *Les Républiques de Donato Giannotti. Une biographie d'un républicain florentin du XVIe siècle*, vol. 1. Florence, 2014, pp. 37–38.

58 Giannotti has Giovanni address the teacher–pupil relationship several times in the dialogue, to which he returns time and again, "because your [Trifone's] varied teaching always gives me an appetite for more" ("[p]ercioche la varieta delle cose, che voi ragionate, mi rinfresca sempre l'appetito"); Donato Giannotti, *Libro de la Republica de Vinitiani*. Rome: Antonio Blado, 1540, p. 101.

59 The curly-haired scholar in the Washington portrait has nothing in common with Trifone's characteristic bald head, and the suggestion that the teacher depicted is possibly the intellectual Niccolò Leonico Tomeo (1456–1531), who is attested as Giovanni's mentor (cf. Jaynie Anderson, *Giorgione. The Painter of "Poetic Brevity" [with a] Catalogue Raisonné*. Paris/New York: Flammarion, 1997, pp. 140–148 and pp. 314–315), is not convincing, since his age alone rules out such an identification and the chronological correspondence of Giovanni's postulated stay in Venice with Tomeo's teaching activity documented between 1504 and 1506 is also based on a confusion of names with Niccolò Leonico da Vicenza (1428–1524); on this, see James Bruce Ross, "Venetian Schools and Teachers, Fourteenth to Early Sixteenth Century. A Survey and a Study of Giovanni Battista Egnazio", in: *Renaissance Quarterly*, vol. 29, no. 4, 1976, pp. 521–566, here p. 538, note 65; Brown 2013 (see note 54), p. 115, note 127.

60 This dating, which is plausible in view of Giovanni's continued contact with Venice and also coherent in terms of style and painting technique, solves the problem, comprehensibly expressed by Antonio Mazzotta in this catalogue, of reconciling the age of the sitters in the Munich painting with the date of origin of the painting described by Vasari in the Borgherini residence, which – on the premise that it is to be identified with the Washington painting – has usually been assumed to be earlier.

61 On this type of image, see Antonio Mazzotta's essay in this catalogue.

62 The Berlin head study (KdZ 12924 verso) has so far not been convincingly associated with either a model or an executed painting; cf. most recently Julian Brooks with Denise Allen and Xavier F. Salomon (eds), *Andrea del Sarto. The Renaissance Workshop in Action*, exh. cat. J. Paul Getty Museum, Los Angeles / The Frick Collection, New York. Los Angeles: Getty Publications, 2015, pp. 96–99, cat. 24 (Julian Brooks). The dating of the sheet results from the fact that the drawings on its recto side are to be associated with the fresco titled *Tribute to Caesar* in the Medici villa in Poggio a Caiano, painted between 1519 and 1521.

63 Giorgio Vasari, *Lives of the Most Eminent Painters, Sculptors and Architects*, 10 vols, trans. Gaston du C. de Vere. London: Macmillan and the Medici Society, 1912–1914, vol. III, p. 118.

64 Cf. Felix Gilbert, "Andrea del Sartos 'Heilige Familie' Borgherini und florentinische Politik", in: Lucius Grisebach and Konrad Renger (eds), *Festschrift für Otto von Simson zum 65. Geburtstag*. Frankfurt am Main: Propyläen Verlag, 1977, pp. 284–288; Allan Braham, "The Bed of Pierfrancesco Borgherini", in: *The Burlington Magazine*, vol. 121, 1979, pp. 754–765.

65 In 1579, Vincenzo di Giovanni Borgherini sold a Madonna painting by Andrea del Sarto, and in 1584 his brother Niccolò di Giovanni sold four paintings by Granacci and del Sarto; see Piga 2018 (see note 54), p. 244, with sources for each. Even del Sarto's *The Holy Family with the Young Saint John the Baptist*, now in the Metropolitan Museum of Art in New York, painted around 1528 for Giovanni Borgherini, can only be traced to the end of the 16th century in family ownership; cf. Andrea Bayer, "Andrea del Sarto's Borgherini 'Holy Family' and 'Charity': Two Intertwined Late Works", in: *Metropolitan Museum Journal*, vol. 52, 2017, pp. 34–55.

66 In addition to Parmigianino's *Virgin and Child with a Monk* (c. 1530), these probably also include Titian's *Vanity* (cat. 57) and Paris Bordone's *Jeweller with a Lady* (cat. 17); the latter two works, like the *Mathematicus* attributed to Leonardo at the time, can be traced for the first time in 1637 in the decorative context of the Old Schleißheim Palace. On the Italian acquisitions of Maximilian I, whose Grand Tour in 1593 also took him to Florence, see Cornelia Syre, "Zur Sammlungsgeschichte. Parmigianinos Madonnenbild und die italienischen Meister in der Kammergalerie Maximilians I. von Bayern", in: Reinhold Baumstark (ed.), *Parmigianino. Die Madonna in der Alten Pinakothek*. Ostfildern: Hatje Cantz, 2007, pp. 117–131.

67 BayHStA, LA 4851, fols 15b r–v, 15c r, first edited (inaccurately) by Jacob Stockbauer, *Die Kunstbestrebungen am bayerischen Hofe unter Herzog Albert V. und seinem Nachfolger Wilhelm V.* Vienna: Wilhelm Braumüller, 1874, pp. 43–44. So far, only two paintings on this list have been identified with certainty: the *Allegories* by Paolo Veronese, now in the Frick Collection, New York (c. 1565, Henry Clay Frick Bequest, inv. nos 1912.1.128 and 1912.1.129), which Rudolf II acquired for his collection in Prague, where they are documented from 1621 onwards (cf. Xavier F. Salomon, *Veronese's Allegories. Virtue, Love, and Exploration in Renaissance Venice*. New York: The Frick Collection, 2006, pp. 21–24). On Jacopo Strada with sources, see Dirk Jacob Jansen, *Jacopo Strada and Cultural Patronage at the Imperial Court. The Antique as Innovation*, 2 vols. Leiden/Boston: Brill, 2019, here especially pp. 383–429 and pp. 576–628; the latter publication also provides a convincing redating of the list (p. 617), but with suggestions for attributions that are purely associative and thus unsubstantiated from an art historical perspective. From a comparison with the inventories of the Kunstkammer of 1598 and the Kammergalerie of 1641/42, however, possible connections to the Munich collection do indeed emerge for further works on the list, which cannot be discussed here.

68 Cf. Piga 2018 (see note 54), pp. 224–225, p. 244. Last mention, but only paraphrasing Vasari: Raffaello Borghini, *Il riposo di Raffaello Borghini, in cvi della pittvra, e della scultura si fauella, de' piu illustri pittori, e scultori, e delle piu famose opere loro si fa mentione; e le cose principali appartenenti à dette arti s'insegnano.* Florence: Appresso Giorgio Marescotti, 1584, p. 373.

69 This is documented, among other things, by the extensive additions and corrections that Giorgione's biography in the *Lives* underwent between the two editions of 1550 and 1568; see Sabine Feser's commentary in Vasari – Feser/Gründler 2008 (see note 55), pp. 9–15.

70 Cf. Vasari 1912–1914 (see note 63), vol. IV, p. 110.

71 This is the designation in inventories of the cinquecento – for instance, that of Gabriele Vendramin's collection (1569) cited in Anderson 1997 (see note 59), p. 333.

72 London, British Library, Sloane MS 4004; cf. ibid., n. sig., the compositions titled "Favola di Paride" and "Sacrifico" (Tancred Borenius, The Picture Gallery of Andrea Vendramin, London, 1923, plates 8, 9 and 14).

73 Cf. his biography by Giacomo Gabriele, in which he parallels Trifone's frugal lifestyle with fashionable modesty: "[...] not adorning the body, but the spirit with beautiful clothes [...]". ("[...] no[n] il corpo, ma l'animo di belle vestimenta ornando [...]"); Giacomo Gabriele, *Vita di M. Triphone Gabriele nella quale si mostrano apieno le lodi della uita soletaria & contemplatiua*. Bologna: Bartolomeo Bonardo & Antonio Grossi, 1543, p. 6. Also see the similar wording in a letter from Trifone to his nephew, where the scholar, echoing the topos of humility, states that he prefers clothing made of coarse woolen material ("grosso panno") to the costly, finely woven coats of his contemporaries ("i lor ricchi manti di sottilissime fila tessuti"; Vatican City, Biblioteca Apostolica Vaticana, Vat. lat. 5182, fols 219r–223v, here fol. 223r, redacted in Morresi 2001 (see note 52), p. 94).

74 The reduced appearance of the brown sleeve is not least due to alterations and overpaintings of later centuries, which were partially removed during a restoration in 2010. The same applies to the design of the background and architectural elements, which are also altered by later interventions and ageing processes. On the brown sleeve, cf. also contemporary astronomers in similar costume in portraits by Marco Basaiti in Lviv (see p. 126, fig. 11) or Giovanni Cariani (c. 1520, private collection, most recently Sotheby's, New York, 31 January 1997, lot no. 201).

Theresa Gatarski: Eros and *vaghezza*

Keith Christiansen and Stefan Weppelmann (eds), *The Renaissance Portrait: From Donatello to Bellini*, exh. cat. Bode-Museum, Staatliche Museen, Berlin / The Metropolitan Museum of Art, New York. New Haven/London: Yale University Press, 2011.

Elizabeth Cropper, "The Place of Beauty in the High Renaissance and Its Displacement in the History of Art", in: Alvin Vos (ed.), *Place and Displacement in the Renaissance* (Medieval and Renaissance Texts and Studies, vol. 132). Binghamton, NY: MRTS, 1995, pp. 159–205.

Enrico Maria Dal Pozzolo, *Lorenzo Lotto. Catalogo generale dei dipinti*. Milan: Skira, 2021.

Bastian Eclercy and Hans Aurenhammer (eds), *Titian and the Renaissance in Venice*, exh. cat. Städel Museum, Frankfurt am Main. Munich/London/New York: Prestel, 2019.

Sylvia Ferino-Pagden and Giovanna Nepi Scirè (eds), *Giorgione. Mythos und Enigma*, exh. cat. Kunsthistorisches Museum, Vienna / Gallerie dell'Accademia, Venice. Milan: Skira, 2004.

Sylvia Ferino-Pagden et al. (eds), *Titian's Vision of Women. Beauty, Love, Poetry*, exh. cat. Kunsthistorisches Museum, Vienna. Milan: Skira, 2022, esp. the contributions by Beverly Louise Brown, Enrico Maria Dal Pozzolo, Wencke Deiters, Sylvia Ferino-Pagden and Anouck Samyn.

Marsilio Ficino, *Über die Liebe oder Platons Gastmahl*, Lat.–Ger., trans. by Karl Paul

Haase, ed. and pref. by Paul Richard Blum. Hamburg: Felix Meiner, 2004.

Agnolo Firenzuola, "Della bellezza delle donne, intitolato Celso", in: *Prose di M. Agnolo Firenzuola Fiorentino*. Florence: Bernardo di Giunta, 1548.

Patricia Fortini Brown, *Private Lives in Renaissance Venice. Art, Architecture and the Family*. New Haven/London: Yale University Press, 2004.

Rona Goffen, *Titian's Women*. New Haven/London: Yale University Press, 1997.

Chriscinda Henry, *Playful Pictures. Art, Leisure, and Entertainment in the Venetian Renaissance Home*. University Park, PA: Pennsylvania State University Press, 2021.

Marianne Koos, "Petrarkistische Theorie oder künstlerische Praxis? Zur Malerei des Giorgionismo im Spiegel des lyrischen Männerporträts", in: Valeska von Rosen, Klaus Krüger and Rudolf Preimesberger (eds), *Der stumme Diskurs der Bilder. Reflexionsformen des Ästhetischen in der Kunst der Frühen Neuzeit*. Munich et al.: Deutscher Kunstverlag, 2003, pp. 53–84.

Marianne Koos, *Bildnisse des Begehrens. Das lyrische Männerporträt in der venezianischen Malerei des frühen 16. Jahrhunderts – Giorgione, Tizian und ihr Umkreis*. Emsdetten: Edition Imorde, 2006.

Dagmar Korbacher (ed.), *Arkadien. Paradies auf Papier*, exh. cat. Kupferstichkabinett, Staatliche Museen, Berlin. Petersberg: Michael Imhof, 2014.

Stella Mary Newton, *The Dress of the Venetians, 1495–1525* (Pasold Studies in Textile History, vol. 7). Aldershot: Scolar Press, 1988.

Ulrich Pfisterer, "Freundschaftsbilder – Liebesbilder. Zum visuellen Code männlicher Passionen in der Renaissance", in: Sibylle Appuhn-Radtke and Esther P. Wipfler (eds), *Freundschaft. Motive und Bedeutungen* (Veröffentlichungen des Zentralinstituts für Kunstgeschichte in München, vol. 19). Munich: Zentralinstitut für Kunstgeschichte, 2006, pp. 239–259.

Mary Rogers, "Fashioning Identities for the Renaissance Courtesan", in: Mary Rogers, *Fashioning Identities in Renaissance Art*. Aldershot et al.: Ashgate, 2000.

Romana Sammern, "Agnolo Firenzuola: Die Frau als schönes Objekt (1541)", in: Romana Sammern and Julia Saviello (eds), *Schönheit. Der Körper als Kunstprodukt. Kommentierte Quellentexte von Cicero bis Goya*. Berlin: Reimer, 2019, pp. 191–202.

Andreas Schumacher, *Michelangelos "teste divine". Idealbildnisse als exempla der Zeichenkunst* (Tholos, vol. 3). Münster: Rhema, 2007.

Jörn Steigerwald and Valeska von Rosen (eds), *Amor sacro e profano. Modelle und Modellierungen der Liebe in Literatur und Malerei der italienischen Renaissance*. Wiesbaden: Harrossowitz, 2012, esp. the contributions by Marie-Christine Leitgeb and Birgit Wagner.

Karine Tsoumis, *Bernardino Licinio. Portraiture, Kinship and Community in Renaissance Venice*, PhD dissertation, University of Toronto, Toronto, 2013, electronic resource: https://tspace.library.utoronto.ca/bitstream/1807/68971/3/Tsoumis_Karine_201306_PhD_thesis.pdf [accessed on 23 June 2023].

Cesare Vecellio, *De gli habiti antichi, et moderni di diverse parti del mondo libri due*, Venice, 1590, fols 144v–145r.

Leonardo da Vinci, "Trattato della Pittura", in: Jean Paul Richter (ed.), *The Literary Works of Leonardo da Vinci*, vol. 1. London: Oxford University Press, 1939.

Winfried Wehle, "Arkadien oder die Kunst natürlich zu sein. Venus-Renaissance in Sannazaros 'Arcadia' und Giorgiones/Tizians 'Ländlichem Konzert'", in: Nicole Hegener (ed.), *Nackte Gestalten. Die Wiederkehr des antiken Akts in der Renaissanceplastik*. Petersberg: Michael Imhof, 2021, pp. 251–269.

Henry Kaap: Portrait painting in Venice

Leon Battista Alberti, *On Painting*, trans. with an intro. and notes by John R. Spencer. New Haven: Yale University Press, 1970.

Hannah Baader, *Das Selbst im Anderen. Sprachen der Freundschaft und die Kunst des Porträts 1370–1520*. Paderborn: Wilhelm Fink Verlag, 2015.

Hans Belting, "A Venetian Artist at the Ottoman Court. An Encounter of Two Worlds", in: *Convivium*, vol. 5, no. 2, 2018, pp. 14–31.

Claudia Blümle and Beat Wismer (eds), *Hinter dem Vorhang. Verhüllung und Enthüllung seit der Renaissance – von Tizian bis Christo*, exh. cat. Museum Kunstpalast, Düsseldorf. Munich: Hirmer Verlag, 2016.

Daniela Bohde, *Haut, Fleisch und Farbe. Körperlichkeit und Materialität in den Gemälden Tizians* (Zephyr, vol. 3.). Emsdetten: Ed. Imorde, 2002.

Caroline Campbell and Alan Chong (eds), *Bellini and the East*, exh. cat. The National Gallery, London / Isabella Stewart Gardner Museum, Boston. London: National Gallery Company, 2005.

Lorne Campbell and Miguel Falomir Faus (eds), *Renaissance Faces. Van Eyck to Titian*, exh. cat. The National Gallery, London. London: Yale University Press for National Gallery Company, 2008.

Keith Christiansen and Stefan Weppelmann (eds), *The Renaissance Portrait from Donatello to Bellini*, exh. cat. Bode-Museum, Berlin / The Metropolitan Museum of Art, New York. New Haven/London: Yale University Press, 2011.

Sylvia Ferino-Pagden et al. (eds), *Titian's Vision of Women. Beauty, Love, Poetry*, exh. cat. Kunsthistorisches Museum, Vienna. Milan: Skira, 2022.

Peter Humfrey, *Painting in Renaissance Venice*. New Haven/London: Yale University Press, 1995.

Holly S. Hurlburt, *The Dogaressa of Venice, 1200–1500. Wife and Icon*. New York: Palgrave Macmillan, 2006.

Henry Kaap, *Lorenzo Lotto malt Andrea Odoni. Kunstschaffen und Kunstsammeln zwischen Bildverehrung, Bildskepsis, Bildwitz*. Berlin: Gebr. Mann Verlag, 2021.

Elsje van Kessel, *The Lives of Paintings. Presence, Agency and Likeness in Venetian*

Art of the Sixteenth Century. Berlin/ Boston: De Gruyter, 2017.

Marianne Koos, "Maske, Schminke, Schein. Körperfarben in Tizians Bildnis der Laura 'Dianti mit schwarzem Pagen'", in: Werner Busch et al. (eds), *Ähnlichkeit und Entstellung. Entgrenzungstendenzen des Porträts*. Berlin: Deutscher Kunstverlag, 2010, pp. 15–34.

Klaus Krüger, *Das Bild als Schleier des Unsichtbaren. Ästhetische Illusion in der Kunst der frühen Neuzeit in Italien*. Munich: Wilhelm Fink Verlag, 2001.

Margaret Morse, "Domestic Portraiture in Early Modern Venice. Devotion to Family and Faith", in: Maya Corry, Marco Faini and Alessia Meneghin (eds), *Domestic Devotions in Early Modern Italy* (Intersections, vol. 59, no. 1). Leiden/Boston: Brill, 2019, pp. 117–138.

Sandra Pisot (ed.), *Die Poesie der venezianischen Malerei. Paris Bordone, Palma il Vecchio, Lorenzo Lotto, Tizian*, exh. cat. Hamburger Kunsthalle, Hamburg. Munich: Hirmer Verlag, 2017.

Giorgio Vasari, *Lives of the Most Eminent Painters, Sculptors and Architects*, 10 vols, trans. Gaston du C. de Vere. London: Macmillan and the Medici Society, 1912–1914, vol. IX, p. 174.

Annette Kranz: Viewed from the north

Der Anfang der Museumslehre in Deutschland. Das Traktat "Inscriptiones vel Tituli Theatri Amplissimi" von Samuel Quiccheberg, ed. and comm. by Harriet Roth. Berlin: De Gruyter Akademie Forschung, 2000, pp. 192–196.

Bernard Aikema and Beverly Louise Brown (eds), *Renaissance Venice and the North. Crosscurrents in the Time of Bellini, Dürer, and Titian*, exh. cat. Istituto di Cultura di Palazzo Grassi, Venice. Cinisello Balsamo: Rizzoli, 1999, especially the essays by Bernard Aikeman, Andrew John Martin and Rona Goffen.

Bernard Aikema and Andrew John Martin, "Crosscurrents with Germany. The Spread of the Venetian Renaissance", in: Bernard Aikema and Beverly Louise Brown (eds), *Renaissance Venice and the North. Crosscurrents in the Time of Bellini, Dürer, and Titian*, exh. cat. Istituto di Cultura di Palazzo Grassi, Venice. Cinisello Balsamo: Rizzoli, 1999, pp. 332–339.

Pietro Aretino, *Lettere sull'arte*, Ettore Camesasca (ed.), 3 vols, 1957–1960. Milan: Edizioni del Milione, 1957, vol. 2, pp. 101–103.

Sibylle Backmann, "Kunstagenten oder Kaufleute? Die Firma Ott im Kunsthandel zwischen Oberdeutschland und Venedig (1550–1650)", in: Klaus Bergdolt and Jochen Brüning (eds), *Kunst und ihre Auftraggeber im 16. Jahrhundert. Venedig und Augsburg im Vergleich* (Colloquia Augustana, vol. 5). Berlin: Akademie, 1997, pp. 175–197.

Giordana Canova, *Paris Bordon* (Profili e saggi di arte veneta, vol. 2). Venice: Alfieri, 1964, pp. 36–38.

Keith Christiansen and Stefan Weppelmann (eds), *The Renaissance Portrait from Donatello to Bellini*, exh. cat. Bode-Museum, Staatliche Museen, Berlin / The Metropolitan Museum of Art, New York. New Haven/London: Yale University Press, 2011, pp. 318–376, cat. 138–168.

Klára Garas, "Die Fugger und die venezianische Kunst", in: Bernd Roeck, Klaus Bergdolt and Andrew John Martin (eds), *Venedig und Oberdeutschland in der Renaissance. Beziehungen zwischen Kunst und Wirtschaft* (Studi/ Deutsches Studienzentrum in Venedig, vol. 9). Sigmaringen: Thorbecke, 1993, pp. 123–129.

Rona Goffen, *Giovanni Bellini*. New York/ London: Yale University Press, 1989, pp. 191–221.

Mary Margaret Keymer Heaton, *The Life of Albrecht Dürer of Nürnberg: With a Translation of His Letters and Journal and an Account of His Works*. London: Seeley, Jackson and Halliday, 1881, p. 76.

Peter Humfrey, "The Portrait in Fifteenth-Century Venice", in: Keith Christiansen and Stefan Weppelmann (eds), The Renaissance Portrait. From Donatello to Bellini, exh. cat. Bode-Museum, Staatliche Museen, Berlin / The Metropolitan Museum of Art, New York. New Haven/London: Yale University Press, 2011, pp. 48–63.

Annette Kranz, "Christoph Amberger und einige Welser-Bildnisse des 16. Jahrhunderts", in: Mark Häberlein and Johannes Burkhardt (eds), *Die Welser. Neue Forschungen zur Geschichte und Kultur des oberdeutschen Handelshauses* (Colloquia Augustana, vol. 16). Berlin: De Gruyter Akademie Forschung, 2002, pp. 409–448, here pp. 411–417.

Annette Kranz, *Christoph Amberger – Bildnismaler zu Augsburg. Städtische Eliten im Spiegel ihrer Porträts*. Regensburg: Schnell & Steiner, 2004, pp. 77–109, 394–400.

Rolf Kultzen, "Relazioni fra Paris Bordon e Christoph Amberger", in: Giorgio Fossaluzza and Eugenio Manzato (eds), *Paris Bordon e il suo tempo*, Atti del convegno internazionale di studi, Treviso, 28–30 October 1985. Treviso: Canova, 1987, pp. 79–82.

Jürg Meyer zur Capellen, *Gentile Bellini*. Stuttgart: Franz Steiner, 1985, pp. 55–69.

Giles Robertson, *Vincenzo Catena*. Edinburgh: Edinburgh University Press, 1954, pp. 58–59, cat. 34.

Andreas Schumacher (ed.), *Staatsgalerie in der Residenz Würzburg. Venezianische Malerei*. Regensburg: Schnell & Steiner, 2021, pp. 72–75 (Annette Kranz).

Giorgio Vasari, *Lives of the Most Eminent Painters, Sculptors and Architects*, 10 vols, trans. Gaston du C. de Vere. London: Macmillan and the Medici Society, 1912–1914, esp. chapters on Bellini (vol. III, p. 82), Giorgione (vol. IV, p. 113) and Carpaccio (vol. IV, p. 58, in which Vincenzo Catena is mentioned).

Sarah Vowles, "'Truly Lifelike and Real': The Portraits von Mantegna and Bellini", in: Caroline Campbell et al. (eds), *Mantegna & Bellini. Masters of the Renaissance*, exh. cat. The National Gallery, London / Gemäldegalerie, Staatliche Museen, Berlin: London: National Gallery Company, 2018, pp. 206–217.

Anik Waldeck, "Vincenzo Catena and Giorgione, Reconsidered", in: *Artibus et historiae*, vol. 37, no. 74, 2016, pp. 59–71.

Image credits

akg-images: p. 27, fig. 2, p. 28, fig. 3 (Henry Clay Frick Bequest); p. 83, fig. 6, p. 156, fig. 1, p. 189, fig. 2, p. 202, fig. 9 (akg-images/Album); p. 48, fig. 4, p. 118, fig. 3 (National Gallery Global Limited/akg); p. 80, fig. 3 (akg-images/Liszt Collection); p. 87, fig. 2 (akg-images/Jean-Claude Varga); p. 191, fig. 4 (Heritage Images/Fine Art Images/akg-images)

Albertina, Vienna: cat. 31, 34, 35, 45, 77, 78

2023 © Archivio Fotografico – Fondazione Musei Civici di Venezia: cat. 73

© Bayerisches Nationalmuseum München, Foto Bastian Krack: cat. 56

Bayerische Staatsgemäldesammlungen, Munich, Fotoabteilung: Haydar Koyupinar (head), Sibylle Forster, Nicole Wilhelms, Margarita Platis, Elisabeth Greil: p. 123, fig. 8, p. 124, fig. 10, p. 137, fig. 7, p. 212, fig. 4, cat. 13, 15–17, 23, 25, 28, 37–40, 43, 47, 48, 51, 57, 61, 82, 85

© Besançon, Musée des Beaux-Arts et d'Archéologie – Photographie P. Guenat: cat. 76

Bibliothèque nationale de France, Paris: p. 131, fig. 2, 3, p. 132, fig. 4, cat. 49

bpk: p. 30 f., p. 141, fig. 11 (bpk/Kupferstichkabinett, SMB/Dietmar Katz); p. 38, fig. 1 (bpk/RMN – Grand Palais/Gérard Blot); p. 72, fig. 1, p. 121, fig. 6, p. 160, fig. 2 (bpk/Scala – courtesy of the Ministero Beni e Att. Culturali); p. 122, fig. 7, p. 123, fig. 9 (bpk/Kupferstichkabinett, SMB/Jörg P. Anders); p. 167, fig. 3 (bpk/RMN – Grand Palais/Hervé Lewandowski); p. 188, fig. 1 (bpk/DeAgostini/New Picture Library/G. Nimatallah); p. 194, fig. 5 (bpk/RMN – Grand Palais/Jean-Gilles Berizzi); p. 201, fig. 8 (bpk/Alinari Archives/Mauro Magliani); p. 210, fig. 3 (bpk/RMN – Grand Palais/Adrien Didierjean); p. 215, fig. 6, cat. 19, 74 (bpk/Gemäldegalerie, SMB/Jörg P. Anders); cat. 9, 11 (bpk/Kupferstichkabinett, SMB/Volker-H. Schneider); cat. 58 (bpk/RMN – Grand Palais/Thierry Le Mage); cat. 59 (bpk/Staatliche Kunstsammlungen Dresden/Elke Estel/Hans-Peter Klut); cat. 63 (bpk/Hamburger Kunsthalle/Christoph Irrgang)

Bridgeman Images: p. 82, fig. 5, p. 197, fig. 6 (Isabella Stewart Gardner Museum/Bridgeman Images); p. 116, fig. 1 (Musei Reali di Torino/Bridgeman Images)

Bristol Museums: Bristol Museum & Art Gallery: cat. 4

Cleveland Museum of Art, Creative Commons: p. 86, fig. 1 (Gift of The Print Club of Cleveland); p. 135, fig. 5 (Bequest of James Parmelee)

Collection Museum Boijmans Van Beuningen, Rotterdam. Stichting Museum Boijmans Van Beuningen 1940 (former collection Koenigs)/Creditline photographer: Studio Tromp: p. 92, fig. 4

© Courtesy of National Gallery of Art, Washington, D.C.: p. 81, fig. 4, p. 190, fig. 3, cat. 2, 27, 79 (Samuel H. Kress Collection); p. 95, fig. 7 (Rosenwald Collection); p. 96, fig. 8 (Gift of W. G. Russell Allen); p. 140, fig. 10 (Gift of Michael Straight)

Doerner Institut, Munich: p. 130, fig. 1, p. 136, fig. 6

Dominique Provost, Collection KMSKA – Flemish Community (CC0): cat. 70

Faringdon Collection Trust, Buscot Park, Oxfordshire: cat. 54

© The Fitzwilliam Museum, Cambridge: p. 45, fig. 3

Fondation Custodia, Collection Frits Lugt, Paris: p. 89, fig. 3

© Fondazione Accademia Carrara, Bergamo: cat. 24, 46

The Frick Collection, New York: p. 76, fig. 2 (Henry Clay Frick Bequest); p. 138, fig. 8 (Michael Bodycomb/Gift of Stephen K. and Janie Woo Scher, 2021)

Gabinetto Fotografico, Musei Civici Padova/Su Concessione del Comune di Padova – Tutti i diritti di Legge sono riservati: cat. 71

Gabinetto Fotografico delle Gallerie degli Uffizi: cat. 18, 29, 55 (Roberto Palermo); cat. 65 (Cristian Ceccanti)

© Galerie Canesso, Paris: cat. 60

Galleria Borghese/ph. Mauro Coen: cat. 21, 68

© Gallerie dell'Accademia di Venezia/su concessione dello Ministerio della Cultura: cat. 5a–d, 6, 22

© KHM-Museumsverband: p. 117, fig. 2, p. 120, fig. 5, cat. 41, 52, 62, 84

© Lyon MBA – Photo Alain Basset: cat. 53

© Martin von Wagner-Museum der Universität Würzburg, Foto A. Mischke: cat. 44

The Metropolitan Museum of Art, New York, Public Domain: p. 94, fig. 6 (Rogers Fund, 1999); cat. 30 (Rogers Fund, 1908)

© Musée des Beaux-Arts de Dijon/Hugo Martens, Legs Anthelme et Edma Trimolet, 1878: cat. 50

Musei Civici di Treviso: cat. 20

Museo Civico Amedeo Lia, La Spezia: cat. 7a–b

© Museo Nacional Thyssen-Bornemisza, Madrid: cat. 80

© The National Gallery, London: cat. 1, 69

Norton Simon Art Foundation: p. 207, fig. 1

Palazzo Mazzolari Mosca Musei Civici – courtesy of Comune di Pesaro: cat. 26

© Photographic Archive, Museo Nacional del Prado, Madrid: cat. 83

© Pinacoteca di Brera, Milano: cat. 3

Royal Collection Trust/© His Majesty King Charles III 2023: cat. 32, 67, 75

Sammlung Bernd und Verena Klüser, Munich: cat. 33, 36

SMK – National Gallery of Denmark, Copenhagen, Public Domain: cat. 14

Sovraintendenza di Roma Capitale – Foto in Comune: cat. 66

© Staatliche Graphische Sammlung München: cat. 10

Szépművészeti Múzeum/Museum of Fine Arts, Budapest, 2023: cat. 8

© The Trustees of the British Museum: p. 93, fig. 5, p. 97, fig. 9

Wadsworth Atheneum Museum of Art, Hartford (CT), The Ella Gallup Sumner and Mary Catlin Sumner Collection Fund: cat. 42 (Allen Phillips)

The Walters Art Museum, Baltimore: p. 43, fig. 2

Private collection, courtesy of Eckart Lingenauber, cat. 12, 64

Cited images

Franceso Rossi (ed.), *Bergamo. L'altra Venezia. Il Rinascimento negli anni di Lorenzo Lotto, 1510–1530*, exh. cat. Accademia Carrara, Bergamo. Milan: Skira, 2001, p. 177: cat. 81

Keith Christiansen and Stefan Weppelmann (eds), *The Renaissance Portrait: From Donatello to Bellini*, exh. cat. Bode-Museum, Staatliche Museen, Berlin / The Metropolitan Museum of Art, New York. New Haven/London: Yale University Press, 2011, p. 329: cat. 72

Simone Facchinetti, Arturo Galansino and Per Rumberg (eds), *In the Age of Giorgione*, exh. cat. Royal Academy of Arts, London. London: Royal Academy of Arts. 2016, p. 144: p. 25, fig. 1

Bernard Aikema and Beverly Louise Brown (eds), *Renaissance Venice and the North. Crosscurrents in the Time of Bellini, Dürer, and Titian*, exh. cat. Palazzo Grassi, Venice. Cinisello Balsamo: Rizzoli, 1999, p. 377: p. 214, fig. 5

Patrizia Nitti (ed.), *Titien. Le pouvoir en face*, exh. cat. Musée du Luxembourg, Paris. Milan: Skira, 2006, p. 207: p. 198, fig. 7

The remaining images come from the archives of the authors and the Bayerische Staatsgemäldesammlungen. It was not possible to locate the copyright holders of the images in all cases. Holders of rights that we could not identify are kindly asked to contact the publisher. Compensation will be made according to standard practice.

Colophon

Cover
Venetian, *Christ Carrying the Cross* (detail), c. 1515 © KHM-Museumsverband

Back cover
Giovanni Bellini, *St Jerome Reading in a Landscape* (detail), c. 1480/85 © The National Gallery, London

Details
P. 2: detail of cat. 80 | p. 4: detail of cat. 62 | p. 10: detail of cat. 58 | p. 18: detail of cat. 37 | p. 34: detail of cat. 1 | p. 70: detail of fig. 5, p. 82 | p. 84: detail of cat. 29 | p. 114: detail of cat. 40 | p. 128: detail of cat. 43 | p. 154: detail of cat. 52 | p. 186: detail of fig. 1, p. 188 | p. 204: detail of fig. 6, p. 215 | p. 230: detail of cat. 39

This catalogue is published in conjunction with the exhibition

Venezia 500 ◀◀ The Gentle Revolution of Venetian Painting
Munich, Bayerische Staatsgemälde-sammlungen, Alte Pinakothek
27.10.2023–4.2.2024

EXHIBITION

General director
Bernhard Maaz

Director of collections
Andreas Schumacher

Curator
Andreas Schumacher

Research assistance
Annette Kranz, Johanna Pawis

Curatorial assistance
Theresa Gatarski

Project coordination
Jessica Vogelsang, Alexandra Schatz

Administration
Angela Cornelius, Ilona von Máriássy, Susanne Engelsberger, Yvonne Hildwein

Registrar
Verena Rayer

Restoration and painting technology
Eva Ortner, Jan Schmidt, Ulrike Fischer, Johannes Engelhardt, Ronja Emmerich, Anneliese Földes, Heike Stege, Patrick Dietemann, Ursula Baumer

Communication and marketing
Tine Nehler, Jette Elixmann, Verena Sanladerer, Bianca Henze, Charlotte Neugebauer

Art education, information and service
Simone Ebert, Anke Palden, Alexandra Hiltmair

Events
Barbara Siebert, Katarina Jelic, Constance Huchette

Photograpic department
Haydar Koyupinar, Sibylle Forster, Nicole Wilhelms

Library
Stephan Priddy

Local administration
Benjamin Roger, Katja Doblaski, Harald Jakesch, Robert Voggenreiter

And the teams of the following departments:
Preventive conservation
Museum and exhibition technology
Safety and operational technology
Central services

Exhibition design
Juliette Israël, scenography + curatorial concepts
Production: Wiendl Expo; Jörg Schwarzenbach

Exhibition graphics
Studio Silke Weigl, Konzeption & Gestaltung
Production: Martin Folienschriften

Key visual
PARAT.cc

Audio guide
Linon Medien

Film
KATALOG Filmproduktion

Sound art
Janko Hanushevsky, Eva Pöpplein/ Merzouga

CATALOGUE

Editor
Andreas Schumacher

Editorial team
Annette Kranz, Theresa Gatarski, Andreas Schumacher

Image editor
Theresa Gatarski

Project management, Hirmer Publishers
Jutta Allekotte

Copy-editing
Ariane Kossack

Translations
Julian Jain (DE–EN)
Laura Bennett (IT–EN)

Graphic design, typesetting and production
Lucia Ott, Hirmer Publishers

Pre-press and reproductions
Repromayer GmbH, Reutlingen

Font
Bembo, Helvetica Neue

Paper
Magno Volume 150 g/m^2

Printing and binding
Printer Trento S.r.l., Trento

Printed in Italy

Bibliographic information published by the Deutsche Nationalbibliothek.
The Deutsche Nationalbibliothek lists this publication in the Deutsche Nationalbibliografie; detailed bibliographic data are available in the internet at http://dnb.de.

ISBN 978-3-7774-4176-4
(English edition)
ISBN 978-3-7774-4174-0
(German edition)

www.hirmerpublishers.com
www.hirmerpublishers.co.uk

The exhibition was sponsored by

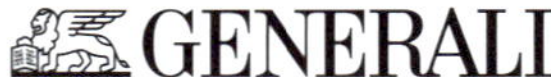

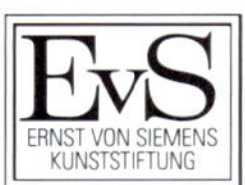

Herbert Schuchardt-Stiftung

Hubert Burda Stiftung

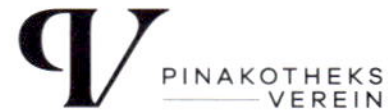

Karl Thiemig-Stiftung

Stiftung Mittelsten Scheid

Dr Wilhelm Winterstein

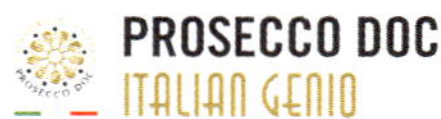

MARINA RINALDI

Restoration work was sponsored by

Eyb&Wallwitz Vermögensmanagement
Charlotte and Nikolaus von Bomhard
Isabel and Andreas Gocke
and other private patrons of the arts

Cooperation partners

Orchesterakademie der Münchner Philharmoniker
Yehudi Menuhin Live Music Now München e.V.
Staatstheater am Gärtnerplatz
Garibaldi
Air Dolomiti
The Charles Hotel

Media partner

All About Italy